DATE DUE

DEMCO, INC. 38-2931

WITHDRAWN

# Becoming Aztlan

# Becoming Aztlan

## Mesoamerican Influence in the Greater Southwest, AD 1200–1500

CARROLL L. RILEY

THE UNIVERSITY OF UTAH PRESS
*Salt Lake City*

10 09 08 07 06 05     5 4 3 2 1

 The Defiance House Man colophon is a registered trademark
of the University of Utah Press. It is based upon a four-foot-tall,
Ancient Puebloan pictograph (late PIII) near Glen Canyon, Utah.

LIBRARY OF CONGRESS CATALOGING-IN-PUBLICATION DATA

Riley, Carroll L.
    Becoming Aztlan : Mesoamerican influence in the greater Southwest,
AD 1200–1500 / Carroll L. Riley.
        p.    cm.
    Includes bibliographical references and index.
    ISBN 0-87480-828-6 (cloth : alk. paper)
        1. Pueblo Indians—Migrations.    2. Pueblo Indians—Commerce—
Mexico.    3. Pueblo Indians—Antiquities.    4. Indians of Mexico—
Migrations    5. Indians of Mexico—Commerce—Southwest, New.
6. Indians of Mexico—Antiquities.    I. Title.
    E99.P9R53    2005
    976'.01—dc22                                            2005004848

The University of Utah Press is committed to preserving
ancient forests and natural resources. We elected to print
*Becoming Aztlan* on 50% post consumer recycled paper,
processed chlorine free. As a result, for this printing, we have
saved:

10 trees (40' tall and 6-8" diameter)
4,185 gallons of water
1,683 kilowatt hours of electricity
461 pounds of solid waste
906 pounds of greenhouse gases

The University of Utah Press made this paper choice because
our printer, Thomson-Shore, Inc., is a member of Green
Press Initiative, a nonprofit program dedicated to supporting
authors, publishers, and suppliers in their efforts to reduce
their use of fiber obtained from endangered forests.

For more information, visit www.greenpressinitiative.org

*To Brent, and to Ben, Vic, Cyn, Don, and Amanda.*
*Also to Marguerite and to the memory of Janet.*

# Contents

# Illustrations

# Acknowledgments

This book owes a debt to a great many people. First, I am much indebted to the two reviewers for the book, Michael S. Foster and David A. Phillips Jr. Their detailed and insightful comments were immensely helpful. Historians Richard Flint and Shirley C. Flint; archaeologists Curtis Schaafsma, Polly Schaafsma, Cordelia T. Snow, and David H. Snow; and linguist Mauricio Mixco read and commented on the manuscript as a whole, and their comments were most valuable. Members of the Santa Fe Seminar, including Shirley Barnes, Jim Dunlap, Barbara Sommer, Linda Hall, Benjamin Keen, John Kessell, Richard and Sandra (Lauderdale) Graham, Vicky Evans, Peter Linder, and Suzanne Stamatov gave detailed critical comment on various chapters. Robert J. Mallouf gave me excellent advice on the La Junta sections of the book. Ellen Abbott Kelley generously supplied illustrations for the La Junta area and Curt and Polly Schaafsma for the Jornada Mogollon, Pottery Mound, and the Casas Grandes area. I want to give special thanks to John Ware, director of the Amerind Foundation, Dragoon, Arizona, and to his staff; also to Marc Thompson, director, Jason A. Jurgena, collections manager, and Lora Jackson, educator, El Paso Museum of Archaeology, for their splendid help in assembling illustrations for the book. Also of great help in this regard were David A. Phillips Jr., curator of archaeology, and Catherine Baudoin, photo archivist, Maxwell Museum, University of New Mexico. In Santa Fe I benefited from the generosity of a number of members of the museum staff and the Archaeological Records Management Section (ARMS). Let me especially thank David E. McNeece of the Laboratory of Anthropology; Cordelia Snow, Louanna Haecker, and Tim Seaman of ARMS; Steve Lakatos and Reggie Wiseman of the Office of Archaeological Studies (OAS); and Amy Verheide, photo archivist at the Palace, Museum of New Mexico. I owe a great debt of gratitude to Mara Yarbrough, librarian at the Museum of Indian Arts and Culture/Laboratory of Anthropology, Laura Holt, former librarian, and Minnie Murray, assistant librarian. Their generosity and support were invaluable. I wish to thank Wetherbee Dorshow, Earth Analytic, who did most of the maps; Keith Kintigh, Barbara Mills, and Deborah Huntley for information on the Zuni area; Paul Minnis, Todd VanPool, and Christine VanPool for information on Casas Grandes; and Michael W. Diehl and Annick Lascaux for data on early Arizona agriculture. John A. Douglas shared information on ongoing work in the Bavispe area, undertaken by Douglas and Cesar A. Quijada in the Bavispe region, as did Elizabeth A. Bagwell on aspects of her research in the Chihuahua-Sonora border region. This is all new and important research and will certainly modify our views on both Casas Grandes and the Sonoran region. For Sonoran research in general I must thank Richard A. Pailes, Daniel Reff, William

Doolittle, and Christy Turner for unpublished information. Rowyn L. Evans drew certain of the pottery designs, and Charmion McKusick gave me advice and generously allowed me to copy various of her illustrations, as did Jonathan Reyman. Christine Marburmin helped with computer aspects of the final manuscript and Robert Woods with camera copy. My archaeologist daughter, Victoria R. Evans, provided the photograph of J. Charles Kelley, taken only a few months before his death. Vick Evans also discussed and advised on various problem areas, especially in ceramics. I wish to give special thanks to my editor, Jeffrey L. Grathwohl, director of the University of Utah Press, for his wise counsel, professional and technical, on this (perhaps my last) book and on earlier ones published by the University of Utah Press. My wife, Brent Locke Riley, has intimate knowledge of the Southwest, the result of many decades of living, visiting, and working in the area. Her advice is of inestimable value.

As always, the shortcomings of the book are my own.

# CHAPTER 1

# Introduction

It is time to put the ancient Southwest back into the larger world. In this book I take issue with the simplistic view that cultural conditions in the prehispanic and early contact period resulted from centuries, even millennia, of natural internal growth. According to the scenario, cultures were shaped by changing environments, but outside influences played only a minor role.[1]

This way of looking at southwestern archaeology, now sometimes elevated to the status of received wisdom, originated partly in reaction to nineteenth-century scholars such as Adolph Bandelier (Figure 1.1), who saw southwestern cultures as the northern edge of a great pan-American nexus of native civilization. Unfortunately, although long on vision, such scholars were short on data. As new scientific approaches entered archaeology at the beginning of the twentieth century, specialists in the northern portions of the Southwest became more and more enamored of a different scenario. This was a continuum from primitive farmers, dwelling in rock shelters and hacking out a rude existence, to the sophisticated town dwellers of fully developed Puebloan society.

By the mid-twentieth century archaeologists had filled in the long centuries before farming and were finding increasing evidence that human beings had occupied the Southwest from late Pleistocene or Ice Age times. The hunters who pursued the large game of the lush Pleistocene eventually gave way to tiny groups, the *Archaic* societies, struggling to meet the arid, draconian conditions that followed the retreat of the glaciers. The discovery of agriculture changed life in the upper Southwest, eventually creating the Puebloan *Anasazi* groups that were still in place at the Spanish invasion.

Observing this continuum of in situ development over thousands of years, archaeologists became increasingly reluctant to consider that the Anasazi received any significant amount of culture from elsewhere. They conceded the spread of agriculture from some southern source, but even extraordinarily talented and perceptive scholars were willing to believe that pottery, a key invention that helped usher in the Anasazi period, originated in the San Juan Basin.

Farther south, in the valleys of the Gila and Salt rivers of Arizona, archaeology was slowly delineating a parallel culture, eventually called *Hohokam*. Like the Anasazi it involved people who were agricultural, pottery-using, with strongly developed art styles (though not town-dwelling in the Anasazi sense of the word until very late). The Hohokam had certain traits that seemed to relate to areas farther south, but again scholars were disinclined to see significant influence from Mesoamerica.

A third major tradition was the *Mogollon*, originally written off as a kind of variant Anasazi. Its bona fides were established in the 1920s and 1930s, but most experts considered

FIGURE 1.1. Adolph F. Bandelier. Museum of New Mexico, neg. no. 9138.

if Gladwin's idea of time is correct, the Hohokam learned to make pottery long before the Basket Makers, since the earliest dated occurrence of pottery in the north is AD 475.... But it must be kept in mind that estimates of the duration of the earlier phases at Snaketown rest on inference only. While the priority of the Hohokam in pottery making seems probable, it will not be proved until positive dating of the early phases has been accomplished.[3]

Morris and many other archaeologists believed strongly that regardless of what may have happened in the Hohokam area and in the archaeological terra incognita of Sonora and Chihuahua, the Anasazi region was the center of southwestern archaeology. Morris put it quite unequivocally:

The Pueblo area may be considered to comprise all of Arizona northward of the Gila Valley, most of Utah, the southwestern corner of Colorado, and all of New Mexico west of the open plains. Beyond these limits there are marginal extensions westward into Nevada, eastward into Kansas and Texas, and, as has been previously mentioned, strong and contributory contacts with the cultures of southern Arizona and northern Mexico. *However these peripheral occurrences may be regarded as no more than radiations and spill-over from the great parent center.*[4]

it to be pretty much a homebred southwestern phenomenon.

My own introduction to archaeology in the immediate post–World War II years was to this concept of an "uncontaminated" Southwest. During the summers of my undergraduate and graduate years I worked as an archaeological park ranger at Mesa Verde and elsewhere in the Four Corners region, the original heartland of Anasazi. By that time A. V. Kidder (Figure 1.2), the excavator of Pecos Pueblo, had put in words what almost everybody believed, calling the idea of Anasazi cultural innovation and domination the "San Juan hypothesis."[2]

Perhaps its clearest formulation, however, was that of the superb field archaeologist Earl H. Morris. Writing in 1939, Morris was willing, perhaps somewhat grudgingly, to concede that the Hohokam may have had an earlier development of *pottery* than in the Anasazi area, basing his comments on Harold Gladwin's work at Gila Pueblo. Gladwin believed that competently made pottery had appeared by the Vahki phase of the Pioneer Period (see chapter 4 below). According to Morris,

I knew Morris personally and admired his archaeological work. Indeed, I continue to greatly admire him, as I do the other pioneering archaeologists who set the stage for later research, including the establishment of the first firm chronologies in the Southwest. But their wonderful achievements should not blind us to the fact that their model of the Southwest badly needs revision.

In the early post–World War II years interest in southwestern anthropological and historical studies was intensified, partly because of greater numbers of students coming into archaeology and partly because more monies

FIGURE 1.2. A. V. Kidder Jr. Museum of New Mexico, neg. no. 7599.

became available from the federal government, states, colleges, museums, and foundations. There also began to be something of a shift in thinking about southwestern archaeology, including new interest by various Mexican and American scholars on the archaeological cultures of north and west Mexico. It was during this time that J. Charles Kelley at Southern Illinois University began his elaborate investigations of the largely unknown Chalchihuites culture of Durango and Zacatecas. At about the same date Charles C. Di Peso, from Amerind Foundation, launched the study of a Mesoamerican-looking site, Casas Grandes or Paquimé, in northern Chihuahua. The archaeologist Edward Ferdon pointed out various features in Anasazi settlements of Chaco Canyon that seemed clearly to have diffused northward from Mesoamerica.[5]

New ideas about the meaning and importance of diffusion worldwide began to surface, beginning in the 1950s, stimulated by scholars such as Robert Heine-Geldern and Gordon Ekholm. In 1968 Kelley and I, with two col-

leagues, organized a panel on diffusion at the national meetings of the Society for American Archaeology, bringing together leading scholars from a number of disciplines. The result was a volume, *Man Across the Sea*, which helped redefine the methods of handling and evaluating data for diffusion to far-flung places.[6] Several of the chapters concerned themselves in part with diffusion into and out of the Southwest. I was (and remain) somewhat skeptical of *intercontinental* diffusion in precolumbian times but, like Kelley, was becoming more and more convinced that Mesoamerica and the Southwest had various contacts, ones that significantly changed basic southwestern human institutions.

The idea of meaningful Mesoamerican influence in the Southwest might have eventually become the prevailing fashion in archaeology. It was sidetracked, however, by another fashion that swept the discipline in the mid to late 1960s: processualism, or, as it was quickly dubbed, the "New Archaeology." Many of the older archaeologists considered archaeology and history to have rich mutual ties. Adherents of the New Archaeology regarded historical methodologies as essentially descriptive and set out to establish a "processual," or ecological-functional, approach that saw cultures as adaptive systems from which the investigator could elucidate general rules of cultural behavior.[7] This approach considered migration "not explanatory" in culture and was reluctant to give any great importance even to such things as diffusion.[8]

Although the processual approach has been generally superseded, its effects linger in the widespread refusal to see southwestern peoples and cultures as significantly influenced by the much larger, older, and far more sophisticated societies of Mesoamerica. Many modern archaeologists accept a Mesoamerica flavor in the Southwest but consider the effects "trivial," with no real significance in the development of the cultural dynamics of the area.

Certainly, this question of significance reaches to the heart of the problem. For example, one could say that the Vikings in the early eleventh century were the first Europeans to settle continental North America and even point to concrete evidence, the site of L'anse aux Meadows in Newfoundland. But from the point of view of meaningful innovation—that is, whether there were significant additions or subtractions to *anybody's* cultural inventory— the Viking perambulations clearly meant almost nothing to either Europeans or Native Americans.[9] Could that have been the situation in the Southwest?

Fortunately, the last two decades have seen a greater willingness on all sides to look at the evidence in a balanced way. For example, scholars no longer steer away from the idea of migration. This is especially beneficial in studies of the Southwest, for there seems to have been a great deal of it throughout that region. And there is vastly increased interest in the in-between country south of the United States portion of the Southwest and north and west of the fully developed societies of Mesoamerica.

In this book I argue that although the Southwest remained "southwestern" in its basic economy, there were drastic changes after about AD 1200 in the south and AD 1300 in the north, changes that especially affected the socioreligious life of the people.[10] There was certainly some continuity. It can be seen in the Hohokam area, in Mogollon, at Casas Grandes and, perhaps even more clearly, in Pueblo society. A Pueblo Indian living in AD 800 had somewhat the same house type, gathered the same plant foods, horticultural or wild, and practiced the same hunting techniques as his or her descendant of, say, AD 1400. But that latter-day individual would have a very different concept of the religious universe, larger physical horizons, and a greater worldview and could surely make plans and dream dreams that would have been quite alien to the earlier Pueblo world.

CHAPTER 2

# Why Aztlan?

Before the Spaniards arrived in AD 1519, the region constituting much of modern Mexico was dominated by the great plunder empire of the Aztecs or Mexica. Only the north and west of Mexico was beyond their reach, but it was precisely in this region, referred to as *Aztlan,* the "Place of the Herons," that traditional histories placed the origin of the Aztec people.[1] According to these Aztec traditions, written down in early Spanish times, an attempt was eventually made to discover this original homeland. This happened during the reign of Motecuhzoma I (AD 1440–1469), who, with the help of his great minister Tlacaelel, launched a major expedition to find Aztlan. After many a magical adventure and with help from the tribal god Huitzilopochtli, the exploration party eventually reached Aztlan and reported back to the emperor: " 'Lord, we have carried out your order, your word, and have witnessed that which you wished to know: we have seen that land called Aztlan and Colhuacan, where our fathers and grandfathers lived and from where they left on their migration. And we have brought the things that grow and are bred there.' They then placed before the king many ears of corn, seeds, and different kinds of flowers, tomatoes, and chilies—food and plants grown in that land."[2]

Alas, this story is largely if not wholly apocryphal, part of a recasting of Aztec history that began around the time of the first Motecuhzoma. This revision was intended to give the Aztecs a set place of origin, a glorious history, and justification for their subjugation of much of Mesoamerica.[3] Nevertheless, the Aztlan origin story was too basic and widespread to be simply invented by the Aztec royalty. The Aztec peoples firmly believed that they came from somewhere in the Northwest, and this may have been true. From a traditional anthropological point of view the ancestors to the Aztecs were tribes of primitive peoples, collectively called Chichimecs, who lived in the wild north of Mexico. And Uto-Aztecan, the language family that includes Nahuatl, the Aztec tongue, extends from the western United States roughly southeastward, with Nahuatl near the southeastern end. Of course the linguistic movements that placed historic Nahuatl speakers in central Mexico occurred too many centuries ago for there to be even reasonably dependable oral history. In any case the old idea that they went from north to south is today under dispute (see chapter 10, with its discussion of regional languages).

Still, the concept of an exciting and mysterious land in the North, whatever it might be called, powerfully affected the Aztecs, as it did the Spaniards in their turn. The earliest Spanish expedition into the Greater Southwest was in search of such fabled regions. Although he does not use the name, Francisco Vázquez de Coronado, in his travels of the region from 1539 to 1542, could hardly have missed the idea that the wealthy land he sought had some sort of identity with Aztlan. After all, his expedition had hundreds of central Mexican Indian "allies," including Aztecs, in tow. And he was definitely influenced by a story, circulating at the time, of rich cities and a trading kingdom far to the northwest of central Mexico.[4]

What and where was this dreamland of the Aztecs, the setting of our book? We cannot define it strictly in Aztec terms (the geographical referents are too vague) but must use information from the Spaniards and what archaeologists have since learned. The area covered in this book is a very large region (somewhat greater than Aztlan itself) generally bounded by the southern Great Plains and the northern Mexican plateaus to the east, and the southern flank of the Rocky Mountains to the north. Its western boundary is the lower Colorado River and Gulf of California. To the south a fuzzy line of demarcation runs from the major Sonoran river basins eastward across the Sierra Madre Occidental through the high plateaus and interior basins of Chihuahua and Coahuila. In modern terms the region includes the U.S. states of Arizona and New Mexico, as well as parts of Utah, Nevada, Colorado, California, and Texas. In Mexico it encompasses much of Sonora and Chihuahua, with influences that reach into portions of Sinaloa, Durango, and Baja California Norte.

It is an area of extraordinary contrast. The wild grandeur of the upper reaches of the southern Rockies contrast with the bland declivities of playas and bolsones, the remnants of Ice Age lakes. Tortured landscapes of bare rock and sand sometimes lie beside rich river valleys teeming with life. There are enormous stands of conifers in the high plateau country to the north and virtually no vegetation at all in salt-impregnated bolsones scattered throughout the region.

For all its differences—in topography, in vegetation, in climate—this region formed a kind of culturally diverse unity. The people who lived here had similar origins, and their intense interactions added to the unity even when differing environments tugged them apart. In some distant past certain of them might have

been ancestors to the Aztecs. Whatever the truth of that ancestry, clearly they were influenced by the great civilized lands of Mesoamerica to the south. One particular wave of influence that began about eight hundred years ago, powerful and widespread, will be the subject of this book.

Archaeologists and historians have long disagreed—sometimes acrimoniously—on what to call this area that so fascinated both Aztec and Spaniard. A number of names have been suggested by various scholars. In a previous book I used the term *Greater Southwest* for this vast area, pointing out that this was the Greater Southwest *not* of the United States but of *North America*. This region forms a sort of hinge where the land falls off sharply to the east. A longitudinal line running through Chaco Canyon in New Mexico intersects Casas Grandes in Chihuahua and reaches the Pacific somewhere around modern Culiacán. If the traveler goes on directly south, he or she will traverse Pacific water until reaching Antarctica. Mexico, Central America, and South America are all far to the east of this imaginary line.[5]

Unfortunately, some of my Mexican friends and colleagues were unconvinced by this argument, believing that a certain kind of Anglo-American chauvinism was implied. I had and have no such agenda, but for the present book I wanted to find a more generally acceptable term. Charles C. Di Peso's old phrase "Gran Chichimeca" comes to mind, but it really does not fit the purpose. Different people at different times have identified "Chichimecs" all the way from the Valley of Mexico to the great interior plateau of north-central Mexico. Oddly enough, the people of the Greater Southwest were generally *not* called Chichimecs. Appropriate or not, Di Peso's use of the words *Chichimec* and *Chichimeca* did spawn several book titles and subtitles.[6]

If one discards the words *Chichimec* or *Chichimeca*, there is the phrase often used by Mexican archaeologists and historians, "Noroeste de Mexico." However, this leaves out the Southwest of the United States. On the other hand, the term *Southwest* generally does not refer to Mexico. "Northwest of New Spain" has been suggested, but unfortunately this geographical area changed drastically over time. In the early period the Spaniards considered that it extended to the North Pole, and in later times it did indeed include upper California, or much of it. In spite of an ingenious argument by William Duncan Strong, many years ago, California, excepting the lower Colorado River area, cannot logically be considered in my prehistoric Greater Southwest, and even the Colorado River region was somewhat marginal.[7] In any case "Northwest of New Spain" hardly applies to the pre-Spanish period.

For all my mulling over names, I ignored the Aztecs and their well-known motherland until a few years ago, when I was asked to contribute to a catalog for an exhibit opening in May 2001 at the Los Angeles County Museum of Art (LACMA). This exhibit was entitled "The Road to Aztlan: Art from a Mythic Homeland." My chapter in the catalog, "Spaniards in Aztlan," concerned the Spanish penetration of the Greater Southwest. I treated *Aztlan* as a metaphor for the great kingdoms and golden cities that the Spaniards dreamed of in this new northern land.

At that point I suddenly realized that here was a ready-made general term for the Greater Southwest. *Aztlan* would be especially apt for that period when Mexican—then Spanish— influences remade vast areas of this north-Mexican frontier (see Figure 2.1). It has the advantage of being popular with the Hispanic communities in the United States, even if their definitions differ from time to time and place to place.

Still, I imagine that there will be objections to this term as to all the others. One obvious objection is that although the Aztecs in their formative years may quite conceivably have *come* from Aztlan, they most likely never *returned* to the faraway Noroeste in prehispanic times—Motecuhzoma and his "expedition" to the contrary. Whatever other peoples and ideas infiltrated the Greater Southwest in the period of greatest "Mexicanization" (about AD 1200 to the beginnings of historic times), it

seems clear that the Aztecs as a political entity were not involved. Or at least not directly involved! There is certain, albeit scanty, evidence that some Nahuatl, or perhaps a trade jargon based on Nahuatl, had infiltrated the upper Southwest by the time of the earliest Spaniards.[8] This may have resulted when Nahuatl-speaking traders, called *pochteca,* penetrated western Mexico in the century or so before the Spaniards arrived in Mexico. We do not know the extent of pochteca influence, but it could be that Aztec traders, or (more likely) western Mexican trading groups that were in contact with the pochteca, had in late prehistoric times pushed far to the north and west along the coast of the Gulf of California.

Another possible objection—if anyone remembers that far back—not to the name *Aztlan* per se but to the subject matter, is that I already had treated the subject a number of years ago in a book called *The Frontier People.* But that book had a very different organization and aim, although the Mexicanization of the Greater Southwest was one theme. Since I discussed only groups still functioning at the beginning of the Spanish invasion of the Southwest, the crucial Casas Grandes area was omitted. In any case neither archaeological nor ethnohistorical studies have stood still in the intervening years, and many new data need to be incorporated.

One important thing to remember is that beginning about AD 1200 in the Casas Grandes area and AD 1300, or a little later, in the upper portion of the area, the late prehistoric Southwest was indeed *becoming* Aztlan. At that time a sea change occurred in this great region. A wave of new religious, ceremonial, and political ideas, as well as new artistic styles and new technology, swept up from Mexico.[9]

It is true that there had been Mexican influences in the Southwest for a very long time, beginning perhaps with the introduction of horticulture three to four thousand years ago. The region had long been open to contacts from the outside. For example, trade in seashell, primarily from the Gulf of California,

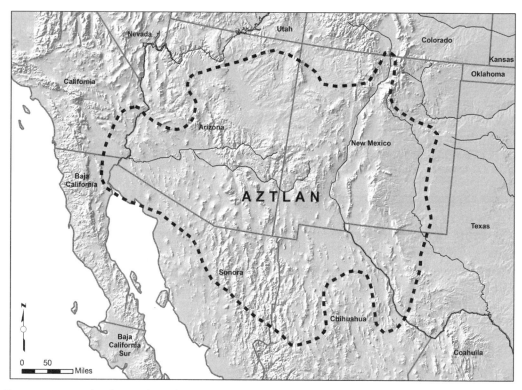

FIGURE 2.1. Map of Aztlan. Earth Analytic, Santa Fe, NM.

dates back to the early Christian or common era, or even before, and various artistic motifs were trickling into the Southwest well before AD 1300.

In southern Arizona the Hohokam had certain Mesoamerican traits, ceremonial platforms, and ball courts by the early first millennium AD. Casas Grandes, and its great central town, Paquimé, perhaps the most intensely Mesoamericanized culture of the Greater Southwest, actually saw a scatter of southern influences in the latter part of the Viejo period (pre-AD 1200). The Viejo was basically a Mogollon-like culture similar to other cultures spread across Arizona and southern New Mexico, much of mountain Sonora, and most of Chihuahua, with extensions into Durango in northwestern Mexico. In the later Viejo period there was a slow introduction of Mesoamerican traits, a trickle that suddenly became a torrent around AD 1200. It was in part through Casas Grandes that the full panoply of the Aztlan complex reached the upper Southwest.[10] How-

ever, we should not overemphasize the importance of the Casas Grandes world, for the major lines of contact gradually shifted westward, and from at least the fifteenth century on, major contacts between Mesoamerica and the Southwest were along the west coast of Mexico.

Another important center, far to the north of Casas Grandes, developed in the San Juan Basin of New Mexico about the same time as the latter part of the Viejo period. Although the Chaco culture was influenced by Mesoamerica, the pervasive influences in what was to be Aztlan began far to the south of Chaco and at a time (AD 1200) when the Chaco tradition was fading. The full manifestation of Aztlan involved not only a series of culture changes throughout the Southwest but also a kind of integration not seen before even in the regional integration of Chaco.

The period in southwestern prehistory that began around AD 1200 in Casas Grandes, and about a century later, following the collapse of the Anasazi San Juan region, in the upper Southwest, is very often misunderstood. It was a time of desertions and migrations from less favored to more favored areas. In the northern part of Aztlan it was a "Golden Age" of those Pueblo Indians who lived along the Rio Grande and in the Zuni-Hopi region, a time of expansion and vigor. The same was true in northeastern Sonora and—until a still unexplained collapse somewhere between 1400 and 1450—in the Casas Grandes world. On the other hand, the old Hohokam and Mogollon regions underwent a series of major cultural changes still not completely understood but so pervasive that the modern archaeological names *Hohokam* and *Mogollon* were only marginally meaningful by the beginning of historical times.

Charles C. Di Peso believed that an important indication of the "Mexicanization" of the Southwest came in the use of adobe in house construction. In his reconstruction adobe appeared quite early in the Casas Grandes area, spreading from western Mexico and eventually reaching the upper Southwest. However, as Curtis Schaafsma and I have pointed out, there is no real evidence for a northern spread of this technique from Mesoamerica.[11] Adobe may actually have been used in the Mimbres area as early as AD 900 and was in use at Chaco in the early twelfth century.[12] Coursed adobe, however, does not appear in Casas Grandes before Medio times (AD 1200), although I suppose it is possible that the adobe foundations for wattle-and-daub houses of Perros Bravos (late Viejo period) houses might have been exemplars and prototypes for later adobe structures. Even so, those would not predate Mimbres adobe buildings (see Figure 2.2).[13]

It does seem to me that the relative popularity of adobe brick in Aztlan times may relate to the "pan-Southwestern" orientation of society during that period. After about AD 1200 (and especially after AD 1300) adobe was used in the upper Rio Grande, at Casas Grandes, in the Río Carmén region of Chihuahua, in the El Paso phase of the Jornada Mogollon, in the Black Mountain phase of the Mimbres, among

FIGURE 2.2. Detail of coursed adobe, Olla Cave, west of Paquimé, Casas Grandes Medio period. Photo courtesy of Curtis F. Schaafsma.

the Salado, and in northeastern Sonora. I suspect that the origins of coursed adobe may eventually be traced to Mesoamerica, but this cannot be done at present.

There are other probable Mexican features, however, that involved town layout and construction techniques. It very likely also included glazed pottery (a specialized form of polychrome ceramic ware in which bands of mineral glazing form part of the decoration), a modified loom for weaving cotton, and probably embroidery on cotton. Cotton and its woven products became an important item of trade in the upper Southwest as it already was in the southern portions of the area, especially in northeast Sonora. By Aztlan times the Hopi area had become a center of the cotton trade, utilizing one of the varieties of *Gossypium hirsutum* that originated far to the south in Hohokam country.

Even more striking were artistic, religious, and political innovations. I will survey them

FIGURE 2.3. Tlaloc figure, southern New Mexico, probably Jornada Mogollon. Maxwell Museum of Anthropology, University of New Mexico, cat. no. 91.2.192.

here and discuss them in considerable detail in chapters 7 and 8. A major component in the Pueblo area was the kachina cult, an extension of worship of the venerable Mexican god Tlaloc (see Figure 2.3).[14] This deity is very old in Mesoamerica, perhaps dating to Olmec times, and everywhere is associated with clouds, mist, rain, and water from caves and springs. The deity may originally have been an earth god (the name can mean "from [or of] the earth"), but in later Mesoamerican cultures and in the Southwest Tlaloc was strongly associated with water. In fact, it has been suggested that the name *Tlaloc* really refers to mist rising from the ground or from the sides of mountains.[15]

Another Pueblo aspect of culture with strong Mesoamerican overtones was the war society incorporating the Mesoamerican twin war gods and their earthly avatars, the twin bow chiefs. The twin war gods were represented celestially by Venus, in its aspects as morning and evening star, and by the god Quetzalcoatl.[16] The latter deity has many aspects. For example, as Ehécatl (Nahuatl "wind") he controlled the breezes; as Topiltzin ("beloved child" or "our prince") he regulated fertility. He also seems to have been associated with the Fire Serpent god, Xiuhtecutli. The name *Quetzalcoatl* means "quetzal bird snake" or, at another level, "sa-

cred twin." In his Mayan manifestation his name was Kukulkan, with essentially the same meaning, "feathered serpent." In the Chalchihuites culture, along the northern frontier of Mesoamerica proper, Quetzalcoatl was represented iconographically as a bird and a serpent together, and he appeared in the Southwest as a feathered or horned serpent. Other Mesoamerican deities that are sometimes related to the Southwest include Chalchihuitlicue ("Lady Precious Green" or "Lady of the Jade [or Turquoise] Skirt"), who is connected (as a sister or a wife) to Tlaloc. She was the goddess of groundwaters, springs, and the like but also to some degree a deity of the earth (see Figure 2.4).

More problematic is Tezcatlipoca (Figure 2.5), whose name in Nahuatl means "Smoking Mirror" and who is a bit of an oddity. He was not a nature god like the others. In the words of Sahagún, "his abode was everywhere—in the land of the dead, on earth, [and] in heaven." He seems to have been a sort of high god, outside the restraints imposed on other deities and on mortal beings. Tezcatlipoca had many avatars; for one thing he was represented as a quadripartite god, associated with each of the primary directions and with color-directional symbolism. In his eastern epiphany

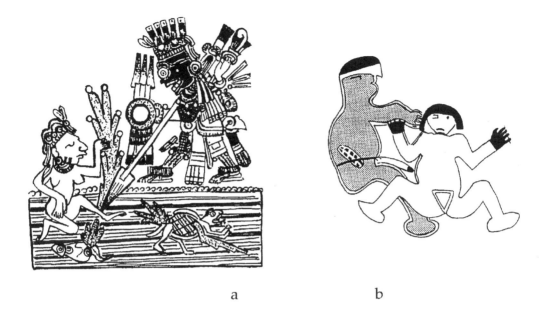

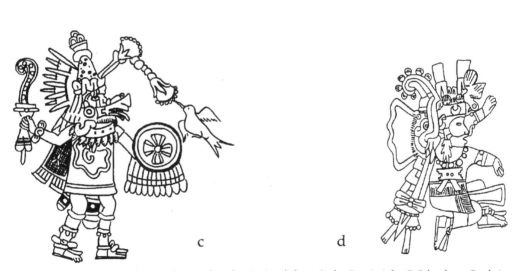

FIGURE 2.4. (a) Chalchihuitlicue and Quetzalcoatl as Ce Acatl, from Codex Borgia (after P. Schaafsma, *Rock Art in New Mexico*); (b) Chalchihuitlique and Ce Acatl from Awatovi kiva mural room 529, Hopi (after McKusick, *Southwest Birds of Sacrifice*); (c) Quetzalcoatl as Ehécatl, Aztec (after McKusick, *Southwest Birds of Sacrifice*); (d) Xiuhtecutli wearing the Fire Serpent as a back piece, from Codex Borbonicus (after McKusick, *Southwest Birds of Sacrifice*).

Tezcatlipoca was associated with yellow, the rising sun, and maize. The southern Tezcatlipoca was blue; the western one was red, linked with the vegetation deity, Xipe Tótec; while the northern Tezcatlipoca was black and the patron of witches and other practitioners of the black arts. His southern manifestation also relates him with Huitzilopochtli the Aztec war god. Huitzilopochtli (his name variously translated as "Hummingbird from the Left," "Hummingbird Wizard," or "Blue Hummingbird") shot into prominence only in Aztec times.[17]

FIGURE 2.5. Tezcatlipoca (after McKusick, *Southwest Birds of Sacrifice*).

The deities Quetzalcoatl, Tlaloc, and Chalchihuitlicue might conceivably date from Chaco times, although present evidence suggests that this is unlikely. The first two certainly appear in Aztlan times, and it seems likely that Chalchihuitlicue did also. These Mesoamerican complexes in their southwestern manifestations were, of course, modified in various ways. In addition to the three deities mentioned above, the claim has been made for Tezcatlipoca and Huitzilopochtli worship in certain parts of the Southwest. However, the evidence for Tezcatlipoca is equivocal and for Huitzilopochtli basically nonexistent.[18]

However this may be, new sodalities, not only the war society but also the hunt society, helped change the nature of social relationships throughout much of the Southwest. A series of new and complex artistic motifs and design elements spread from Mesoamerica to Casas Grandes and, a century later, to the upper Rio Grande and to the Zuni and Hopi towns. Color-directional symbolism in the Southwest probably dates from this general time. It is of great antiquity in Mesoamerica, and its spread

northward was early enough for it to have a secondary diffusion to some of the Apachean peoples.[19]

The trade in exotic and brightly plumaged birds, already noted in Chaco, now became much more widespread, covering the width and breadth of Aztlan. The shell trade was also important. Strings of shell (called *hishi* among the historic Pueblos), which were used as a sort of primitive currency, perhaps date from this period.[20] According to the Ramusio edition of Marcos de Niza, turquoise was also used as a medium of exchange, at least in the sixteenth century.[21] Turquoise, found in various parts of Mesoamerica, has been provisionally identified by the neutron activation technique as from the Cerrillos region south of modern-day Santa Fe.[22] I should caution, however, that turquoise variation, even within the same mine, makes such identification rather chancy.

Such finds indicate the Southwest was exporting turquoise, and there is evidence that other semiprecious stone such as peridot and garnet, as well as bison hides, salt, and possibly slaves, were also moving from north to south. The Southwest also exported pottery. Early-fifteenth-century Largo Glaze-on-yellow pottery from the Rio Grande region has been found in western Jalisco.[23] Only a century later Marcos de Niza, traveling along a major trading route somewhere in northern Sonora, noted very handsome pottery vessels in the trade network.[24] Excavators at the site of Guasave, in Sinaloa, dating around AD 1350, discovered a number of turquoise beads and 15 pendants, the turquoise tentatively associated with the Cerrillos area of central New Mexico.[25]

Aztlan, therefore, was a region that largely owed its character, and its very definition as a sociogeographical entity, to events beyond its borders. It became a frontier region, an appendage of the civilized states of Mesoamerica. This was no political or military conquest because none of the peoples such as the Aztecs and the Tarascans, who were in the business of overrunning their neighbors, and who had the sophisticated political organization to do so, lived near enough to directly impinge on the Southwest. Rather, it was the cumulative effect of contacts, planned or unplanned, that had existed in the past but that now took on a new dimension and new depth.

There are a couple of curious negatives in this contact picture however. Even though it was known and popular in Mexico, the upper Southwest (we are not totally sure of Casas Grandes and the Sonoran region) did not seem to have adopted any alcoholic beverage.[26] This is particularly odd since the use of alcoholic beverages has been extraordinarily popular among human populations for thousands of years. The other lack in at least the upper Southwest—data from the southern parts of the area are, again, uncertain—is the domesticated chili. This should have been natural since the southwestern diet is rather bland, but the chili plant has not been found archaeologically, and the first known documents mentioning it are from the latter part of the sixteenth century.[27] Chili and melons seem to have exploded into the Southwest very quickly after Spanish contact, and it seems quite possible that both were introduced as early as Coronado's time. Melons, of course, are Spanish-introduced plants, but why chili did not reach the Southwest sooner is somewhat of a mystery. On the other hand there is a possibility that the hallucinogenic plant peyote may have a prehispanic distribution in the Southwest,[28] although documentary evidence for it does not come until the early seventeenth century.

One important aspect of this period is the existence of widespread contacts throughout the new cultural entity of Aztlan. Even before its formation, peoples in the Southwest were involved in various kinds of long-distance interactions; consider, for example, the trading network that supplied Chaco. Other examples that can be traced archaeologically, and that overlapped with the early Aztlan period, were the St. Johns redwares (black-on-red and polychrome ceramics), which probably originated in the region of the Mogollon Rim in Arizona and in adjacent New Mexico. These wares were traded from central and southeast Arizona

in the west to the Pecos River and its tributaries in the east, and from the Four Corners area in the north to southwest Texas and northern Chihuahua in the south. As discussed in chapter 6, polychrome pottery and a ceramic design style, the Pinedale style, were found in early Aztlan times from the Hopi region and the upper Rio Grande to the Salado of the Salt River basin, the Jornada Mogollon, Casas Grandes, and extended, as trade ware, into northeast and north-central Sonora. Patricia Crown has tied this ceramic "horizon style" to what she calls the *Southwestern Cult*, a pan-southwestern manifestation.[29] I will return to the Southwestern Cult in later chapters.

Also forming in the fourteenth century, a web of trade networks extending from Mesoamerica linked all areas of the Southwest. Paquimé, in Chihuahua, was surely involved in the earlier trade. But even before the collapse of Paquimé, more and more of the trade was being pumped up the west coast through Sinaloa and northeastern Sonora. In the latter area small vigorous trading-oriented polities that I have called "statelets" were in the process of forming. By the time the Spaniards arrived, this route had become the major trade artery, although some goods, scarlet macaws for example, may still have traversed the eastern, intermontane, route.[30] In a 1976 publication I postulated a hiatus, or at least a considerable lessening of contacts into and out of the Southwest from about AD 1200 to AD 1350 with the major wave of influences, reinvigorating the trade networks beginning even a little later, about AD 1400.[31] This still looks to be largely true of trade contacts extending from the eastern Pueblo area across the plains toward the Mississippi Valley. However, for most of Aztlan I now consider the idea of a slackening in trade during the thirteenth and early fourteenth centuries to be considerably overblown.

In any case these trade routes eventually extended in every direction as southwesterners became middlemen in the exchange systems. Trade parties certainly reached the lower Colorado River and the Pacific coast of California, where shell, coral, and probably steatite were exchanged for turquoise, ceramics, skins, and brightly colored feathers. The routes also ran east into modern Kansas, Oklahoma, and Texas, and trade goods are found as far east as Missouri and Arkansas. The eastward distribution included Pacific and Gulf of California shell, turquoise, obsidian, agate, petrified wood and a wide range of pottery, maize, cotton cloth, piñon nuts, and perhaps tobacco. Flowing to the west out of the Great Plains (and regions further east), were bison and deer hides, bison meat, Osage orange bow wood, freshwater shell, and Gulf Coast marine shell, alibates flint, the schistose fibrolite, and, plausibly, elbow ceramic pipes and Caddoan shouldered and carinated pottery. One item of shell, a particular species of Strombus found at Pecos Pueblo, may have originated in Florida.[32]

It might be well to pause here and talk about civilizations and frontiers. There are no implications of differential human moral or mental worth in this word *civilization,* or indeed in *advanced society* or *high culture,* terms used more or less interchangeably in this book. An advanced society is one that, in relationship to the simpler societies around it, has a technology with complicated architectural and agricultural techniques, sophisticated weaponry, carpentry, weaving, ceramic making, and metallurgy. Many high cultures also have invented or borrowed writing systems. Their religions have well-defined and cogently interrelated deities and rich traditional mythologies and eschatologies. Art in advanced societies contains more techniques, employs more varied media, and has, overall, more functions. Populations are larger and the socioreligious organization has greater complexity, reflecting this greater demographic size.[33]

An example of an advanced society with its interacting borderlands would be the late Republic and Imperial Rome in relationship to the simpler societies of northern and eastern Europe.[34] A New World high culture/low culture situation, and the one I deal with in this book, is Mesoamerica and its various border groups.[35] Another New World example would be the Inca Empire and the cluster of tribal

cultures that surrounded it on the north, east, and south. There are, of course, many other examples in every habitable continent around the world. Even the remote and primitive island continent of Australia developed a sort of high center and dependent hinterland when the British came, a bit before AD 1800.

Frontiers generally demonstrate that the advance to civilization is never a straight-line proposition. It is not an unbroken quickening of the borderlands by cultural innovations from the center, like the inexorable spread of ripples when a pebble is tossed into a still pond. Rather, there are nodes of more hierarchical culture that appear for a time in selected places, then fade, only to pop up elsewhere. The overall fermentation over long periods will advance the frontier. Collapse of the center, as happened with Rome in the fourth and fifth centuries AD, and in both Mesoamerica and the Central Andes at various times, created devastation in the hinterland, but it was a differential devastation and one that took various forms. For example, the Mesoamerican frontiers existed for perhaps 2,500 years, and there were, in fact, several collapses, and subsequent reestablishment, of borders. The Central Andes, also a very old civilized area, seems to have had a series of cultural advances and retreats, the advances marked by the great horizon styles in ceramics, architecture, and weaving. These pan-Andean styles were followed by retreats to local cultures, though some of those—the Moche of north coastal Peru, for example—were themselves brilliant civilizations.[36]

In Mesoamerica there had been a slow spread outward from certain original nodes of high culture from about 1000 BC. The initial centers of Mesoamerican civilization were in the central mountains and western highlands of Mexico and in the eastern and southern lowlands. Whether they were in turn the outgrowth of some mother culture, perhaps Olmec or proto-Olmec, is still a matter of controversy. In any case, quite early in time these centers expanded into regions of politically less centralized cultures that surrounded them and grew also toward each other, cross-fertilizing a vast region.

More complex culture spread in irregular and imprecise waves, some higher and some lower, southward into Central America, northeastward along the Gulf Coast and to the northwest and the Gulf of California. The initial wave that produced this northwestern frontier occurred at the end of Classic times (AD 500 to 700), with a second one about three to four centuries before the arrival of the Spaniards. The northwestern extension of Mesoamerica crept up the Pacific coast and along the high plateau and basin country into the north and west of Mexico. As indicated above, the Mesoamerican tide after incomplete attempts (Chaco, for example) eventually inundated present-day northwest Mexico and southwestern United States, turning them into Aztlan. Some scholars believe that it even reached the U.S. Midwest around this time, though if so it was only in a diffuse and generalized way.[37]

The rich religious ceremonies, mythology, and iconography of the Tlaloc cult (and to some degree the Quetzalcoatl and Chalchihuitlicue cults) appeared in the lower Southwest perhaps around AD 1200 and in the upper Southwest a century or so later. It is important to understand that these divine complexes came in recognizable but vastly distorted forms. To the extent that we do understand them, it is clear that in the Greater Southwest the great religious traditions of Tlaloc and Quetzalcoatl were transformed into something quite different, something that fitted the needs and cultural imperatives of the region. The Spaniards, when they came to the Southwest, had an opportunity to observe the kachina dances among Pueblo Indians. Some of them may well have been acquainted, at least indirectly, with the great rain and fertility god Tlaloc. Certainly this religious figure would have been described in Sahagún and in other writings of the sixteenth-century Franciscans, though to what extent these writings were available to the early Spanish conquistadors is uncertain. In any case, as far as we know, none of the conquistadors tumbled to the fact that the kachinas were attenuated forms of Tlaloc. The differences in both form and func-

tion had, at this far remove, swamped the generic relationship.

The same was probably true with Quetzalcoatl and Tlaloc in Casas Grandes. The iconography that in central Mexico was associated with Quetzalcoatl, was certainly present in Casas Grandes, though, unlike the Pueblo Southwest, we do not know the specificities of worship in the great Chihuahuan center. There were also Tlaloc manifestations at Casas Grandes. But the icons themselves suggest that the Casas Grandes people had somehow changed the religious nature of Quetzalcoatl and Tlaloc.[38]

Before ending this chapter, I need to say a word about methodology. Although the research for this book is mostly archaeological, I also make use of Spanish documentation. In fact, I originally considered using the name *Protohistoric* in the title. However, if we are to understand the late fluorescence and intense Mesoamericanization of society in the Greater Southwest, my starting point needs to be a bit earlier than one can comfortably designate as *protohistoric*, if by the term we mean societies that are to some degree illuminated by written historical records. To really understand the events that precipitated the Golden Age of the Pueblos, the rise and fall of Casas Grandes, and the particular organization of the Sonoran statelets, we must delve back a bit before AD 1200. This takes us into the late phases of the Hohokam, the latter part of the Chaco culture, the late blooming and collapse of Mesa Verde, and the early springtime of the great northern Mexican societies in Chihuahua and Sonora, perhaps the nearest thing to civilizations that the Greater Southwest ever produced. These were the seed cultures, laying the conditions that would generate Aztlan.

To incorporate this "pre-protohistoric" period, a semantically flexible term like *Aztlan* seems to make more sense. The earlier materials do not lend themselves to any recognizable reflection from Spanish sources. Spanish materials on the kachina cult can give us information that dimly reflects the situation as of about AD 1300, but, as indicated above, the

Spaniards misunderstood most or all of what they saw in Pueblo ceremonials. Although the Spaniards used the Sonoran statelets as a stopover in their early explorations into the Southwest, they provide amazingly little information on the region and its people and certainly nothing that could reasonably go back to the early thirteenth century.

Sadly, even this scanty information does not hold for the Casas Grandes world. Although one Spanish expedition actually saw the ruins of Paquimé in the mid-1560s, it produced very little information on the Paquimé heartland. The Mimbres region was totally unknown to the early Spaniards, nor were they acquainted with the El Paso phase of the Jornada Mogollon. In the sixteenth century there was a group, called Manso by the Spaniards, who still lived in the El Paso area. One might expect information on the Manso to provide some insights into the final phases of the Jornada Mogollon. However, the Manso were a remnant people by the time of the first Spanish contacts and had lost much of their cultural complexity. Only among the people of La Junta, where the Rio Grande and the Conchos River meet, did the Spaniards find tribal peoples whose cultures continued on with something of the vigor of earlier times. The Spaniards, however, learned nothing of any great importance from these groups. Ethnographers the Spaniards were not! They occasionally collected oddments of information, but more often than not they left out important details on religious life, language, and sociopolitical organization.

As I pointed out above, the Spaniards were not the only people with civilization. Both central and west Mexico had highly sophisticated cultures that affected the Greater Southwest for several hundred years before the arrival of the Europeans. Forms of writing existed in Mesoamerica, although they were only partly developed in the regions nearest northwest Mexico and the Southwest. In any case there is no evidence that any writing system was ever introduced into the Greater Southwest before Spanish times. No Mesoamerican written source related to the Southwest has been found, if we except the vague Aztec stories of the wanderings from the seven caves of Aztlan.

There were in fact a few oral traditions that point to a southwestern-Mesoamerican interaction in earlier times. Perhaps the most dramatic is the Tejo story discussed in chapters 8 and 9. And the Spaniard missionaries and government officials, in the sixteenth and seventeenth centuries did give us *some* information, especially about ceremonial life, even though their interpretations were almost always far off the mark. More important, in some parts of the Greater Southwest, ethnographic evidence collected in the last century and a half links protohistoric but pre-Spanish southwesterners to the high cultures of Mesoamerica. Alas, this is not true of the Casas Grandes world, the Hohokam, nor to a large degree of the Sonoran statelets; their voices are mute, and we have only physical evidence. But it *is* true of the Pueblos, and through them we can see how pervasive were certain aspects of Mesoamerican religion and ceremonialism.

# CHAPTER 3

# Landscapes, Cultural and Natural

Aztlan constitutes a cultural unity more than it does a geographical one.[1] Although the Southwest bordered on and contained specialized hunters and Archaic-like gatherers, most of its inhabitants were sedentary and agricultural. They lived in settlements of substantial houses (see Figure 3.1), often stone or coursed adobe, though some areas utilized pithouses or wattle-and-daub structures. Earthen platforms, presumably constructed for ceremonial reasons, were a feature of the sedentary Greater Southwest but mostly in the south, being intrusive and exotic among the more northern groups.[2] The ball court was used, ceremonially, in the Casas Grandes region, probably in the northeast Sonoran area and certainly among the Hohokam, although it was dying out in that region by the times covered by this book. It never took hold in the Pueblo world, its functions probably usurped by the plaza, the center for the great ceremonial dances.[3]

Ceramic production was essentially universal among the sedentary peoples, although technical skills in pottery making varied a great deal from one area to another. Generally, the finest pottery was produced at Casas Grandes centers and in the Pueblo world, especially in the western regions. Both areas had polychrome pottery, and their best wares, particularly the Hopi Jeddito pottery and certain of the Casas Grandes decorated ceramics, represent perhaps the premier ceramic traditions in all of aboriginal North America (Figure 3.2). Curiously enough, the Sonoran region was backward in pottery, as was the nearby Trincheras. The Indians of this region imported some Casas Grandes wares, but their own pottery traditions were not greatly developed. In the Gila-Salt area the skilled pottery of Hohokam times was gradually replaced by crude culinary wares. This was also true in the El Paso region, where a technically adequate El Paso pottery gradually faded out as the region approached early historic times. In the border region of the lower Colorado River, ceramic traditions were relatively undeveloped, certainly uninspired, and at La Junta, on the eastern fringe of the Greater Southwest, the El Paso wares had been replaced by a roughly made culinary pottery by early Spanish contact times.[4]

The region extends from the habitat of the late prehistoric Anasazi Pueblo Indians, who at the beginning of our story were in the process of exiting a vast extent of the San Juan Basin, parts of the Colorado River area, and the high plateau country of central Arizona. By the time of first Spanish contact in this western region, only two tiny clusters of pueblos remained, those of Hopi and Zuni, clusters both pressured by and interacting with nomadic Apachean- and Ute-speaking Indians. At about the time the San Juan region was deserted, the Casas Grandes region was becoming a powerful cultural factor.

There are certain generalizations that can be made about the physical landforms of the

FIGURE 3.1. Pueblo house block. Maxwell Museum of Anthropology, University of New Mexico, cat. no. 71.18.119.

FIGURE 3.2. Chihuahuan polychrome pottery. Amerind Foundation, Dragoon, AZ.

Greater Southwest. Except for the upper reaches of the mountains and the western fringe of the Great Plains it is generally a dry land, desert or semidesert with the typical flora and fauna associated with deserts. With the exception of the bottoms of ancient lake beds, or *playas,* it is a rough and broken country, and even some of the old lake beds are highly dissected. A great deal is Basin and Range topography, and the isolated ranges vary in altitude, some being too low to develop fully montane biological and climatic environments.

The northern portion of Aztlan is in the high mountain country of the southern Rockies. Parallel chains extend into modern New Mexico, the easternmost being the Sangre de Cristo Mountains, containing the highest terrain in that state. Two peaks, Wheeler and Truchas, are above 13,000 feet, and several are above 12,000 feet. The Rio Grande, originating in the uplands of southeastern Colorado, divide the Sangre de Cristo Mountains from the slightly lower Tusas and Jemez ranges. The rivers in this area drain into the Rio Grande although the easternmost, the Pecos, flows for more than 900 miles before joining the parent stream. The one exception to this pattern is the Canadian River and its tributaries, which drain a portion of northeast New Mexico and adjacent areas of Texas and Oklahoma to eventually flow into the Arkansas River and on to the Mississippi. The Rio Grande itself rises in present-day Colorado in the high country at the Continental Divide. It flows southward through New Mexico, then turns east, forming part of the international boundary between the United States and Mexico. Eventually the river devolves into the Gulf of Mexico.

Only a few miles from the headwaters of the Rio Grande, the San Juan River drains the opposite way, its waters, via the Colorado River, reaching the Gulf of California and the Pacific. This headwater country is at the very edge of the Southwest, though it may have been utilized to some degree by people of the Mesa Verde area. The San Juan River and its tributary rivers and creeks, especially the Animas, La Plata, Mancos, McElmo, Yellow Jacket, and Mon-

tezuma, were important to Puebloan peoples in the period before about AD 1300. The major tributaries all enter from the north, draining the higher country of Colorado and Utah. From the south there is little in the way of perennial streams, although one intermittent stream, Chaco Wash, was an important part of the cultural Southwest in pre-Aztlan times. It heads in the high country west of the Continental Divide, less than fifty miles from the headwater of the Puerco River, the latter east of the Divide and part of the Rio Grande system. This is a bleak landscape, arid and much eroded. In modern times it is utilized by the Navajo for sheep herding, but aboriginally it was the center of the complex Chaco culture.

The Rio Grande flows south and east into the San Luís Valley, then in a southward direction, where it enters the Rio Grande Gorge, several hundred feet in depth. The stream leaves the gorge south of the Taos area and skirts the eastern flank of the Jemez Mountains and Pajarito Plateau, eventually coming out in the Basin and Range country south of the Jemez River. Major streams draining into the Rio Grande are the Chama, Jemez, and Puerco, coming in from the west, and the Taos, Santa Cruz, Santa Fe, and Galisteo from the east. In the Greater Southwest a "major stream" is generally one that flows all year round; however, the Santa Fe, Galisteo, and Puerco hardly do even that, at least at the present day.

South of the Jemez, scarcity of the ambient water supply means that the Rio Grande has few tributary streams, something also true of the Pecos, which parallels its parent as it flows south and east. There is one major exception to this situation in the Rio Grande watershed. The Conchos River, which joins the Rio Grande at La Junta in south Texas and northern Chihuahua, is indeed a major river, tripling the flow of the Rio Grande.

West of the Rio Grande, in northern New Mexico and Arizona, lies the high country of the Colorado Plateaus, some of the region reaching 8,000 feet or more but tailing off into the river valleys of the San Juan, Colorado, and Little Colorado. This area was home to some of the Pueblo peoples, as well as nomadic groups, some moving into the area during Aztlan times. The eastern frontier of Aztlan is made up of that section of the Great Plains that butts up against the Rockies. Elevations in the very western part of the Great Plains reach 5,000 to 6,000 feet, and aboriginally this relatively flat grassland was the home of bison herds moving restlessly north to south and north again. Two rivers, the Canadian and the Pecos, drain the region, the Canadian cutting across the southwestern plains, and the Pecos forming their westernmost edge. Both rivers begin in the southern spur of the Rockies, the Sangre de Cristo of southern Colorado and northeast New Mexico. Much of the drainage area of the Pecos River is deficient in rainfall, and this is true to some degree for the Canadian, although the southern plains have more precipitation in general than do the desertlike regions to the south and west. However, the upper reaches of both rivers receive considerable moisture, something on the order of 30 inches of rainfall (or its snowfall equivalent) per year (see Figure 3.3).

One geographically specialized portion of the southern plains is the Llano Estacado. This is an extraordinarily flat area, a tableland covering some 30,000 square miles in southwestern Texas and southeastern New Mexico. This stretch of grassland, delineated by escarpments on the west and a series of stark and rugged canyons on the east, was home to enormous herds of bison during the period covered in this book and for many other periods in the past. During the fourteenth to sixteenth centuries AD, which saw the northern manifestation of Aztlan, trade for bison products, flints, and various other commodities was important to southwestern Indians, who in turn sent shell, turquoise, and pottery into the plains.

The eastern edge of Aztlan is formed by the escarpment of the Sangre de Cristo Mountains and, farther south, the valley of the Pecos River as it flows from New Mexico into Texas. A line along Toyah Creek to the La Junta area, then looping south and west to encompass the Casas Grandes sphere, would delineate the southeast-

ern and southern boundary. Much of the region is Basin and Range, with jagged peaks thrusting up from the adjacent more or less flat range or plain. But even this area is not really flat, thanks to the forces of erosion, which have carved out innumerable arroyos or gulches, lacing the otherwise flat terrain. This Basin and Range country extends south and west from central New Mexico, below the Sangre de Cristo and Jemez-San Juan chains. It is an arid country, with a series of isolated mountain ranges, which form a rather random scatter across the landscape. Because of the generally dry conditions the lower portions of the mountains have only a scrub vegetation, or *monte* (as it is called in Mexico). Many of these ranges are not high enough to catch the moister currents in the upper atmosphere and so have a very sparse plant life. The Sierra Blanca Range, however, forming the eastern rampart to the Tularosa Basin in southern New Mexico, has one peak (Sierra Blanca) with an altitude slightly greater than 12,000 feet. At this altitude there is considerable winter snow and heavy stands of conifers.

The Basin and Range country includes the Chihuahuan Desert, of New Mexico and Chihuahua, and the Sonoran Desert, of Arizona and Sonora. These regions have extremely hot summers but mild winters, especially in southern Arizona and Sonora.

In the easternmost part of this region, in what today is eastern Chihuahua, lies the large drainage area of the Rio Conchos and its tributaries. These drain the eastern slope of the northern Sierra Madre, and, as mentioned above, the Conchos joins the Rio Grande, vastly increasing the flow of the "main" river. The headwaters of the Conchos lay at the very southern edge of Aztlan, its aboriginal population made up of latter-day Archaic and incipient agriculturalists. The area was settled early by the Spaniards because of silver mines, in particular those in the vicinity of the Río Florido.

A bit farther to the north and west lie the dry interior basins of western Chihuahua, where several rivers, small but important to the development of the Casas Grandes culture, flow into

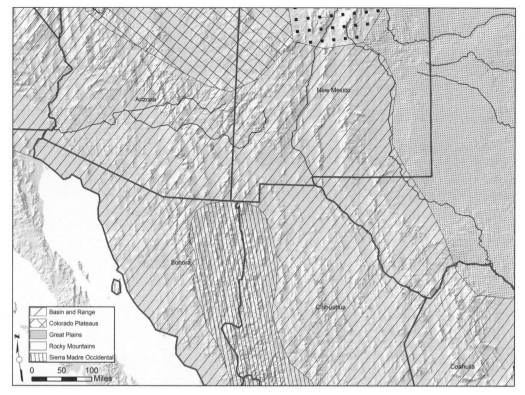

FIGURE 3.3. Physiographic provinces of Aztlan. Earth Analytic, Santa Fe, NM.

shallow bolsones or basins. The rivers include—from east to west—the Carmén, the Santa María, and the Casas Grandes, all of which flow northward into northwestern Chihuahua, eventually draining into the Laguna de Los Patos, the Laguna Santa María, and the Laguna Guzmán, respectively. These are shallow ephemeral lakes, forming during the rainy seasons but largely marshland or salt flats the rest of the time. Between the river drainages are low ranges, increasing in size and ruggedness as one goes from east to west. Westward of the Casas Grandes drainage lies the Sierra Madre and the Continental Divide. This particular region contains some of the most rugged country in North America, though trails crossed it in aboriginal times as a few roads do today.

The Sonoran Desert flanks the northern portion of the Sierra Madre Occidental to the west. These mountains begin at about the present international border and trend far into west-central Mexico. It was in the Sonoran

Desert and in the mountainous country of the Sonora-Chihuahua border country that certain relatively rich late prehistoric cultures developed, especially in the upper and middle courses of the Sonora, Moctezuma, and Yaqui rivers. In those river valleys small energetic units, "statelets," formed around primate towns, controlling separate stretches of the rivers. Farther west, the desert country of the lower Colorado drainage, including the lower Gila River basin, formed the westernmost frontier of what was to become Aztlan (see Figure 3.4).

The flora of the Southwest shows considerable variation, reflecting the differences in altitude, precipitation, and amount and intensity of sunlight. Sunlit days considerably outnumber cloudy ones. The southwestern part of the region, especially the valleys of the Yaqui, Sonora, Magdalena-Altar, Gila, Salt, and lower Colorado rivers, has a climate that is largely warm steppe and warm desert. The Sierra Madre itself is relatively well watered in its

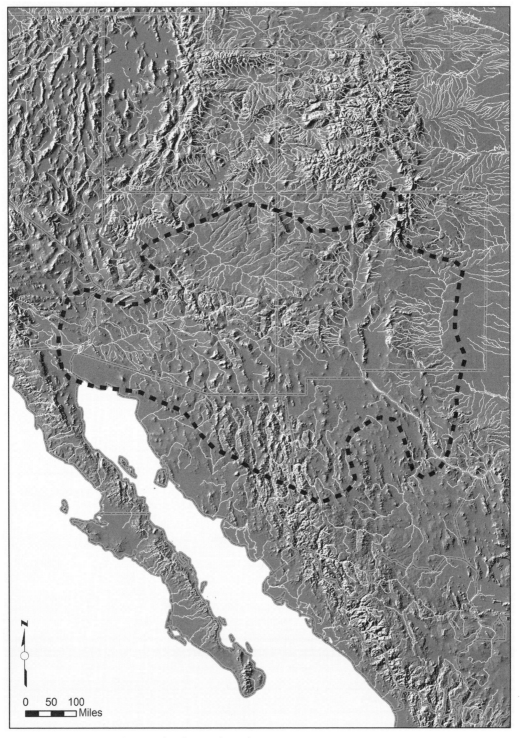

FIGURE 3.4. Mountains and rivers of Aztlan. Earth Analytic, Santa Fe, NM.

upper reaches, but in the lower elevations east of the mountains, in the Casas Grandes area, and eastward to the drainage of the Conchos and La Junta, there is a dry warm desert, shading into a cooler desert as one goes east and north toward the Rio Grande. All these regions are characterized by xerophytic vegetation, including the many cacti, arid-land grasses, mesquite, and other scrub ground cover, or monte. As altitude increases in the Sierra Madre and in various isolated ranges in the Basin and Range country to the north and east, there are stands of piñon, juniper, live oak, and, as one goes even higher, various of the larger conifers.

Farther north, the mountains of central Arizona were, and mostly still are, heavily forested. North of the Mogollon Rim are stretches of semiarid grass and scrub vegetation, including sagebrush and yucca and various cacti, with stands of cottonwood and hackberry in the valleys and conifers in such higher elevations as the Zuni Mountains. This is the region of the Colorado Plateaus, grassland with wooded stretches in the upland areas, where the lay of the land is generally high. It is the original heartland of the Anasazi. In this region winters are usually cold, while summers are apt to be hot. East of the plateau country the valley of the upper Rio Grande, as we have seen, flows between two southern spurs of the Rockies, eventually devolving into the extensive Basin and Range south of Santa Fe. The mountains were heavily covered with conifer forests, many of which still remain. Along the river are stretches of "bosque," or deciduous forests (cottonwood, maple, plum, and, in the south, walnut, screwbean, and mesquite, among other species). As the river cuts through the Basin and Range country of central and southern New Mexico and the Texas-Mexico border area, the climate becomes increasingly arid and, reflecting the steady drop in elevation (5,000 feet at Albuquerque down to 3,500 feet at El Paso), a milder winter climate.

The Pecos River more or less parallels the Rio Grande in development of plant life and heavy forests at the headwaters, with grasses and increasingly xerophytic vegetation as one goes south along the river (Figure 3.5). East of the Pecos the high plains contain grasses such as side oats, blue grama, and buffalo grass. Protected areas grow wild plums, willow, maple, and other trees, as well as a variety of compositae and other flowering plants. Winters here are apt to be variable, with a number of days well below freezing and sometimes with considerable snow.

In aboriginal times the fauna of the Greater Southwest showed a great variety, with large game animals and their predators in the mountains, deer, antelope, elk, wolves, bears (both black and grizzly), and mountain lions. Many of these remain today, although the grizzly bear now has a more northerly range. Even today jaguars are found in the Sierra Madre and have been seen, though rarely, as far north as southern Arizona. During the period covered in this book vast herds of bison ranged on the southern plains. Smaller mammals included and include large numbers of hares and rabbits (important for human consumption from at least early Archaic times), a variety of ground squirrels, and other fur-bearing creatures, among them, beaver, otter, badger, and skunk. There are numerous lizards and snakes, especially at the lower elevations, including several poisonous snakes and in the Gila-Salt area a poisonous reptile, the Gila Monster. Certain scorpions have painful stings, especially in the Gila region, and one life-threatening variety, the bark scorpion, does extend well into Aztlan. However, there is a full component of arachnids and insects, as well as bats and various birds to prey on them. Larger birds include the carnivorous owls, hawks, eagles, and a variety of game birds. Some are seasonal for the Rio Grande and other river and lake systems and have long been part of migratory flyways. There are fish in the permanent streams, and some, though not all, of the native peoples utilized fish for food.[5]

As I have indicated, there is a general deficiency in rainfall except at high elevations. The patterns of rainfall are similar over much of the area. In the Greater Southwest the scanty rains come mainly in the late summer and early

FIGURE 3.5. Pecos River, near San José. Photo by the author.

winter, much of the precipitation in the latter period falling in the form of snow. This pattern varies somewhat; for example, in the La Junta region of Texas-Chihuahua there is relatively little winter rain.[6] Aztlan is a region where dry farming was generally chancy, many of the aboriginal inhabitants depending on irrigation. Some of the irrigation systems were very simple, for example those in the La Junta area and in the lower Colorado. One technique was effected by placing fields in the runoff plains of ephemeral streams, whereas another, called riverine irrigation, involved planting the fields in the flood plain of the rivers (Figure 3.6). Much more sophisticated ditch irrigation systems were employed in Gila-Salt Valley, and in the Sonora, Yaqui, Montezuma, and San

Miguel systems. The small internally draining streams of northern Chihuahua were also used for ditch irrigation by the Casas Grandes people. The Pueblo Indians, both east and west, tapped the various rivers, especially the Rio Grande, for ditch irrigation.[7]

In all parts of Aztlan water control was important in the prehistoric past, as it remains today. In areas where we have historical echoes of prehispanic religion, rain or other water control ceremonies were important. In fact, water is today the overriding ecological consideration in southwestern human occupancy, and this has been true for a very long time, perhaps from the end of the lush climates of the terminal Pleistocene.

FIGURE 3.6. Northern portion of Sonora Valley in upper statelet area. Photo by the author.

CHAPTER 4

# Before Aztlan

Human beings entered the New World during the latter phases of the Pleistocene or Ice Age, moving into the Southwest at least by around 11,500 years ago, as indicated by ¹⁴C dating. This is the period of the large-game-hunting *Paleoindian* Clovis culture, but it now seems quite possible that there were even earlier peoples in the Southwest. Older dates for human beings also seem very likely in other parts of the New World.[1]

By seven to eight thousand years ago warmer climatic conditions created new challenges for southwestern peoples. Tiny nomadic groups, organized to best utilize the diverse plant and animal resources and cope with shrinking water supplies, spread throughout the Southwest. These *Archaic* peoples maintained themselves for a number of millennia throughout much of the Americas. In the very northern part of the Southwest the *Oshara Archaic* extended through parts of northern New Mexico and adjacent states beginning around 5,500 BC. South and west of the Oshara, and originating perhaps a thousand years earlier, was the *Cochise Archaic* in western New Mexico, Arizona, Sonora, and extreme western Chihuahua. A third Archaic tradition, the *Chihuahua Archaic,* was in place to the south in southern New Mexico and in Chihuahua, and an incipient agriculture of maize and squash had begun in the Chihuahua area by the Fresnal phase, sometime after 2,000 BC. Eastern New Mexico and the western Great Plains saw a series of related groups, sometimes referred to collectively as the *Plains Archaic.* These different Archaic peoples interacted with each other in various and not-very-well-understood ways, especially the Cochise and Oshara, the two groups having a certain interdigitation of territory in central New Mexico. The economies of these four Archaic groups were roughly the same, and they were likely similar in social organization. They all represented very small populations tied to a subsistence economy of small game hunting, diverse plant collecting, and—in some areas during the latter part of the Archaic—the beginnings of agriculture. Those societies living near running streams had a more dependable water supply, but all groups were probably to some degree tethered to water sources as they searched for scanty food resources in daily and seasonal rounds. Nowhere was life easy.[2]

Native American domestication of plants was earliest in Mexico and in parts of Central and South America. Maize, for example, derived from a wild cereal weed called *teocintle,* which appeared in southeast Mexico several thousand years ago, and cucurbits (squash) may have been an even earlier domesticate. Beginning about 2,000 BC, and spreading from south to north, one after another of the Archaic cultures were influenced and directed by an incipient maize and squash agriculture, originally involving primitive and not overly productive strains, especially of maize. Eventually beans were added to this agricultural diet. All this happened somewhat sooner in the south than in the north, which is to be expected since the agricultural impulses originated even farther south along the northern fringes of Mesoamerica.

The westernmost culture of what would be in modern times an archaeological-geographical construct, "the Greater Southwest" probably developed from a local Archaic, west of the Cochise, and has been called the *Patayan* or *Hakataya*. The Cochise people themselves gradually differentiated from the parent culture and, as briefly discussed in chapter 2, developed two major agricultural traditions. One such, in the desert country of southern Arizona and northern Sonora was the *Hohokam*. A second was the *Mogollon* in the mountainous country of western New Mexico and western Arizona, the Basin and Range and riverine areas of southern New Mexico and eastern Arizona, and in Chihuahua and Sonora to the south. In both cases the original, and very long-lived, Archaic lifeways became gradually enriched by the aforementioned spread northward of maize and squash. In the northeastern area the Oshara groups slowly became agricultural and eventually developed into the Basketmaker-Pueblo societies of the *Anasazi* (see Figure 4.1).[3]

The Patayan, still not well known and a bit peripheral to the other Southwest societies, was developing at least by the early centuries AD. Ceramics appeared in the low country along or near the Colorado River and spread to the highlands by, or not long after, AD 500. The pottery, buff or brown wares, show some similarities to Hohokam. Living structures were quite minimal, for the most part brush or reed construction, often with a low rock wall forming a foundation. The population collected in scattered, rather than compact, living units called *rancherías*, preferring dispersed farmsteads to towns. The lowland Patayan groups were contacted quite early in the historic period when the lower Colorado area was explored by Coronado's captain, Alarcón, in AD 1540. By that time they can be identified with historic lower-river Yuman-speaking peoples who still occupy part of the area. The region, agricultural for a number of centuries, had a relatively dense population. The upland Patayans of the region north and east of the lower Colorado River may have formed at least part of the ancestry of the more northern Yuman language groups, Yavapai, Havasupai, and Walapai.[4]

The Hohokam proper was primarily centered in the Gila-Salt River region. In the earlier periods this tradition can be characterized by the use of square or ovoid pithouses and villages with little obvious signs of town planning but with ball courts and platform mounds. The pottery was normally plain or buff and was constructed by the paddle-and-anvil technique. In this method the pot is roughly formed by broad coils and then is thinned and shaped by a wooden paddle, hitting against a bracing pottery or stone "anvil" (Figure 4.2). The Hohokam people were involved in an active trade in shell, primarily from the Gulf of California. There was also a strong emphasis on cremation burials and maize, bean, corn, and cotton agriculture. Hohokam began in what is called the Pioneer period, perhaps by diffusion of advanced cultural items onto a local Cochise Archaic base.[5] In any case the nascent Hohokam slowly expanded throughout Pioneer and Colonial period times and reached its greatest areal extent in the early Sedentary period, around AD 900, when it extended throughout much of the Gila-Salt drainage area, excepting only the lower Gila and the upper mountainous reaches of the two rivers. Agriculture in southern Arizona may have begun around 4,000 years ago but for many centuries competed with collecting of wild plants. It was only in the early centuries AD that planted crops became truly important as food sources.

Irrigation agriculture was early, with Chapalote, Reventador, and Onaveño, all rather primitive species of maize, having already appeared by early Pioneer times (indeed, maize agriculture predated Hohokam by a number of centuries). The common brown bean *(Phaseolus vulgaris)* and squash *(Cucurbita* sp.) may have been present by this time, though physical evidence for them in Hohokam sites is

## HOHOKAM – MOGOLLON – ANASAZI CHRONOLOGY

| | Hohokam | Mogollon | Anasazi |
|---|---|---|---|
| AD 1500 | O'Odham | Upland Pai? | Protohistoric Pueblo |
| 1400 | Terminal Aztlan | Terminal Aztlan | Aztlan (P-IV) |
| 1300 | Aztlan (Classic Hohokam ) | Aztlan (Late Mogollon) | Pueblo III/Aztlan |
| 1200 | Classic | Late Mogollon Mimbres Postclassic | Pueblo III |
| 1100 | Sedentary (Sacaton) | Mimbres Classic | Pueblo II (Late Chaco) |
| 1000 | Sedentary (Sacaton) | Mimbres Classic | Pueblo II/Pueblo I |
| 900 | Colonial (Santa Cruz) | Late Pithouse/Preclassic (Late Three Circle) | Pueblo I |
| 800 | Colonial (Gila Butte) | Late Pithouse (Three Circle) | Basketmaker III |
| 700 | Pioneer (Snaketown) | Late Pithouse (San Francisco) | Basketmaker III |
| 600 | Pioneer (Sweetwater) | Late Pithouse (Georgetown) | Basketmaker III |
| 500 | Pioneer (Estrella) | Late Pithouse (Georgetown) | Bm III/Bm II |
| 400 | Pioneer (Vahki) | Early Pithouse (Cumbre) | Basketmaker II |
| 300 | Pioneer (Red Mountain) | Early Pithouse (Cumbre) | Basketmaker II |
| 200 | Early Agriculture/Ceramics | Early Pithouse (Cumbre) | Basketmaker II |
| 100 | Early Agriculture/Ceramics | Early Agriculture/Ceramics | Basketmaker II |
| 1 AD | Early Agriculture | Early Agriculture | Basketmaker II |
| 100 BC | Early Agriculture | Early Agriculture | Basketmaker II |
| ------------------------ | | | |
| 1000 BC-1500 BC | Incipient Agriculture | Incipient Agriculture | Basketmaker II |

FIGURE 4.1. Chronology of the Hohokam, Mogollon, and Anasazi, ca. 1500 BC–AD 1500.

somewhat later. The same is true for cotton (*Gossypium* sp.), the fatty seeds probably originally used as a food.[6]

An argument has been made that advanced irrigation techniques in the Hohokam were in-vented independently,[7] but it could have been one of several Mesoamerican-influenced traits that filtered north into the Hohokam in the period around AD 500 to 800. These included ball courts and perhaps prototype platform

FIGURE 4.2. Anvil for production of paddle-and-anvil pottery (origin unknown). Maxwell Museum of Anthropology, University of New Mexico, cat. no. 84.1.7.

mounds.[8] At about this time there was an augmentation of Hohokam agriculture, with *Cucurbita moschata* and *C. mixta,* perhaps the tepary bean *(Phaseolus acutifolius),* and more sophisticated varieties of maize, such as the Harinoso de ocho, added to the basic food crops.

As time went on, the Hohokam population expanded into new areas. The Tonto Basin, that long valley formed by the Salt River and Tonto Creek, was already settled, with scanty populations of pithouse dwellers whose antecedents seemed to be basically Mogollon. There may have been a primitive irrigation practiced perhaps before AD 400, and Hohokam influences began to seep into the area by around AD 700. Among the things becoming increasingly important was domesticated cotton, a crop that may have been cultivated even before Hohokam times.

Other markers of the Preclassic Hohokam were an extensive use of shell, including techniques of etching, and large numbers of clay figurines, sometimes with elaborate headdresses or body ornaments. There were also thin flattened shinglelike objects made of stone or clay, called *palettes* (Figure 4.3). These were generally rectangular in shape but sometimes were made in the form of stylized effigies, animal or human. The function of palettes is not entirely certain, but they were probably pigment hold-

FIGURE 4.3. Slate palette, Hohokam Sedentary period, AD 900–1000. Maxwell Museum of Anthropology, University of New Mexico, cat. no., 63.11.74.

ers of some sort. The Hohokam cremated their dead or buried them with grave goods that included pottery, figurines, shell ornaments, palettes, and stone tools.[9] The first of the brightly colored macaws and parrots, so important in the later Southwest, were found at the extensively excavated Hohokam site of Snaketown in the Gila Valley, early in the Hohokam cultural sequence.[10]

Exactly what did the Preclassic Hohokam represent? David Wilcox has suggested that a regional system based on the ball court was operating at least until the eleventh and twelfth centuries, when new ideas and structures, especially platform mounds (actually beginning in the Sedentary period), suggest a new orientation of society.[11]

During the Classic period a new phenomenon, the Salado, appeared, centered in the Tonto Basin. These people built specialized aboveground rooms, constructed platform mounds, and used brilliant three-colored pottery (the Salado polychromes). The Salado, which seemed to have been greatly influenced by Anasazi, is generally dated from about AD 1250 to AD 1450, so at least in the heartland Salado lasted almost into historic times.[12]

My own position has been that the riverine Hohokam were Tepiman-speaking Indians and eventually became the historic Pima-Papago or O'odham Indians. This point of view is not held by all archaeologists and ethnohistorians working in the region, but it seems to me the most parsimonious explanation.[13]

North of the Hohokam area, in the region around Flagstaff, Arizona, and in the Verde Valley region, there grew up a separate archaeological tradition, that of the *Sinagua*, a Spanish term meaning "without water." The Sinagua originated before AD 500 and developed for several centuries, some inhabitants clinging to the area perhaps as late as AD 1400. However, the most extensive occupation of the region seems to have been from the eleventh century to the beginning of the fourteenth, perhaps related to a series of soil-enriching volcanic eruptions in the decade of the 1060s, volcanic activity that produced Sunset Crater. Sinagua is variously classified. Some archaeologists consider it a sort of Mogollon; others believe it to be a valid independent regional tradition although much affected by Hohokam, Mogollon, and Anasazi.[14] The archaeologist Fred Plog considered it primarily Anasazi.[15] Because of its probable derived nature, Sinagua is not shown on Figure 4.4 but can be located where Mogollon, Hohokam, and Anasazi interface.

There were ball courts in Sinagua. Villages of pithouses aggregated, over time, into small masonry pueblos, though the pithouse continued to be used. Originally, ceramics focused on a simple brown ware, but pottery influences and trade pieces eventually came from all sides of the Sinagua. The Sinagua people were at least on the outer edges of the Mesoamerican sphere of influence; certainly they traded for scarlet macaws. Charmion McKusick sees a major trade in macaws that perhaps originated in Casas Grandes in pre–Medio period times (although the evidence for macaws at Casas Grandes during that period is minimal). The trade went along a south-to-north route, extending from the Casas Grandes area through Mimbres and on to Chaco Canyon and to the Mesa Verde country and that of the great site of Yellow Jacket in the Four Corners region. However, macaws, or macaw feathers, apparently, were not traded into Mesa Verde/Yellow Jacket, this region generally seeming indifferent to the goods and perhaps the ideas of Mesoamerica. According to McKusick the macaw trade swung sharply westward from Chaco to the Sinagua. It is indeed the case that the largest single collection of scarlet macaws north of Casas Grandes was found at the Sinaguan site of Wupatki (see Figure 4.5). McKusick believes that Wupatki was a center of worship of Quetzalcoatl in his epiphany as Ehécatl, the wind god. In any case there are hints of Mesoamerican connections at that site, including, perhaps, the ball court.[16] For a more extended discussion of this north-south route see chapter 5.

Originally the Mogollon tradition was simply considered a southern extension of the much better known Anasazi. The Mogollon complex was classified separately from the Anasazi, primarily as a result of research by Emil Haury in the early 1930s. There was considerable initial resistance to the idea of Mogollon, but increasing work during the 1930s and the 1940s in various Mogollon subregions gave the culture a firm foundation. By the time of Joe Ben Wheat's 1955 seminal publication, *Mogollon Culture Prior to A.D. 1000,* the concept of Mogollon as separate from Anasazi, at least for the earlier period, was largely unchallenged. Separation of the two great traditions by modern archaeologists was based on a series of archaeologically identifiable traits: a difference in pottery manufacture, certain differences in mortuary practices, variation in the construction of pithouses, and in Mogollon the continued use of pithouses rather than aboveground contiguous pueblos until relatively late. To what extent the two societies differed in religion, sociopolitical organization, or language(s) was (and remains today) unknown. What the ancient inhabitants of western New Mexico and eastern Arizona would have

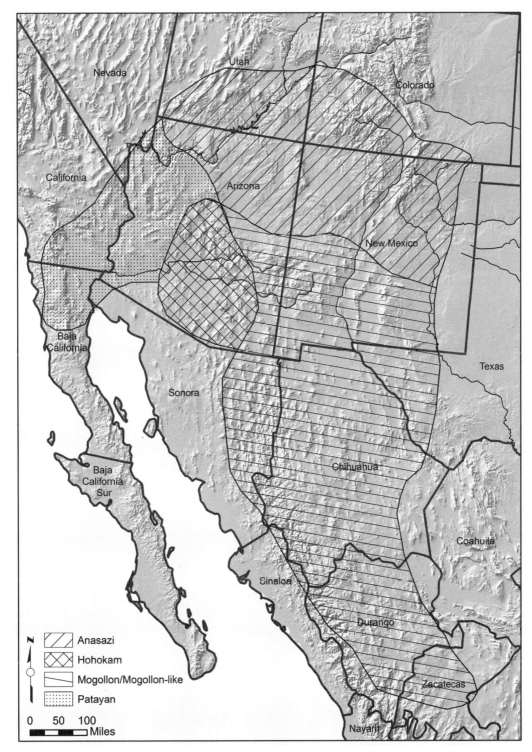

FIGURE 4.4. Macrotraditions of Aztlan. Earth Analytic, Santa Fe, NM.

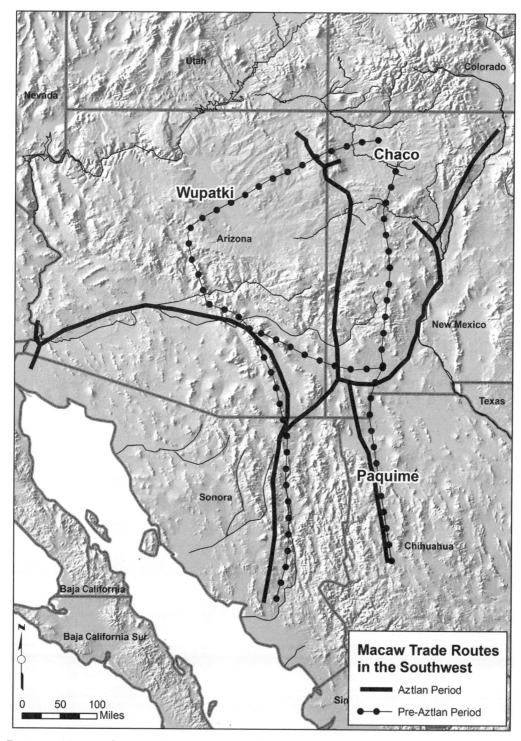

FIGURE 4.5. Macaw trade in pre-Aztlan and Aztlan times. Earth Analytic, Santa Fe, NM.

thought about this modern pigeonholing is equally unknown.[17]

The Mogollon, an extraordinarily widespread tradition, was first identified in the high and relatively well-watered country along the Arizona–New Mexico border. In that area it began about 2,000 years ago, perhaps even a bit earlier. One of the ancestral components of this branch of Mogollon was likely a local primitive agricultural Cochise Archaic population. The Early Pithouse period of Mogollon, dating from perhaps AD 300, was characterized—no surprise here—by pithouses and, in the larger villages, large pit structures that seem to have had a ceremonial function. Usually called *kivas* (see Anasazi area), they might possibly relate to the large "ceremonial" pithouses of the late Basketmaker period in northern New Mexico. In any case these "kivas" are found from the Early Pithouse period till the very end of Mogollon, a century or so before the Spanish entry into the area. The Mogollon people were farmers, sharing the same trinity of plants (corn, beans, and squash) as did their Hohokam and Anasazi neighbors. There was also tobacco, while cotton seems to have appeared at least by the time of the Classic phase (AD 1000–1150) of the Mimbres branch of the Mogollon. However, hunting and gathering remained important to Mogollon societies throughout their history.[18]

The earliest Mogollon began to utilize pottery, constructed by a coiling technique. Sausagelike ropes of clay, fashioned by rolling in the hand, were built up coil by coil to form the walls of the pot. The pots were then thinned by scraping and fired generally in an oxidizing atmosphere, a technique in which atmospheric oxygen is allowed to interact with the pot, leading to red, brown, or buff ceramic ware. This technique was commonly used in the Greater Southwest from the beginning of ceramic production. Oxidizing wares can also be used to produce a white surface if there is absence of iron oxides in the clay. Even the earliest pottery was relatively sophisticated, brown and red wares, undecorated but well made. Of these early wares, Alma Plain, and San Francisco Red

were traded to the Hohokam and eventually had a very large distribution, reaching into northern Mexico. Their point of origin is still uncertain.

A Late Pithouse phase of Mogollon, AD 600–1000 (but ending somewhat later in the Arizona mountain region), saw expanded populations, probably a greater reliance on agriculture, and a shift from mesa top locations of villages to the valley floors. After AD 1000, pit villages began to be replaced by masonry pueblos, first in the Mimbres area, then in the mountains of eastern and central Arizona. Parts of this post–AD 1000 manifestation have sometimes been called *Western Pueblo*. This name in its archaeological manifestation has gone out of fashion in recent years—somewhat of a pity, since the term was well established in the earlier literature as a specific areal Mogollon-Anasazi (or perhaps Mogollon-Anasazi-Hohokam) blend.[19] I will use it here in a very narrow sense to mean peoples of the Hopi-Zuni-Acoma regions, both in late prehistoric (Aztlan) and in historic times.

The later Mogollon towns were sometimes quite large. Grasshopper Ruin, on a tributary of the Salt River, contained 500 rooms or more. The brown and red wares of earlier times were replaced by black-on-white, black-on-red, and polychrome pottery. There were clear Anasazi influences and in some cases an actual interdigitation with the Anasazi peoples, especially after the collapse of the San Juan Anasazi in the late thirteenth century.

Some specialists consider the heartland of the Mogollon culture to be the region along and on both sides of the present-day Arizona–New Mexico border including upper tributaries of the Salt and Gila rivers, especially the valley of the San Francisco. However, the Mogollon-Mimbres peoples also lived in the San Simon Valley of southeast Arizona at what may be a very early period. A northern extension of Mogollon occupied the Cibola region of western New Mexico, north of the San Agustin Plains, and the Forestdale area of Arizona, along the upper reaches of tributaries to the Salt River, draining southward off the high country delineated on the north by the Mogollon Rim.[20] In addition, cultures that are called "Mogollon" or "Mogollon-like" extended well south of the Mexican border and will be discussed when I talk about the Chihuahua Archaic below. As we will see, a Mexican origin of Mogollon is quite conceivable.

The Mogollon Rim and adjacent areas were important for the development of later cultures. Out of a curiously hybrid Anasazi-Mogollon base the region became increasingly Anasazi-like in later centuries. A key happening was the rise and spread of what are called the White Mountain redwares beginning in the eleventh century AD. As we will see in chapter 6, these ceramic traditions eventually influenced much of the Southwest.[21]

The Mimbres themselves were a branch of Mogollon, centered in south-central New Mexico. This segment of the Mogollon lies south of the San Agustin Plains, extending west as far as the San Francisco, Gila, and San Simon rivers. To the east there are many Mimbres sites along the Rio Grande north of Hatch, especially in the Palomas Creek area, and several to the east, penetrating into Jornada Mogollon territory. On the south, Mimbres is found as far as the Chihuahua border and perhaps beyond.[22]

A good example of Mimbres life comes from the Swartz ruin in the Mimbres River valley, north of present-day Deming. Swartz was excavated in the late 1920s (when the area was still thought of as "frontier Anasazi") and shows much of the temporal range of the culture as a whole. Mimbres people at the Swartz site originally lived in small clusters of rectangular semisubterranean structures. However, around AD 950 a compact village of aboveground stone houses appeared. In the eleventh century, population in the area was probably increasing, for a more extensive town grew up, two room blocks sharing a plaza area. One decided advantage of aboveground rooms over pithouses is the ease with which they can be extended, especially as conjoined additions to existing structures.

Another site with a long Mimbres occupation that has seen considerable excavation is the Galaz ruin. Galaz, perhaps the largest of the Mimbres towns, lies about ten miles north of Swartz on the Mimbres River and started around AD 550, a century or so before Swartz. It had, seemingly, a continuous occupation for the next 600 years, extending from the beginning of the Late Pithouse through the Mimbres Classic phase. In addition there was a later, Postclassic, occupation in the area.[23]

It has been suggested that this Classic phase was influenced from the developing Casas Grandes to the south, though the revised dates for Casas Grandes make it somewhat doubtful unless the pre–Medio period occupation was more extensive and more sophisticated than present evidence shows. As mentioned above, archaeologists originally thought that Mimbres represented an actual Anasazi intrusion into the region, but this point of view has lost favor. It seems to me that there was *some* sort of Anasazi influence—perhaps through idea diffusion—in the aboveground masonry construction that largely replaced pithouses in the eleventh century, structures that look very much like kivas, and in the final development of the brilliantly decorated black-on-white (sometimes a red-on-cream) pottery that heralded the Mimbres Classic. Mimbres potters originally used the standard Mogollon technique of firing in an oxidizing atmosphere, but after AD 750–800 a modified reduced atmosphere was used, producing the black-on-white effect.

However, the graphic animal and human depictions that are the hallmark of Classic Mimbres pottery are certainly not Anasazi. Exactly what they represent is still debated, but archaeologist Marc Thompson believes that they include renderings of Mesoamerican-derived supernatural beings, moon, sun, and the divine twins. The latter (who in the Pueblo world became the Twin War Gods) journeyed to the underworld of the dead, a mysterious region signified iconographically by fish. They were strongly dualistic, one twin symbolizing

FIGURE 4.6. Divine twins indicating life/death, right/left, sun/moon, male/female duality. Left-hand twin has tasseled sash of female. El Paso Museum of Archaeology.

FIGURE 4.7. Divine twins emerging from fish man. Imagery found from Maya country to Pueblos. El Paso Museum of Archaeology.

the sun and its representative animal, the deer; the other twin symbolizing the moon and its representative, the rabbit. These twins also signify male and female (see Figures 4.6, 4.7, 4.8). This obsession with duality appears in slightly later times in Casas Grandes.

The ceramic forms, primarily bowls, were used with the dead and depicted journeys to the underworld and perhaps also served as mnemonic devices for the recitation of funerary rituals. Harry Shafer, in his extensive work at the NAN Ranch site, has pointed out that funerary vessels often show marks of previous culinary use so presumably were not made specifically for burials. The use of "killed" (ritually punctured) vessels, often covering the face of the dead person, appears in late Pithouse or Preclassic (Three Circle phase) times and continues throughout the Classic period. Shafer believes that an important use of the elegant Mimbres decorated ware was as gift exchange, especially to link corporate extravillage groups, perhaps associated with a valleywide irrigation system.[24]

In any case the Mimbres-decorated pottery represented close attention to the natural world, with careful representation of plants and ani-

FIGURE 4.8. Fish, representing Mimbres interest in nature and perhaps also divine twins reborn as fish. El Paso Museum of Archaeology.

mals. To one degree or another this iconography presages the mythology of the world of Aztlan and of historic Pueblo Indians.

Some scholars have suggested that the later pan-Pueblo *kachina cult* was already in evidence in Classic Mimbres times. The primary reason for this line of argument seems to be that the divine twins or twin war gods are in evidence in Mimbres. This is surely true, but I do not see that the divine twins are particularly related to the kachina cult. They seem to be part of a Quetzalcoatl movement into the Southwest and in the Aztlan period did become somewhat intertwined with kachinas. But this was more a matter of syncretism, a great deal of which was going on in the period after AD 1300. I discuss the matter of religious cults in the Southwest in later chapters.[25]

As I mentioned above, one link between Mimbres and the upper Southwest was the trade in scarlet macaws. A number of specimens are found in Mimbres, and Charmion McKusick believes that the macaws may have actually been bred there for shipment out to Chaco Canyon. McKusick notes one macaw bone in the Viejo period in the Casas Grandes area and believes that area may have been some sort of way station on the north-south macaw route. Of course, the "Mesoamerican" occupation at Paquimé, the great quickening of the Medio period (see chapter 8), had not yet occurred.[26]

Mimbres sites also contain a considerable amount of shell. Like the Hohokam, the Mimbres commonly used *Spondylus, Glycymeris, Olivella,* and *Pecten.* Another "Hohokam-like" aspect of Mimbres is the appearance of shale, slate, or sandstone palettes in considerable numbers in the Late Pithouse and Classic periods. Palettes in Hohokam are normally associated with cremation burials, and about half those of Mimbres are also associated with burials, in this case primarily inhumations. The age distribution of these burials seems more or less random, in other words matching the overall distribution; and there is no evidence that palettes were buried with specific specialist groups. Whether the palettes had the same use(s) in Mimbres and in Hohokam is unknown.[27]

There was considerable turquoise, a thousand pieces found at Galaz alone. The sourcing is still not clear, but the Burro Mountains 40 miles to the west are reputed to have turquoise workings that date to prehistoric times. Other evidence of trade into Mimbres is the occasional crotal (tinkler or bell) or other worked copper, presumably from western Mexico.[28]

The Classic phase of the Mimbres ended sometime around AD 1130 to 1150, and what happened next is not clear. There are alternative points of view, and I will indicate two important ones here. For a more detailed discussion of these differences in interpretation see chapter 6. Darrell G. Creel believes, based on evidence of his excavation at the Old Town site, near present-day Deming, New Mexico, that sometime in the early twelfth century the Mimbres classic peoples evolved into the Black Mountain phase, one that saw the development of red and polychrome ceramics and the appearance of Chupadero Black-on-white and El Paso Polychrome. The brilliant decorated black-on-white pottery of Classic Mimbres now disappeared, but here was a continuity in design style and subject matter, now found not in ceramics but in rock art.[29]

Harry T. Shafer doubts this continuity scenario and believes that there was a break in occupation at the end of the Classic period Mimbres in the Mimbres Valley and the upper Gila drainage. This break, he believes, was due to an out migration of Mimbres by around AD 1150. At some later point the Black Mountain phase peoples, probably desert-dwelling cousins of the Classic Mimbres, reoccupied the area, utilizing the intrusive potteries like Chupadero Black-on-white and El Paso Polychrome, plus early Chihuahua polychromes. Their only locally produced ceramics were variants on Playas Red, a pottery that originated in the Medio period at Casas Grandes (Figure 4.9).[30]

East of the Mimbres was a related group, the Jornada Mogollon. Like Mimbres the Jornada people underwent an evolution from pithouse structures to aboveground dwellings. The Jornada seems to have developed out of a local manifestation of the Chihuahua Archaic, the Hueco phase, the Jornada Mogollon being formed by the addition of pottery to this underlying simple culture. Jornada peoples spread down the Rio Grande and across the mountains and valleys of southeastern New Mexico

FIGURE 4.9. Playas Red pottery. El Paso Museum of Archaeology.

to about the Roswell area. The earlier phase of the Jornada Mogollon was one of a pithouse-dwelling, apparently rather mobile, population still somewhat influenced by its Archaic roots.[31]

The eastern portion of this Mogollon region seemed to have a considerable interaction with Anasazi along the northern and especially the northeastern frontier of the Jornada. In the latter area a Glencoe phase of "pure Mogollon" sites was replaced by increasingly Anasazi-like Corona phase and Lincoln phase sites, perhaps representing movements of peoples from the Salinas area or environs. The inhabitants lived in room blocks of adobe and had ceremonial "kivalike" structures in a time period of perhaps AD 1200 to 1400. Associated pottery varies from site to site, but common were Chupadero Black-on-white, El Paso Polychrome, Lincoln Black-on-red, Three Rivers Red-on-terra-cotta, Jornada and Corona wares and smaller amounts of Glaze A, and St. Johns and Gila polychromes. Twenty or thirty miles southeast of the Tompiro towns of the Estancia Valley, at Pueblo Pardo in the Chupadero Mesa area, excavations show a village on the Mogollon-Anasazi frontier and one that shares aspects of both traditions.[32]

The later Jornada Mogollon eventually became part of the Casas Grandes sphere of influence and will be discussed in a later chapter. To the north, along the Rio Abajo (a rather vaguely defined segment of the Rio Grande extending from somewhere north of Socorro, downriver to below Milligan Gulch), there were both Paleoindian and Archaic occupations along the river. Archaic peoples in this region seem to have been influenced from west, south, and north, the Cochise, Chihuahua, and Oshara. The extent to which they established their own discrete tradition is not clear. The succeeding sedentary tradition, the San Marcial phase, is marked by horticulture and by both a Mogollon-like series of brown wares and the type pottery, San Marcial Black on white, reminiscent of the late Basketmaker farther north.

Beginning about AD 800 there appeared a downriver equivalent of the Basketmaker/ Pueblo transitional period, extending into Pueblo II and involving experimentation with scattered aboveground stone-based adobe structures. The ceramic ware suggests a Mogollon-Anasazi mix, mostly of Mogollon-related brown wares but with considerable amounts of various Anasazi wares. An added complication is that from about AD 1150 sites that are palpably Anasazi, for example with Mesa Verde–like pottery, appear in the Rio Abajo. In fact, along a broad frontier that includes the northern part of the Rio Abajo but also the old "Western Pueblo," and the Mimbres, terms like *Mogollon* and *Anasazi* become archaeological abstractions, increasingly hard to sort out, and are not particularly expository.[33]

South of the Mogollon, in the northwestern tier of Mexican states, were cultures that developed somewhat separately from those farther north but as time went on interacted more and more with the more northern regions. The Chihuahua Archaic dates to perhaps 6,000 BC in that region of northern Mexico. The Gardner Springs complex or phase and the subsequent Keystone phase saw the utilization of a broad variety of desert animals and especially desert plants. These plants included agave, nopal, and a number of seeds ground by mano and metate. During the subsequent

Fresnal phase (2500–900 BC) maize and squash were added to this earlier plant-food base. The period also saw a considerable development of string and cords made from agave and lechuguilla, which were used to make square-toed "fishtail" sandals, baskets, and other woven or corded materials. There was trade in the form of Olivella shell probably from the Gulf of California. The Hueco phase (c. 900 BC–AD 200) saw an augmentation of these trends, for example the development of new types of maize, such as maíz de ocho, and a higher development of basketry and footwear.[34]

Many of the inhabitants of the Chihuahua and Coahuila region remained Archaic hunters and collectors up into historic times. However, by processes still unclear new ideas, whether spread by diffusion or by actual movements (or perhaps both), trickled along the mountainous backbone of northwest Mexico. Today we call the cultures that resulted from these processes Mogollon or "Mogollon-like," since they were first identified in the Mogollon region of southeastern Arizona and southwestern New Mexico. This phenomenon should not be taken as a north-to-south movement, however, for the spread may have been in the opposite direction at some point in BC times.[35]

In any case these various peoples were all simple agriculturalists, utilizing maize, beans, squash, and perhaps cotton and using varieties of plain or simply decorated brown or red pottery. They lived in houses in pits or in simple rectangular rooms constructed of adobe, sometimes with cobblestone footings and/or vertical posts. Houses that I have investigated in the Zape area of northern Durango sometimes have upright slabs forming parts of the walls. These particular wall bases were not footings but a ground level, facing what was likely a jacal-like structure supported by wooden posts. Such Mogollon-like societies were forming in the early centuries AD, and they gradually spread over a part of the old Archaic area, following river valleys such as the Rio Grande and the Rio Conchos, where they eventually are recognized as the Jornada Mogollon.[36] In northwestern Chihuahua they penetrated the

interior draining valleys of western Chihuahua, the Carmén, the Santa María, and the Casas Grandes. The Viejo period of Casas Grandes, its boundaries still largely undefined, derived in large part from these simple agricultural cultures. In the Mexican state of Sonora these Mogollon-like peoples, called the Rio Sonora culture, extended along the upwaters of the Sonora and Yaqui river systems. They eventually developed small but vibrant polities that I have called "statelets." Mogollon-like cultures may reach even farther south to include the Tacuichamona culture of the Fuerte River in Sonora. On the eastern flank and foothills of the Sierra Madre they formed the Loma San Gabriel. Howard D. Winters and I have argued that the Loma San Gabriel were at least in part ancient speakers of a Tepiman tongue, related to the historic Tepehuan Indians.[37]

Scattered pithouse villages appeared in the Casas Grandes area, rising out of a late regional Archaic and dating to AD 500 or perhaps even a bit earlier. By around AD 700, what Charles C. Di Peso called the Convento phase of the Viejo period of Casas Grandes was in evidence. This was basically Mogollon-like and involved small settlements of pithouses sometimes with a larger "community house" pit structure. The pottery was quite similar to that of the Mogollon region to the north. As time went on, through the succeeding Pilón and Perros Bravos phases, these villages increased in size. Rectangular adobe and jacal aboveground structures appear, and there was a strong tendency toward organized villages rather than the somewhat haphazard pithouse arrangement of earlier times. The ceramics included various redwares, bichrome wares, and, toward the end of the Viejo period, Mata Polychrome, the Viejo period's one true polychrome ware (red and black designs on a brown background). Trade with the western part of Mexico is indicated by a scatter of copper artifacts and a considerable amount of shell from the Mexican west coast, especially in Perros Bravos times.[38]

The various ethnic movements in this extended region are not entirely clear, but they must somehow be related to the spread of linguistic groups in Mexico. Various branches of the great Uto-Aztecan language family are found especially in the southwestern quadrant of the Southwest. Distribution and relationships among languages form an important part in any reconstruction of the prehistoric Southwest, and in chapter 10 I will discuss the general language situation especially during the Aztlan period.

On the northern edge of the Greater Southwest, the San Juan Basin was a major center of Basketmaker-Pueblo or Anasazi (Figure 4.10).[39] Developing from an Archaic, hunting-gathering base, southwestern populations in the San Juan region by the early centuries AD were incorporating maize and squash agriculture and substantial pithouse dwellings into their lifestyles. They wove well-made baskets, hence the name *Basketmaker*. Hunting was done with clubs and heavy sticks for dispatching rabbits and other small animals. The main projectile was the spear-thrower or throwing stick (sometimes called by its Aztec name, *atlatl*), an implement that seems to have been centered in the old Anasazi region. This was a flattened segment or shaft of wood or bone, three or four feet long, hooked or grooved at one end to attach a four or five foot dart. With the dart attached, and held loosely in place with the fingers, the hunter rotates the shaft forward somewhat as one would throw a baseball, sending the dart a considerable distance at considerable speed.

Many of the traits that were to become the essence of Anasazi Pueblo culture began to appear especially in the second and richer phase of Basketmaker life. The early archaeologists in the area utilized the terms *Basketmaker II* and *Basketmaker III*. There was no Basketmaker I. We would now identify Basketmaker I

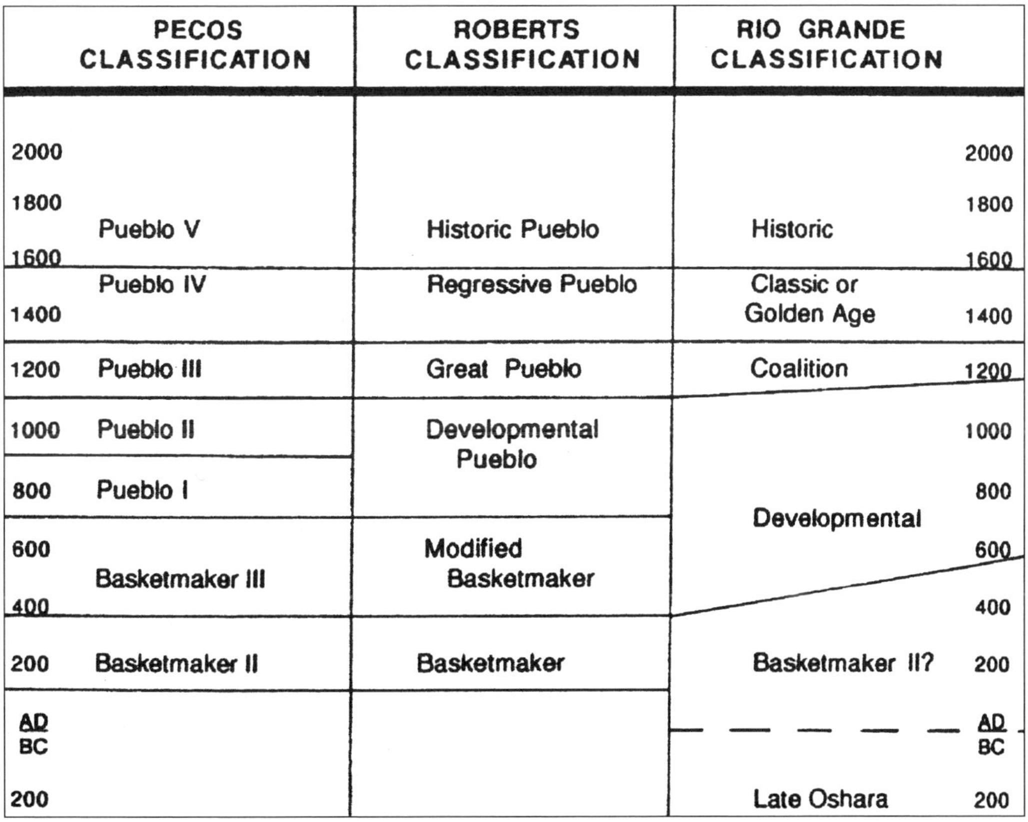

| PECOS CLASSIFICATION | | ROBERTS CLASSIFICATION | RIO GRANDE CLASSIFICATION | |
|---|---|---|---|---|
| 2000 | | | | 2000 |
| 1800 | Pueblo V | Historic Pueblo | Historic | 1800 |
| 1600 | | | | 1600 |
| 1400 | Pueblo IV | Regressive Pueblo | Classic or Golden Age | 1400 |
| 1200 | Pueblo III | Great Pueblo | Coalition | 1200 |
| 1000 | Pueblo II | Developmental Pueblo | | 1000 |
| 800 | Pueblo I | | | 800 |
| 600 | | Modified Basketmaker | Developmental | 600 |
| 400 | Basketmaker III | | | 400 |
| 200 | Basketmaker II | Basketmaker | Basketmaker II? | 200 |
| AD BC | | | | AD BC |
| 200 | | | Late Oshara | 200 |

FIGURE 4.10. Comparative classifications Anasazi Pueblo. Note short-term chronology used for Basketmaker II. Aztlan period is essentially P-IV (after Riley, *Rio del Norte*).

as the earlier, preagricultural phase of the Oshara Archaic.

The Basketmaker II period in the upper Southwest has been traditionally dated to begin around the start of AD times, when a Chapalote-type maize and squash agriculture spread northward, probably from the Mogollon region. A more recent long chronology puts the dates back to around 1500 BC, with a "late" Basketmaker II dating from ca. AD 50 to 500.[40] The Basketmaker II period was characterized by a maize and squash (but not bean) agriculture and the use of the spear-thrower in hunting. With the later period people began to live in shallow pithouses. Basketmaker III, after about AD 500, built on the earlier Basketmaker II but added new items to the complex. One of these was the bow-and-arrow, which seems to have diffused from the north and which supplemented the spear-thrower, or atlatl, as a hunting and military weapon. Bows were the simple self-bow type, but even so, they were considerably more efficient than the atlatl. The latter implement can discharge a short spear at the speed of perhaps 70 feet per second while a self-bow of the southwestern type can shoot an arrow at about 115 feet per second.[41] Other innovations included the protein-rich bean, which was added to the agricultural inventory, and a deeper pithouse, used as a dwelling. Pottery also appears a couple of centuries or more after its first use in Mogollon lands to the south. Because of this, it seems reasonable to conclude that Anasazi pottery was diffused from Mogollon or at least drawn from Mogollon models.[42]

It looks as if the pithouse was utilized not only for living quarters but for ceremonies as well. A small opening, usually somewhere at one side of the central fireplace, probably represented what in later times became known by its historic Hopi name of *sipapu*, a ceremonial opening to the underworld. In later Pueblo times a form of this pithouse was retained as a ceremonial chamber. The sipapu seems to be an attenuated form of a much wider Mesoamerican distribution in which an opening to the underworld is a common architectural feature.[43]

The Basketmaker phase of Anasazi extended over much of the San Juan Basin, westward to the lower Virgin River of southern Nevada, although there is not much evidence for Basketmaker occupation in some areas, for example the north rim of the Grand Canyon. If the enigmatic pithouse-dwelling Fremont tradition can be included, much of Utah and parts of Colorado belonged in the Basketmaker-Pueblo world. In the Rio Grande drainage Basketmaker settlements extended to the adjacent Pecos and its upper tributaries. There were pithouse users as far east as the Tecolote and Gallinas rivers and as far south as the Pecos-Gallinas juncture. In fact, by the early Pueblo times Anasazi had reached roughly its greatest extent and, although filling in internally, would expand relatively little beyond those boundaries during the next several hundred years.[44]

With the coming of the Pueblo phase of the Anasazi, after ca. AD 700, aboveground building became the norm, although pithouses were still used in various places. As already described, the pithouse was now maintained as part of a specialized religious-oriented ceremonial structure. In historic times this ceremonial building was and is generally known by its Hopi term, *kiva*. In some areas it continued to be a pithouse, a rounded semisubterranean structure, in others a square building, either underground or incorporated in the room blocks.

Quite early in time we can discern two major Anasazi subprovinces. Sometimes called Eastern Anasazi and Western Anasazi, they differed in house construction, pottery, village layout, and several other aspects of material culture. There is considerable disagreement as to the boundary line between Eastern and Western branches of Anasazi. In the synthesizing Handbook of North American Indians series Fred Plog and Linda S. Cordell argue that southwestern Colorado, the Four Corners region, and parts of southern Utah should be included in Western Anasazi, while Chaco and the general Rio Grande drainage formed a part of Eastern Anasazi.[45] Eric Reed, however, pointed out more than a half century ago the broad differences between designations of east

and west: "The central area containing the majority of Anasazi remains—the Navajo country—may be divided in two after AD 500 and
especially after about AD 900, with the boundary approximately at the Chinle Valley in
northeastern Arizona. There may have been a
certain degree of east-west separation among
the pre-ceramic Basket Makers before the late
fifth century also, probably less important and
certainly less obvious."[46]

Jeffrey S. Dean, in a recent publication,
draws roughly the same line between east and
west, suggesting broad ecological and cultural
differences. The loess and clay soils of the San
Juan area are richer than the sandy soils to the
west, and rainfall is greater, particularly in the
uplands north of the San Juan. The western
region never attained the heavy populations
and large towns that were found in the eastern region until the Aztlan period, that is after
about AD 1300.[47]

From my own point of view, separating out
settlements in the upper San Juan region from
those of the Chaco area and from the northern
Rio Grande Basin tends to confuse the issue.
Not only was there significant sharing of cultural items, but the northern San Juan populations likely had considerable contact with
those of the Rio Grande, and it was to the Rio
Grande area that they migrated following the
great trauma of the thirteenth century. I discuss
this matter in greater detail in chapter 5, where
I follow the extensive movements of people that
brought an end to the Anasazi domain in the
San Juan and most of the Colorado drainages.

The Anasazi population in the northern
reaches of the San Juan Basin perhaps reached
its climax in late Pueblo II times (say from
about AD 1000 to 1100), when climatic conditions especially in the Four Corners region
grew somewhat warmer and more humid,
allowing a belt of dry farming that began at
altitudes of about 5,500 feet. After around AD
1150 there were more unsettled climatic conditions, and population tended to shift to somewhat higher elevations, on Mesa Verde proper
and in the Dolores region to the north. Only
in favored spots (for example the canyon heads

with their living springs, as in the Hovenweep
region) or in the main Animas–San Juan river
bottom, did villages maintain themselves in
somewhat lower elevations. Sites in favored
locations can be found along the Dolores, Yellow Jacket–McElmo and Montezuma drainages. A very important site, Yellow Jacket, north
of modern Cortez, was a ceremonial center.[48]
Stretching for a mile or more along Yellow
Jacket Creek, the site contains around 130
structures that show characteristics of kivas,
including a Great Kiva. I have already mentioned the fact that McKusick considers Yellow Jacket to be the northern terminus of a
long trade route that stretched up from Chihuahua, probably through the Mimbres country, to Chaco Canyon and the San Juan River
settlements, with a branch extending westward
to the Sinagua region of central Arizona. A great
many goods of Mesoamerican origin flowed
up this route; however, with the exception of
a few items (a southern domesticated variety
of turkey and perhaps certain building techniques) they never got to Yellow Jacket. This
is really somewhat of an oddity and probably
reflects a self-imposed insularity of the area
north of the San Juan River. It looks as if the
most obvious items of Mesoamerican trade—
for example the scarlet macaw, west coast and
Gulf of California shell, coral, techniques such
as pseudocloisonné (lacquering the surface of
pottery or stone), and platform substructures
related to elite political, military, or religious
organizations—simply made relatively little
impression north of the San Juan Valley. The
same thing may have been true of turquoise,
supplied by central New Mexico mines but
traded widely both to the Chaco centers and
very likely south and west into Mexico. In spite
of the beauty of the stone it was not valued (or
at least very little of it is found) in the Mesa
Verde area and the Four Corners.

If this was the case, what exactly did the
people of Yellow Jacket and nearby sites want
from the south, and what did they have to
trade? Peripheries to major centers often deal
in foodstuffs, and this could have been the case
here, though in a period where human carriage

was the only practical method of moving goods there are certain space and time limitations on such kinds of trade. Golden eagles or their feathers would be a possibility and certain kinds of processed skins.[49] The domesticated turkey, called by McKusick the Large Indian Domestic *(Meleagris gallopavo merriami),* appeared in Basketmaker times and became a very important domesticate in the Anasazi world. At one stage of the bird's physical development, shiny black feathers appear, and these may have been traded. What the northerners received is also somewhat puzzling. Perhaps esoteric knowledge was a "tradable" item and might relate to the introduction of Mexican cults, but this is highly speculative to say the least. McKusick thinks that the Large Indian Domestic turkey was sacred to Tezcatlipoca, and conceivably idea diffusion could introduce "updated" elements of some Tezcatlipoca cult already present.[50]

It has been suggested that the Mesoamerican rain deity Tlaloc emerged very early in the Southwest, appearing perhaps as early as late Archaic times in the Escalante-Fremont River area of southeastern Utah, as shown in the Barrier Canyon Anthropomorphic style rock art.[51] I think that this is very unlikely—evidence for it rests on rather generalized large-eye features in rock art. Charmion McKusick believes that the cult of Tlaloc spread to the Mesa Verde area from somewhere in Mesoamerica and was associated in the Southwest with turkeys and eagles.[52] Again, I seriously doubt this; a far better case can be made that Tlaloc was at the center of the kachina cult that swept up from the south as part of the post-1300 Aztlan period Mesoamericanization of the Southwest. This cult did not reach the San Juan area for the simple reason that by that time the San Juan was essentially deserted.

However, even earlier and quite spectacular evidence for *pre-Aztlan* Mesoamerican contact and regional integration came in the Chaco period of Anasazi Pueblo, especially from the late tenth century to the beginning of the twelfth. The Chaco phenomenon, centered in the San Juan Basin of northern New Mexico,[53]

actually represented a major, though somewhat spatially limited, intrusion of Mesoamerican influences that some scholars think involved actual Mesoamerican intruders into the Southwest. Mesoamerican elements include such architectural features as columns, courtyard altars, room platforms with forecourts, core-and-veneer wall construction, and perhaps ceremonial roads and certain aspects of the engineering of Great Kivas. In art Chaco most likely owed pseudocloisonné and shell inlay to Mexican influences. In Chaco (as was also the case farther south in Mexico) the decorative elements are applied to slabs of sandstone rather than to metal as in "true" cloisonné (Figure 4.11). Actual objects from the south included the scarlet macaw from the lowlands of southeastern Mexico, shell from the Gulf of California, and copper bells, probably from western Mexico.

There can be no doubt that Chaco Canyon and its surroundings represented the culmination of the Pueblo II–Pueblo III Anasazi and owed something to Mesoamerica. The amount of Mesoamerican-derived materials and the obvious sophistication of the Chaco centers suggest something more than the tribalism that probably existed in other parts of the Anasazi. The exact *nature* of Chaco society, however, is still somewhat of a question. The hallmark of Chaco society was what is called the *Great House.*[54] Great Houses, described originally from Chaco Canyon centers like Pueblo Bonito (Figure 4.12) and Chetro Ketl, involve massive clusters of rooms, kivas (including Great Kivas), courtyards, and walls laid out symmetrically. Some of them were connected by roadways. Exactly how widespread were these Great Houses?

Stephen Lekson sees Chaco-inspired Great Houses extending eastward to Guadalupe Ruin, on the Puerco River, northeast of Chimney Rock, in Colorado. To the west are Chaco outliers across southwestern Colorado and into southeastern Utah, there being a Great House in the Bluff area. The western frontier of the Great House, according to Lekson, continues on south to the Holbrook area and the

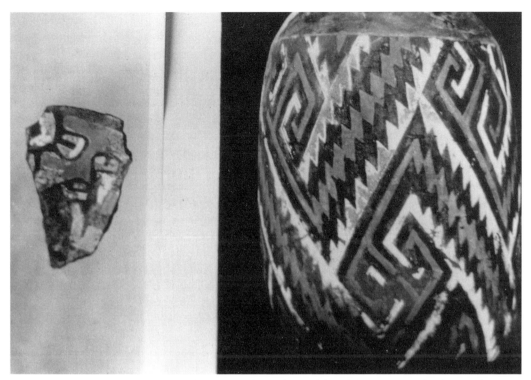

FIGURE 4.11. Pseudocloisonné from Pueblo Bonito: (left) sandstone slab with decoration; (right) decorated stone mortar. Found by Pepper at Pueblo Bonito. Photos by Jonathan Reyman.

FIGURE 4.12. Pueblo Bonito. Museum of New Mexico, neg. no. 1116.17.

Mogollon Rim, including perhaps Wupatki. He also sees possible Great Houses in the Mimbres area, a part of the interdigitation of Chaco and Mimbres societies. The Chaco outlying area extends, in this scheme, throughout the Anasazi area, excluding only the far west, the Kayenta region, and the upper Rio Grande Basin.[55] Lekson, however, takes a very generous view of Chacoan influence. Other archaeologists are more cautious in their evaluation of what represents Chaco influence, and, indeed, what represents a "Great House" (Figure 4.13).[56]

Were the Chaco centers dominated by an elite that exploited and to one degree or another controlled a large region that may have extended from the San Juan River, and Chaco itself, eastward to the Puerco River and westward to Zuni? Was Chaco some sort of class society, or can it be that we are overestimating both the population levels and the degree of social and political complexity? A number of

specialists believe in the elite interpretation.[57] Lekson is one of these, and his scenario holds that the Chaco area was indeed controlled by an elite that dominated the area from about AD 900 to 1100 or a little later by manipulating the distribution of Mesoamerican and other prestige trade wares. Sometime after the beginning of the twelfth century, the center of Chaco power was moved from the canyon some 60 miles almost directly north to what is now the large ruin of Aztec in the Animas Valley.[58]

It seems to me that something like Lekson's idea might well have held for the Chaco culture, including the shift of the power center to Aztec, although I do have some reservations. Certain archaeologists, however, have doubts as to whether Chaco had any sort of class-structured elite.

Charmion McKusick, as seen above, suggested the introduction of the Mesoamerican Tezcatlipoca cult, with its stress on the sacrificial scarlet macaw and the Large Indian Do-

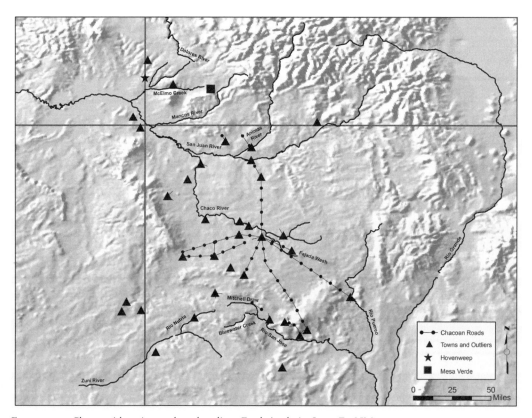

FIGURE 4.13. Chaco, with major roads and outliers. Earth Analytic, Santa Fe, NM.

mestic turkey as a unifying element in Chaco society. As Tezcatlipoca represented warfare, suffering, witchcraft, and the dark arts, it is possible that cannibalism was also associated with this god.[59]

The appearance of cannibalism, this dark side of Chacoan culture, now seems reasonably certain. The meaning of cannibalism is not totally clear, but there could have been some sort of Mesoamerican component in this dissonant alimentary behavior. Christy and Jacqueline Turner suggested a few years ago that cultists from Mesoamerica associated with Tezcatlipoca-Quetzalcoatl and Xipe Tótec introduced cannibalism into Chaco. In their scenario cannibalism might have been introduced by actual military and/or trading groups in the Chaco–San Juan region and was perhaps part of a larger religious and ceremonial complex.[60]

This proposition, of course, is highly speculative. The nature, extent, and implications of southwestern cannibalism need further research. Indeed, it could have been an extreme response to serious climatic deterioration in the San Juan Basin and had only incidentally to do with Mesoamerican influences. Or there may have been still other reasons. A recent (and in my opinion rather unlikely) explanation is that Chacoan cannibalism constituted "training exercises to initiate members of the [Keres] Obi warrior priesthood."[61]

Whether we are dealing with actual cultists or tenacious idea diffusion, the Tezcatlipoca identification is, of course, possible, but given the lack of iconographic evidence, I personally doubt that Tezcatlipoca cults had appeared at so early a time. In fact, I am quite doubtful as to the appearance of *any* of the more obvious Mesoamerican deities very much before the Aztlan period, though some specialists hold a contrary opinion.[62] Quetzalcoatl, along with Tlaloc, is more likely associated with the kachina cult, one of the hallmark features of Aztlan times, and I really do not see any evidence that kachinas—or even protokachinas, whatever they are—had appeared at the time of Chaco hegemony.

In any case the Chaco period faded after AD 1125 to 1130, though perhaps it was perpetuated, as Lekson believes, in the San Juan–Animas valleys for another century or so. In any case the San Juan Anasazi had completely relocated out of the region by around AD 1300. The reasons for this depopulation of the San Juan Basin seem to have been complex and represented not only serious shortfalls at home but also "pull" factors that made the Rio Grande Basin more attractive for long-term habitation.

Certainly weather patterns, including a serious drought in the last quarter of the thirteenth century, were involved. Some specialists argue that the period beginning around AD 1200 saw the beginning of what in Europe is called the Little Ice Age, and this led to marked deterioration in southwestern climate. Other climate experts are cautious or skeptical of this explanation. Possibly related to long-term climatic shifts, there were large-scale volcanic eruptions in various parts of the world in the period under discussion. By throwing large amounts of sulfuric oxide aerosol into the atmosphere, such eruptions reduce solar radiation, with cooling effects that may occur thousands of miles away from the actual volcanoes. A very large volcanic event occurred in 1259, possibly from a source in Mexico, and there were others. In fact, of the 11 major eruptive events in the last 1,000 years, four occurred in the thirteenth century (1228, 1259, 1278, and 1287). The role of volcanic activity in the desertion of the San Juan region is still largely a matter of speculation, but to one degree or another it must be factored in.[63]

In any case the Anasazi in the drainages of the Rio Grande and certain of its tributaries (Chama, Jemez, Puerco–San José, Taos, Santa Fe, Galisteo, and Pecos rivers) experienced rather slow and somewhat uneven growth in the earlier periods. Not till the desertion of the San Juan Valley was there a dramatic increase in Rio Grande settlements and in the importance of the area. As will be discussed in chapter 5, several lines of evidence suggest that the upper San Juan Basin populations, centered in Mesa Verde and the Four Corners region, had contact with those of the upper Rio Grande a century or more before the migration period.

Although a parallel growth appeared in the Hopi-Zuni region, the major activity does seem to have occurred in the Rio Grande. That the area received a major infusion of human population from the San Juan Basin is now widely accepted although the details are not always clear. The upper Rio Grande Valley in later times became the northeast sector of Aztlan and extremely important in the later prehistory of the Southwest.[64]

# CHAPTER 5

# The Great Anasazi Migration

The southwestern Basketmaker-Pueblo peoples known in pre-Aztlan days as the Anasazi were marked with a series of traits that tended to set them off from surrounding peoples. *Tended* is perhaps the operative word here, for not all these traits extended throughout the length and breadth of the Anasazi domain, and some of them were shared with the Mogollon to the south. In fact this sharing became so extensive that after around AD 1000 to 1050, sometimes, and in some areas, it was not particularly meaningful to distinguish between the two groups. The modern Pueblo Indians can be said to be Anasazi (or Anasazi descendants), but the Western Pueblo groups at Hopi and Zuni, even to some degree Acoma, clearly had some infiltration of Mogollon and perhaps influences from people even farther to the south and west. In the southeastern quadrant, along the Rio Grande and farther east in the Salinas Basin, the Piro and their linguistic brethren the Tompiro also showed considerable influence from the Jornada Mogollon.

The Anasazi were Native Americans who lived first in underground chambers or *pithouses* and then from roughly AD 700 began to reside more and more in aboveground structures later called by the Spaniards *pueblos* ("villages" or "towns"). These pueblos were made up of a series of contiguous rooms, sometimes three or four stories high, and held numbers of families. They were built either on mesa tops or tucked into rock shelters, as were some of the well-known ones at Mesa Verde (Figure 5.1). Walls were built of stone, usually more or less dressed sandstone, and were laid in courses with mud mortar. Typical of the individual rooms were flat load-bearing roofs made of beams, with smaller timbers at right angles, then brush and a topping of adobe. Occasionally, houses of roughly coursed adobe were used, but this house-building technique was more common farther south.

As I mentioned in chapter 4, one of the functions of the pithouse was apparently ceremonial from the beginning, and when the Anasazi groups moved above ground, they maintained this specialized pithouse as a ceremonial chamber or kiva. The incoming Spaniards used the term *estufa*, for these structures, probably meaning some sort of warming room. In the Anasazi homelands in pre-Aztlan times the kivas were generally round and varied in size (and probably in function) from small structures only 10 or 15 feet across to the Great Kivas of the Chaco area, which might span 70 feet or more and reach depths of several feet (Figure 5.2). There were variable numbers of kivas in the Anasazi ruins. In the Mesa Verde area and around Yellow Jacket individual sites would have a dozen or more of these structures. The settlement at Yellow Jacket had a remarkable collection of kivas. What so many ceremonial rooms were doing in such a small area is not clear, and it may well be that some were domiciles or had other nonkiva functions.

FIGURE 5.1. East end of Cliff Palace. Mesa Verde National Park, Colorado. Nordenskiöld, 1893.

The smaller kivas often had roofs of interlocking logs forming a "beehive" type of ceiling that would be strong enough to support considerable weight on its flat top. They normally were entered by a door in the middle of the roof, where a ladder went down to the packed-dirt floor and where a slightly offset fire pit could use the opening to discharge its smoke. Some kivas had a tunnel that led to the outside, to a room, or to another kiva. On a wall adjacent to the fire pit a small shaft for ventilation allowed fresh air to circulate through the kiva. Offset from the center was the *sipapu,* a small depression, only a few inches wide and deep. In modern kivas this feature symbolizes the opening to the underworld from which came the ancestors of Pueblo Indians. These small kivas are often referred to as "clan" kivas, but we do not know enough of the so-cial organization of the Anasazi to be sure that there were clans.

The Great Kivas radiating out from the Chaco world are often found with smaller kivas, both within the Chaco heartland and on the outskirts of that world. The Great Kiva's function must have been somewhat different from that of the smaller kivas, and it could have served the needs of *moieties,* that is divisions of a pueblo into two halves for social or ceremonial purposes. Moieties and clans exist among the historic and modern pueblos, but we cannot say for sure that they derived from the social usages of Anasazi times. In any case the Great Kivas were massive structures, often with great posts made of tree trunks or occasionally of masonry, holding up the heavy roofs of beams, smaller poles, and branches, the whole covered with mud mortar. The interior

48

FIGURE 5.2. Great Kiva at Chetro Ketl, Chaco Canyon. Museum of New Mexico, no. 1115.493.

included large basinlike structures of unknown function. They may have held water or some other substance, or they may have been used as resonators for foot drums. Entry was normally from the side and sometimes through a tunnel, possibly for the dramatic appearance of priests or dancers.[1]

Another hallmark of the Anasazi, and one that developed in the latter part of Basketmaker times, was the use of pottery. As I mentioned in chapter 4, the idea of pottery and probably specific techniques of pottery making very likely came from the Mogollon country to the south. Though made by coiling like the Mogollon ceramics, Anasazi pottery did have significant differences; for example, it was generally fired in a reduced (oxygen-starved) atmosphere, leading to white or gray wares (an example is Lino Gray [Figure 5.3]) unlike the Mogollon red or brown ceramic traditions.[2] Decoration in Anasazi pottery was usually with a black paint, made either with organic carbonaceous materials or with an iron-mineral base. However, Mogollon-looking early (Basketmaker III) red and red-on-orange ceramics, fired in an oxidizing atmosphere, plus Mogollon trade(?) wares such as San Francisco Red also appear in Basketmaker sites. Alongside the black-on-white pottery were a number of plainwares and ones decorated by pinching out or corrugating the coiled surfaces (Figure 5.4). The use of red either as a background color or as decoration and the appearance of polychrome potteries were generally quite late in Anasazi times.

Since an alternate name for Anasazi is *Basketmaker-Pueblo*, the use of baskets may be assumed; indeed, these containers, both coiled and twilled, appear even before Anasazi times. Simple weaving by hand, using fibers such as apocynum and yucca, was also early. By Pueblo III times, in places like Mesa Verde and Chaco, true loom weaving with cotton had appeared. This cotton was most likely imported, as the San Juan uplands have too short

FIGURE 5.3. Lino Gray globular pitcher, ca. AD 500–700. Maxwell Museum of Anthropology, University of New Mexico, cat. no. 42.12.40.

FIGURE 5.4. Corrugated jar, Cibola gray ware, probably Pueblo II, ca. AD 900–1100. Maxwell Museum of Anthropology, University of New Mexico, cat. no. 94.15.5.

a growing season to sustain any kind of cotton industry. During the Aztlan period cotton, probably both raw and processed, came from the Hopi region. The provenance of earlier cotton is not entirely clear.

A word about terminology might be useful here. The Anasazi were originally slotted into the Pecos classification introduced by A. V. Kidder in 1927. In the 1930s a modification of this classification was produced by F. H. H. Roberts Jr. For the Rio Grande a somewhat variant classification was developed by Fred Wendorf and Eric K. Reed in the 1950s. The chronological divisions of this Wendorf and Reed Rio Grande classification most important to this book are (1) the *Developmental* period (c. AD 600–1200), taking up essentially the Basketmaker and earlier Pueblo); (2) the *Coalition* period (AD 1200–1325), which signals the demographic change and increase in population and includes the end of Pueblo III and the beginnings of Pueblo IV; and (3) the *Classic* period (AD 1325–1600), basically our Aztlan as it applies to the upper Rio Grande.

The periods known as Pueblo II and the early part of Pueblo III saw the greatest expansion of the Anasazi. The westernmost extent of settlements recognizable as Anasazi were in

the lower Virgin and Muddy rivers in Nevada and in the upper reaches of the Virgin, the Paria, and Escalante rivers of southern Utah. In the lower Virgin-Muddy river areas rainfall is so low (about 4 inches per year, only a third of it falling in the summer months) that agriculture must needs be based on irrigation. Though there was an Anasazi presence as early as Basketmaker times, the main occupation of the western periphery seems to have been P II, reaching a climax sometime around AD 1050–1100.[3] The region of north-central Arizona was also considerably populated, particularly the Kayenta area north of Black Mesa.[4] There are a number of Anasazi sites in the plateau country of northern Arizona, south of the Virgin River and north of the Grand Canyon. Pueblo Indians lived on the Kaibito, Rainbow, and Shonto plateaus, on Black Mesa, in the Laguna-Chinle drainage, and parts of the Little Colorado drainage in Arizona and extreme western New Mexico.

South of the Kayenta region in the Cibola area of west-central New Mexico, in the vicinity of Arizona's White Mountains, and along and north of the Mogollon Rim, Mogollon-like peoples were adjusting more and more to an Anasazi type of life with black-on-white pottery and very Anasazi-like transition from Basketmaker pithouses to Puebloan aboveground structures. The pottery derived at least in part from the Chaco region. At some point in late Pueblo II times, around or a little before AD 1100, a series of redwares, often with black design elements, appeared in the region. Their evolution is not entirely clear (and perhaps involved both Anasazi and Mogollon ancestry), but they seem to have developed from a technique of adding red slip to the original whitish surface of the pot. In any case these White Mountain redwares became very popular. Sometime after AD 1100 the addition of a white pigment to this black-on-red pottery

created a true polychrome. The White Mountain redwares evolved through several very distinctive design styles that can be traced over large areas of the Southwest. The widest-spread of these redwares were St. Johns Black-on-red and St. Johns Polychrome (Figure 5.5), perhaps originating somewhere in the Zuni-Gallup area (at least their greatest concentration was there). They had a considerable time depth, AD 1145 to 1300, and a north-south distribution from the Mesa Verde area to the El Paso area and Chihuahua, and an east-west spread from central Arizona to the Pecos River drainage of eastern New Mexico (see Figure 5.6).[5]

St. Johns pottery carried the widespread Tularosa design style, with its complex interlocked hatches and solid elements, bird motifs, and parallel hatching. Very late in the St. Johns sequence the Pinedale style appears. The latter

FIGURE 5.5. St. Johns Polychrome bowl. El Paso Museum of Archaeology.

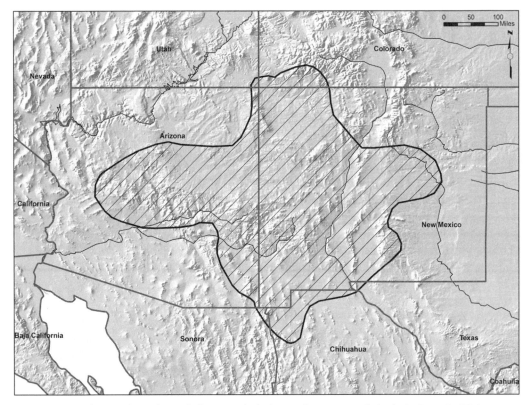

FIGURE 5.6. Distribution of St. Johns Polychrome and Black-on-red pottery. Earth Analytic, Santa Fe, NM.

distinctive style, with its "mosquito bar" designs, double hatching, stepped fillers, and diamond motifs, became very widespread in later times. Patricia Crown calls the Pinedale design style "a true horizon style."[6] It belongs, however, along with its successor the Fourmile style, more to Aztlan times, and its significance will be discussed in later chapters (see Figure 5.7).

The twelfth and thirteenth centuries are sometimes thought of as a low ebb in terms of southwestern and Mesoamerican contacts. This ebb spans the period between the polity centered in Chaco Canyon, which, traditionally, was supposed to have collapsed around AD 1130, at least in the canyon, and the development of Aztlan after AD 1300. But the St. Johns ceramics demonstrate that influences of *some* sort were linking up large portions of the Southwest during these troubled times.

There was intense settlement north of the San Juan River, along the Montezuma, Mc-Elmo, Yellow Jacket, and Mancos drainages of

Colorado and on the high plateau country of Mesa Verde. New Mexico settlements included the main San Juan–Animas, as well as the Chaco, Puerco, Salado, Rio Grande, and Pecos river systems. This irregular area stretched for more than 500 miles, east and west and, at its greatest extent, 300 miles north and south (the latter depending on one's definition of *Anasazi*).[7]

The heaviest Anasazi populations were in the central San Juan region of the upper Southwest. Not only was there the "Chaco Phenomenon," but farther to the north, in the region of Mesa Verde, the Four Corners area, and a wide swath of southeastern Utah, there were heavy concentrations of Pueblo Indians. These Mesa Verde–Four Corners Indians lived in scattered towns and villages, some of them, like the settlement on upper Yellow Jacket Creek in extreme southwestern Colorado, very large indeed. For the most part they were more "parochial" than the Chaco centers in the sense

FIGURE 5.7. Pottery styles in late pre-Aztlan and Aztlan times: (a) Tularosa; (b and c) Pinedale; (d) Fourmile. Drawing by Rowyn L. Evans.

great reorganization of Anasazi during the period around AD 1300 (except of course for Pecos itself [Figure 5.8]).[8]

The southern limits of the Anasazi, at least in pre-Aztlan times, are often put somewhere in the Socorro–San Marcial area of the Rio Abajo country along the Rio Grande. By Late Elmendorf times the culture was basically Anasazi though on a Mogollon base, as might be expected on this Anasazi and Jornada Mogollon frontier. In addition the region contains what looks to be Mesa Verde–type "refugee" sites. The Elmendorf groups were at least partly ancestral to the Piro, who in post-1300 times were drawn into the more northerly Pueblo orbit, sharing the Rio Grande gray and glazed wares (particularly Glaze A) with pueblo peoples of Anasazi antecedents in the Rio Arriba country to the north. Piro territory extended from somewhere around the Rio Puerco junction with the Rio Grande, roughly the line of modern U.S. Highway 60, south to the area around Milligan Gulch, near Black Mesa.[9] The Tompiro, those linguistic brethren of the Piro, in the Salinas, east of the Manzano Mountains, are also a late phenomenon and like the Piro belong to the Aztlan period. However, there was earlier settlement in the Chupadera Mesa and Salinas regions and in the mesa country to the south. A pithouse village near Gran Quivira dates back to perhaps AD 600, and there was a pithouse occupation to the southeast along the Sierra Blanca and Sacramento Mountains with beginning dates before AD 900.[10] Along the eastern edge of the Capitan Mountains there was an early phase of small jacal settlements, but from about AD 1200 to 1400 a series of stone and coursed adobe multiroom pueblos with problematic kivas occupied this area. Some relatively late sites (extending into the early fourteenth century or possibly later)—for example, Henderson Pueblo, near Roswell—are adobe structures of considerable size. As we saw in chapter 4, however, these areas, though possessing varying Anasazi "flavors," are normally considered more properly related to the Jornada Mogollon.

Beginning in the twelfth century, cresting at

that there was hardly any obvious Mesoamericanization. Still, there were outliers with Chaco-type architecture and, presumably, ideology that penetrated the area.

The upper Rio Grande Valley was populated, generally quite minimally, from Paleoindian and Archaic times on with somewhat different history throughout the earlier Basketmaker-Pueblo. This is the area on the receiving end of the population shifts that reached their greatest intensity in the latter part of the thirteenth century and the beginning of the fourteenth. On the eastern edge of the Anasazi there were settlements on certain eastern tributaries of the Pecos, especially the Tecolote and Gallinas rivers. Around or a bit after AD 1200 a series of villages of pueblo-dwelling type pushed into that area, replacing or perhaps mixing with a residual Pueblo population. At about the same time various towns in the upper Pecos were formed, following what seems to be a hiatus of several hundred years. These included Pecos itself, Forked Lightning, Dick's Ruin, and Rowe Ruin among others. All of these sites, situated in the Pecos River drainage, disappeared in the

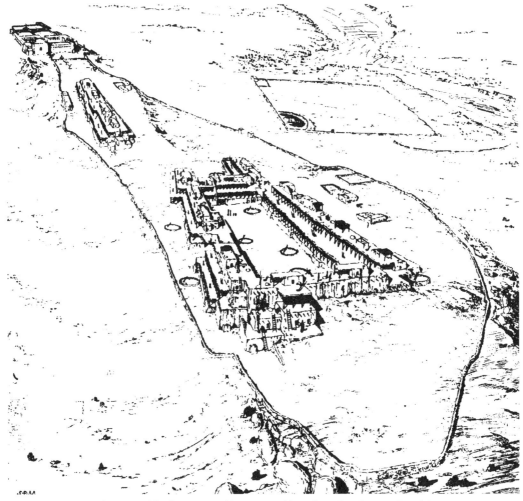

FIGURE 5.8. Sketch of Pecos Pueblo, from original by A. V. Kidder (after Riley, *Frontier People*).

the end of the thirteenth, but continuing on to the edge of historic times, there were a series of population shifts that greatly changed the cultural landscape of the Southwest. In this chapter we are concerned with the Anasazi manifestations that started with the edges, west and east, both rolling back toward the center. In the west the twelfth century saw the desertion of much of the Nevada, Utah, and northwestern Arizona areas. During the thirteenth century and early fourteenth the Tecolote-Gallinas region of the upper Pecos drainage was deserted, as was the Pecos, except for the upper valley, the people in all probability moving into the valley around modern Pecos and westward into the Rio Grande Basin, from

where they had originally come. I have suggested elsewhere that this western shift was related to the movement of Apachean peoples (called *Querecho* by the earliest Spaniards, two and a half centuries later) onto the western edges of the southern plains. A shift in rainfall patterns (see below) was also probably implicated.[11]

More dramatic, however, was a shift in the whole San Juan region, which was emptied of all Pueblo life by around AD 1300. The San Juan people are generally thought to have gone both southeastward into the Rio Grande Basin and southwestward, where they formed components of the emerging Hopi and perhaps Zuni. The paths of these migrations can be to some degree traced by site dating, pottery types, and other features. Of course, such comparisons might mean something else: generic similarities that extend over large areas or selective borrowing through trade and other contact mechanisms that might not involve any significant gene flow from one area to the other. However, the people of the San Juan area, perhaps 30,000 of them, went *somewhere,* and the Rio Grande and region around Black Mesa do seem the most likely possibilities. It is true that the *biological* evidence, skeletal materials, not to mention the underlying DNA, has not yet been very extensively evaluated.[12]

What caused the depopulation of large areas for the upper Southwest, thousands of square miles, during this time period? In part, this depopulation was probably due to a vibrant early overexpansion of Anasazi culture into marginal areas. This seems to have been the case in western reaches of the Anasazi, primarily the drainage of the Virgin River and adjacent territory north of the Grand Canyon,[13] and also in the extreme east, along the edges of the Great Plains.

It was to some degree due to climatic factors. The Anasazi region is a climate-sensitive area, with large stretches of semidesert, as well as heavily forested regions in the higher elevations of the Colorado Plateaus. The early expansion that included the transition from pithouse living of the Basketmaker III period to early aboveground dwellings of Pueblo I (AD 700–900) seems to have been during a period of increased moisture. After a period of unsettled weather another wet spell (apparently somewhat warmer with a longer growing season) in various parts of the Anasazi region stretched from sometime before AD 1000 to around AD 1150 and saw the beginning of heavy settlement in the McElmo, Montezuma, Dolores, Mancos, and Cottonwood Wash drainages.[14] An example of this was the Yellow Jacket area, near the Four Corners. The Yellow Jacket site, one of the major population concentrations, is located on Yellow Jacket Creek a few miles northwest of modern Cortez, Colorado. A tributary flowing from the north

cuts into the main stream, and relatively flat land extends for about a mile between the two creeks. This tongue of land, several hundred feet wide, contains almost continuous ruins. The late P-II to early P-III population has been variously estimated, the highest figures being 3,000 to 4,000 people.[15]

Climatic conditions in the western Anasazi area became rather unsettled after about AD 1100 and in particular after AD 1150. There seems to have been a falloff in population across the western periphery about this time and, as I said above, a desertion of the area by Pueblo peoples, perhaps complete by AD 1200. What happened here is not clear, though arroyo cutting and shifts in rainfall may have been factors. Possibly these westernmost Pueblo groups drifted off to the east and south, or they may have remained in the general area while returning to basically an Archaic way of life.[16]

The Kayenta region represented another series of challenges to life in Anasazi times. The region is somewhat varied, much of it being semidesert uplands drained by a series of small streams, usually intermittent, that flow north and northwest to the San Juan and Colorado rivers. Examples of these streams, going from west to east, are Navajo Creek in western Arizona, and Laguna-Chinle creeks, which drain Kayenta proper and the mountains that form the eastern boundaries of present-day Arizona and New Mexico. This area is bounded on the south by Black Mesa, a high dissected plateau whose northern ramparts rise sharply, a thousand feet and more, from the rather broken valleys around Kayenta (the modern town of that name lying at 5,800 feet). Black Mesa drains southward, and the land falls off sharply to the fringy edges of the Hopi Mesas on its southern boundary. The archaeology of this general region is complex. There were periodic fluctuations of population and, indeed, regional depopulation in some areas.

The region, like that of the San Juan farther to the east was deserted by around AD 1300. The reasons are unclear, but in all probability climatic changes were involved, as well as general environmental degradation caused by overuse and a concomitant loss of topsoil. On the southern fringes of Black Mesa the Puebloan cluster that was to become Hopi survived and probably received additional population at this time. The subsequent rise of the Hopi group of pueblos, especially as important purveyors of cotton and cotton cloth, came later in the Aztlan period.[17] At least some of the Kayenta people moved on to the south, where they form an element in these settlements of the mountainous region of Arizona south of the Mogollon Rim and of the Salado of the Lower Salt drainage.

In the Chaco area an unsettled climate was likely one of the reasons for collapse of the Great House tradition and what seemed to be some sort of elite group control. All in all, the period from around AD 1100 was one of considerable unrest, especially in the San Juan region. People whose ceramics and house and kiva structures showed a common ancestry in the uplands north of the San Juan, such as Mesa Verde, gradually moved southward in the twelfth and thirteenth centuries, reaching into Chaco Canyon and settling Chacra Mesa, which borders Chaco Canyon on the southeast. Chaco peoples of the Great House tradition had, as we saw earlier, expanded north of the San Juan and had an impact on the people of the Four Corners region. Even Yellow Jacket has its Great Kiva, as do Lowry, Yucca House, Escalante, and other ruins in the general area. Still the cultural affinities of this region, constituting the general Four Corners region, including the canyons and mesas of Mesa Verde and the canyons of the Hovenweep area, seem to be largely of what perhaps could be called a "Mesa Verde" type.[18] There is not only a distinctive architecture but also a general lack of the ritual and ceremonial elite goods that seem to have been so important in Chaco Canyon.

On the face of it Chaco Canyon is a rather odd place to center an advanced society. The region is relatively barren; today rainfall and snowfall together measure only some nine to ten inches of precipitation annually. Winter nights are often brutally cold, and summers are dry and hot. The core area of Chaco is colder than the surrounding region because of the drainage of cold air into the canyon. Within the canyon most years have fewer than 100 frost-free days, not an optimal situation for agriculture.[19] Yet the ruins indicate that an enormous effort was put into the construction of the canyon buildings, as witness the many thousands of logs, presumably carried or dragged by human teams (see below). The logistics of such operations have yet to be fully investigated.

What Chaco Canyon and its cultural environs represented is very much under dispute. At its height, in the tenth and eleventh centuries, a number of spectacular Great Houses were built, most of them north of Chaco Wash. The developmental climax at Chaco came roughly during the period AD 1000 to 1100, a period seeing the full expansion of such great sites as Pueblo Bonito and Chetro Ketl (Figure 5.9), among others. Out from the Great Houses were a series of roads and trails, some of them avenues 30 feet or more in width, sometimes with packed-earth foundations, berms, and retaining walls along slopes.[20] The fourteen Great Houses in the general Chaco area can be four stories high, and average more than 200 rooms per site. The largest (Pueblo Bonito) has something like 700 rooms, though of course the site was occupied for 150 to 200 years.

Great Houses come in a variety of shapes—in the form of a D or E, oval or rectangular—and they often show modifications in design over time. The structures are built with a core and veneer, often banded, sandstone and mud mortar masonry. Doorways are often carefully finished with a timber or slab of stone for lintel. One interesting feature in the Chacoan houses is the T-shaped doorway. Generally speaking, Great Houses, wherever they are found, show a series of features, though any given Great House may not show all, or necessarily even a major part, of these. Along with T-shaped doorways, features include core-and-veneer masonry and geometric ground plans mentioned above, as well as high-ceilinged spacious rooms, plazas, roads, kivas enclosed in room blocks, and Great Kivas.[21]

FIGURE 5.9. Chetro Ketl. Maxwell Museum of Anthropology, University of New Mexico, cat. no. 99.9.4.

Throughout the central Chaco region are smaller sites (given the name "small houses" by Gwinn Vivian), contemporary with the Great Houses but normally not associated with Great Kivas. This small house–Great House differentiation is often but not always found in outlying areas. At Chaco Canyon these smaller sites cluster along the south side of the wash. They tend to be single story with open plazas and associated small kivas.[22]

Building of Great House structures may have started before AD 900, although the climax of Great Houses came in the eleventh and early twelfth centuries.[23] A serious drought period, beginning around the latter date and lasting for some thirty years, seems to have marked a terminus to the most vigorous period at Chaco itself, though the canyon may have seen a scattered occupation of small sites until perhaps AD 1300, primarily by peoples whose origin, as suggested by pottery and house construction, was originally north of the San Juan River. It looks as if some of those people moved south and east after around AD 1300, following the line of the Puerco River of the East and eventually settling in the Galisteo region of the Rio Grande Valley.[24]

What exactly was the Chaco "phenomenon"? On one hand, the Great Houses, the connecting roads, sophisticated pottery (see Figure 5.10), southwestern trade or tribute items such as turquoise, caches of Mesoamerican goods (including macaws, copper, and shell), as well as "southern" features (for example columns, pseudocloisonné decoration, platforms, and veneer wall construction) all suggest some considerable level of difference from earlier Anasazi. On the other hand, the rock art of Chaco seems not to represent the Mesoamerican themes so prevalent in the rock art of Aztlan times.[25] Are we dealing with a complex of features coming from Mesoamerica, or were these features largely "home-grown," an outgrowth of local evolution? This

FIGURE 5.10. Pottery head of woman, Gallup Black-on-white. From Pueblo Bonito, Chaco Canyon, ca. AD 1000–1150. Maxwell Museum of Anthropology, University of New Mexico, cat. no. 92.1.1201.

by Great Houses, roads, and other forms of material culture. Whatever the *resident* population of the Great Houses themselves, a considerable workforce was necessary to construct them and to build the roadways. Vast amounts of ponderosa pine and other timbers (in one estimate 200,000 trees) were used. Certain kinds of wood, especially fir and spruce (which together make up greater than 20 percent of the total at Chaco) were lumbered from the region around Mt. Taylor to the south and from the Chuska Mountains to the west. It looks as if nearer stands of timbers had been stripped away by around AD 1000, and it became necessary to go farther afield. However, the high-altitude Mt. Taylor and Chuska spruce and fir were used quite early in the Chaco period, the first known cutting date being AD 974.[28] Mt. Taylor is about 50 miles to the south of Chaco, and the Chuskas are some 45 to 50 miles to the east. The Chuska area also produced a great deal of the pottery used at Chaco. Interestingly, the San Pedro Mountains, some 50 to 60 miles to the east, were not particularly utilized, perhaps because of nearby outliers in the Taylor-Chuska region. This selectivity may be cultural in nature—the developing system of roads and outliers favoring the southern and western highlands (Figure 5.11). Or it may be that the Chuska and Taylor timbers were more desirable or more easily available, so outliers were built in near proximity to these regions (Figure 5.12). In any case much-used roads and trails from early times on must have connected Chaco to the Chuska and Mt. Taylor areas. The Herculean task of transporting logs might have been the stimulus for the well-maintained roads, carefully planned as to grades and arroyo crossings.

Contemporary with the Great Houses are the small-house village sites, mainly on the south side of Chaco Wash. These structures, averaging about sixteen rooms, are more diverse than the Great Houses, some resembling earlier Pueblo II sites and, unlike the Great Houses, showing rather unplanned growth. They are associated with small kivas, some reminiscent of Mesa Verde, others of the broad-bench interior

latter position has been argued by archaeologists steeped in the intellectual tradition of the Anasazi and especially the San Juan Basin.[26] The reality probably lies somewhere between— but where?

What was the political situation at Chaco? Regardless of the origins of Chaco culture, there is a general feeling that something a bit more complicated than modern-day Pueblo sociopolitical organization was involved. Some archaeologists see Chaco Canyon as a ceremonial city with a population of perhaps 3,000 in the central core of the region. However, various other estimates exist, some higher; one is as low as 250 people, peak population, for the Chaco Canyon Great Houses combined.[27] Nor is there basic agreement on the area of Chacoan regional influence. Estimates range from about 11,000 to more than 55,000 square miles. This is not necessarily the region of *political* control but of "Chaco-ness" as defined

FIGURE 5.11. Pueblo Alto, on north mesa above Chaco Canyon. Maxwell Museum of Anthropology, University of New Mexico, cat. no. 92.1.1179.

FIGURE 5.12. Greenlee site, an outlier south of Chaco. Maxwell Museum of Anthropology, University of New Mexico, cat. no. 92.1.1199.

"Chacoan" type. One Great Kiva, Rinconada, on the south side of the canyon, may have served a number of nearby small-house sites. Originally called the Hosta Butte phase to distinguish them from the Great House Bonito phase, it is now clear that the two types of structure are generally contemporary, although small houses began earlier. It now seems likely that small-house villages contained at least part of the population that serviced the Great Houses.[29]

This seems to be what John R. Stein and Andrew P. Fowler suggest in a recent publication on classificatory problems in the Chaco area:

> There is another explanation for the monumental structures of Chaco Canyon, one that is faithful to the forces that predictably shape the built environments of traditional societies. In our explanation of developments in Chaco canyon, the Great Houses are but elements of a larger planned architectural composition which functioned in the ritual, not the residential, realm. We suggest that Pueblo Bonito was not a pueblo, that Chaco Canyon was never a proto-urban center of culture and commerce, and that the canyon population, the so-called Chacoans, resided in smallish but otherwise normal communities spaced along the length of the canyon. There is no argument that the monumental architecture of Chaco Canyon is magnitudes larger than a contemporary Anasazi dwelling, however, the "mystery" of Chaco is a reference to our discomfort with the empirical reality of the scale and timing of the Chaco monuments, contrasted with our expectations based on the Pecos Classification. We caution that the idea of a "Chaco Phenomenon" is an artifact of the Pecos Classification.[30]

The Stein and Fowler statement, however, represents only one point of a rather wide spectrum of opinions concerning the meaning of Chaco. Archaeologist Lynn Sebastian has somewhat variant thoughts on the matter:

Although there is clear evidence for contact, the distances [to Mesoamerica] are too great for intensive interaction and there is little evidence of heavy traffic in the intervening areas. More important, there is clear evidence that Chacoan complexity was a long-term, multigenerational in situ development. The argument that Chacoan complexity was an adaptive response, however, is still the explanation of choice among most Chacoan researchers.

My problem with this is that increasing investment in complexity is a *really* bad response to subsistence stress and population/resource imbalance. And while we all know that bad adaptive strategies are not uncommon, they are usually self-limiting, while Chacoan society flourished and became increasingly complex over a period of 200 years. Complexity is a bad idea as a response to stress because it is expensive; the Chacoans spent vast quantities of calories on monumental constructions—Great Houses and Great Kivas, hundreds of kilometers of well-engineered roads, mounds, earthworks, and irrigation complexes.[31]

Let me say first of all that I am not totally convinced of the marginalization of Mesoamerica as a player in the development of Chacoan society. Ideas, as against material goods, often do not leave perceptible marks of their passage, and it is the diffusion of sociopolitical and religious *ideas* that might be involved here. As far as the intervening area is concerned, I can only point to the fact that the archaeology of northwestern Mexico still has many gaps, and vast parts of this vast region are still basically unexplored. And certainly in Mesoamerica there was a long-standing tradition of very long-range trade.

Still, it must be conceded that even mental structures, especially religious ones, usually come with their particular icons, and, as mentioned above, these do seem to be lacking at Chaco. For example, the Chacoan rock art is more traditional old-line Anasazi, with little or nothing that relates to Mesoamerica. As we will see, this is a very different situation from what went on in the Aztlan (post-1300) period, where the iconography itself, with its Tlaloc- and Quetzalcoatl-oriented figures, allows us to trace large-scale religious movements that clearly originated in Mesoamerica. This iconography in the south was also utilized to represent elite individuals and groups, something also missing at Chaco.[32]

In any case Sebastian sees Chacoan culture originally as one of small residential groups, involved in reciprocal exchange. During the tenth century these small residential entities began to experience an imbalance of exchange obligations as some groups controlled better-watered and more-productive lands than others. This led gradually to greater social power on the part of some communities and greater obligations on the part of less-fortunate neighbors, obligations that originally could be met by labor contributions. As time went on, leadership roles became hereditary in fortunate families, access to and consumption of goods and labor became increasingly differential, and Chaco Canyon itself became increasingly a center for social relationships. In the early twelfth century, however, the intensity of construction and probably the centers of political power and social relationships shifted north to the San Juan Basin.[33] Sebastian's explanation of Chacoan evolution in some ways goes back to the classic economic surplus explanation of V. Gordon Childe.[34]

Others have different viewpoints about Chacoan complexity. W. H. Wills considers that the massive building at Chaco was the result of a "corporate social enterprise" in which the community cooperated in a "secular ritual system that suppressed or eliminated much of the divisive dynamics of competition among religious leaders."[35] Catherine Cameron suggests that "the power of Chacoan leaders may have been situational, emerging only in the context of various different communal activities."[36] That sounds somewhat like historic Pueblos, but which historic Pueblos? As Linda Cordell

points out, there are considerable differences between the western and eastern group of Pueblos:

Chaco is more often compared to Western Pueblos, such as Hopi and Zuni, and it seems unlike those modern Pueblos, which have few leadership roles and little centralized control. Eastern Pueblos do have something like elites. They emphasize ranked non-kin "sodalities" (organizations and institutions that are *not* kinship-based), whereas Western Pueblo organization is kinship-based. Eastern Pueblo society is divided between initiated elite leaders and commoners based on membership in these sodalities. The inter-village ties among the religious leaders link villages in ways that might resemble multiple communities. It seems possible that something as complex and apparently centralized as Chaco could have been the product of ranked sodalities, like those of the Eastern Pueblos.[37]

Even in Chaco times there seems to have been a considerable amount of contact with the Rio Grande Valley. The area of Chaco regional influence, even for the most expansionist archaeologist, does not actually extend to the main basin of the Rio Grande, though Guadalupe Ruin, in the Puerco River valley, is often (usually?) considered part of the Chaco hegemony. Still, there are settlements in the Galisteo region, the Bronze Trail group, that in all likelihood serviced the Chaco thirst for turquoise.[38]

The Great House period at Chaco Canyon is generally considered to have come to an end around AD 1130 to 1150, although some would argue that it was somewhat later. Lekson considers that the Chaco elite (consisting of perhaps a thousand individuals) moved north along a meridian line to another center, another "capital," the great ruin now called Aztec in the Animas Valley, just north of the San Juan River. According to Lekson, "the movement, up and down the meridian, *was not* a migration; it was a political maneuver, by a small but powerful elite. When the capital shifted first to Aztec and then to Paquime, the elite moved—perhaps 1,000, less than a multitude, but more than enough to reproduce, both biologically and socially."[39]

Though I am not an expert on Chacoan culture, I will hazard a few outsider comments on the *nature* of Chacoan sociopolitical relationships. Given the size and complexity of the Chaco ruins, it seems reasonable that some sort of elite system was operating there. By elite, I mean a group that had some sort of differential access to both resources and power. Chacoan peoples were fairly obviously involved in some sort of elaborate exchange system, one that extended deep into what is now Mexico.[40] As Stephen Plog has pointed out, the great Chaco Canyon centers, seemingly so remote and environmentally hostile, are actually within easy distance of three major drainage systems, the Rio Grande, the San Juan, and the Little Colorado.[41] However, given these factors, one might reasonably expect some sort of funerary differentiation, an indication in death practices of the social inequality of the society. But, this is not the case—relatively few Chacoan burials that might be interpreted as elite

have been found. Of course, the burials may be there and simply remain undiscovered, or they may have been destroyed or deeply buried by erosional processes.[42]

The ruins of Aztec became one of the major foci of an area sometimes called *Totah,* a Navajo word meaning "rivers coming together," the area in the vicinity, both up- and downstream of the San Juan junction with the Animas and La Plata rivers. The site itself was misnamed by romantic early settlers who saw in the aboriginal ruins of the area, similarities to the Aztec civilization to the south. The modern town of Aztec, just across the Animas River and east and south of the ruined pueblo, was founded in the late nineteenth century. It was named for the ruins, thus perpetuating the misidentification. Aztec, now a national monument, was excavated during the early part of the twentieth century and is best known to the general public for its Great Kiva, reconstructed by the archaeologist Earl Morris (see Figure 5.13). However, only a small portion of Aztec, one of the largest Anasazi ruins in the Southwest, has actually been excavated. The Chacoan period at Aztec began about AD 1110

FIGURE 5.13. Aztec ruins, Chaco outlier north of Chaco Canyon on Animas River. At center of photograph is the Great Kiva, reconstructed by Earl Morris. Maxwell Museum of Anthropology, University of New Mexico, cat. no. 92.1.1200.

and continued for more than a century and a half, the site being deserted, like the rest of the San Juan Basin, sometime between AD 1270 and 1300. Indeed, Aztec, while perhaps the largest site, was hardly the only Chacoan settlement in the area. A number of other Great House sites are in the area, but with the exception of Aztec itself and Salmon, on the north bank of the San Juan a few miles upstream from the Animas–San Juan juncture, there has been little systematic excavation.[43]

In the final century and a half of occupation of the San Juan area there seems to have been restlessness, a movement back and forth, especially in the region to the north of the San Juan. Along the western portion of this elongated region, in the drainages of McElmo–Yellow Jacket and Montezuma creeks, there was concentration on available water sources, especially in seeps along the canyon walls and in canyon heads. Water control in the Hovenweep area was characterized by check dams. Many of these were located too near the canyons for an optimal agricultural function, so perhaps they were used to supplement domestic water supply.[44] A very noticeable aspect of Hovenweep is a series of towers and other substantial structures built along the canyon walls or rising from terraces within the canyons (Figure 5.14). These have small "windows" placed regularly and at strategic places along the walls. More than a half century ago, while working at Hovenweep for the National Park Service, I did a study, analyzing these small wall ports in a number of the structures. I concluded that the towers had a defensive function, as did nearby large communal buildings that I called "Great Houses," following the archaeologist J. Walter Fewkes.[45] I did not have Chaco Canyon in mind—in the 1940s the obsession with Chaco outliers had not begun, and in any case these structures generally owed nothing to the Chaco architectural tradition. The ceramics were unquestionably Mesa Verde style (see Figure 5.15), and there were no Great Kivas in the Hovenweep heartland. There are Great Kivas nearby, relating to Chacoan outliers, but not at Hovenweep itself. I thought

FIGURE 5.14. Square Tower and associated ruins in Square Tower Canyon, Hovenweep. Museum of New Mexico, neg. no. 60695.

that these Hovenweep "Great Houses" might be blockhouses used in defense of water supplies. As far as I know this question of the function of the Hovenweep structures has never been satisfactorily settled. Certainly the move to cliff dwellings, often easily defendable ones, in the San Juan area, generally, during the thirteenth century, suggests a defensive stance.

In any case certain kinds of environmental stress were wracking the upper Southwest during that eventful thirteenth century. In chapter 4 I discussed the possibility that increased volcanic activity in other parts of the world may have impacted the southwestern climate of the time. This could have produced colder summers and generally a shorter growing season. Another possibility is that the great weather phenomenon La Niña, brought about by cooler seasonal temperatures in the Pacific Ocean, lasted longer and was more intense during that period. In later times, at any rate, such extended La Niñas produced dryer conditions

FIGURE 5.15. Mesa Verde Black-on-white mugs from the Farmington, New Mexico, area. Maxwell Museum of Anthropology, University of New Mexico, cat. no. 88.71.9.

in the Southwest. Certainly there were periods of considerable drought, particularly a twenty-four-year period of dry weather in the latter 1200s.[46]

The century seems to have been one of steady population decline. A part of this decline may have been caused by exhaustion of certain crucial basic environmental supplies, especially wood for construction and for fuel. Certain areas, especially the south-facing canyons and mesas of Mesa Verde, thrived for a while, but one gets the feeling that the periphery was steadily peeling away.

The role of outside enemies has been suggested, either the earliest of the Apachean groups or perhaps Ute-speaking peoples sifting in from the west. Of the two kinds of intrusion the latter looks marginally more feasible, but archaeological evidence for either Apachean or Ute speakers is very scarce on the ground for this period. As William D. Lipe, following Ralph Linton's classic article on the subject, points out: "I would expect the hostile nomads would have had to be relatively numerous in order to have displaced thousands of Pueb-

loans: if they were in fact sufficiently numerous, we might expect them to be well above the threshold of archaeological visibility."[47]

However, increasing environmental pressures could well have led to intergroup Pueblo hostilities. A scarcity of water can be an especially serious matter, particularly if it comes during the crucial growing season. Water for both domestic and agricultural use may become more and more precious, especially in the Four Corners area, as suggested by the building of reservoirs and the tendency for later construction to be near springs. These springs were the only living water sources readily available to the mesa-top settlers in the Mesa Verde region.[48] Of course, that would not have been true along the always-flowing San Juan River and certain of its tributaries, especially the Animas.

There is some evidence that out-migration had begun perhaps by the beginning of the thirteenth century. It is quite possible that there was already significant population flow to the Rio Grande area and, perhaps, the Zuni-Hopi area a century before the final depopulation of the San Juan Basin. Whatever else it may mean, this does signify that as hard times came on, people knew they could find refuge in the Rio Grande Valley and, perhaps, in the Little Colorado drainage also.[49] I should stress that certain southwestern archaeologists discount massive migration from the San Juan to the Rio Grande and believe that the considerable increase in Rio Grande population especially in the fourteenth and early fifteenth centuries was in part a matter of in-migration from the surrounding plateaus and even from the Little Colorado region to the west.[50]

The availability of animal foods is not totally clear, but there seems to be a drop-off in hunting of the larger mammals, especially deer, in the later occupation phases, emphasis being placed on domestic turkeys and the less-productive, "unit-wise," smaller animals such as rabbits and rodents.[51] Another interesting possibility that has not been investigated fully is that there may have been striking differential access to basic foodstuffs in the thirteenth century, with women and children simply getting less to eat.[52] This would be a bit reminiscent of the situation among aboriginal Eskimos, where it has been documented that, during times of scarcity and hunger, preferential treatment was given to adult men. If carried to extremes, it might have had an adverse effect on population growth.

Elsewhere I have tentatively suggested that in BC times an ancestral Tanoan language extended from the San Juan Basin and the Four Corners area into the northern Rio Grande. Ancestral Keresan was spoken in the Chaco area and perhaps to the west. By the last centuries of Puebloan occupation of the San Juan area this original Tanoan language had become Tewa and Towa in the San Juan region and Tiwa and the related Piro in the Rio Grande. Keresan dialects, probably fairly similar to ones known historically, were spoken at Chaco Canyon. In the period following AD 1100 Keresan-speaking Indians spread southward and eastward into the Acoma area and down the Jemez River to the Rio Grande. People using Tewa and Towa also moved east and south, through the valleys of the Puerco and the Chama into the Rio Grande proper, these intrusions splitting the Tiwa speakers into northern and southern groups. By around AD 1350 the linguistic grouping of the eastern pueblos was not too far from what the Spaniards found two centuries later.[53] Let me warn the reader that this reconstruction is highly suppositional. If true, however, it does suggest long-standing cultural relationships between the San Juan and Rio Grande valleys.

The northwest quadrant of the Anasazi is even less clear as to the linguistic situation, but at least some of the peoples, especially in the Kayenta region, may have spoken a northern Uto-Aztecan language, perhaps an ancestral form of Hopi. I think it likely that sedentary Indians speaking the Zuni language had reached the Zuni River drainage by at least the early AD centuries, perhaps spreading from the Mogollon region to the south. There may also have been Keresan-speaking natives in the upper and middle Zuni Basin.

Although opinion is by no means unanimous on this point, a San Juan–influenced ceramic type, Santa Fe Black-on-white, does seem to have spread through the upper Rio Grande (Figure 5.16). This pottery, beginning about AD 1200, had its immediate antecedents in K'wahe and Gallina Black-on-white traditions. But Santa Fe Black-on-white also had influences from the McElmo and Mesa Verde Black-on-white ceramics in its use of carbon paint and in various design elements. John R. Roney has recently pointed out that the thirteenth-century middle Puerco Valley, an area intermediate between the Rio Grande proper and the San Juan, saw a series of sites that have mixtures of Mesa Verde–McElmo ceramics and Santa Fe Black-on-white. At a somewhat later time sites in the Magdalena region of the Rio Grande suggest strong Mesa Verde contacts, their settlement coming near the collapse period in the San Juan and lasting into the fourteenth century.[54]

If there was a significant movement of peoples from the San Juan Basin to that of the Rio Grande, it might account for the persistent and widespread modern Eastern Pueblo origin

FIGURE 5.16. Santa Fe Black-on-white jar, Otowi area. Photo by Blair Clark. Courtesy Museum of Indian Arts and Culture/Laboratory of Anthropology, Department of Cultural Affairs, cat. no. 43354/11.

stories that involve the "White House," an ancestral settlement north or northwest of their historic positions. Although all the Pueblos could hardly have come from one site (and surely a part of their ancestry was already in place by the thirteenth century), it does suggest migration from somewhere in the San Juan area.[55]

A significant movement from the San Juan, both into the Rio Grande and into the Western Pueblos, has been accepted by many archaeologists, and perhaps all students of the region believe that there was *some* movement. However, the same is not true of another idea proposed a few years ago by Stephen Lekson. According to Lekson members of a Chaco Canyon elite group, sometime after AD 1100, had shifted from Chaco to a new power center at Aztec. Then (in the late thirteenth century) this peripatetic aristocracy moved again. Using the same meridian, they trekked directly south for some 430 miles to Paquimé. The north-south meridian aspects of this proposed route are quite amazing. From Aztec to Chaco the offset from a true meridian line is only about two and a half miles, due perhaps to the necessity of getting down into the San Juan Valley.

From Chaco to Paquimé, a distance of ca. 375 miles, it is something on the order of three-fifths of a mile.[56]

The Casas Grandes Medio period, a time of rapid cultural expansion, represented, according to Charles C. Di Peso, the entry of an influential group from northern or western Mesoamerica. These newcomers, in Di Peso's mind, were intent on establishing a mercantile state based in part on exploitation of goods and commodities from the Pueblo world (see also chap. 8). Lekson turns this idea on its head, seeing the migration from the north rather than the south and representing the Chaco-Aztec elite. The date of this movement of populations was somewhere between AD 1250 and 1300, dovetailing nicely with the desertion of the San Juan area.[57]

Lekson is a perceptive archaeologist, and he has written an exciting book, one that opens new vistas into this portion of the Pueblo past. Still, in my view things really did not happen this way. Lekson's dating of the initial quickening at Casas Grandes seems a bit late.[58] I think the greater likelihood is that the Medio period appeared around AD 1200. More recent work by Michael Whalen and Paul Minnis at the Tinaja site, a few miles west of Paquimé, has now established a strong thirteenth-century Medio Casas Grandes presence, a series of [14]C dates extending throughout that century.[59] One point on which Di Peso and Lekson are in agreement is the rather sudden appearance of Casas Grandes. Although this quickening may have been in part the result of a large-scale migration, it was also built on the earlier, indigenous culture, as Whalen and Minnis's work makes clear. The fact is that the last phase of the Viejo period in the Casas Grandes area may have been more complex—that is, more "Casas Grandian"—than often thought. It is true that there was some sort of road or trail that ran probably from the Casas Grandes area to and through Mimbres to Chaco Canyon. This was the route for the earlier movement of macaws and other exchange items (see chapter 4). That it was functioning as late as the latter part of the thirteenth century seems to me quite another matter. Nor do I believe with Lekson that "Paquimé is profoundly Puebloan"[60] (for further discussion see chapter 8).

But regardless of where and under what conditions its human inhabitants migrated, the San Juan Basin was essentially empty of human beings by around AD 1300. It is possible that a few scattered remnant groups, ardent homebodies, returned to something like the late Archaic lifeway and remained behind to cope in the midst of a collapsing environment and an all-encompassing loneliness. It is also quite conceivable that from the Rio Grande and Western Pueblo refuges, individuals or small groups journeyed back to hunt or to visit hallowed ceremonial shrines. I must stress, though, that we have no particular evidence, either for remnant hangers-on or for opportunistic or nostalgic visitors. The area remained uninhabited for a time, but eventually there was a drift eastward of various northern Uto-Aztecan-speaking peoples, primarily the Utes.

At some undetermined date, perhaps as late as historic times, the Apacheans (ancestors of modern Navajo and Apache) began to sift into the region, this time most likely an east-to-west migration. But for a while a choice bit of southwestern property, along a major river system, was without human population.

# CHAPTER 6

# The Shaping of the Midlands

The midlands of the Greater Southwest, those areas developing out of the Mogollon and Hohokam traditions, were increasingly influenced from both north and south in the period after AD 1300 (see Figure 6.1). Even before that time a considerable amount of Anasazi contact, including actual migration, had marked and changed the aboriginal culture. Late Mogollon settlements in the high country south of the Mogollon Rim in Arizona became to one degree or another Anasazi-like, as did the Salado, farther south in the Salt-Gila drainage. The Jornada Mogollon of southern and southeastern New Mexico was also affected by the Anasazi but as time went on became more and more a part of the Casas Grandes world, an influence whose nature is still not clear. In the northern part of Aztlan the populations of the northern and central Rio Grande Valley and of the upper Pecos and the Estancia Basin formed an Anasazi subculture but with influences from the south and east. Western Pueblo, the Hopi-Zuni cluster of towns, might be called basically Anasazi but with traits not found in the old San Juan Anasazi heartland: a different kind of kiva, new and vigorous ceramic traditions both in design style (Pinedale and, later, Fourmile) and in surface treatment (glazing), and, especially at Zuni, such exotic practices as cremation burial. Cremation certainly spread from the south, as likely did glazing. The design styles seem to have had multiple origins, in part from the vicinity of the White Mountains south and west of Zuni.[1]

One midland tradition, the peripheral Patayan, was perhaps the least affected by either northern or southern influence, although even the Patayan groups had contacts with the burgeoning Aztlan populations to the north and east, most specifically with the Hopi and Zuni Pueblos. In fact, this continuing back-and-forth interaction is the main justification for my including the lowland Patayan in this book. These Indians were Yuman-speaking for the most part in the early sixteenth century and probably had been so for at least some centuries.[2] Their linguistic relatives to the north, the "Pai" peoples, did have some contact with the Pueblo groups but, as was also true of the incoming Apacheans and Ute speakers, were not part of the Aztlan culture world.

The lower Colorado region is one of low rainfall, brutally hot summers, and mild winters. The weather recording station at modern Yuma shows the July mean temperature to be 91.4°F, and the January mean is 55.4°F. The annual rainfall is under 4 inches, and any agriculture must be based on permanent streams. Fortunately, the silt-rich Colorado River provides ample water.[3] Patayan culture had more of a California "flavor" than a southwestern one, but the Patayan of the lower Colorado were very important middlemen in the trade of much-desired items, especially coral and

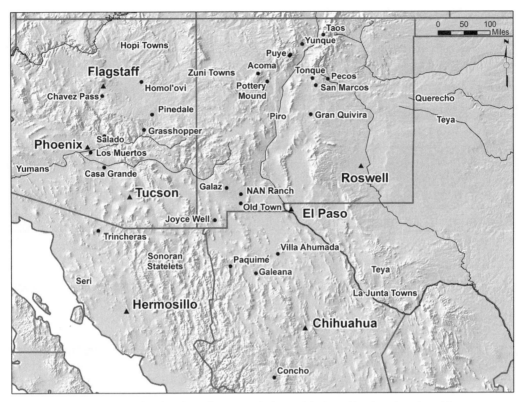

FIGURE 6.1. Native groups and archaeological sites, pre-Aztlan and Aztlan with selected modern cities. Earth Analytic, Santa Fe, NM.

*Olivella, Glycymeris,* and other types of shell from the Gulf of California. The lower Colorado people also transshipped abalone and *Olivella* shell, and probably steatite (soapstone) and other goods as well, from the California coast to the northern Southwest. What the Yumans received in return is less clear, but items may have included worked bison hides, in the form of shields, and turquoise. In the sixteenth century these groups also obtained macaw and/or parrot feathers, though the source of this sought-after commodity is not entirely clear. Such feathers could have been obtained from the Hopi, transshipped from farther east, or they could have come down the Gila River.[4] The point here is that such trade was vigorous, very important to the Pueblo Southwest, and it tied the Patayan, however loosely, to the larger Aztlan world.

The archaeology of this lower Colorado region is known at least in its general outlines. *Patayan,* or *Hakataya* as it is sometimes called, is the collective name for a number of pottery-making people who developed from some branch of western Archaic, most likely Pinto-Armargosa. Pottery making appeared around, or a bit after, AD 700; brown, red, and buff wares, largely bowls and jars, were constructed by the paddle-and-anvil method. Burials were primarily by cremation, perhaps a matter of Hohokam influence. There was a considerable interdigitation—at least by the earliest historical times—of Yuman- and Piman-speaking peoples along the lower Gila River. Agriculture likely went back a number of centuries but never replaced a vigorous gathering society, based on wild seeds, including both *Chenopodium* and *Amaranthus,* mesquite beans, screwbeans, and likely various *quelites* (wild edible greens). Though we have relatively little information on hunting, it might be pointed out that rabbits were much hunted by a variety of southwestern peoples, and the early Spaniards noted what were probably rabbit clubs. Several of the early accounts mention the widespread use of fish, which is not surprising considering that the Colorado River is the largest stream in the Southwest. At least by the time of earliest Spanish contact, the populations along the lower Colorado River had maize, squash, beans, cotton, and probably the gourd *Lagenaria*.[5]

Lower Colorado populations were of considerable size. The Spanish accounts, those of Alarcón and Díaz in 1540 and of Oñate in 1605, indicate numbers of the Yuman speakers at 30,000 or more and of the Piman-speaking Oseca at 2,000 to 3,000.[6] Still, the culture of these Colorado peoples was a rather sketchy reflection of the various vigorous southwestern societies that existed to the east and northeast. There is no credible evidence that they were much influenced by the complex social and religious organization of the Pueblos. They may have shared certain religious traits with the semiurbanized cultures of northeastern Sonora, those I have called "statelets," for example, sun worship and the sacrifice of hearts; but lower Colorado religions were apparently shaman-based, without any indication of priesthoods or of the kachina cult. In fact, what little we do know of the religion suggests roots farther west, in California. Nor did the social organization suggest any great degree of complexity, in spite of heavy overall populations. The lower Colorado Indians were primarily a ranchería people.[7]

That being said, these large Colorado River populations had the rudiments of southwestern culture (agriculture and ceramics). Would the Patayan, perhaps, eventually have become full citizens of Aztlan? I suggested in a previous publication that the Navajo were on their way to becoming the first Athabascan-speaking Pueblos when Spanish contact changed the cultural situation in drastic and far-reaching ways.[8] I think that this might eventually have been true also of the lower Colorado groups, espe-

cially since in the later Aztlan period, the cultural center of gravity was shifting somewhat to the west. Though their participation in southwestern culture was minimal, the Indians of the lower Colorado Basin certainly were involved in an obviously vigorous and profitable trade network. Pueblo peoples visited the lower Colorado, and there is reason to believe that individuals from the latter region reached at least the western portion of the Puebloan area. The extraordinary speed with which peoples of the lower Colorado and those of the Southwest proper could communicate is given in various early Spanish documents. For example, Alarcón, in the lower Colorado country in early September 1540, heard of Spaniards in Cibola (Zuni), no more than two months after the Coronado party actually arrived in the Zuni Pueblos. Two years later, at the end of September 1542, Juan Rodríguez Cabrillo, beating up the Pacific coast off what is now San Diego, heard that Spaniards had been killing Indians in the lower Colorado region. These murderous intruders were led by Coronado's captain, Melchior Díaz, who reached the Colorado very shortly after Alarcón had departed in the fall of 1540.[9]

The obvious long-standing contacts, and the premier position of the Colorado populations on shell routes leading both to the Gulf of California and to the Pacific coast, make it likely that river Yuman groups would have become increasingly interested in the traditions of Aztlan, not only in material culture but, eventually, in the rich socioreligious life of that great region.

The southeasternmost region, like the lower Colorado to the west, was always somewhat peripheral to the Greater Southwest. It contained a rather aberrant Jornada Mogollon settlement at the oasis region of La Junta, where the Rio Grande is joined by its major tributary, the Rio Conchos, flowing north and eastward from the Sierra Madre Occidental of northern Mexico. Even in the Aztlan period, when there seems to have been some integration into a Casas Grandes Interaction Sphere, it remained largely outside the major southwestern culture.

Curiously, the La Junta is somewhat similar climatically to the lower Colorado region, although La Junta at the actual junction of the rivers is at about 3,300 feet altitude instead of the near sea level of the Colorado delta and lower valley. It is a region of low rainfall (a little more than eight inches annually) and of hot, dry summers and relatively mild winters, with the mean temperature for June, marginally the hottest month, about 87°F and for January 50°F.[10]

The region of the lower Rio Conchos had for some millennia been a shatter zone among a series of Archaic traditions, north and south. Into these primitive conditions and scanty populations came influences, or perhaps peoples, from the Jornada Mogollon in the more upriver area of the Rio Grande. J. Charles Kelley (Figure 6.2), who did significant early archaeological work in the region, believed that this development was due to an actual migration of Jornada populations southward, where they probably mixed with the local population. Archaeologist Robert Mallouf, however, believes that Jornada Mogollon agricultural, ceramic, and architectural traits were adopted by La Junta hunting and foraging people in somewhat the same way that people of the Antelope Creek culture, near the Canadian River, just north of the Llano Estacado, adopted Puebloan traits.

By whatever mechanism, these Jornada influences had reached the region of El Cajon, 140 miles downriver from El Paso, by around AD 1100 and had spread to the broad river valleys around La Junta sometime after AD 1200. Here a specialized variant, which Kelley called the La Junta phase of the Bravo Valley aspect developed, spilling over from the Rio Grande Valley proper into the lower valley of the Conchos River and the lower part of Alamito Creek. The latter small stream drains into the Rio Grande from the north, several miles below the Rio Grande–Conchos junction. The connection of La Junta with the more upriver towns was weakened sometime after AD 1400, when the Jornada Mogollon collapsed and several hundred miles of Rio Grande between

FIGURE 6.2. J. Charles Kelley, Pecos Conference, Chaco Canyon, August 1997. Photo by Victoria R. Evans.

the El Paso area and La Junta became the home of Indians known historically as Suma and Manso. These were at least in part the descendants of the Jornada peoples but were now only marginally agricultural, without the advanced ceramic techniques that marked Jornada. Nevertheless, contact up and down the river was maintained, and the route from La Junta, up the Rio Grande to El Paso and environs, then northward to the Pueblo country, was used by Spanish parties for several decades.[11]

La Junta phase sites consisted of three types of houses. One type comprised contiguous rectangular adobe aboveground rooms. A second type, also rectangular, had structures set in pits but did not utilize the pit walls as structural features. The walls were jacal, made by insetting rows of poles. A third type, a variant on the second, was the circular or oval semi-subterranean room, again with jacal walls. The first and second types of dwelling had prepared adobe floors, sometimes with raised fire-hearths. A curious feature involved smoothed-off blocks of adobe along the south side, which J. Charles Kelley, the excavator, called "altars" (see Figure 6.3). Quite conceivably they did have a

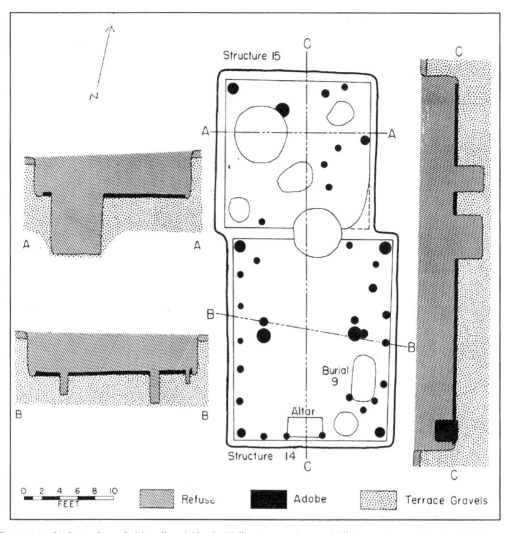

FIGURE 6.3. La Junta, Jornada Mogollon. J Charles Kelley's excavations at Millington Site, near Presidio, TX. La Junta phase. Structures 14 and 15. Note "altar" near south wall of Structure 14. Pre-AD 1400. Drawing courtesy of Ellen Abbot Kelley.

religious function. The third, circular, type of building showed neither floor features nor "altars" and perhaps represented storage pits.[12]

The ceramics of the La Junta phase were, as might be expected, primarily related to the Jornada Mogollon. Ceramics include El Paso Polychrome and Chihuahuan wares such as Villa Ahumada Polychrome and Ramos Polychrome, as well as the ubiquitous Chupadero Black-on-white.[13]

Originally Kelley saw a late prehistoric transitional period, dating to around AD 1400, which he called the Concepción phase. Kelley believed that at the end of the La Junta phase (correlating to the collapse of Casas Grandes sometime after AD 1400), the La Junta area became at best semisedentary. More recently, as a result of new work, R. J. Mallouf takes a somewhat different approach to this situation. He believes that an important factor was the Cielo Complex, representing groups of hunters and gatherers who were found in the La Junta area extending downriver to the Big Bend region. This complex generally dates from around AD 1250 until the late seventeenth century.

Eventually, sometime after AD 1500, a new

synthesis of ideas and perhaps peoples from the south and incoming nomads from the north restored the agricultural and ceramic bases at La Junta. This re-dated Concepción phase had somewhat simpler house types, without the prepared floors, fire pits, and "altars" of earlier times. House layout, however, was much the same. The use of ceramics may in fact have died out for a time, though by the earliest Spanish contact the villagers at La Junta were producing simple bichrome pottery (Paloma Red-on-gray and Capote Red-on-brown), as well as plainwares and the Chinati series, somewhat reminiscent of the Alma wares of classic Mogollon. Interestingly, the lithic toolkit in Concepción times, as in the ancestral Cielo Complex, was very similar to that of La Junta phase, perhaps indicating a continuity of populations from La Junta phase times. At the time of first Spanish intrusions into the La Junta area there were two groups, named by the Spaniards Patarabueye and Jumano. These Indians were represented archaeologically by the historic Conchos phase and were sporadically documented by the Spaniards from the 1530s. We have reasonably good historical data on them, beginning around AD 1581.[14]

The Patarabueye may have been a mixed population, some elements going back to La Junta phase times and others representing newcomers moving up the Conchos River. The Jumano were seasonal bison hunters who wintered in the warm river valleys of the Rio Grande and the Conchos. These two groups lived in an ecological balance, one that probably involved trade and also very likely some sort of kin relationship. The Jumano, originally contacted at La Junta by Cabeza de Vaca in 1535, are a particularly interesting group. Cabeza de Vaca failed to give a tribal name, but Vázquez de Coronado, in late spring of 1541, met what was clearly the same group under the term *Teya*, a name of Indian origin. Coronado contacted these Indians several hundred miles to the north in the Blanco Canyon area, near modern Lubbock, Texas. From the latter part of the sixteenth century on they were known as *Jumano*, like *Teya* a term of unknown

but presumably Indian origin. It appears in various spellings in Spanish documents of the time (Jumano, Xumana, Jumana, Humana, Umana, Xoman, among others). A number of suggestions as to the linguistic affiliations of the Teya/Jumano have been made, the situation being confused by the fact that in the late seventeenth century people calling themselves Jumano were Apachean speaking. But this was clearly due to the fact that the Apaches during the course of the seventeenth century were in the process of absorbing a number of other, linguistically different, peoples.

It seems likely that as of initial Spanish contact times, Patarabueye and Jumano spoke similar languages. I think these tongues were related to the Tanoan language, Piro/Tompiro, spoken in historic times by the southern- and easternmost extensions of Pueblo peoples into New Mexico. It should be pointed out that the Jumano had a very close relationship with the Tompiro in the Estancia Valley during early historic times—in fact one of the pueblos in that area was called "Town of the Humanas." It is plausible that other early historic people, the Suma and the Manso upriver on the Rio Grande from the Patarabueyes, also spoke dialects of the same language.[15]

The La Junta people were to one degree or another outliers of the great Mogollon tradition, but the exact nature of this tradition is still not entirely clear. It was named as a result of work by American archaeologists trained in the Anasazi and/or the Hohokam areas and first identified in the upcountry of west-central New Mexico and east-central Arizona, as described in chapter 4. As I pointed out in that chapter, a whole series of archaeological traditions, stretching throughout southern New Mexico, western Texas, southeastern Arizona, and portions of the Mexican states of Sonora, Chihuahua, Durango, and Sinaloa, seemed to have affinities with Mogollon. These included antecedent cultures to such highly developed manifestations as the El Paso phase of Jornada Mogollon, the statelets of northeastern Sonora, Casas Grandes, and perhaps at least a component of the far-flung Chalchihuites culture of

Durango and Zacatecas. The relationships are generally rather generic, pithouse-dwelling simple agriculturists who made a series of simple brown or red ceramic wares. In previous publications I called this macrotradition "Mogollon-like" and suggested that it might extend to the Loma San Gabriel of Durango and Zacatecas and the Tacuichamona culture of Sinaloa.[16]

For one thing, the pottery is often quite similar:

For northern Sonora, Pailes . . . has pointed out the similarity of the Río Sonora material culture to that of the Mogollon phases— Georgetown, San Francisco and Three Circle [what are now generally called the Early Pithouse and Late Pithouse periods]. In particular, the Río Sonora plain and incised or punched brown wares look very much like the Mogollon Alma pottery. At Casas Grandes, Di Peso's Convento phase—and to some degree the Pilón phase of the Viejo period contained pottery very similar to Alma and Reserve ceramics. Lister's sites in the region of the Bavispe and the Río Piedras Verdes actually contained a variety of Alma, Reserve, and Three Circles wares from the Mogollon inventory.[17]

The Jornada Mogollon in its earlier phases contained basically heartland Mogollon pottery and their local copies (for example El Paso Brown [Figure 6.4], a dominant early Jornada pottery, was an outgrowth of Alma Plain). One other subarea of the Mogollon, that of Mimbres, shared a considerable amount of ceramic ware, both in borrowing and copying, something not surprising considering the near proximity of the two traditions (see also note 18). As discussed in chapter 4, the populations seem to have been rather small pithouse-dwelling groups, perhaps seminomadic.

Around AD 1200 a new and somewhat different manifestation of the Jornada Mogollon appeared. Called the El Paso phase in the riverine areas of the Rio Grande and in the Tularosa Basin to the east and north, this seemed to represent a quickening of culture in the region.

Fairly substantial villages of aboveground coursed adobe houses were either grouped around plazas or arranged in east-west oriented tiers. The dominant pottery type was now El Paso Polychrome, with considerable evidence of trade and contact in all directions. The room "altars" described for La Junta by J. Charles Kelley are also found in El Paso phase sites. Their point of origin, whether the El Paso region, around La Junta, or elsewhere, is unclear. There was a considerable amount of intrusive pottery: Ramos Polychrome, from the Casas Grandes region; Gila Polychrome, whose heartland is the Gila-Salt drainage of Arizona; Heshotauthla Glaze-polychrome and St. Johns Polychrome, from the Zuni area. An occasional sherd of Galisteo Black-on-white suggests contact far up the Rio Grande.[18]

Other important ceramics are the widespread Chupadero Black-on-white, Lincoln Black-on-red, and Three Rivers Red-on-terracotta. The extent to which these ceramic types might be considered "intrusive" is not clear since their points of origin are not securely known. Chupadero is usually thought of as originating in the Chupadera Plateau, south of the Estancia Valley, and Lincoln and Three Rivers seem to center in the vicinity of the Tularosa Basin.[19]

Other evidence of trade include copper bells, palettes, and animal effigies. Scarlet macaw feathers were found in the grotto at the back of Feather Cave near Capitan, in the northern Jornada Mogollon region. More homey objects included sandals and basketry (Figure 6.5). Ceramic deposits in the cave have a range of dates, but some Three Rivers Red-on-terra-cotta and Chupadero Black-on-white probably represent the Jornada San Andres phase (the northern variant of the El Paso phase). In fact, Feather Cave may have been at least intermittently used for a long period. The grotto itself perhaps represented a *sipapu*, the symbolic entrance to the underworld found in kivas in the Pueblo world. In fact the grotto deposits had a definite Puebloan look and probably represented Anasazi influence in this frontier area.[20] According to Florence Hawley Ellis, who di-

FIGURE 6.4. El Paso Brown pottery. El Paso Museum of Archaeology.

rected the recovery of artifacts, "There seems little question but that Arrow Grotto was a combination Shipap [Sipapu] and Sun Father cave used by people whose solar ceremony customs were not far different from those of living Pueblos."[21]

Another cache gives an indication of the wealth of the region. The Hueco Basin cache on the old Tobin Ranch, a few miles northeast of El Paso, contains about a hundred pieces of turquoise, 21 of them pendants, and several thousand pieces of shell, including *Olivella* and *Glycymeris*. Pottery included El Paso Polychrome, Tucson Polychrome, and Chupadero Black-on-white, as well as Ramos and Villa Ahumada polychromes from Chihuahua.[22] Compare this cache with the one in the Sacramento Mountains of southeastern New Mexico. This rich cache, called Bald Eagle, nesting high in the mountains, was discovered in 1976. It contained a great variety of artifacts, including beads of varying kinds, turquoise, marine

shell, calcite, and slate. There were pendants of turquoise and shell, both marine and freshwater, *Glycymeris* shell bracelets (see Figure 6.6), and other objects, including quartz crystals. Two pottery vessels were tentatively identified as variants of a Jornada brown ware. Dating is somewhat uncertain, but it has been suggested that the cache belonged to the Mesilla phase of Jornada Mogollon (ca. 900–1100).[23] I suspect, however, that it, like the Tobin Ranch cache, is datable to the later El Paso phase.

This El Paso phase of the Jornada Mogollon extended southeastward as far as La Junta, northeastward to near Roswell, northwestward to around Alamosa Creek between the modern towns of Truth or Consequences and Socorro, and southward into what is now Chihuahua. In that area it merged with more specifically Casas Grandes–type of material. Sites in this shatter zone have not been extensively explored, but the large mound at Villa Ahumada near the Río Carmén, near the

75

FIGURE 6.5. Sandals from Feather Cave, Jornada Mogollon. Maxwell Museum of Archaeology, University of New Mexico, uncat.

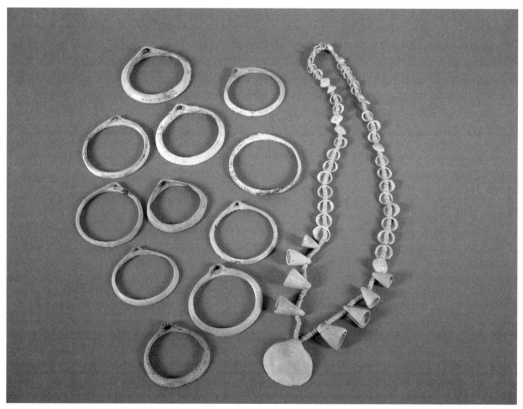

FIGURE 6.6. Native southwestern *Glycymeris* bracelets and shell necklace, provenience uncertain. Maxwell Museum of Anthropology, University of New Mexico, cat. nos. 40.4.62, 40.64.64–73, 64.21.4.

modern Mexican town of Villa Ahumada, has been partly excavated. Villa Ahumada people were involved in both the El Paso phase and Medio period Casas Grandes ceramic traditions.[24] However, not only Villa Ahumada but all of the late period Jornada Mogollon seem to have somehow entered the orbit of what C. F. Schaafsma and I have called the "Casas Grandes Interaction Sphere," which I will discuss in a later chapter.

In the old Mimbres region the flamboyant Classic period had died out by around AD 1130 to 1140 for reasons unclear, though a sustained time of drought may have been a factor. The Classic period was replaced at some point by a partially new culture, which has been called the Black Mountain phase. The two phases differ in certain important respects. In Classic times there were aboveground masonry pueblos and rectangular semisubterranean kivas, the Mimbres people having changed from pithouse dwellings to surface structures sometime around AD 1000. Rooms in the Mimbres villages had rectangular or square slab-lined hearths. As we saw earlier, it is around that time that Mimbres potters began to manipulate the slip and modify the firing of the pottery to produce red-on-white and then black-on-white wares.

The Black Mountain phase of Mimbres, whose initial dates (though post–AD 1150) are still contested, saw the development of contiguous houses of coursed adobe, the rooms containing round hearths. There were no kivas (at least no rooms immediately recognizable as such). Many of the ceramics were from other areas and included El Paso bichrome and polychrome wares, Chupadero Black-on-white, Playas redwares, and White Mountain redwares, including St. Johns Polychrome. Architecturally, the Black Mountain towns have a definite relationship to those of Casas Grandes.

Archaeologist Darrell Creel, who excavated the Mimbres Old Town site near modern Deming, believes that at least in the lower, southern, Mimbres sites, the beginnings of Black Mountain phase activities were already being foreshadowed in the very last part of Classic period

Mimbres. Although the elegant black-on-white ceramics of Mimbres Classic times died out, there was a continuation of certain kinds of pottery. For example, various corrugated wares and certain wares of the Playas tradition, probably locally made, seem to link the two periods. In addition, some ceramics that normally are considered a marker of Black Mountain are found in Classic contexts. These include El Paso Polychrome (Figure 6.7), Chupadero Black-on-white, and St. Johns Polychrome. As I pointed out earlier, there was also a continuity in rock art between the two areas. Creel believes that substantial populations survived the Classic demise, at least in the south, to form the beginning of the Black Mountain phase. The phase ended sometime around AD 1300. At about that time, Creel suggests (following Steven LeBlanc), cotton, already grown in Classic times, was possibly becoming an important Black Mountain phase commodity. It may have been traded to the developing Casas Grandes group. This might explain the curious shift from the higher country of the upper and middle Mimbres Valley to the lower drainage of that ephemeral river during what likely was a drought period.

FIGURE 6.7. El Paso Polychrome, ca. AD 1200–1400. El Paso Museum of Archaeology.

There were other "holdover" traditions. Creel thinks that a type of arrow point, one that added a basal notching to an originally side-notched point, spans the two periods. Though not at all typical of Classic Mimbres, coursed adobe does appear, in fact as early as around AD 900. Inhumation burials into floor subsurfaces, the face of the deceased being covered with killed (ritually punctured) vessels, appear in both periods. The percentage of cremations may possibly have increased somewhat in the Black Mountain phase although Creel cautions that the inhumation-cremation ratio in Classic Mimbres times may need re-evaluation.[25]

Recent work among the eastern extension of the Mimbres, especially along Palomas Creek, which drains into the Rio Grande south of modern Truth or Consequences, suggests that in that area the post–AD 1150 occupation showed a continuity with earlier times.[26]

Harry Shafer, however, believes that there was an out-migration of the late Classic Mimbres by around AD 1140, and after a hiatus of 50 to 75 years a new population, called Black Mountain by archaeologists, moved into the lower and middle sections of the Mimbres Valley, perhaps sometime around or after AD 1200. The subsequent occupation of the area is not well known. According to Shafer:

The Black Mountain phase was apparently short-lived: the people took advantage of a short wet-cycle and maintained distant relationships with Casas Grandes but soon moved out again, probably back to the desert. Sometime later they returned once again for a brief time in the 1300s as Cliff phase groups with strong Salado ceremonial connections only to abandon the valley forever after about two generations. It is important to note that neither of the Postclassic occupations created their own brand of decorated pottery to reinforce new ancestral ties to the land. It seems that their affiliation was with distant power centers—Casas Grandes, Cibola, Salado—where such ties became established.[27]

Whatever the situation in Mimbres, the Black Mountain phase has a number of obvious relationships with the El Paso phase of the Jornada Mogollon—in house type, town layout, and ceramics.[28] The relationship between these two areas and Casas Grandes will be discussed later.

Farther west, the flow of influences was more north to south. As I said at the beginning of this chapter, Anasazi influences in the old Mogollon heartland began well before the migration period. Collapse of the San Juan area produced an acceleration, perhaps an inevitable one. There were actual Anasazi site intrusions, presumably from the Kayenta-Tusayan region, to villages near the important settlement of Grasshopper in the Salt River drainage and at several sites in the San Pedro Valley farther south. Anasazi influences included masonry pueblos, black-on-white pottery, kivas of the western square or rectangular variety, and perhaps the kachina ceremonials, which are normally associated with rectangular kivas. New techniques of dryland farming had begun by the early twelfth century.[29]

Nor was the flood of influences only one way. As mentioned above, certain distinctive culture complexes flowed northward. Especially noticeable was the institution of cremation, which eventually reached the Zuni region and from there moved sporadically eastward. Cremation, presumably originating among the Hohokam, where it has a considerable antiquity, gradually spread through much of the midlands. Interestingly enough, it is not found at Casas Grandes.[30] In the statelet area of northeastern Sonora only a handful of burials have been found. They include three cremations and a bundle burial at the large site of San José and an extended inhumation at a site near Banamichi. Another inhumation was discovered by a local citizen near Huepac, but it has not been well described. The excavator at San José, Richard A. Pailes, believes that burials in the Sonora River area are deeply covered with alluvium.[31]

There are also cremation burials in the Trincheras region of northern central Sonora and southern Arizona, perhaps an indication of influence from the nearby Hohokam. The Trincheras polity, which had its major expression in the Altar Valley of Sonora, is known for spectacularly terraced hillsides. These hillsides represented habitation sites built perhaps with an eye to defense. The historical distribution of peoples in that region suggest that Trincheras populations were O'odham speaking and ancestral to the Lower Pima missionized by the Jesuits in the early seventeenth century. Trincheras as an entity may have lasted into the mid-fifteenth century. In the early sixteenth century Marcos de Niza visited a town that I believe to be a Piman village on or near the Altar River, a strong suggestion of continuity from Trincheras into historic times.[32]

I briefly discussed the important Sedentary period of Hohokam in chapter 4. Major traits of the Sedentary (and earlier periods) include towns of scattered pithouses; irrigation agriculture based on maize, beans, squash, and cotton; ball courts; platform mounds; red-on-buff pottery; clay figurines; extensive use of shell for ornamentation; and stone or clay palettes, likely used for holding or mixing paints.

Following the Sedentary period in the Hohokam region (that is to say after about AD 1200), a number of cultural changes marked the Hohokam landscape. Living structures, especially in the larger sites, were now ground-level, square or rectangular, often contiguous rooms of crude coursed adobe, surrounded by adobe open-air compound walls. These were sometimes associated with ball courts, at least in the earlier portion of this Classic phase, and with platform mounds. There were also jacal structures and caliche or adobe-walled houses with post reinforcements. There was a drop-off of decorated pottery, one, however, being a derivative of Sacaton Red-on-buff, now called Casa Grande Red-on-buff, a ware that, according to Emil Haury, eventually was to develop into the historic Pima Red-on-buff. In the latter part of the Classic, locally made Salado wares become important. Figurines were now less common, perhaps disappearing for a time, and use of palettes, for whatever purpose,

comes to an end. There was a scattered use of pottery *comales,* flat dishes used in making tortillas, perhaps for some sort of specialist or ritual food. The Classic, whatever it represented demographically (and both population increase and decrease have been argued), did see a reduction of the overall Hohokam area with sites in the lower Verde Valley, the San Pedro, and the Gila Bend region fading out. Population concentration was now largely in the Gila-Salt Basin.[33]

A rather scantily known Postclassic Polvoron phase was identified a few decades ago. There was a resurgence of pithouses during the Polvoron phase, and platform mounds and ball courts cease to be made. In terms of ceramics there were red and red-on-brown wares, resembling the rather atypical pottery of the Tucson Basin. A small amount of Salado polychromes and occasional figurines found in the Polvoron may have been heirlooms. It was an impoverished period in some ways but not necessarily demographically.[34] I have argued that quite large populations were found in southern Arizona by the early Spanish explorers, and I think it likely that these early contact period peoples were descendants of late period Hohokam.[35]

Perhaps the defining event of the latter part of the Hohokam (and, to some degree, the Mogollon) was the appearance of the rather enigmatic Salado. What Salado actually represented is still not clear. The name *Salado* was first used in a 1930 publication by Winifred and Harold Gladwin. The Gladwins believed that Salado peoples had originally migrated from the Little Colorado area around AD 1100, with an additional wave of population in-migrating from the Anasazi Kayenta region ca. AD 1300. Other versions of the migration idea have appeared over the years, generally seeing the Salado arriving from the north and representing some Anasazi or Anasazi-influenced group. One radical departure was that of Charles Di Peso, who believed that Salado had southern (Casas Grandes) origins. However, Di Peso's arguments depended on his early dating of Casas Grandes, which seemed to show that the

FIGURE 6.8. Salado polychromes: Gila Polychrome bowl and jar, Tonto Polychrome sherd. Maxwell Museum of Anthropology, University of New Mexico, cat. nos. 65.24.119 and 72.43.111. Sherd is from museum type collections.

main marker ceramics of Salado, the Salado polychromes (Figure 6.8), were earlier at the site of Paquimé than in the Salt River valley. With the redating of Casas Grandes this argument no longer holds water.[36]

In more recent years archaeologists have been more equivocal, though it is hard to deny that there occurred at least some spread of peoples from the north, providing a leavening to the resident populations. An attractive current reconstruction is that of Patricia Crown, who believes that a widespread design style on pottery, the Pinedale style (ca. AD 1275–1400) is the key to understanding Salado. This style, spreading from the region of the Mogollon Rim, reached many parts of the Southwest. See Figure 6.9 for distribution of the Pinedale wares themselves. The Pinedale *style,* of course, has an even wider distribution. In the Salado area it appears on Salado ceramics, particularly the late, Gila phase, of Salado. In Crown's view the heart of Salado represented a religious cult, which she called the Southwestern cult:

Evidence that the Pinedale Style is related to the adoption of a cult rests primarily in the redundant and ubiquitous icons that

appear on the earliest Pinedale Style pottery and increase in frequency throughout the production of the Salado polychromes....

[The] iconic system includes images of parrots, snakes, horned serpents, eyes, the sun, stars, masked and unmasked anthropomorphs, cloud terraces, and butterflies, as well as human and bird effigies. Co-occurrence of these icons on the pottery and contemporaneously in other media demonstrates their systemic nature. In contemporaneous mesoamerican religion and in historic Puebloan religion, this suite of icons relates to beliefs concerning water control and fertility. The unprecedented spread of the Pinedale Style thus pertains to the adoption of a religious ideology that incorporates this suite of icons.[37]

The cult began around the end of the thirteenth century as part of the general restlessness of that period. It very likely followed well-worn trade routes and may have utilized preexisting trading protocols. Certain of the cult imagery appeared earlier, perhaps as early as AD 1100, in pockets of population such as Mimbres. The imagery was concerned with

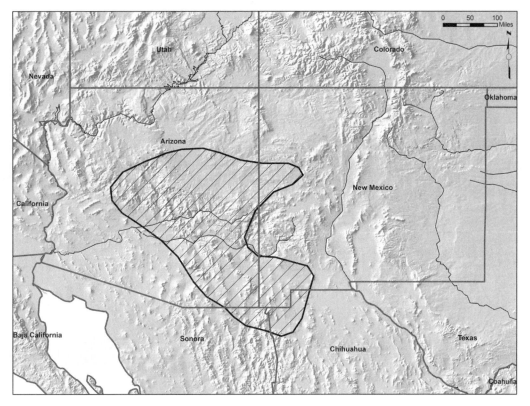

FIGURE 6.9. Distribution of Pinedale Polychrome and Pinedale Black-on-red. Earth Analytic, Santa Fe, NM.

weather control and fertility, Venus, moon and sun rituals, and the twin concept, and it may have involved the kachina cult. Crown notes the icons similar to the southwestern cult in the earlier Classic Mimbres ceramics. She points out, however, that the elaborate Mimbres ceramics are generally found in funerary contexts and probably represented a fixed burial ritual in which "killed" (ritually punctured) pots are placed on the head or body of flexed burials, normally buried under the house floor. The Pinedale style, as a marker for the southwestern cult, appeared in various places, including the Salado area. Crown suggests that whereas the Mimbres pottery was used in some sort of ancestral cult, that of the Salado was more likely part of some fertility rite. For the possible relationships of the southwestern cult to the kachina cult see chapter 7. VanPool et al. have recently pointed out that Salado and Casas Grandes seem to represent competing religious systems, with similar imagery, especially

the horned serpent, but expressed very differently. For example, the horned serpents in Salado art have backward-pointing horns and usually occur in pairs, whereas the serpent in Casas Grandes normally has either a single forward-pointing horn or two horns, one pointing forward, the other backward.[38]

In some ways the most dramatic pottery distribution was that of the White Mountain redwares, which extended from the Mesa Verde area to Chihuahua and from Central Arizona to the Pecos River. I stress this wide distribution, first of the St. Johns wares and then of the Pinedale style, because it seems to me that here we have a distinct foreshadowing of the Aztlan period in the Southwest. A few of the St. Johns Polychrome sherds from the late thirteenth century are painted in such a way that they seem to presage the glazed pottery of Aztlan times. Most St. Johns ceramics (Figure 6.10) come from the Western Pueblo area, but occasionally examples are found that seem to

FIGURE 6.10. St. Johns Black-on-red. Maxwell Museum of Anthropology, University of New Mexico, cat. no. 40.4.295.

be made locally in the Rio Grande Valley.[39] Later on, in full Aztlan times, Salado pottery, especially the Salado polychromes, extended throughout much of the Greater Southwest.

The Chaco culture had already helped to provide links between the Anasazi and lands and peoples to the south. Regionalism was still strong, especially in the northern tier of the Southwest, but cosmopolitanism was emerging in certain areas: Chaco, the Sinagua, perhaps Mimbres. Beginning sometime after AD 1100 and continuing for the better part of two centuries, these societies broke down. As we saw earlier, the thirteenth century was one of great environmental turmoil throughout much of the Southwest. At the end of it much of the Anasazi land had been deserted, and new populations were flowing into the midlands, including Salado. Farther south new polities were forming, such as Paquimé and the Sonoran statelets. Yet during this period of social turmoil the Southwest seems to have been linked as never before. The very wide net thrown by the St. Johns redwares and the growing importance and widening distribution of the Pinedale style suggested a new kind of "internationalism," with contacts of one kind or another (trade, migration, cultic movements, probably others) becoming widespread. Within the region about to become

FIGURE 6.11. Tlaloc figure, probably early representation of kachina cult. Alamo Mt, NM. Photo courtesy of Polly Schaafsma.

Aztlan, only the far west, the admittedly marginal Patayan seemed relatively unaffected.

The twelfth century and especially the thirteenth century set the stage for Aztlan in the fourteenth. The various movements and widespread connections during these earlier centuries surely made it easier for new religious, political, and social ideas, new art forms, and even new technologies to spread northward from the Mesoamerican heartland. But aside from that generality we are still unclear as to the why and how of the matter. For example, when in fact did the kachina cult spread northward? This cult has as its center masked dancers representing ancestral figures who serve as agents of both weather manipulation and social control. I think that the balance of the evidence suggests that the full panoply of the cult, with all its implications for interaction and integration over large areas, came early in the fourteenth century (Figure 6.11). But as we have seen, some archaeologists believe that "proto-kachina" elements of the cult existed as early as the thirteenth century, in the San Juan region.

In any case Jornada Mogollon rock art seems to represent kachinas ancestral to the Pueblo area itself. These are found in the Three Rivers area, at Hueco Tanks, and there may have been a kachina component in the grotto behind Feather Cave. Certainly by the end of the thirteenth century organizations such as Crown's southwestern cult could have had kachina affiliations. As a number of specialists have pointed out, there have been palpable changes in the kachina cult during the course of historic times, and surely this was true among protohistoric southwestern cultures. Such cultures were dynamic systems, and nowhere was that dynamism demonstrated more clearly than when the Southwest was first becoming Aztlan.

CHAPTER 7

# Building Aztlan in the North

By AD 1300 the transformation of the Anasazi Pueblo world was essentially complete. The great expanse of the San Juan drainage was now deserted except perhaps for occasional visits by small parties. Indeed, throughout the San Juan and Little Colorado drainages, only certain areas of the Little Colorado and its tributaries had Puebloan settlements. In the Little Colorado, existing residents seem to have been joined by Kayenta peoples to the north and certain of the more easterly San Juan groups.[1] For example, the Zuni area in the eleventh and twelfth centuries had a certain Chaco flavor, and it seems reasonable that some of the Chacoan populations from north-central New Mexico continued to drift into the area.[2] In the east only the upriver country of the Pecos River remained in the old Anasazi domain. There were, to be sure, Anasazi outriders in the Mogollon and Salado worlds, but these, too, would collapse within a century or so. Only along the Rio Abajo country of the Rio Grande, in the mid-Pecos drainage, and in salines and scattered basins east of the Rio Grande, could the Anasazi be said to expand, that by a merging and swamping-out process with Mogollon neighbors. And even these settlements, except for the Piro and Tompiro groups, would disappear within a few decades.

By the early years of the fourteenth century the Rio Grande Pueblo area was taking shape and in terms of linguistic distribution would look much as it did in historic times. The Rio Grande portion of the Pueblo world is normally divided into three geographic segments. The region of the Rio Grande Gorge and the valley created by the juncture of the Rio Grande and the Rio Chama, its great tributary flowing around the northern side of the Jemez and San Pedro Mountains, is called Rio Arriba, the "upper river." East of the river several streams drain in from the Sangre de Cristo range. They contained a considerable Pueblo population in aboriginal times, and several pueblos remain today. Much of the area west of the Rio Grande, the Pajarito Plateau, is covered with compacted ash, the result of a monstrous volcanic explosion that created the caldera of the Valle Grande. This volcanic activity took place perhaps a million years ago, long before any human population in the Americas, but the series of deep, rugged canyons cut into those volcanic deposits were to be favored living places for later Pueblo Indians (see Figure 7.1).

Farther south, along the eastern escarpment of the Pajarito Plateau, the juncture with the Jemez River, and the broad valley that extends to the Rio Puerco, lies the "middle river" sometimes included in Rio Arriba but occasionally called the Rio Medio or Río en Medio (these are also terms for two small streams in the northern Rio Grande Basin). At present this

FIGURE 7.1. Tyuonyi Pueblo, Frijoles Canyon. Shelters of compacted volcanic materials from the Valle Grande are visible in the background. Museum of New Mexico, neg. no. 28693.

part of the river contains a sizable segment of the population of modern New Mexico, a region including the modern cities of Berna-lillo, Rio Rancho, Albuquerque, Los Lunas, and Belen. It extends roughly to the lower Puerco Valley and is bordered on the east by the Sandia and Manzano mountains. To the southwest is the Rio Abajo, or "lower river," section, extending from the Puerco to Milligan Gulch and the area of the San Cristobal Moun tains. This was the region of the Piro Pueblos during the Aztlan period. Still farther south and east were Jornada Mogollon and, after the Jornada collapse, settlements of the historic Manso Indians.

There are only a few more or less perma-nent rivers draining into the upper Rio Grande from the east, although certain intermittent streams like the Galisteo River were important roadways east and west (see Figure 3.4 for the drainage patterns in the Rio Grande region). There are breaks in the mountains in the Taos

and Picuris areas, but the major east-west route both in aboriginal and historic times was north of the Galisteo Valley, where an escarp-ment opened eastward through Glorieta Pass into the upper Pecos River. The upper Pecos Valley was inhabited by Towa-speaking peo-ples in Aztlan times. An earlier, more exten-sive, occupation that included portions of the Tecolote and Gallinas valleys had ended by around AD 1300.

Another route eastward out of the Rio Grande Valley, though not much used today, was between the Ortiz and Sandia mountains and still another—this one carrying a major modern highway—threaded its way through narrow Tijeras Canyon, near present-day Albu-querque. Farther south another aboriginal trail followed Abo Arroyo, cutting between the Manzano and Los Piños mountains to the great salt flats of the Estancia Basin, a route now followed by U.S. Highway 60. This route was important in the Aztlan period, for it connected the Rio Grande Piro peoples with their linguistic brethren, the Tompiro, of the Estancia Valley and the Mesa de los Jumanos.

In Pueblo times the Puerco, with its associated tributary the San José, provided an opening between the Rio Grande Valley and the San Juan River to the north and the Little Colorado to the west. As we have seen, the San Juan drainage does not seem to have been used after about AD 1300. However, the Western Pueblo region was of immense importance to peoples of the Rio Grande, providing as it did trade goods, ceramic innovations, and perhaps sociopolitical and religious ideas. The Western Pueblo towns gradually assumed their historic configuration during Aztlan times. When the various Coronado parties arrived in 1539–1540, main settlements were on the Hopi Mesas, along the Zuni River and at Acoma, essentially occupying the same area they had for the previous century or so.

During Aztlan times the Rio Grande apparently had somewhat colder winters than it does today, presumably affected by the Little Ice Age. Moreover, climatic data suggest that the period 1350–1550 was generally somewhat dry, perhaps accounting for the clustering of Puebloan settlements along the major rivers. Exceptions to this distribution are the Hopi and Tompiro areas, where specialized agricultural and water conservation techniques were practiced.[3]

During the final decades of occupation of the San Juan, a new fashion in village construction appeared in the Southwest. It spread over much of the upper Southwest within a relatively short time, the mid-1200s to around AD 1325. In the old Anasazi region the new settlements were somewhat reminiscent of the earlier Chacoan towns, though with defensive elements emphasized. The new fashion stressed fortified villages, many of them with houses whose blank outer walls closely surrounded enclosed plazas. Various of these were on mesa tops or ridges, thus adding to the defensibility of the sites. The Spaniards, in the sixteenth century, had considerable trouble with these closely defended towns, at Hawikuh, Arenal

(Puaray), Moho, and Pecos, among others. They usually prevailed, however, when willing to invest sufficient resources and time, even at the seemingly impregnable mesa-top site of Acoma (see Figure 7.2). The new defensive structures most likely indicated inter-Pueblo hostility—a tendency to warfare that raged for the next three centuries, finally being quenched by Spanish intervention and settlement.[4]

This shift to warfare and warlike conditions marked the coming of the Aztlan period in the Southwest. At this remove it is impossible to say that war conditions were a part of the initial Mesoamericanization of the Southwest. It is true that chronic and sustained hostilities were attributes of many Mesoamerican cultures. These are documented in the Spanish contact period, perhaps the best example being the Aztecs, to whom warfare was a way of life. When no real war was in the offing, Aztec warriors fought the ritually arranged "flower wars," thus supplying human beings for sacrifice to the various deities. But the Aztecs were only one example. Just about every group that the Spaniards found on the great central plateau of Mexico was more or less warlike.[5] The situation along the west coast is less clear. Spanish disease, spreading before the actual conquest, plus the pathological brutality of the primary conqueror, Nuño de Guzmán, created such devastation along the coast that the original lifeways of the west coast peoples are difficult to reconstruct. Nevertheless, what we do know suggests rather warlike societies, though probably not ones whose deities demanded mass human sacrifice. Certainly, mountain groups such as the Acaxee and Xixime, still relatively intact when the Spanish explorer Francisco Ibarra crossed the Sierra Madre Occidental in the early 1560s, were belligerent enough.[6]

Earlier societies, known archaeologically both in central Mesoamerica and along the north Mexican frontier, the area nearest the Greater Southwest, seemed to have been actively involved in some sort of real or ritualized warfare, as evidenced by fortifications in great sites like La Quemada and by the mass

FIGURE 7.2. Acoma Pueblo, on its easily defended mesa. Maxwell Museum of Anthropology, University of New Mexico, cat. no. 27.10.24.

burials, presumably sacrificial, at the Chalchihuites town of Alta Vista. In the lower part of Aztlan it seems likely that Medio period Paquimé was basically a warring state, although some of Di Peso's evidence for the intense warlike nature of Casas Grandes has been disputed. Farther west, the Sonoran statelets were enthusiastically warlike entities at least by early Spanish times. We cannot be sure this was true in earlier times, but the archaeological evidence suggests it.[7]

That the Mesoamerican concept of warfare affected the Southwest seems very likely, but it probably did not in itself precipitate chronic warfare in that area. This way of life predated the full appearance of Aztlan in at least the upper Southwest. An excellent recent statement on the matter of hostilities comes from Steven LeBlanc:

Following a period of unprecedented peacefulness, suddenly the Southwest was engulfed in warfare. Vast areas soon were abandoned, massacres transpired, and the survivors moved into increasingly larger de-

fensive sites for safety. In my Late Period—from around A.D. 1250 to Spanish contact—things drastically changed and there is very good evidence for intense warfare. The entire concept of the Pueblo people—large numbers living in compact communities—derived directly from the several hundred years of warfare that began around 1300.

Virtually every class of archaeological data that could reflect increased evidence for warfare has it beginning in the late 1200s.... War was having a major impact on the lives of the Southwest people in the Late Period. Of equal importance during this interval is that settlements, the way people were organized, and the way they made war changed dramatically from the preceding centuries.[8]

It has been suggested that one impetus for warfare in the period beginning around AD 1250 was not only aridity but—more unsettling from the viewpoint of primitive agriculturalists—great climatic uncertainty. The balance of summer and winter rainfall fluctuated from year to year, and especially after AD 1350 there occurred an extremely erratic distribution of "wet" and "dry" years.[9] That warlike conditions existed at the very dawn of the Aztlan period is made clear by events in the pre-Aztlan late P-III or Coalition period. One dramatic example in the Galisteo Basin is Burned Corn Pueblo. At some point, probably near the beginning of the fourteenth century, this very large pueblo near the later Aztlan period town of San Marcos was the victim of a catastrophic attack, with widespread conflagration and associated signs of wholesale looting that brought the life of the pueblo to a close.[10]

The new emphasis on hostilities practically demanded some new social order, one in which the war leader took on additional significance and in which some sort of sociopolitical bonding linked groups beyond that of the village. It is clearly no accident that the kachina cult, with its religious bonding among villages, appeared at about this time. This is not to deny that the rainmaking aspects of the kachinas might have been a specific response to drier climatic conditions. The cult, however, was primarily a bonding mechanism. Along with the cult came new emphases on Mexican deities, the rain god Tlaloc and the multifaceted Quetzalcoatl, especially in his manifestation as Morning Star with its war and warrior associations and as Ce Acatl, the savage war dragon.[11] In Mexico Tlaloc was also strongly associated with warfare and with child sacrifice, the latter involving both Tlaloc and Quetzalcoatl aspects.[12] As I have stated elsewhere:

This human sacrifice motif must have been discarded by the Pueblos by 1540; at least, the suspicious Spaniards, who knew human sacrifice first hand from Mexico, could find no trace of it in the Southwest. But elements of human sacrifice still exist in Pueblo folklore. One Pueblo motif is that of the kachinas coming for and carrying away children, and stories that suggest former child sacrifice were fairly common among the historic Pueblos. Pueblo tales of human sacrifice

usually involve the horned serpent in a water manifestation, and pools of water.[13]

The kachina cult, as we know it from the historic Pueblos, involves a series of ceremonies, centering on masked dancers (the kachinas in their human manifestations). During the dances the dancers and the masks they wear are imbued with the supernatural kachina spirits. Kachina organizations and the dancers themselves are normally male although under certain conditions, varying from pueblo to pueblo, females may join the kachina associations.

There is a certain ambiguity in what kachinas actually represent, a fact that might be expected from a cult that came originally from outside the Pueblo world. But we can say that they are powerful spirits, often associated with the ancestors, connected to clouds, springs, and water sources generally. They are important in weather control, especially the production of rain. They are also connected to death and to an afterlife in the underworld, from whence the dead return as kachinas and cloud people to bring the rain.[14] Polly Schaafsma points out the relationship of kachinas with the Tlalocs of central Mexico:

As with Tlaloc and his assistants, the Tlaloque of Mexico, Pueblo kachinas are associated both with mountains, around which clouds and mist form, and with the watery underground realm, accessed via springs and lakes, to which the dead return. The latter suggest affiliations with the domain of Chalchihuitlicue, Tlaloc's female counterpart. Certain springs and lakes are simultaneously regarded as the *sipapu,* or place of humankind's emergence to the earth's surface. All of these terrestrial water sources are thought of as being connected under the earth.[15]

As Jonathan Reyman pointed out a number of years ago, kachinas also have astral associations, as do altars, kivas, and the war cult:

Astronomical symbolism is present in other Southwestern cultural traits. Orion and the

Pleiades are depicted on the star effigy placed on the War Chief's altar in the Goat kiva at Walpi and the Milky Way (Galaxy) is painted on the wall in the War Chief's house.... [Ursa Major] and the Pleiades are painted on the face of the Mastof Kachina who represents the Spirit of the Earth God, and who appears during the Winter solstice ceremony at Second and Third Mesas.... The Hopi Star Kachina has a Venus as Morning Star motif for a face. The Chief kiva at Walpi has stars painted on the walls in possible directional association: Pleiades (west); Orion (south); moon (northwest); and Morning Star. The kivas at Zia have or had stars painted on the walls... and the ceremonial chamber of the Laguna Fathers at Isleta also had a Morning Star depiction on a wall.[16]

As early as Chacoan times, and likely before, there was an interest in astronomy and star lore. But during the Aztlan period this astronomy began to show clear connections to Mesoamerica. The astral aspects of deities were well known in the south and were of high antiquity. Observation of various astral bodies, especially the sun, the moon, Venus, Jupiter, and Mars, had its highest development in the Maya area, but importance of the heavens was a widespread concept in Mesoamerica. Star lore presumably was also ancient in the Southwest, but, as Reyman says, the wave of influence that brought in specific kinds of esoteric knowledge seems to have been late, probably no earlier than the fourteenth century:

What is significant here is that the surviving rosters of stars for both the Southwest and Mesoamerica, like those for the constellations, are virtually identical. Furthermore, in both regions there are similar functions ascribed to the stars, especially Venus which is both a god and a timing device and the Pleiades which also serves as a time keeper. Again, as for the constellations, that there should be almost identical correspondence between the two areas indicates that something other than chance is operative, the

chance probability for such correspondence being infinitesimally small. Once again the evidence points to Mesoamerican-Southwestern contact and south to north diffusion of astronomical complexes, especially since the archaeological record documents the use of these complexes for a much earlier date in Mexico.[17]

In my opinion color-directional symbolism, widespread and ancient in Mesoamerica, entered the Southwest at about this time. It spread throughout the Pueblo world and at some point, perhaps as early as the fifteenth century, reached Apachean groups, including the Navajo, where it became important in the cosmology. Among the Pueblos the symbolism of colors and directions was interdigitated with various societies and ceremonies, including the kachina cult.[18]

Another invention that likely spread from Mexico, at some point in the fourteenth or fifteenth centuries, was *patolli*, a game widespread in Mesoamerica and well known to the Aztecs, from whom the name comes. I have suggested elsewhere that patolli (in the Southwest called *patol,* a variation on the Aztec name) might have been introduced by Coronado's Mexican soldiers. This sixteenth-century date now seems to me too late. The subsequent spread of the game to the Navajo and Apache, and its considerable differentiation within the Pueblo area, suggests a considerable time depth in the Southwest. Even if the Apachean groups received it as late as the sixteenth century, a prehispanic spread to the Pueblo world is not unlikely.[19]

Today the kachina cult is known in its most organized form in the western pueblos of Hopi, Zuni, and to some degree Acoma. It seems clear that, originally, in the fourteenth century the cult was practiced in most (probably all) areas of the Pueblo world. However, during the seventeenth century the cult was suppressed by Spanish authorities at the request of Franciscan missionaries. Although pressure lessened after the Pueblo Revolt, the Eastern Pueblos never regained the full panoply of the cult.

One important thing about the cult is that it works outside the basic social systems, clans in Western Pueblo, and a moiety arrangement among the Rio Grande Pueblos. The cult links these disparate social elements and also forges links to groups of related pueblos. Some form of the name *kachina* is used very widely, though at Zuni the alternative term *kokko* is preferred. The word *kachina* is often thought to be Hopi in origin, but it is a borrowed word among that group (there is no initial *ka* syllable in Hopi), presumably from outside the Pueblo area.[20] We do not know where the name *kachina* originated, though most likely it came from the south, like the cult itself.

In chapter 6 I mentioned the possibility that the kachina cult, or some sort of "proto-kachinas," had spread into the Pueblo world, perhaps from the Mimbres region before the Aztlan period. But whatever the truth of earlier manifestations of the cult, solid evidence for its appearance comes from the period around or a bit after AD 1300. At around that time figures that can reasonably be identified with kachinas, or with Tlaloc, began to appear

on rock art (Figure 7.3), and at very nearly the same time similar designs can be found as pottery motifs. The idea that the Tlaloc and the kachina cults were related is accepted today by many experts and is in fact quite an old one among scholars. Elsie Clews Parsons suggested it in the 1930s,[21] and both J. O. Brew and Ralph Beals in the 1940s considered it to be an important part of the "Golden Age of the Pueblos" (that is, around AD 1300 to the Spanish Conquest).[22]

One place from which the rock figures spread is the Jornada Mogollon area. These figures, generally thought to be Tlaloc representations, include round or square masks and rectangular or trapezoidal figures with huge "goggle" eyes, sometimes with small, round, and toothed mouths, and hourglass noses. The torsos are decorated with geometric designs or with cloud motifs (see Figure 7.4). Also appearing are horned and feathered serpents, presumably to be identified with Quetzalcoatl. The nonhuman carvings include stepped cloud designs. Small wooden effigies are sometimes found in the Jornada, possibly precursors of

FIGURE 7.3. Tlaloc, Black Mesa, Doña Ana County, NM. Maxwell Museum of Anthropology, University of New Mexico, cat. no. 91.2.209.

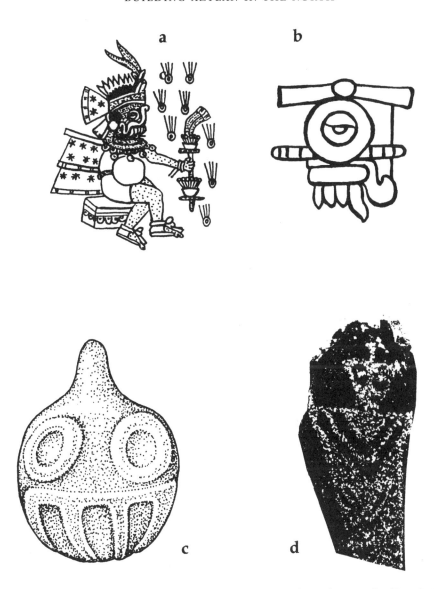

FIGURE 7.4. Aspects of Tlaloc: (a) Tlaloc in masked form (after McKusick, *Southwest Birds of Sacrifice*); (b) Day Sign symbol for Tlaloc (after McKusick, *Southwest Birds of Sacrifice*); (c) copper crotal with Tlaloc face (after Di Peso, *Casas Grandes*, Vol. 2); (d) Tlaloc in rock art, Three Rivers area, southern New Mexico (after P. Schaafsma, *Rock Art in New Mexico*).

kachina dolls. Many of these motifs had their origin in Classic Mimbres.[23] According to Polly Schaafsma:

The Jornada Style is a major rock art style in the Mogollon region. It represents a serious break with earlier rock art both in regard to content and the style in which figures are depicted. As well, the Jornada Style (A.D. 1000–1450) represents the beginning of a 1,000 year-old art tradition in New Mexico that continues in the native ritual art of today, as expressed in Pueblo dance costumes, kachina forms, altar painting, and so forth, and, to a lesser degree, in Navajo sand painting. The complex life-forms on a few examples of Mangas Black-on-white and on many Classic Mimbres Black-on-white bowls, another case where this encompassing tradition finds visual expression in the Mogollon, provide us with secure beginning dates (ca. A.D. 1000) for its appearance. Three hundred years later this art tradition is clearly evident in the fourteenth century Pueblo world of the Upper Rio Grande and Little Colorado River drainages, where it occurs on pottery as well as rock art.[24]

Was the Jornada area the source (or, more likely, the final staging area) for the fully developed Pueblo kachina cult? It seems a good candidate from the rock art evidence. Schaafsma thinks that the rich rock art at the Piro site of Cerro Indio, north of Socorro, represents a spread from the Jornada area, earlier than that of rock art sites in the west.[25] Charles Adams, however, suggests a possible Mimbres origin for the cult (or at least for the ideas that led to the cult). Spreading northward into the upper Little Colorado River around AD 1325, the cult continued eastward in the following quarter century to the Rio Grande. Adams believes that this movement paralleled the spread of pueblos with enclosed plazas, which may have started in the south and moved northwestward then northeastward. It is not clear how, or to what extent, the earlier Chaco plazas might have influenced these later structures. Rectangular kivas also seem to be a blend of Anasazi and Mogollon features, having, at least in part, a southern origin. Adams suggests that "katsinas and katsina masks appear on classic Fourmile style (Fourmile Polychrome) probably as early as 1325,"[26] following an earlier appearance of enclosed plazas, rectangular kivas, and the Pinedale style of pottery, precursor of the Fourmile style, in the middle to late thirteenth century:

> The convergence of enclosed plazas, classic rectangular kivas (having south or east facing raised platforms) and Fourmile style iconography overlap in a relatively small area in the upper Little Colorado River valley bounded on the west by the Silver Creek drainage, on the north and east by the Lit-

tle Colorado River, and on the south by the Mogollon Rim....It is noteworthy that Fewkes...recorded Hopi and Zuni accounts of katsina beings originating near Fourmile ruin in the upper Little Colorado River area.[27]

According to Adams the important fact, however, was that katsina iconography "appeared almost throughout the Pueblo world of the fourteenth century, that stimulus came from northern Mexico (or at least south of the historic Pueblo area), and that its appearance coincides with many other changes in Pueblo culture, namely change in village size and layout, as part of a general reorganization of the Pueblo world following its sudden abandonment of the Four Corners region."[28]

Whatever the point of origin, kachinas began to be portrayed iconographically not only on rock art but as pottery design, in murals on kiva walls, and in at least one case on a sandstone slab (Figure 7.5). A selection of pottery decorations includes those on the Fourmile style of the White Mountain redwares, on Hopi yellow wares, occasionally on the Tonto polychromes, and on various ceramics from the Rio Grande, including Galisteo Black-on-white, and Glaze A wares.[29] Murals depicting parts of kachina cult rituals appear on kiva walls at the Hopi towns of Awatovi and Kawaika-a; Homol'ovi II, on the Little Colorado; Kuaua, on the Rio Grande, near Bernalillo; and Pottery Mound, on the Puerco River, west of modern Albuquerque. It is interesting that most of the kiva murals at Pottery Mound and all at Kuaua, as well as room murals at Gran Quivira (which have kachina-like figures), appear in rectangular structures. Rectangular kivas, of course, are a Western Pueblo phenomenon. What implications this has for possible west-to-east spread of this particular form of kachina art is not clear. Murals on round kivas, those of Gran Quivira, in the Salinas region, and Pueblo de Encierro, near Cochiti, are less clearly related to the kachina cult, not having masked anthropomorphic figures.[30]

The kachina cult borrowed from or merged

FIGURE 7.5. Kachina figure on sandstone, Mogollon, fourteenth century, Maverick Mountain component, Point of Pines. Amerind Foundation, Dragoon, AZ.

with earlier Anasazi religious elements, the most obvious of which is the kiva complex itself. There was also the probable borrowing of earlier motifs that now took on kachina attributes. A specific example is the Kokopelli kachina, found in modern Hopi. Kokopelli is a humped-back individual, often playing a flute. In archaeological literature (although not by the Hopi) the name *Kokopelli* is also often given to rock art figures that have a considerable antiquity in the upper Southwest. Such figures appear as humped flute players around AD 1000 in Anasazi art and also in Mimbres and Hohokam. Archaeologists have suggested various identifications for these rock art individuals, calling them deities, shamans, or even traders, with the hump actually being a trader's pack. There is no absolute proof that the Hopi Kokopelli kachina grew out of these earlier rock art figures, but the points of similarity are rather striking.[31]

"Kachina dolls" are occasionally found in archaeological excavations and surveys. Today the dolls serve a number of purposes, including sale to tourists. The ones found archaeologically cannot be identified as firmly as historic dolls, for they may be altar pieces or may have some ritual function other than the kachina cult. One problem with identifying archaeological kachina figures in whatever medium, is that historic kachinas are not static but evolve and change over time.[32]

Certain thirteenth-century innovations in village design, particularly the enclosed plaza construction, gave a new and satisfactory setting for kachina ceremonies. Associated are plaza or house-block kivas, rectangular in the west and rectangular or round in the east, which likely were becoming the focus of kachina activities. A part of the kachina ceremonies now shifted to kivas, as indicated by kiva murals, showing the cult in what perhaps was its private and more esoteric aspect. I doubt if arrival of the kachinas was the triggering mechanism for the aggregation of pueblos from a more open to a more closed form. I would imagine that the necessities of defense dictated that, but the needs of the cult may have been a contributing factor in the specificities of town layout and placement of kivas in relation to plazas.[33]

Two other innovations appeared in the Pueblo realm about the same time as the kachinas: the sandstone *comal* used for making piki bread, a thin waferlike cornmeal bread, and the shoe pot (Figure 7.6). Adams thought that these may have arrived in the western area about the same time as, and were possibly associated with, the kachina cult. It is true that piki bread was historically a part of the kachina rituals in Western Pueblo, being distributed by the kachinas during dances, especially at Hopi. The use of comales became quite widespread in the Southwest in the Aztlan period, this kitchen device being found at Pecos, Acoma, San Lázaro, and a number of other Rio Grande sites.[34]

The use of the shoe (slipper or duck-shaped) pot is less clear. No specific association with kachinas has ever been demonstrated, and it may have been quite independently diffused to

FIGURE 7.6. Slipper or duck pot from Zuni area, Hawikuh, late prehistoric. Amerind Foundation, Dragoon, AZ, cat. no. 7.4856.

the Southwest. It is certainly a superior vessel form for certain uses; the elongated shape allows the vessels to be put among glowing coals, to heat the contents evenly. Not all such pots have handles; however, those that do have the further advantage that the handle, projecting from the top, stays cool when the rest of the pot collects considerable heat. Shoe-shaped forms are probably basically Meso-american, though they have been found at Babocomari and elsewhere in the Hohokam. Di Peso reports ceramic shoe-shaped "duck effigies" in Medio period Casas Grandes. Although basically utilitarian, these shoe pots are found in burials in the Zuni and Hopi areas, but their general distribution is not securely known.[35]

A few scholars argue for the in situ development of the kachina cult, but the weight of scholarly opinion is that kachinas came from the south.[36] The Tlaloc and, secondarily, Quetzalcoatl associations seem very clear, and various lines of evidence point to a Jornada Mogollon spread to at least the Rio Grande area. In the west it is quite possible that earlier Classic Mimbres elements may have entered into the construction of the cult. As I said in chapter 4, I do not think that there was an actual kachina cult operative in Mimbres, but some of the precursor divine imagery is there.

Polly Schaafsma has suggested that the ultimate origin of the kachina cult was associ-

ated with the Mesoamerican integration of "spirits of the dead with natural forces in order to transform the deceased into rainmakers."[37] There is a considerable iconography in Mesoamerica that suggests this—for example, burial bundles (probably representing ancestors) associated with Tlaloc masks that extend from the Classic period in central Mexico to the Postclassic, as shown in the codices. This association of ancestors with the fructifying power of rain and water is the very centerpiece of the southwestern kachina cult.[38]

What were to become recognizable kachinas in their southwestern manifestation can be seen in the Jornada Mogollon area quite early, a century or more before the rapid fourteenth-century spread of the cult in the Southwest. It does not seem likely that the cult crystallized out in that rather peripheral region, so somewhere farther south is a more probable point of origin. Perhaps the Casas Grandes region was the real homeland, although the Paquimé style of rock art in the Casas Grandes area does not show the clear kachina connections found in the Jornada. Tlaloc images in Paquimé rock art may indeed appear, but they are rare. Geometric motifs related to Tlaloc and what may be Tlaloc heads are found on the Chihuahuan polychromes, however. The dominant motif, though, is the plumed or horned serpent, not only on pottery but in rock art, often in association with springs and other water sources. It may be that a Casas Grandes version of the kachina cult had these serpent-Quetzalcoatl associations as primary iconographic elements.[39] Or, perhaps, the cult actually originated farther down in west Mexico. I will discuss these matters further in chapter 8.

Nor were the conditions necessarily the same in the kachina land of origin as in the Southwest. In this latter area the associations with growing defensive-oriented Pueblos and groups of Pueblos, with the rising hunt and especially the ubiquitous war societies, make it clear that kachinas were somehow involved in a new ordering of society. And one function of this new order was the bonding of old kin-oriented villages into something that was larger and reached beyond the control of individual families and individual clans. Certainly, by the time the Spaniards arrived, in the sixteenth century, Pueblo sociopolitical control had evolved into a series of confederacies linking linguistically related Pueblos and with certain wider linkages (trade relationships, for example) that joined the entire Pueblo world and beyond. Relatively few Pueblos stood outside these primary confederacies, and those who did, mainly at Acoma and Pecos, had special geographical reasons for doing so. I think it likely that such groupings went back to the beginning of Aztlan times.

One puzzle in any reconstruction of events in the fourteenth century Southwest is the relationship of the kachina cult and Crown's southwestern cult. Whereas kachinas almost certainly came from the south, the southwestern cult seems to have a northern, basically Anasazi (or perhaps Anasazi-Mogollon/Mimbres), origin. Elements of it may have coalesced in the Kayenta area in the thirteenth century. Crown believes that in this northern homeland important aspects of the cult (or what was to become the cult) were belief in the flower world and in the relationship between caves and the underworld. Both of these concepts are ancient in Mesoamerica, and in that area they suggest Quetzalcoatl and Tlaloc or Chalchihuitlicue associations. In my opinion these Mexican deities most likely spread to the northern Southwest at the beginning of Aztlan times (early fourteenth century). Perhaps the flower associations relate to an older substratum of culture, common to both the Southwest and Mesoamerica. In fact, it seems possible that the flower associations themselves, including flower metaphors in song, may have been spread by early Uto-Aztecan migrations, which also affected other ethnic groups in the Southwest and in Mesoamerica. They are found among historic groups from Arizona to Chiapas.

In Crown's reconstruction the southwestern cult as it spread southward picked up elements of the kachina cult and horned serpent and Venus manifestations (both considered aspects of Quetzalcoatl). The cult likely had to

do with water resources and fertility but, unlike the kachina cult, was not involved in ancestor veneration. It may have been partly syncretized with the kachinas but hardly identical with them. In fact, it has been suggested that the term *cult* is too strong since, unlike the kachina groups, we have no ideas about its organization or degree of cohesion. But it must have helped give a sort of identity to the whole Greater Southwest during the early Aztlan period.[40]

The fourteenth century witnessed considerable social experimentation and innovation. A number of organizations developed, or at least were considerably elaborated, during these times. The various clown societies are extremely important among the historic Pueblos. Ceremonial clowns are widespread in the Southwest and probably predate the Aztlan period in the Pueblo world. After AD 1300 their functions seem to have been interwoven with the kachina organizations, at least in the west. Among Eastern Pueblos they became important in the dual organizations that formed the underpinning of socioreligious and political life. Hunt societies are another form of sodality that probably formed in early Aztlan times; at least the iconographic evidence suggests it. Kiva walls and rock art sites show such animals as the mountain lion, traditional patron of hunters and hunting. These societies, still found among the historic and modern Pueblos, actually had several functions. One was the organization of communal hunts, another was the control of the hunt rituals and ceremonies, and still another was curing. At all times, apparently, the hunt groups were associated with war, and this makes it difficult to know when a given image relates to hunting or to war. Both hunt and war societies recognize the patronage of the beast gods, and distinctions between them tend to blur. As Parsons says, "Among all Pueblos there is a close conceptual relationship between killing men and killing prey animals, between hunting and warring organizations."[41] Among the historic Keres Pueblos the Corn Mother Iyatiku institutes the hunt society with all its ceremonies.[42] As mother of the twin war brothers, avatars of the twinned Quetzalcoatl,

FIGURE 7.7. Mimbres, elder sacred twin, with deer representing the sun. Presumed ancestor of Elder of Twin War Gods. El Paso Museum of Archaeology.

FIGURE 7.8. Mimbres, younger sacred twin as rabbit representing the moon. Presumed ancestor of Younger of Twin War Gods. El Paso Museum of Archaeology.

she forms another link between the hunt and war societies (see Figures 7.7 and 7.8).

The war sodalities were probably the most important of the societies in the Aztlan period, as might be expected by the increasingly bellicose nature of Pueblo society. From about AD 1325 into historic times, the entire Pueblo area (but most especially the Rio Grande Valley) developed a rich war iconography in rock art and in kiva paintings. This includes shields and shield bearers, as well as warriors with spears, axes, bows, arrows, quivers, and various kinds of war clubs. Star symbolism was common in the Rio Grande Valley, though less so in the rock art of the Little Colorado.

Animal war patrons include the mountain lion. The latter animal is also a patron of hunt societies and unless the creature is pictured in clear war context, it can be ambiguous. The same is true of the bear. In historic Pueblos the bear is a widespread patron of curing societies and of shamanism. However, a large bear image at San Cristobal, in the Galisteo region, has star associations. These four-pointed stars are normally considered to be Venus as Morning Star, widely associated with war among historic Pueblo peoples and with the twin war gods, with their Quetzalcoatl affiliation. What are suggested to be jaguars appear in the mu-

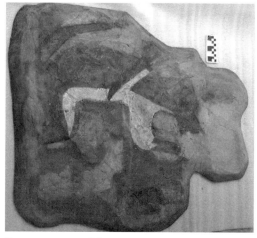

FIGURE 7.9. Animal from section of wall mural (probably a jaguar). Originally from Pottery Mound. Amerind Foundation, Dragoon, AZ.

rals at Pottery Mound (Figure 7.9). The jaguar was a potent war symbol in Mesoamerica, the animal representation of the famous Jaguar Knights of Aztec times. The actual animal is known in the Southwest, occasionally making appearances at this extreme northern edge of its range.[43]

As indicated in rock art, the important weapons were long lances, probably mainly for thrusting, both body shields and the smaller arm varieties, war clubs with blunt rounded double bites or with sharp points, single blade axes and bows, both recurved and simple. The recurved bow, sinew-backed for greater striking power, was diffused into the upper Southwest sometime around AD 1300. As likely as was the case of the self-bow a thousand years earlier, the compound bow appeared from somewhere farther north. Indeed the spread may relate to the appearance of the earliest Apachean groups into the northeastern quadrant of the Southwest. Though simple bows continued to be used during Aztlan times, the recurved bow is considerably more powerful. Whereas a southwestern self-bow released an arrow at around 115 feet per second, a recurved bow of the general type used by southwesterners attained initial velocities of over 140 feet per second.[44]

The paramount importance of the war societies, their interlinking with the various hunt groups and their association with transplanted Mesoamerican deities and mythologies, seems to have been accomplished during the fourteenth century. Like most or all other aspects of Pueblo life, war societies interdigitated with the pervasive kachina cult and, like the kachina cult, helped link various Pueblos together. When the Spaniards came to stay in the last years of the 1500s, they were generally antagonistic to native sociopolitical and especially religious organizations. For the native political structure the Spaniards imposed their own set of officers, based in part on the Spanish *cabildo,* or town government. For religious structures the newcomers brought the Catholic Church, under the control of Franciscan missionaries. No alternative form of worship was to be permitted.

The one great exception to this wholesale substitution of institutions is that of the war organizations. It is not clear to what extent the actual structure of the war societies was maintained, but the chances are that Spanish authorities removed only overt religious symbolism. Certainly the war leaders, under the new title of *capitanes de guerra,* continued to be favored.[45] The reason for this is actually quite simple. During the entire seventeenth century,

and much of the eighteenth as well, Spaniards in New Mexico were seriously undermanned. They faced a restive Pueblo world, but, more important, they were forced to contend with implacable enemies on all sides of their new province, the Apache and Navajo, increasingly the Utes and (after AD 1700) the Comanche. So the war captains, the heads of the old warrior societies, maintained their positions, vying with the newly Spanish-inspired officials and the old religious leaders for power among the pueblos. During the course of the seventeenth century the warrior groups learned new tactics and obtained new weapons. Although technically not allowed to ride horses, the Pueblo Indians quickly learned because of their duties caring for the new Spanish animals. As auxiliaries in the Spanish forces they did not have a chance to show off riding skills, but during the Pueblo Revolt (1680–1696) they often were mounted and had a certain number of guns. With the Spaniards, however, the Indian warriors normally utilized their native weapons, the lance and shield, war ax and war club, and the bow and arrow. From very early times they were important components of Spanish war parties and even as late as the early eighteenth century often made up 75 percent of the Spanish-led war parties.[46]

By the latter part of the seventeenth century the various war captains were somewhat acclimatized to Spanish ways, and various of them flirted with the idea of deserting Quetzalcoatl and the kachina religion for Christianity. Still, in 1680 they were firmly enough in the camp of the Pueblo religious leaders so that most of them swung their prestige and military resources against the Spaniards, providing military firepower that forced the Europeans to flee the Province of New Mexico. When the Spanish forces returned (1692–1696), they were largely successful because many of the war captains switched sides, accepting leadership roles in their various pueblos as part of the Spanish power structure.

We know relatively little about tactics during the Aztlan period, but accounts of Spanish battles with Pueblo Indians give some data.

In defensive warfare the Indians attempted to hold advantageous positions; for example, when the Spaniards attacked Hawikuh, the westernmost Zuni town, in 1540, a Pueblo war party tried to defend a narrow defile south of the settlement. Seeing that they were unable to do this, they gave a signal with some sort of trumpet, perhaps one of shell, and retreated. At the pueblo itself they grouped in the flat ground outside the town and discharged flights of arrows. When they were scattered by a Spanish cavalry charge, they withdrew within the walls, where they continued to shoot arrows and to throw down heavy stones. Even after the Spaniards, heavily reinforced by hundreds of Mexican Indian auxiliaries, broke into the pueblo, there was fighting in the narrow alleys between houses, the Zunians continuing to hurl missiles from above. Coronado estimated the number of bowmen at Hawikuh at 300.

At Hopi a war contingent met the Spaniards "in wing formation," armed with shields, maces, and bows and arrows. At the pueblo of Moho or El Cerco in the Rio Grande Valley, a pueblo with its back to the cliffs, the strongly defended Indians met the Spaniards and their allies with the usual hail of missiles from the town walls. The Spaniards attacked with a cavalry unit, then feigned flight, drawing numbers of Indians into the flats beyond the walls. After inflicting considerable casualties, the Spaniards attempted to take the pueblo by direct assault but within the front wall found a palisade of logs. They used a battering ram against this obstruction, but a fierce enfilading fire drove them back. They then tried ladders, but again savage volleys of arrows drove them away. The invaders were forced to siege operations, and Moho held out for two to three months, finally succumbing for lack of water since the Spaniards cut off the defenders' access to the river.

Several things appear in these sixteenth-century accounts of Pueblo Indian warfare. They demonstrate the importance of the bow, of the Indian skill at, and a certain dependence on, defensive warfare. A number of pueblos made an effort to bring their water supply within the town fortifications (Hawikuh, for example, and Pecos). Nevertheless, water was somewhat of an Achilles heel in defensive warfare, at least when Pueblo Indians faced Spanish military forces. It seems fairly clear that the southwestern natives were not geared to putting forces in the field for very long periods. Their logistic systems were quite primitive, and offensive warfare took the nature of extended raids. One obvious reason for this was the problem of transport. To besiege a place, it is necessary to carry a considerable number of goods, especially food, to the siege site. Lacking pack animals, the Pueblo war parties were quite limited in haulage capabilities. Only after the coming of the Spaniards were the Indian auxiliary warriors trained in the uses of the commissariat. This hit-and-run warfare was also true of the Apachean groups, sometimes enemies and sometimes allies of the Pueblos. After the Spaniards came, these Apaches (and later the Utes and Comanche) became skilled horsemen and were able to strike rapidly and at long distance from their home bases. Even then, however, their attacks mostly took the form of raids, devastating but short lived.

Confederacies along linguistic lines were important in warfare. This seems to be true of Zuni, Coronado's Cibola, where the great flat-topped mesa of Dowa Yalanne (Figure 7.10) served as a refuge for all the Zuni towns after the fiasco at Hawikuh. It was also true of the Hopi country, where various pueblos seem to have acted in concert to oppose the Spaniards. It was clearly the Tiguex (Tiwa-speaking) federation that defied Coronado in the winter of 1540–1541. In 1541 Barrionuevo's expeditionary force met with hostilities from the northern Tewa-speaking Indians. Coronado's forces, however, forged some kind of an alliance with the Rio Grande and Jemez River Keresans, one aimed against the Tiguex. The only Pueblos that acted alone during the Coronado period were those of Acoma and Pecos, isolated from linguistic kinsmen and holding strong defensive positions. Both pueblos were bellicose, and neither was overrun by Coronado, though two leaders at Pecos, one who seems to have been a war chief or perhaps bow

FIGURE 7.10. Zuni sacred mountain Dowa Yalanne. Foreground figure is the late Virgil Wyaco of Zuni Pueblo, a friend of the author from student days immediately after World War II. Photo by Victoria R. Evans.

chief and the other a religious leader of some sort, were kidnapped and held in the Spanish camp for a time.[47]

If the attitude toward war was changed, or at least heightened, during the Aztlan period, there also were major changes in the socio-religious and political structures. These changes can only be understood in terms of the arrival of kachinas and of the societies, especially the war societies of early Aztlan times. I believe that, like the kachina-based religion, certain ideas about group organization spread from the south and became part of the new milieu.

Exactly what were the political structures of Pueblo III and what changes were made in the post–Pueblo III period of the old Anasazi territory? This has been a question since the delineation of Pueblo culture was first made in the period around the First World War. One of the first answers came with archaeologists such as Walter Fewkes, then with Pueblo ethnologists such as Fred Eggan, who were deeply involved in studies of Western Pueblo. In the west the primary social entity today is the matrilineal and matrilocal clan. To many of the investigators, believing that the San Juan people were ancestors of the Zuni and Hopi peoples, it seemed logical that the clan was the structural base of the San Juan Anasazi as well. The proliferation of small kivas, thought of as clan-gathering structures, in the Mesa Verde seemed to argue for this position. However, Chaco Canyon remained somewhat of an anomaly. A hallmark of the Chacoan Great Houses were the Great Kivas, more suited to some sort of larger units. In the historic Rio Grande pueblos large kiva structures are normally related to *moieties*, dual divisions of a pueblo. It is true that some of the Chaco people likely migrated into the Rio Grande Valley, but others had contacts with the west—in fact, Chacoan Great Kivas reach into the Zuni area, and post-Chaco Zuni in all probability had a leavening of Chacoan settlers.

Today the Western Pueblos of Hopi, Zuni, and Acoma are basically clan oriented. At the Hopi towns clans are grouped into larger units, the *phratries,* which, like clans, are exogamous (that is, marriage is outside the group) but whose other functions are somewhat nebulous. Clans control the kivas, but kivas are also utilized by the various societies and priesthoods that crosscut the clans to some degree. Leadership was provided by the head of the bear clan, who usually functioned as village chief. The bear clan, a powerful sodality, has economic control of at least some of the Hopi lands and also maintains charge of the great winter solstice or Soya'l ceremonies. There is a kachina cult that both boys and girls join around the ages of 6 to 10, although boys and men normally perform the actual ceremonies.[48]

Zuni had a somewhat more complex system, as it was described in the late nineteenth and early twentieth century, which is still more or less true today. Again the matrilineal clan is central to the social organization, with the clans again being grouped into phratries. As in Hopi there is a dominant clan, in this case Pikchikwe or Dogwood. The pueblo is also organized into six kiva groups, twelve curing societies, and sixteen priesthoods. Probably the most important office is that of *Pekwin,* or sun priest of the zenith, who heads the religious hierarchy and who must belong to the Dogwood clan. Other cults include the priesthoods of the rainmakers, the kachina priests, and those of the war gods and the beast gods. The priesthoods represent a number of clans but tend to be dominated by the Dogwood clan, which holds three of the six directional priesthoods, including the dominant Pekwin.

The kachina cult is tribal at Zuni. Its membership is normally male, though occasionally females may belong. Very important, especially in the past, was the cult of the war gods, in the hands of the Bow Priests, avatars of the Twin War Gods. The Bow Priests are appointed by the chief priest of the north, controlled by the Dogwood clan.[49]

At Acoma there are matrilineal exogamous clans, crosscut by medicine, clown, hunting,

and warrior societies. The most important clan, historically, was the Antelope clan, which provided the town or tribal leader. This individual is referred to among the Keresans as *cacique,* a term introduced by the Spaniards and borrowed by them from West Indies Arawakan-speakers. There is a tribalwide kachina cult that accepts both sexes, though females do not play much of a ceremonial role.[50]

Eastern Pueblos, at least in historic times, have a considerably different type of political and socioreligious organization, focused on the moiety rather than the clan. Eggan believed that this may have been a recent reorganization of society from an originally more clan-based one:

> My own guess is that the dual organization began to expand [among the Eastern Pueblo] soon after reaching the Rio Grande. The dual principle of organization is the simplest form of segmentary organization, beyond the band or village, and operates most effectively in relatively small groups. The organization of social, ceremonial, and political activities in terms of a dual division, and the further conceptualization of this division in terms of winter and summer, and the associated natural phenomena, suggest a fairly long period of development.
>
> The clan system would be reduced in importance by these events but would be further affected by the extensive period of Spanish acculturation. Catholic regulation of marriage practices would take away the last remaining functions of the clan system, and intimate contacts with Spanish (and later Spanish American) settlements would give a patrilineal tinge to the remnants.[51]

A historical study by Gutiérrez goes even further, suggesting that weakening of matrilineality (and by implication, the matrilineal exogamous clan) was totally an artifact of Spanish acculturation along the Rio Grande.[52]

In the latter nineteenth century and early twentieth, when ethnological accounts of various Pueblo people were written, the Eastern Pueblos had a quite different approach to social organization than did the west. This is perhaps least true among the Keresan groups, where matrilineal clans still serve to regulate marriage. However, unlike Western Pueblo these clans no longer have an ownership function, the socioreligious and political functions having been taken over by the crosscutting medicine societies (which also function in weather control), the kachina groups, hunt societies, and warrior societies. Two "clown" societies, also called "managing societies" because of their role in supervising the various ceremonies, are the Koshare (Figure 7.11) and the Quirana. There are dual "moiety" structures, Squash (Pumpkin) and Turquoise, each associated with a kiva. Among Zia these are called Wren and Turquoise and associated with the north and south sides of the pueblo respectively. The pueblo headman, the priestly cacique, is normally chosen from the Flint medicine society. Among his assistants are two war priests, representing the twin war gods, Masewi and Oyowewi, these probably originally filled from the warrior society. Again, Zia differs some-what in that the cacique is drawn from either the Saltbush or Corn clan.

The Towa, now the single pueblo of Jemez, but as late as the early nineteenth century also including Pecos Pueblo, are strongly related in social and ceremonial structures to the Keresan group. The ethnologist Edward P. Dozier suggested a number of years ago that this was due to intensive acculturation in relatively recent times because of proximity and intermarriage. The exogamous clans, for example, do not fit well into the Jemez social structure and seem to be new. Otherwise the system has a large number of societies, as well as the Squash and Turquoise moieties, patrilineal, tending toward endogamy (marriage within the group), and associated with kivas. There is the lifetime cacique and under him the war chief. Positions filled annually are the war captain and his assistants, selected in alternating years by the two moieties.

Among the Tewa the moieties are Summer and Winter, and the cacique is the moiety head. Moieties are patrilineal but somewhat flexibly

FIGURE 7.11. Koshares at unidentified pueblo, possibly Santo Domingo. Maxwell Museum of Anthropology, University of New Mexico, cat. no. 71.8.127.

so. There are clans, but they have no marriage function. There are medicine, clown, hunt, and war societies and a somewhat attenuated kachina society.

The clans among the northern Tiwa are actually kiva groups, organized into a north side and a south side, and there are summer and winter moieties. The affiliations of the cacique seem to be with the south-side kivas, perhaps mainly from the Water kiva, although this varies with the individual holding the office. Among the southern Tiwa are also summer and winter moieties, and so-called clans, which are actually called "corn groups," matrilineal but not exogamous. The politico-religious cacique has as executive officers the war chief, war society head, and a Bow Priest who normally succeeds him. Kachina groupings are very weakly developed in both areas.[53]

Perhaps the most important point about the modern Pueblos is that their social, religious, and political systems are very much reduced from the sixteenth century. Even in this earliest Spanish period Western Pueblos, and to some degree those of the east, were already in considerable decline. The question of whether given Pueblos originally had a clan-based organization or one based on dual sodalities is something that must remain a matter of speculation. My own feeling is that clans are basically western, with a considerable antiquity, originating possibly in the period of Anasazi-Mogollon interchange that produced the Western Pueblo (if not earlier). Whether or not parts of the San Juan area, especially Mesa Verde, with its considerable numbers of small kivas, shared this situation is unknown. The more important problem for us is the extent, following the Mesoamericanization after around AD 1300, that the region, west and east, took on Mesoamerican aspects.

In a recent publication Curtis Schaafsma and I suggested that the Casas Grandes area, beginning in the Medio period, was organized by what we called the *Cacique Model*. Drawing on the Mixtecan work of Jill Furst and on research among various Pueblo peoples, we saw caciques as controlling the rituals of power,

which could include linkages with deities, ritual objects, and myths. These rituals functioned to validate the caciques, both in their own eyes and *in the eyes of their subjects*. This situation necessitates that the recipient group had some understanding of the way power was validated in the larger world, and it is particularly during early Medio period Casas Grandes and of the post-1300 Pueblo world, with its wave of new ideas and contacts, that such esoteric knowledge might be known and understood. In the historic Pueblo world virtually all groups had this sort of leader—in Western Pueblo the head of the dominant clan, in the East often a moiety head. Such individuals were priests who controlled esoteric and powerful objects and ceremonials. These persons and their entourages would be perfectly placed to control the elite groups that sprang up in the Pueblo world about 1300, the kachina cult, and the various specialist societies, including the increasingly crucial warrior society. These all had, as a major function, binding together of peoples from a series of towns, promoting political and religious unity, protecting and enhancing trade between towns and between more far-flung areas, and, coincidentally, solidifying the power of the elites that were at the centers of these operations.[54]

One factor in the analysis of protohistoric Pueblo society is the fluctuation in population from the beginning of the fourteenth century to modern times. This was especially dramatic in the western part of the area. When the Spaniards first came to the Western Pueblo area, they found three clusters of towns: six villages at Zuni, five (possibly six) at Hopi, and the single mesa-top town at Acoma, a total of 12 or perhaps 13 towns. The population of the Western Pueblos in Coronado's time was perhaps 10,000 and in the entire Pueblo world around 60,000. It shrank considerably during the Spanish period. By the time of Oñate (1598) the overall Pueblo population had dropped to around 50,000. If East and West Pueblos had comparable percentages of drop, the end of the sixteenth century would have seen roughly 42,000 Pueblo Indians in the east and some

FIGURE 7.12. Zuni Pueblo, originally Halona, probably late nineteenth century. Maxwell Museum of Anthropology, University of New Mexico, cat. no. 97.10.22.

8,000 in the west. At the time of the Pueblo Revolt (1680) I have estimated the total Pueblo numbers to be somewhere on the order of 17,000. By that period, among Western Pueblo, the Zuni region had shrunk to one town, Halona (see Figure 7.12), the precursor of modern Zuni, although the five Hopi towns maintained themselves. The Pueblo population continued to decline during the Spanish and Mexican period, reaching its nadir in the late nineteenth and early twentieth centuries, after which there has been steady growth.[55]

If one turns back to prehistoric times, there is a drastically different picture. As Stedman Upham has pointed out, in the fourteenth century the Western Pueblo consisted of a number of subareas and large clusters of towns, some 67 population centers. There were clusters in the Verde region, at Anderson Mesa, southeast of Flagstaff; along the middle Little Colorado, on the upper reaches of that river; at the Hopi Mesas, in the Pinedale and Fourmile area north of the Mogollon Rim; in the eastern portion of the Zuni area, and around

Acoma. There seem to have been primate towns, for example Homol'ovi II on the Little Colorado, Nuvaqueotaka (Nuvakwewtaqa or Chavez Pass)—with its Sinagua affiliations— at the edge of Anderson Mesa, and a number of others. Western Pueblo was an area in which an elaborate series of trading networks distributed valued pottery: White Mountain redwares, Zuni glazes, Winslow orange wares, and the Jeddito yellow ceramics. Although Upham's own study concentrated on pottery, he sees the potential for various other goods, foodstuffs, textiles, including cotton goods, semiprecious stones, shell, minerals, skins, and other materials.[56]

The linkages among the segments of this Western Pueblo regional system were, in Upham's eyes, bound by political alliances, facilitating the transmission of esoteric knowledge and the control over large Pueblo populations. The collapse of this fourteenth-century system—leaving only three peripheral areas, Hopi, Zuni, and Acoma—happened because of "a series of failures, either in agricultural production or in political management, that had a *domino* effect on the remaining polities of the system. This effect would prove most costly to population centers that were proximate to one another and that may have established dependency relationships with their neighbors."[57]

It is not clear whether political rivalries, setting one elite group against another, flashed into hostilities, or that the large size of the population and overall area was such that the mechanisms available (crosscutting organizations like the kachina cult) proved insufficient in the long run to bind the region together. We also need to work out the details of special relationships among Western Pueblo settlements. For example, Homol'ovi II, on the Little Colorado, represented some sort of Hopi intrusion into the Little Colorado area, beginning about AD 1330, perhaps to control the important production and trade of cotton. During that period the area received the great majority of its decorated ceramics from the Hopi Mesas, and according to historic Hopi tradition the Homol'ovi people eventually resettled in Hopi.[58]

In the Zuni area a shift from hundreds of small pueblos to a relatively few very large towns took place around or after AD 1250, especially in the eastern section. According to Keith W. Kintigh, who has done extensive work in this region:

Our understanding of the late prehistory of the Zuni area . . . indicates several obvious features of the settlement pattern sequence that demand consideration: (1) the dramatic population aggregation that occurred in the late A.D. 1200s; (2) the unusually high rate of settlement relocation within the eastern part of the study area that started during the late 1200s and continued through the 1300s (during this short interval, more than 25 large pueblos were built, inhabited, and abandoned); (3) the major settlement shift about A.D. 1400 to the lower, more uniform settlement pattern of the historic pueblos.[59]

We must, of course, guard against overestimating the degree of centralization and organization of this Western Pueblo area. For one thing the various subregions were not totally in lockstep in a temporal sense; the various Silver Creek sites (Pinedale, Sholow, Fourmile, and others) were deserted between 1325 and 1385, and a number of the Zuni, Hopi, and Acoma area sites were deserted during the same century. In the Verde Valley, at Nuvaqueotaka on Anderson Mesa, at Homol'ovi and Chevelon in the middle Little Colorado, and at Cubero in the Acoma area, occupation ended around AD 1400, the survivors gathering in the three centers that remained. The first half of the fifteenth century saw the consolidation of towns in the Zuni area, at Hopi and at Acoma, that would essentially reflect the situation as of the Spanish entradas of the sixteenth century.[60]

During the early part of the Aztlan period, the fourteenth century, and indeed even before, Western Pueblo greatly affected the Rio Grande area. This can be especially noted in pottery, where the various White Mountain redwares made their way eastward (reaching as far south as Late Elmendorf in the Rio Abajo), and then their descendants, the early glazes. The movement went both ways, for the earlier glazes, at least those produced in the Zuni area, utilized lead ores from the Cerrillos hills, while later ones seem to have preferred other such ores from the Magdalena region. The glazes had a long-term popularity, continuing for centuries, well into the historic period. They seem to have had ritual functions, though most likely utilitarian ones as well. The earliest of these made their way to the Rio Grande around AD 1300 and eventually spread over much of the Keresan, southern Tiwa, Towa-Pecos, Galisteo Tewa, and Piro-Tompiro areas. With glazed pottery came emphasis on the *olla* (rounded bowl with restricted neck), a form likely utilized to store water, dry foodstuffs, or other materials. Glaze wares may have been used both as trade goods and as the carriers of such goods (see Figure 7.13).[61]

FIGURE 7.13. Espinoza Glaze Polychrome, University of New Mexico excavations at Puaray, ca. 1450–1550. Maxwell Museum of Anthropology, University of New Mexico, cat. no. 36.12.55.

Other influences from the west spread eastward. The practice of cremation, which had its main western center in the Zuni area, had almost certainly spread from the south. Hawikuh and Kechipawan, in the western Zuni region, were centers for the new practice, 30 to 35 percent of burials there being cremation, the remainder mainly extended inhumations. Whether a new religious cult was implicated is unknown, but the practice was common enough to make it appear that native Zunians, not traders or other outsiders, were involved. Cremation was initiated in the upper Southwest relatively late in the Aztlan period, probably the mid-fifteenth century at Zuni. It spread eastward along the trade routes, appearing at some point at the entrepôt of Pottery Mound, on the Puerco. The dating is unclear, but it was fifteenth century, probably the latter part of the century. At about the same time, cremation burials appear at Pueblo Pardo, in the Salinas, and at the important site of Gran Quivira (Humanas). A scatter of Zuni glazes is also found in the Salinas area, and at least by the beginning of historic times a trail from Zuni, more or less following the line of modern U.S.

Highway 60, reached from Zuni to these Tompiro sites. I have elsewhere suggested that possibly a trading colony from the Zuni area was settled in the Pueblo Pardo–Gran Quivira region.[62]

Another intrusion from the south is that of Gila Polychrome and other Roosevelt redware types, very widespread particularly in the western portion of the Southwest from Chihuahua and Sonora to Arizona and New Mexico in the period 1300 to 1450. It extends through much of Western Pueblo but not to the upper Rio Grande. There is some indication of a relationship between the ware and cremation burials: at least at Kechipawan and Hawikuh a number of such burials are found in association with Gila Polychrome.[63]

But even though Western Pueblo was a vibrant part of the Anasazi Southwest and one that made considerable technological, artistic, and probably religious and ceremonial contributions to the wider region, the focus of population and culture after AD 1300 was the upper Rio Grande Basin. In early Spanish times roughly 80 percent of the Pueblo population lived in the Rio Grande drainage. Such population aggregates necessitated fairly advanced agricultural systems, though the same southwestern trio of plants—maize, beans, and squash—continued to dominate. There were irrigation ditches and check dams at Chaco Canyon and, during Aztlan times, in the upper Rio Grande Valley. As I pointed out in chapter 5, excavations in the Zuni area have revealed irrigation channels that may date back to the beginning of AD times or even earlier. In the Aztlan period certain areas, especially in the Chama-Jemez region, developed quite sophisticated grids of mulched garden plots, situated to optimize collection of ambient water and sunlight.[64]

Although the Rio Grande region suffered to some degree the same population decline over time as did the west (see below), the area started from a higher base and maintained a considerable vigor until the disasters of the Spanish entradas. Paul F. Reed has calculated that from AD 1325 to 1540 there were 70 sites in the northern Rio Grande *alone* that had more than 400 rooms (some as many as 2,000 or more). Reed's survey stretches from the Chama River to the vicinity of present-day Albuquerque. Expanding the region to extend from Taos on the north to the Piro-Tompiro region to the south and east, important sites include Yungue, Sapawe, Ponsu, and Posi, in the Chama Valley; Tshirege, Puyé, Tyuonyi, Tsankawi, and Otowi, in the Pajarito region; several towns in the Taos region; Picurís, in the mountains south of Taos; several pueblos in the Santa Fe area; Patokwa, Tovakwa, Wabakwa, and Guisewa, in the Jemez country; Zia and the other large eastern Keresan towns; Tonque, Puaray, and Kuaua, in the Tiguex area north of Albuquerque; Mann-Zuris, near Albuquerque; Pottery Mound, on the Puerco; San Marcos, San Lázaro, San Cristóbal, Galisteo, and Shé, in the Galisteo Basin; Arroyo Hondo and Pindi, near Santa Fe; Pecos and the other settlements in the upper Pecos drainage; a number of towns downstream in the Piro region; and the cluster of Tompiro pueblos along or near the salines east of the Manzano mountains.[65]

Of course, not all these towns were occupied at the same time; nevertheless, the area continued to be heavily populated until the beginning of the Spanish entradas, with the major collapse in town numbers occurring in the late sixteenth and seventeenth centuries. The chronicler with the Coronado expedition, Castañeda, lists 54 pueblos, not counting Zuni, Hopi, and Acoma, as does Pedrosa with the Chamuscado party 40 years later.[66]

As in the western areas, there was a series of alliances grouped, to some degree at least, along linguistic lines. As late as the Pueblo Revolt, 140 years after Coronado, these linguistic alliances among groups in contiguous territories were still very much in place. It is clear that the southern Tiwa, Coronado's bellicose Tiguex province, formed a unit. The Jemez Towa-speaking towns seemed to have formed another, as did two separate groups of Tewa,

those of the Chama area and those of the Galisteo Basin. Taos, with whatever satellite towns, was another such entity, as was Pecos. The situation with the Keres is not so clear. In the eyes of the Coronado party the large town of Zia exercised some sort of Keresan leadership, but we have no idea how much Keresan unity there actually was. In the late-seventeenth-century De Vargas reconquest period we find three Keresan towns—Zia, San Felipe, and Santa Ana—acting in concert, but special circumstances may have been involved in that situation.[67]

How far back into the prehistoric period these nascent Pueblo federations can be projected is uncertain, but I think it highly probable that nuclear groups around which alliances formed, and which were first and foremost linguistic in nature, go back to the early AD 1300s, if not before. Their political organization is not known, but likely there was an elite leadership, anchored in the moieties and in the powerful societies, hunt, clown, and especially war and kachina societies. It seems likely that it was through this leadership that the kachina and other sodalities channeled religious ceremonies. It was a congeries of individuals, and probably related families, that also directed relationships with other groups, including trade and warfare, and to one degree or another controlled the instruments of economic land, irrigation and other water resources, and hunting and gathering territories. Just how this was done is not known today.

However, as in the Western Pueblos, the Eastern Pueblos suffered decline. Demographic projections for 1300 to 1600 show a steady reduction from a peak population around AD 1300 in the northern Rio Grande area and a sharper drop in the Little Colorado. Something was going on in Aztlan, especially in the fifteenth and early sixteenth centuries, that caused a general downhill movement of society. Among Eastern Pueblos, as in the west, there was depopulation in some areas. To use only one example, the large and important pueblo on the Puerco River west of modern Albuquerque, whose native name is unknown but is now called Pottery Mound, became a ruin sometime in the late fifteenth century (Figure 7.14).

To some degree it may have been the parts affecting the whole; the collapse of the Salado, mountain Mogollon, and Jornada areas, and especially the Casas Grandes world must have produced shock waves in other parts of the Greater Southwest. The reasons are not clear, although some specialists see the Little Ice Age as an important factor. The continuing pressure of nomadic newcomers, Apachean and Ute, may also have been involved, although a major hunting-gathering group, the Navajo, was on its way to becoming agricultural and "Puebloized."[68]

One thing that should be taken into account is that from the beginnings of Pueblo times the life expectancy of even the largest towns was somewhat limited. There are a number of reasons for this: climate, water availability, shifting patterns of intergroup rivalry. But perhaps the overriding factor was the necessity to seek wood for heating, cooking, pottery making, and building construction. Pueblo peoples traditionally tended to strip away the tree and bush cover near their towns, and as generations went by, the barren areas stretched out ever farther from the town centers. In only a few generations, with only human haulage available, this became a problem.[69] One solution—in many cases perhaps the only solution—was to shift the pueblo itself to a more wooded region. Desertion of pueblos does not *in itself* mean a drop in population.

We should also remember that the breakdown was selective. Western Pueblo survived, albeit in a somewhat reduced state. The Sonoran area actually seemed to have thrived, for with the collapse of Casas Grandes it took over much of the trade between Mesoamerica and the Southwest. It was a very active trade and at its greatest reach in the fifteenth and sixteenth centuries extended (likely through a variety of middlemen) from the Gulf of Cortez to the lower Red River and Arkansas valleys, in what is now the west-central part of the United States. The statelets were also involved

FIGURE 7.14. Pottery Mound, with the Puerco River in the distance (mid-1980s). Photo by the author.

in another tentacle of the trade routes that reached from the California coast and the lower Colorado region southward into Mexico and eastward to the Pueblo settlements. It was the pattern of far-flung trade that first led the Spaniards into the Southwest in the 1530s and 1540s, for they followed the trails and were guided by knowledgeable natives from various parts of the region. Placement of the trails to a large degree dictated the actual areas explored in those first decades of Spanish conquest. It led the Spaniards up the west coast of Mexico, reaching the Southwest by this roundabout route. Later, when Spanish towns had been established in the north interior of New Spain, native trails that largely followed the rivers were utilized to take the exploring parties from central Chihuahua into the upper Southwest. It took two or three generations to establish the major shortcuts such as the Camino Real, which stretched in a taut north-south line from Chihuahua to the El Paso area and then up the Rio Grande.

The most awesome, yet most underestimated, indications of the close connections of Mesoamerica and the Southwest and of the various segments within the Southwest are these trails and the goods they carried (see Figure 7.15). Because of them, individuals from Sonora knew about and had visited the Pueblos. Hopi and Zuni Indians reached the lower Colorado River and perhaps even the California coast. Eastern Pueblo parties visited the Western Pueblos and went eastward into the plains, while Plains Indians traveled to the Pueblos. Native Americans in eastern Oklahoma and eastern Texas could enjoy the luxury of turquoise from New Mexico mines and, more dramatically, the seashell that came from the Sonora coast a thousand miles away. The Sonorans, and people even farther south along the Mexican coast, as well as those in the lower Colorado Basin, received hide products, turquoise and other semiprecious stones, and pottery. Although not documented archaeologically, bison hides were noted in Sonora in very early historic times. These were most likely traded as worked hides because of the

weight of unprocessed skins. The provenience of west coast turquoise has not been firmly established. As considered in more detail below, the turquoise found in fourteenth-century sites in Sinaloa may well have come from the Cerrillos mines (or at least from somewhere in the Southwest) since we know from historical accounts that turquoise was flowing down the west coast trails. Descriptions of the donor groups suggest quite clearly that the turquoise, as well as the "emeralds" (uvarovite garnets?), found in Sonora by Cabeza de Vaca came from the Pueblo area. The coral found in that area was traded from somewhere on the coast, according to the Spanish sources.[70]

Fifteenth-century Puebloan glaze pottery has been found in Jalisco, and what is very likely southwestern pottery is described by Marcos in Sonora. In fact southwestern ceramics also reached into southern California, likely transshipped from the lower Colorado River region. Included was pottery both from the Hohokam area and from the upper Southwest, with dates ranging from around 900 to 1150 (Sacaton Red-on-buff) to the early historic period (the Hopi polychromes). A great deal of shell came from the lower Colorado River, some brought in from the California coast and sent on into the Southwest.[71] The earliest Spaniards discovered deerskins that were said to have come from the Western Pueblo region. They also saw shields of what were likely bison hide from even farther east. Since trade from the Eastern to the Western Pueblos was documented from earliest Spanish times and certainly had been going on for centuries, these shields may have come from the very eastern edge of the Pueblo world. The earliest Spanish accounts indicate that the lower Colorado River Indians knew about turquoise and valued it, though as far as I know, no turquoise has been found in Colorado River archaeological sites. Given the ubiquity of the shell and coral trade (the latter commodity much desired at Zuni), it seems very likely that turquoise, easily available in the upper Southwest, was part of the trade network. Certainly, communication between the upper Southwest and the Lower

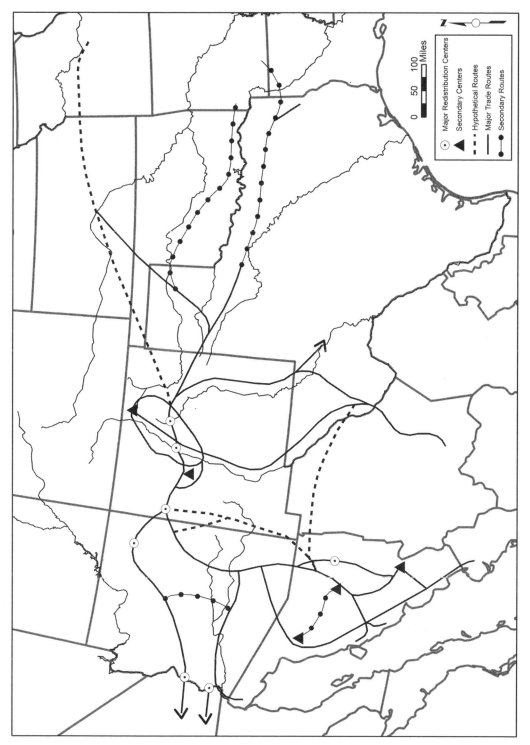

FIGURE 7.15. Trade routes in late Aztlan times. Earth Analytic, Santa Fe, NM.

Colorado was rapid, for Alarcón on the Colorado in 1540 heard about Coronado in Cibola-Zuni within weeks after the latter man's arrival.[72] Likewise, steatite or soapstone greatly interested the Spaniards, who heard descriptions of the stone from lower Colorado natives. They thought it might be silver and more or less documented its source as Catalina Island, off the southern California coast. It was probably traded into the Southwest, but we have no documentation for this. There are steatite implements at Pecos, and Kidder also reported a bivalve carved from "gray soapstone" at that pueblo, though the provenience is unknown.[73] Nor were the lower Colorado trade goods entirely from the Pueblo area and the California coast. The lower Colorado people also possessed "parrot feathers," which were probably from the Sonoran region since that region had an active trade in both exotic birds and their feathers.[74]

Apropos of turquoise, Sydney H. Ball, writing for the Bureau of American Ethnology in 1941, made the claim that Aztec and Toltec turquoise from central Mexico and also a turquoise mosaic plaque found at Chichen Itza, in Maya country of Yucatan, came from the New Mexico mines. Unfortunately, Ball offers no evidence for these assumptions.[75] The doyen of turquoise studies, Joseph E. Pogue, also believed that Aztecs received at least a part of their turquoise from the New Mexico Cerrillos mines.[76] Again, this seems to be merely speculation, but more recent neutron activation (NAA) studies done by specialists at Brookhaven National Laboratory do indicate that turquoise from the Cerrillos mines has been identified from Chichen Itza.[77] These Brookhaven researchers sourced turquoise from various Mexican archaeological sites. These include studies from the Chalchihuites culture, a Classic to Postclassic Mesoamerican outpost in the north Mexican states of Durango and Zacatecas. These researchers believe that turquoise from two nearby Chalchihuites sites, Cerro de Moctezuma and El Vesuvio in Zacatecas, came from the Cerrillos area and from the Azure mine, near Tyrone, in southwestern

New Mexico. Dating on this Chalchihuites turquoise is not secure, but it may belong to the pre-Aztlan period in the Southwest.[78] At El Ombligo, near Guasave, in northern Sinaloa, a considerable amount of turquoise was found dating to the Guasave phase of the Guasave culture, ca. AD 1200–1400+. This Guasave culture has a very Mesoamerican flavor, especially in pottery design. Studies by the Brookhaven group suggest that some of this turquoise came from specific mines within the Cerrillos area.[79] I should stress again, however, that not all specialists accept turquoise sourcing because of the variability even within local source areas. Still, with the historical data indicating turquoise trade along the west-coast trade routes such a source for Sinaloa turquoise would hardly be surprising.

One article of trade that was avidly desired by the entire Aztlan area, and had been traded for many centuries, was shell, which began trading very early and extended into historic times. The shell was not only greatly desired for ceremonial use and for personal decoration, but a great deal of it was traded eastward into the plains. Donald D. Brand has documented the trade in terms of numbers of species traded, and it is indeed formidable. Thirty-eight species of shell from the Gulf of California have been found in southwestern sites, nine species from the Pacific coast, and an additional ten species that are common to both seashores. Shells came also from Atlantic waters, some nine species, primarily from the Gulf of Mexico.[80]

Other very important trade items were exotic birds—macaws, parrots, and their feathers, a trade that dates at least from the Chacoan period and continued on into historic times. It seems fairly clear that the Casas Grandes area was the supplier from the beginning of the Mesoamericanized Medio period, about AD 1200, the town of Paquimé actually breeding the scarlet macaw (see chapter 8). Before the Medio period, as discussed earlier in this book, it does seem that macaws may have traveled through the Casas Grandes region, on to the Mimbres, Chaco, and the Sinagua sites, although to what extent the Viejo period Casas

Grandes people were directly involved is unknown. In any case highly colored feathers were in great demand throughout the Aztlan period, as, indeed, they are among the historic and modern Pueblos.[81]

The trade from the Pueblo world eastward was also extensive. Here the easternmost towns, Pecos, Picurís, Taos, and the Salinas pueblos, especially Humanas (the modern Gran Quivira), were prominent. It has been suggested that the Salinas group of pueblos traded extensively for meat from plains neighbors. The reasoning for this is indirect. Aztlan period Pueblo Indians were avid consumers of domestic turkeys except for the Salinas area, suggesting that the latter had ample meat supplies from elsewhere.[82]

Pecos Pueblo was probably the most active in the trade with the plains, but this may simply seem to be the case because of the extensive excavation of that pueblo. We know of trade westward from Pecos because the Coronado party met a trading party at Zuni with "dressed skins, shields, and headpieces." I have elsewhere suggested that the latter probably were of bison hair and/or skin. Pecos traded for an enormous amount of shell (Figure 7.16). There is *Olivella, Glycymeris, Turritella*, and *Conus* from the Gulf of California; *Haliotis* (abalone) from the Pacific coast; and *Alectrion, Oliva*, and *Strombus* from the Gulf of Mexico. Some 1,000 pieces of wastage indicate that shell was being worked at Pecos. The single largest deposit of shell was *Olivella dama,* around 2,000 pieces, and here Pecos seems to have been a distribution point since *Olivella* shell has been found as far east as the big bend of the Red River, around modern Texarkana, and in the Canadian and Arkansas drainages.[83] A large number of *Olivella* shells (around 15,000, primarily from one burial) found at the Spiro site in extreme eastern Oklahoma were originally identified as the *Olivella nivea* from Atlantic waters. These have recently been reclassified as *Olivella dama,* very common in the Southwest, which originate around the Gulf of California.[84]

Turquoise is also found in the Arkansas River area as far as the Spiro site in extreme eastern Oklahoma, on the Red River, and on the Trinity River of eastern Texas. In fact turquoise appears even farther east, in central Missouri, in northern Mississippi, and in the Great Lakes region. It cannot be certain that this was actually southwestern turquoise, though associated Alibates flint and (perhaps) Puebloan pottery in the Missouri find makes it likely at least for that area. Puebloan pottery, glazes, Hopi yellow ware, and Chupadero Black-on-white are also found in the southern plains, as well as a considerable amount of Pueblo-style but locally made plain wares. There were also piñon nuts, agate, petrified wood, and obsidian, some of the latter from the Jemez Mountains. The great bend of the Arkansas River in present-day Kansas has a cluster of sites dating to late prehistoric and extremely early historic times that are very rich in southwestern materials.[85] They include turquoise, *Olivella,* and glazed ware, some of it from the Tonque area, from the Pajarito Plateau, and perhaps from Zia. Also found is Chupadero Black-on-white, as well as Biscuit B pottery (the latter likely from the Tewa region; see Figure 7.17), jasper, obsidian, and quartzite, steatite arrow-straighteners similar to those of Pecos, also an incised pottery pipe of the Pecos type. The Rio Grande glazes could have come from Pecos, and the beautifully banded Alibates flint, from the quarries north of Amarillo, also suggests Pecos, since that pueblo was importing Alibates. However Taos and Picurís may also have been involved, perhaps even the Salinas pueblos. In addition, the pueblo of Tonque was probably a major supplier of pottery for Pecos Pueblo. Tonque (the name is also spelled Tunque) was Tiwa or perhaps Keresan speaking and was located near the northern end of the Sandias.[86]

Cotton cloth was also popular, being found as far east as the Trinity River. In the latter part of the sixteenth century the Spaniards noted that such cloth was widely traded to Plains Indians, along with maize and turquoise, for bison and deerskins. Osage orange wood, or bois d'arc, for making of bows came from eastern Texas, while the freshwater shell *Lampsilis*

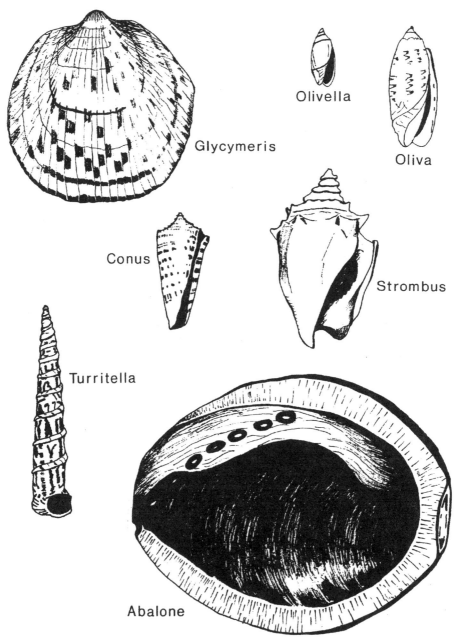

Figure 7.16. Shells traded into the Southwest (after Riley, *Rio del Norte*).

*purpura,* also from eastern Texas, was a desirable item at Pecos; at least a fair amount, including wastage, has been found.[87]

Shell coming into the Great Plains, whether from Pecos or other Puebloan sites, was transshipped from far to the south and west. The importance of shell was such that an argument can be made that shell necklaces, or *hishi,* were a form of exchange with fixed value throughout the Pueblo world.[88] The turquoise that flowed into the Great Plains almost certainly came from the Cerrillos mines, the pottery from various Rio Grande sites and the obsidian mainly from the Jemez Mountains. Cotton and cotton cloth in all probability came from the Hopi country.

FIGURE 7.17. Prayer meal bowl, Bandelier Black-on-white (Biscuit B), University of New Mexico excavations at Sapawe, ca 1525–1550. Maxwell Museum of Anthropology, University of New Mexico, cat. no. 69.36.10.

Some of the Rio Grande area could support the growth of cotton, and cotton fields in the Piro and Tiwa country are mentioned by Gallegos in the Chamuscado party. However, Hopi seemed to have been the main cotton-growing center. Hopi cotton, grown from a desert-adapted variety of the plant *Gossypium hirsutum*, was introduced perhaps from the Gila-Salt area, where it had diffused from western Mexico. It seems likely that cotton cloth and other cotton products were originally traded into the northern Southwest from farther south. The actual plant and the skills necessary to grow it may have reached the northern portion of the Southwest by around AD 1100, the plant by this time having been adapted to the colder northern climate. The distribution of prehistoric cotton was largely in the western part of the old Anasazi region. However, woven cotton cloth, including kilts, mantas, wall hangings, and blankets, can be identified from the kiva murals and from rock art both east and west. The kilt, as a dress form, seems to have reached the Pueblo area around the beginning of Aztlan times.[89]

Some scholars believe that the classic Anasazi upright loom, later borrowed by the Navajo, appeared quite early. Kate Peck Kent suggests that it might actually have been an Anasazi invention, made by adding heddle and shed rods (introduced from the south?) to an earlier Basketmaker frame used for twining. By the beginning of the Aztlan period cotton was being produced at Homol'ovi along the Little Colorado, among other sites, and traded at least within the Western Pueblo area.[90]

The fifteenth century saw a major shift in production to the Hopi Mesas. The Hopi were in a good position to obtain various dyestuffs and minerals, including those from the Verde River area, and decorated cotton mantas became somewhat of a Hopi specialty. The Spaniards were especially impressed by the amount of Hopi cotton goods. According to Espejo in 1583, "The natives gathered together from various parts of the province more than four thousand cotton blankets, colored or white, hand towels with tassels at the ends, and many other things including some of the blue and green ores sought by them for coloring their blankets."[91]

This may seem an exaggeration, but another member of the party estimated some 2,800 pieces of cotton, in addition to considerable spun and raw cotton.[92] It seems unlikely that the Hopi felt any need to propitiate the tiny Spanish party, so these were probably surplus trade goods, routinely given the Spaniards either in trade or as courtesy gifts. In any case cotton was widely desired across the Southwest, and Hopi seemed to have thrived on the demand. Farther south, the Sonoran area was also cotton rich and likely had its own trade in cotton.

Another important commodity of which the upper Southwest had ample supplies was salt. Because of its perishable nature, salt as a trade commodity is difficult to document, though it has been suggested that the wide distribution of Chupadero Black-on-white pottery may be related to the trade. Certainly there were very desirable salt deposits in the Salinas area, where salt collecting and trading continued up into modern times. Zuni Salt Lake, south of the present-day town, was also an area with very pure salt, which was used historically as well as in prehistoric times.

One curious anomaly in the contact picture is the relative lack of contact between the Casas Grandes world and that of the Rio Grande Pueblos. There certainly was a considerable amount of contact up and down the Rio Grande. This was one of the areas from which the kachina cult reached the upper Southwest, and in Aztlan times Rio Grande glazes spread southward at least to the southern edges of the Piro area. However, contacts between the upper Rio Grande people and Paquimé are very uncertain. There was most likely some trade in scarlet macaws. These are found in various Rio Grande sites and the birds themselves (or their feathers) may well have come from the breeding pens at Paquimé. But there was relatively little else, for the contacts of Casas Grandes seem to have been primarily westward, into the Salado and mountain Mogollon regions and on to Western Pueblo. A particular kind of *Glycymeris* shell pendant, which likely was manufactured at Casas Grandes, is found in these various western regions. It appears at Pecos and at Tijeras (a site just east of Albuquerque) but could easily have been retraded eastward from Western Pueblo middlemen.[93] The great mass of shell that poured into the Eastern Pueblos seems rather to relate to the Sonoran statelets and to the Lower Colorado and California coastal areas.

Very few of the Chihuahuan polychromes appear in the upper Rio Grande and nearby areas. More surprising, perhaps, there is little evidence for the Chihuahua polychromes in Western Pueblo. In the eastern San Juan drainage, in a thirteenth-century context in Mesa Verde, there were two sherd fragments of what is perhaps Ramos Polychrome. Frank C. Hibben reported five sherds of Ramos Polychrome at Pottery Mound on the Puerco River, and two of the horned-serpent masks in the murals there are very similar to horned-serpent heads depicted on Ramos Polychrome vessels at Paquimé (Figure 7.18). There is a certain amount of Chihuahuan pottery in the upper part of the Rio Abajo, for example Playas Red

FIGURE 7.18. Horned serpent similar to those on Ramos Polychrome vessels. Pottery Mound mural. Photographed during excavation of site but otherwise not attributed.

and three sherds of Ramos Polychrome at the Pinnacle site, southwest of Socorro, New Mexico. Pinnacle and other sites in the general area are interesting in that they have strong Mesa Verde affiliations.[94] In addition, a relationship has been suggested between the late Tewa province pottery, Potsuwi'i Incised, a hard thin-ware gray to gray-brown pottery, with incised decorations, that dates from mid-1400s to late 1500s, and the Casas Grandes pottery, Playas Red incised, dating somewhat earlier.[95]

Charles Di Peso also believed that Paquimé was a center for the manufacture and distribution of copper bells (mainly in the form of crotals or tinklers) that are found in the upper Southwest. Recent work by Victoria D. Vargas, however, strongly suggests that the Casas Grandes area was not a manufacturing center for these bells and that both Paquimé and the northern Southwest received their bells from western Mexico. In this case copper wares probably moved through northeastern Sonora to the Western Pueblos. A few reached the Rio Grande area, but that region was really not much involved in the copper trade.[96]

In fact, much of the exotic material that flowed into the northeastern Southwest may actually date from a time when Paquimé was in decline or deserted. At that time the Sonoran area became the great middleman area for trade for shell and brightly plumaged birds. I suggest that in the general trade picture with the upper Southwest we are actually looking at two periods. In the earlier phase, fourteenth century primarily, there was considerable interchange among Casas Grandes, including its Jornada hinterland, the Salado-Late Hohokam region, and Western Pueblo. Chihuahuan polychromes are occasionally found in the Gila Valley and in southeastern Arizona generally—though not in Western Pueblo. As we will see in chapter 8, pottery either imported or copied from these areas appears in the Casas Grandes region, especially at Paquimé. Some of the horned-serpent motifs in Western Pueblo have Casas Grandes features—for example, the forward-curving horn (Figure 7.19)—but also have elaborations not found at Paquimé. The

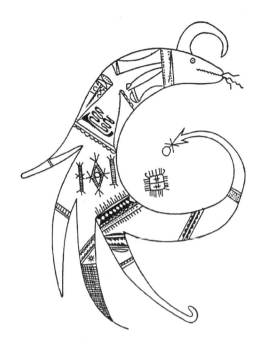

FIGURE 7.19. Elaborate horned and plumed serpent, Walpi, Hopi. Note the Paquimé-like forward-curved horn (after Fewkes, "Designs").

Rio Grande region was only peripherally involved. There were, of course, vigorous contacts up and down the Rio Grande between the Pueblos and the Jornada Mogollon as indicated by the rock art; indeed, there was the spread of the kachina cult itself.

In the latter part of the period, essentially the fifteenth century, trade from the Casas Grandes region dwindled and largely stopped because of the collapse of Paquimé, its place being taken by the thriving middlemen in the Sonoran statelets and peoples in the lower Colorado drainage. Here the Rio Grande region became the primary recipient, the Western Pueblos now having shrunk to enclaves at Hopi, Zuni, and Acoma. Contacts from the Rio Grande Pueblos eastward into the plains, already building in the previous century, now became very important. During this period the variety of trade goods discussed above spread east and west, north and south. Surely other things, religious and political formulations, perhaps even bits of language (trade jargons, for example), saturated the whole region. I believe that it was during this period that non-Pueblo groups such as the Navajo began to collect their Mesoamerican religious and ceremonial flavor, a secondhand transmission from the Pueblos themselves. This of course brings up the vexed question of just when and where the Navajo (or proto-Navajo) first encountered the Pueblos. It is my belief that the Querechos contacted by Espejo's party in the Hopi area and also near Acoma in the early 1580s were Navajo, but there is no consensus on this point, nor, indeed, where the proto-Navajo were living in the fifteenth and early sixteenth centuries.[97] If it was along the eastern edge of the Pueblo area, their contacts would have been with one or the other of the Eastern Pueblos.

In spite of the many problems that confront the student of the upper Southwest in the Aztlan period, there are important things that can be said. That there was active trade extending from both western and southeastern Mexico and the Pacific coast of California to the central and eastern plains is proven by the wealth of trade materials to be found in archaeological sites. It is also obvious that the Pueblos were not only recipients but also middlemen in much of this trade. That Mexican deities and ceremonials, such as those involved in the kachina cult, spread throughout the Southwest also seems beyond dispute. Mesoamerican influence on the sociopolitical life of southwesterners is less certain, though it seems feasible that Mesoamerican ideas about the validation of political and religious power made their way into the Greater Southwest.

Aside from Mexican influences, there was clearly a great deal of interaction among southwesterners, exchanging cultic ideas, ceramic styles, trade goods, and the like. It seems reasonably clear that the Native Americans of the upper Southwest in Aztlan times, although frontier people, were not isolated in some stagnant cultural backwater. They lived in a vibrant, rather dangerous, and exciting world in which small confederacies fought but also traded and exchanged social and religious ideas. Natives of the upper Southwest knew about alien peoples and themselves sometimes traveled and visited over distances of hundreds of miles. Some probably had seen major bodies of salt water—the Pacific Ocean and the Atlantic shores of the Gulf of Mexico. There may even have been visits to the large urban centers of western Mexico. Even if they never visited these places, the Aztlan people certainly heard stories of them from trading partners. In short, these southwesterners were citizens of a larger world. From the stories and legends of their historic descendants, we can be sure that they felt some kinship—some affinity, nebulous though it might have been—to that greater world beyond their frontiers.

# CHAPTER 8

# The Casas Grandes World

In previous chapters I have discussed various aspects of the site of Paquimé and its hinterland, the region of Casas Grandes. Paquimé represented the most overt Mesoamericanization in all of Aztlan. Here were not only indications of Mesoamerican religion but also of Mesoamerican social and political systems, attenuated, to be sure, but in place and operating. The area shows a sophistication in building greater than that of its contemporaries in the Greater Southwest. There were actual Mesoamerican structures, including I-shaped ball courts (two at Paquimé itself and two more in outliers), several of the "semi-I" or T-shaped variety, and a number of simpler courts in the general area.[1] There were mounds faced with masonry, including one in the form of a cross, perhaps an astronomical observatory. The living areas were mostly of adobe, a complex tangle of houses, courtyards, and alleyways. Some of the structures were large, elite quarters or public buildings, spacious and built with high ceilings, colonnaded galleries, and atrium rooms. The city had a rather elaborate water system or acequia, brought into the living areas from springs to the northwest of Paquimé. There was also a rudimentary sewer system, including town drains that channeled water from the plazas to a series of cisterns. The site of Paquimé at its heyday covered around 88 acres, and the population was several thousand.[2]

The first written account of Paquimé dates to the mid-1560s and describes a visit to the town by Francisco de Ibarra, the governor of the newly formed province of Nueva Vizcaya. At that time the site had been deserted for a century or more. But even in ruins it was impressive. *Paquimé* was the name given by local nomadic Indians, though whether they were referring to the site, the surrounding area, or both is not clear. According to the chronicler Baltasar de Obregón the ruins were those of a large city containing buildings that might have been constructed by the ancient Romans:

The city is located in some fertile and beautiful plains near handsome and useful mountains and small mountain ridges.... There are many houses of great size, strength and height. They are of six and seven stories, with towers and walls like fortresses for protection and defense against the enemies who undoubtedly made war on its inhabitants. [Paquimé] contains large and beautiful patios paved with large, beautiful slabs resembling jasper. There were knifelike stones that supported the great elegant pillars of heavy timbers brought from afar. The walls of the houses were whitewashed and painted with pictures in many shades and colors. They were constructed of adobes, although mixed and interspersed with stone and wood, this combination being stronger and more durable than wood alone.

There were wide and spacious canals, running from the river to the town, which they used to carry water to their houses. They have large, broad warming rooms [*estufas*] under their houses and buildings to protect themselves from the cold weather.

Metal slag [?] which the natives probably utilized, and stones to grind it were found. It was likely copper because we found two copper plates among the [nearby] savage Indians.[3]

The origin of the word *Paquimé* is no longer known.[4] The syllables, *pa, qui,* and *me* all occur in the Opata language, and Charles C. Di Peso, whose extensive excavations at Paquimé are discussed below, reports a personal communication from the linguist Morris Swadesh that *Paquimé* could mean big (pa), house (ki), plural (me), in other words, "Big Houses." There is also a possibility that the name relates to a Tarahumar word, *Pakime,* meaning roughly "place where I am going to enter." There are other possibilities, one of which is rather suggestive: the city name *Amaqueme,* which was known to the Aztecs as the capital of the Chichimecs in the far northwest of Mexico.[5] Of course, simply because the nomadic Indians of Ibarra's time contributed the name, this does not guarantee that it was used by the Casas Grandes people. The natives contacted by Ibarra were probably Suma; at least Suma Indians were in residence in the seventeenth century.[6] Scholars, however, have been disinclined to relate the Suma to the Casas Grandes people, the general idea being that they were relative latecomers to the Casas Grandes Valley. These nomadic people, using signs, told Ibarra that the people who built Paquimé retreated northward, driven out by enemies who "venían desotra parte de las sierras,"[7] presumably from the Opata-controlled west. Obregón's report is of a sufficient antiquity to bring us within a few generations of people who *did* know and use the correct name for their city and homeland. What language, or perhaps languages, were spoken in Paquimé and its hinterland is not known, though Opata is certainly a candidate.

Although Paquimé had been deserted for a century or more when the Ibarra party arrived, enough of the site remained intact to make quite an impression. Although the Spaniards settled the Casas Grandes Valley in the seventeenth century, there is very little further mention of Paquimé. It was a recognized ancient site, however, because Adolph Bandelier in the spring of 1884 made it a major goal on his archaeological trip through northeastern Sonora and northwestern Chihuahua. In fact the Swiss scholar spent several weeks exploring the Casas Grandes area (see Figure 8.1).[8] Bandelier reported a tradition among the Opata that they had been bitter enemies of the Casas Grandes people and that a number of their towns had been destroyed by Casas Grandes warriors.[9]

A few years later, in the 1890s, Carl Lumholtz, on a trip through the Sierra Madre, camped on the ruins of Paquimé and estimated that the site must have contained three or four thousand people.[10] In the next century a number of surveys of the Casas Grandes regional area were made, particularly by the geographer Donald D. Brand and the archaeologist Edwin B. Sayles. Exactly where Casas Grandes fit in general southwestern classification schemes remained a problem. Mexican archaeologists Carmén A. Robles and Eduardo Noguera believed the region to be Puebloan, as did Americans Edwin B. Sayles and Harold S. Gladwin, a position that has recently been reiterated by Stephen H. Lekson. Henry A. Carey, however, in a 1931 publication, saw both southwestern and Mesoamerican elements in the Casas Grande culture.

The major excavation that brought widespread attention to the Casas Grandes world came with the Joint Casas Grandes Project shared by the Amerind Foundation of Dragoon, Arizona, and the Instituto Nacional de Antropología e Historia (INAH) in Mexico. This endeavor, beginning in 1958, was directed by Charles C. Di Peso (Figure 8.2), head of the Amerind Foundation, and Eduardo Contreras, who represented INAH, with a number of associated specialists including John B. Rinaldo

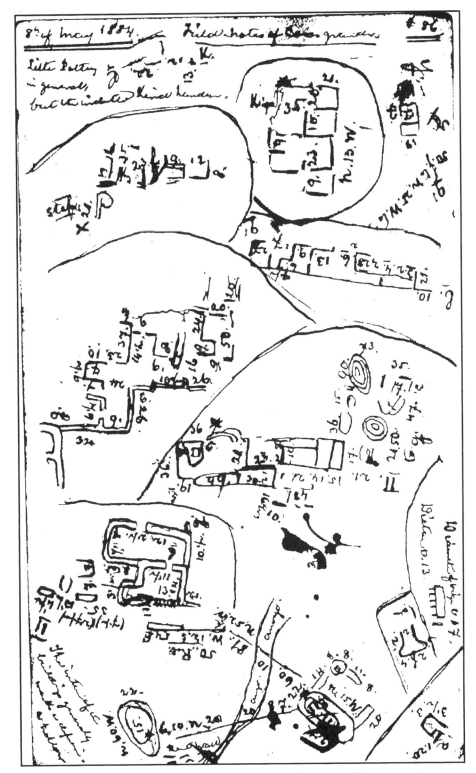

FIGURE 8.1. First of several pages of sketches on Casas Grandes done by A. F. Bandelier in 1884 (after Lange and Riley, *Journals of Adolph F. Bandelier*).

FIGURE 8.2. Charles C. Di Peso examining a macaw pen at Paquimé. Amerind Foundation, Dragoon, AZ.

and Gloria J. Fenner, the latter two individuals coauthoring with Di Peso a part of the resulting massive publication. There was intensive fieldwork at Casas Grandes from 1958 to 1961, then a vast amount of laboratory work and other preparation before final publication of the eight-volume work in 1974. The major concentration was on the site of Paquimé, but three other nearby sites in the Casas Grandes Valley, north of Paquimé, were also investigated.[11]

As a result of this monumental work Di Peso and his associates developed a sweeping vision of the Casas Grandes culture, built around and dependent on developments in the great center of Paquimé. According to Di Peso there were ancestral Mogollon-like settlements that formed the Plainware period. Out of these early settlements grew Di Peso's Viejo period, in which small groups, originally living in pithouses, gradually grew in sophistication, the increasing populations developing jacal structures (a frame of interwoven poles covered with mud),

trade with surrounding areas, and bichrome and the beginnings of polychrome pottery.[12]

This suddenly changed, around AD 1060 in Di Peso's chronology, when new overlords, a merchant-type elite, arrived from the south, bringing in the Medio period and control by the burgeoning city of Paquimé over an expanding hinterland. There was some trade with the southern regions, mainly Durango, Zacatecas, and Jalisco, but contacts were strongest with the Pueblo region to the northwest. There was a certain amount of the White Mountain redwares, including Pinedale, St. Johns, Springerville, and Heshotauthla polychromes; a few sherds of Kwakina and Kechipawan polychromes from the Zuni region; and various Salado wares. Among the latter was Gila Polychrome (Figure 8.3), which made up some 4 percent of the Casas Grandes ceramic inventory, more than 23,000 sherds being found. We are talking primarily about Paquimé here; Gila Polychrome is very rare in other major sites, such as Galeana and Villa Ahumada.[13]

There were traces of ceramics from the upper Rio Grande, fifteen sherds of Galisteo Black-on-white and a considerably greater number from the more southerly part of the Rio Grande drainage, including Lincoln Black-on-red, Chupadero Black-on-white, and Jor-

FIGURE 8.3. Gila Polychrome bowl. El Paso Museum of Archaeology.

nada Polychrome. The main trade ware from the middle Rio Grande Basin however was El Paso Polychrome (more than 17,000 sherds). The general paucity of upper Rio Grande wares paralleled the lack of Casas Grandes pottery in that northern region. In fact, aside from the Gila wares, some of which seem to have been locally made, the only significant amounts of trade wares from a percentage point of view are Mimbres Black-on-white for the Viejo period and El Paso Polychrome for the Medio.[14]

According to Di Peso this Medio period collapsed in a blaze of warfare around AD 1340. The great center of Paquimé was deserted, and the fragmented Casas Grandes population scattered. Challenges to Di Peso's interpretation of his Casas Grandes chronology began almost immediately. It was the Medio period trade wares, especially Gila Polychrome, that created most confusion. I will use the word *trade* here to include both traded wares and local copies from Salado archetypes. The Gila pottery first appeared in the initial Buena Fé phase of the Casas Grandes Medio period, therefore dating in the latter part of the eleventh century in the Di Peso chronology,[15] and made up about 47.3 percent of the ceramic trade inventory at Paquimé itself. As the Salado polychromes in the northern "homeland" are normally considered to have begun in the latter part of the thirteenth century, Di Peso was faced with the problem of Casas Grandes Salado ware *one-and-a-half to two centuries earlier* than in the north. This led Di Peso to suggest a Mexican origin for Salado ceramics and to propose entry of these kinds of pottery into the northern Southwest from Casas Grandes itself.[16]

The chronological problem came about because Di Peso depended on a series of tree-ring dates, all coming from trees whose outer layers had been stripped away when the trees were dressed for use in construction. In the minds of a number of dendrochronological experts Di Peso's interpretation of the cutting dates of these trees, particularly for the Medio period, made his time periods unacceptably early. Eventually, using mathematical formulae to estimate the missing tree rings, a new

chronology was developed that drastically changed the picture at Paquimé, particularly in the interpretation of its relationships with other parts of the Southwest. Di Peso's Medio dates were therefore shifted forward, circa 150 years, with the period beginning sometime around AD 1200 (Figure 8.4).[17] Around the same time, some experts began to question the prehispanic Robles phase that began Di Peso's Tardio period, pointing out that the chronological markers used to support it were untenable. It now seems most probable that the site of Paquimé was deserted not in AD 1340 as Di Peso suggested but perhaps a century later. Not only has the Robles phase of the Tardio period become problematic, but as various writers have recently pointed out, it is difficult to distinguish among the three phases of the Medio period (Buena Fé, Paquimé, and Diablo), especially since the pottery assemblages do not seem to differ greatly from one phase to the other. Further pottery analysis may allow for a firmer phase chronology.[18]

Though less of an immediate issue than the chronology, the merchant-elite takeover of the settlement of Paquimé also had its share of doubters. Di Peso thought of this group as a *puchteca* (more commonly called *pochteca*), naming it after the merchant class that rose to power among the Aztecs. Di Peso used the name *puchteca* as an analog, but even so, it tended to confuse the issue, since contacts between the Casas Grandes world and the Aztecs of central Mexico were minimal at best. Aside from terminology more recent work at Casas Grandes favors explanations of its origins that are more complex and at the same time more indirect than a movement en masse of Mesoamerican power brokers into the Casas Grandes Valley.[19]

Charles C. Di Peso was a longtime friend and colleague of mine, and if the preceding sections seem to show him in a negative light, that certainly is not my intention. As all students of the region recognize, the massive excavation, analysis, and especially the full publication of Di Peso's Casas Grandes material drastically changed our conceptions of the site

| Time | Casas Grandes Area | | Mimbres Area | Jornada Area |
|------|-------------------|---|--------------|--------------|
| 1598 | Sumas, Conchos Tarahumaras, Janos, and Jocomes | | Janos, Jocomes, and Mansos | Sumas, Mansos, Chinarras |
| 1540 | | | | |
| 1500 | | | | |
| 1450 | | | | |
| 1425 | | | | |
| 1400 | MEDIO PERIOD. See note below | M E D I O   P E R I O D | Cliff Phase | El Paso Phase |
| 1350 | | | | |
| 1325 | | | | |
| 1300 | | | | |
| 1250 | | | Black Mountain Phase | |
| 1200 | | | | |
| 1150 | | | | Doña Ana Phase |
| 1100 | Perros Bravos Phase Small Pueblos | V I E J O   P E R I O D | Mimbres Phase | |
| 1050 | | | | |
| 1000 | | | | |
| 950 | Pilon Phase Pithouses | | Late Pithouse Period | Late Mesilla Phase (Pithouse Period) |
| 900 | | | | |
| 800 | Convento Phase Pithouses | | | |
| 750 | | | | |
| 700 | | | | |
| 600 | Plainware Period Pithouses | | Early Pithouse Period | Early Mesilla Phase (Pithouse Period) |
| 500 | | | | |
| 400 | | | | |
| 300 | | | | |
| 200 | | | | |
| 100 | Late Archaic Pre-Ceramic | | Late Archaic Pre-Ceramic | Late Archaic Pre-Ceramic |
| 100+ | | | | |

FIGURE 8.4. Casas Grandes chronology with comparison to Jornada and Mimbres regions (after Schaafsma and Riley, *Casas Grandes World*).

and the area. It brought in a vast amount of new data, and Di Peso presented us with a new model, an elaborate and exciting framework for considering problems of Paquimé and its hinterland. It was a major pioneering effort, and like all such undertakings on the frontiers of knowledge, it had shortcomings. I am certain that Di Peso eventually would have modified much of his own thinking on Casas Grandes matters. His untimely death from cancer, however, removed his insightful presence, and others—by necessity—had to carry on his work.[20]

With the publication of the eight-volume Casas Grandes report, interest in the area increased dramatically, and there were new investigations both in the region around Paquimé and farther afield. In the Río Casas Grandes and adjacent valleys Michael E. Whalen and Paul E. Minnis conducted a series of surveys (and a certain amount of excavation) beginning in the late 1980s, work that continues in the new millennium. Other studies included Jane H. Kelley, Joe D. Stewart, and their associates in the southern portion of the Casas Grandes world; Rafael Cruz Antillón and Timothy D.

Maxwell in the Carmén region, east of Paquimé; and a number of others in the northern and western peripheries of the Casas Grandes region. Recently my colleague Curtis F. Schaafsma and I edited a comprehensive volume on the larger Casas Grandes world, and Whalen and Minnis have published a synthesizing volume on the region. Thanks to the work of the Mexican government, Paquimé itself has been designated a World Heritage Site and is now a considerable tourist attraction. Some aspects of the Casas Grandes culture are becoming clearer; others remain obscure.

There is no great agreement on the size and constitution of Casas Grandes. Whalen and Minnis's survey area, their "heartland," is relatively small, perhaps 500 square miles, and only in the Casas Grandes drainage itself. David Wilcox has suggested a "heartland area" of something over 7,000 square miles. Di Peso himself calculated a region radiating out for about a hundred miles from Paquimé as being dominated by the center, an area of some 32,000 square miles. A somewhat more generous Casas Grandes–influenced area of around 65,000 square miles has been suggested by Curtis Schaafsma and me. This estimation takes into account the Casas Grandes–like cultures of the southern extension of the culture into the upper and middle Santa María, the Babícora and Santa Clara drainages, and eastward expansion into the Rio Carmén. It also suggests a Casas Grandes presence westward in the mountainous region of northeast Sonora and the Jornada Mogollon to the north. The exact nature of this interaction is unknown, but it obviously varied in intensity. Clearly, the nearby outliers in the Casas Grandes Valley had a relationship different from that of the distant Jornada Mogollon area. In the Jornada it was perhaps one of economic exchange and various ideological influences but certainly not of any sort of political control. J. Charles Kelley, who did extensive work in the La Junta area, came to believe that this extreme eastern extension of the Casas Grandes Interaction Sphere was an important supplier of roasted *mezcal* and mesquite beans, as well as bison

products transshipped from the plains (see Figure 8.5). There is, however, little direct evidence for this, except perhaps for the numbers of large mezcal roasting pits in the La Junta region.[21] What all this amounts to is that there is disagreement—even to a greater extent than in other areas of the Greater Southwest—as to what constitutes the Casas Grandes world. The widely varying figures are partly due to the fact that different people measure different things ("inner areas" versus "regional systems," for example).[22]

Even more basic than the question of size is the question of the fundamental *nature* of Casas Grandes. Was Paquimé, as Di Peso thought, the capital and center of some sort of mercantile empire? Or perhaps there were numbers of culturally similar but independent towns, of which Paquimé, with its large size, was simply the first among equals? What was the nature of Casas Grandes–like settlements in the Santa Maria Valley or those in the Carmén Basin, where Casas Grandes and Jornada Mogollon elements were intermixed? How close was the relationship of the Casas Grandes Valley people to those of the Animas and to the Jornada Mogollon? What of Casas Grandes and the Postclassic cultures, Black Mountain and Cliff phases, in the old Mimbres region? And what relationship did Paquimé, with its large amount of Gila and Tonto polychromes, have with Salado? What connections were there to cultures on edges of Mesoamerica to the south and west? The latter question is especially difficult because the chronologies of both the Chalchihuites tradition of interior-northwest Mexico and those of west-coastal Mexico are not sufficiently finely tuned and the interchange of artifacts not sufficiently identifiable to allow for definitive statements either of chronology or of type and intensity of contact.

One thing that seems reasonably clear, both from Di Peso's work and from the archaeology done in later years, is a certain continuity from the early stages of Casas Grandes, the Viejo period of Di Peso, and indeed from his base Plainware period. The latter period, character-

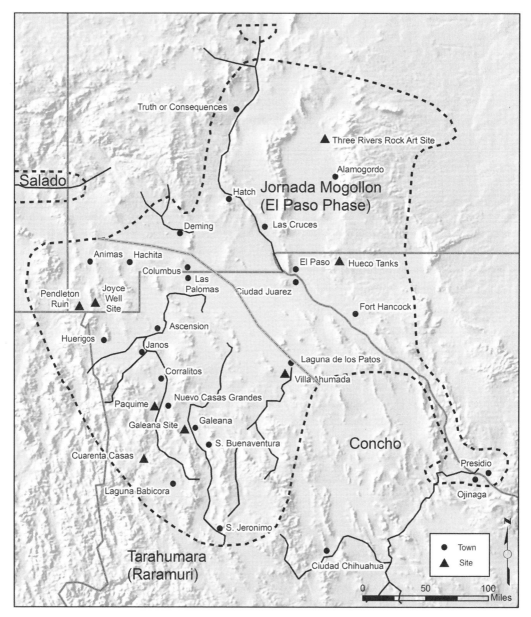

FIGURE 8.5. Casas Grandes Interaction Sphere, Medio period (after Schaafsma and Riley, *Casas Grandes World*). Earth Analytic, Santa Fe, NM.

ized by pithouse dwellings and, at least during the latter part of the period, Mogollon-like brown ware pottery, is very roughly dated from around the beginning of AD times to AD 700. It was superseded by a scatter of sites in the Casas Grandes and tributary valleys of the Viejo period. Di Peso investigated three of these: the Viejo component at Paquimé itself and the Viejo Convento and Los Reyes #2 sites,

about three miles north of Paquimé. Whalen and Minnis identified fifteen additional single component Viejo period sites. Four of these were in Whalen and Minnis's *inner zone* (within ten or fifteen miles south and west of Paquimé and five miles north of the site). An additional eleven were in the Whalen and Minnis *middle zone*, extending northward to the junction of the Río Casas Grandes and the Río San Pedro, westward along the San Pedro to around Janos and Casa de Janos, and southwestward in the region of the Arroyo El Cuervo. These sites were marked with red-on-brown pottery, assigned by Di Peso to the Viejo period. In some sites there were also Classic Mimbres Black-on-white pottery, normally considered to have a terminal date of around AD 1150, presumably before the beginning of Medio times.[23]

In addition to these single-component sites, 55 of the Medio sites in the Whalen-Minnis survey area also contained red-on-brown pottery, and a number of them, especially in the middle zone, had Mimbres Black-on-white ceramics as well. It is, of course, possible that the red-on-brown pottery types, identified as Viejo by Di Peso, actually were made as late as the Medio period. Nevertheless, the balance of evidence (especially given the Mimbres pottery also found) suggests that such sites were ones with both Viejo and Medio components.

Viejo sites were quite small, generally not more than an acre or so. Some were pithouse sites, while others, probably dating from Di Peso's late Viejo Perros Bravos phase, had small clusters of aboveground houses of wattle and daub on adobe foundations. Larger pithouse structures, which Di Peso called "community houses," might be 30 feet or more in diameter. Of Di Peso's three phases of the Viejo period (Convento, Pilón, and Perros Bravos), the latter is the most secure. A different kind of architecture appears: the rectangular houses of jacal or wattle and daub on footings of adobe mentioned above. The circular "community house" remains but is incorporated in a town plan that includes plazas, rectangular "public buildings," and ordinary dwellings.[24] The ceramics include such eleventh- or twelfth-century trade wares as Reserve Black-on-white and Classic period Mimbres Black-on-white. Indigenous pottery includes the various red-on-brown wares. The one polychrome pottery that can be dated to the Viejo period, Mata Polychrome, probably appeared late in the Pilón phase but continued into the Perros Bravos phase. However, as Christine VanPool has pointed out, a Medio period pottery, Dublán Polychrome,

more closely resembles earlier pottery in layout and design and may well have been a Viejo-Medio transitional type.[25]

The extent to which the signature Medio period of Casas Grandes drew from and depended on events of the Viejo period is still very much a question. Charles Di Peso thought that the Medio period was essentially a Mesoamerican construct, an elite group moving into the area from the south and imposing a new order on the scattered indigenes of Viejo times. Michael Whalen and Paul Minnis seem to believe that evolution rather than migration is a major key to understanding the development of the Casas Grandes culture:

> Unfortunately, the Viejo remains poorly defined at this writing, but there is reason to question both the idea of its low population density and the notion that it was replaced by a fundamentally different culture in Medio times.
>
> First, it may well be that the Casas Grandes area was not the sparsely populated cultural backwater that Di Peso envisioned. Instead, it is possible that northwestern Chihuahua was one of the more highly populated and dynamic areas in northern Mexico and the U.S. Southwest.[26]

Whalen and Minnis point to a late (ca. 1000 BC) Archaic site of some 25 acres at the San Pedro–Casas Grandes confluence, about 40 miles north of Paquimé and evidence of possible Archaic occupation in the region around Paquimé, these things suggesting a considerable Archaic population:

> This work raises the distinct possibility that the late Archaic population in the Casas Grandes region may have been larger and more organized than in most of the adjacent territory. Moreover, it is quite possible that the large late Archaic population and the spectacular developments of the Medio period bracket a larger and much more complexly organized Viejo period than we presently have any concept of. If so, then the internal cultural dynamics of northwestern

Chihuahua may well be the context within which the development of Casas Grandes is to be understood.[27]

It is true, as discussed above, that the Perros Bravos phase of the Casas Grandes Viejo period saw a quickening, something that Curtis Schaafsma and I also pointed out a few years ago.[28] Still, the Viejo sites do seem rather small potatoes; none are impressive, and most are tiny indeed.

I am certainly not trying to deny that there were Viejo influences in Medio Casas Grandes or that some of the cultural traditions of that earlier period continued on into Medio times. Nevertheless, the present evidence seems to point to Di Peso's having gotten it right—that something big and dramatic happened in the period we now date to around AD 1200. While it was manifested most dramatically at Paquimé itself, a town of almost 90 acres (see Figure 8.6), there were other fair-sized sites in the near hinterland, the largest several acres in size.[29]

The same is true of sites to the east of Paquimé, the large sites of Galeana in the middle Santa María drainage, about 30 miles southeast of Paquimé, and Villa Ahumada in the Carmén Valley, about 90 miles east northeast of Paquimé. Only a small part of Galeana has been excavated. The site stretches out over a half mile and is similar to Medio period Paquimé in having multiple-storied rooms, plazas,

and T-shaped doors. It does not contain ball courts however.[30] Villa Ahumada, called by Brand "Cerro de Montezuma," was considered by that researcher to be a blend of Mogollon and what he named the Chihuahuan complex, which can generally be identified with Casas Grandes culture. Recent analysis of Villa Ahumada ceramics, however, suggests that the site may have started as a Jornada Mogollon town. In the upper strata there were increasing, though still relatively small, amounts of Chihuahuan pottery, including Villa Ahumada Polychrome. In any case the site seems to date to the Medio period.[31]

About 12 miles west of Paquimé, in the drainage of the Arroyo Tinaja, is the large (200-room) Tinaja site. As of this writing the site is under excavation and has not been fully reported, but it is one of the largest towns in the Paquimé core area, with a large I-shaped ball court and fragments of doors to macaw or parrot cages. An important aspect of this Medio period site is the fact that $^{14}$C dates place the earlier part of the site in the thirteenth century. The earlier occupation was somewhat simpler in nature than the later, fourteenth-century, portions of the site but did have the adobe walls, T-shaped doorways, and adobe stairs that characterize the Casas Grandes culture. In the fourteenth-century portions of the site were other standard Casas Grandes features— alcoves, platform hearths, and what may be bases for columns like those of Paquimé itself.[32]

FIGURE 8.6. Overview of Paquimé. Amerind Foundation, Dragoon, AZ.

This situation seems to be true in the regions south and west of Paquimé. West of Villa Ahumada, in the upper Santa Clara and southwestward to the Santa María drainage and the Babícora region, there is a kind of attenuated Casas Grandes culture, again, it would seem, a mainly Medio occupation, though scattered Viejo sites do appear. The culture in this area lacked such distinctive features as ball courts and sophisticated irrigation systems. There were, however, certain Casas Grandes architectural features, with adobe-walled structures and sometimes T-shaped doorways. As at Paquimé, there was a habit of burial beneath the room floors, and the ceramics are related to those of the Casas Grandes drainage, with Babícora Polychrome the dominant ware, but usually in association with Ramos Polychrome, the latter a signature pottery at Paquimé.[33] Trade pottery is relatively scarce, though in the easternmost portion of the region, the Santa Clara Valley, there is some El Paso and Villa Ahumada Polychrome.[34] One oddity is the find of fragments of what seem to be macaw pen entry stones at three separate sites in the Laguna Bustillos Basin country northwest of the town of Cuauhtemoc. The excavators are skeptical that macaw breeding pens actually were being used in this frontier area, and the meaning of these finds remains a mystery.[35]

In the rugged mountain country southwest of Paquimé, extending to the Chihuahua-Sonora border area, are a number of well-preserved cave sites and houses of coursed-adobe masonry, sometimes reinforced with stone or wood. They are primarily Medio period and contain Paquimé pottery, T-shaped doors, and evidence of considerable agriculture. Most of the caves that feature houses also have globular or ovoid adobe structures, some standing 10 feet high, that are called *graneros* (granaries) and probably did function as grain-storage areas.[36]

Forty to fifty miles north of the Paquimé area in extreme northwestern Chihuahua is the Carretas Basin, where one Casas Grandes–like ball court has been found. The Carretas sites again are primarily Medio period containing various Chihuahua ceramics with an emphasis on Carretas and Huerigos polychromes (Figure 8.7). A bit farther north, north of the present-day Mexican-USA border in the New Mexico boot heel and adjacent southeast Arizona, are a series of sites of the Carretas-like Animas phase dating to about AD 1200–1400. The first of these sites to be systematically excavated was the Pendleton site in the Animas Valley.[37] Pendleton, though related to Casas Grandes, was somewhat peripheral. However other Animas phase sites, farther east on the eastern fringe of the Animas Mountains, show a clearer relationship to Casas Grandes. Of these, the best-known is Joyce Well, excavated by Eugene B. McCluney and recently published in some detail in a volume edited by James M. Skibo and William H. Walker. At Joyce Well there appeared a wealth of polychrome pottery, adobe architecture, Casas Grandes–like T-shaped doors, ball courts, platforms, and rock art reminiscent of Paquimé style, including cartouches (see below) though lacking feathered or horned serpents. As in Casas Grandes proper there were no kivas. Though the full range of Chihuahuan wares including Babícora, Carretas, Corralitos (see Figure 8.8), Dublán, Huerigos, and Villa Ahumada polychromes, Madera Black-on-red, and Médanos Red-on-brown are found at Joyce Well, the premier decorated pottery is Ramos Polychrome. This type constituted 97 percent of all the Chihuahuan polychromes and with El Paso Polychrome and Gila Polychrome was one of the three major polychrome groups at the site. It seems very likely that both Ramos and El Paso polychromes were locally made, whereas the Gila Polychrome seems to have come from the Salado regions of Arizona, and the other Chihuahuan pottery was traded from the south and east. The Animas area's affinity for Ramos Polychrome, the major polychrome group in the Paquimé core area, is especially interesting.[38] Di Peso believed that some of the Casas Grandes people moved into the New Mexico boot heel and were still living there in the sixteenth century when Obregón made his report.[39] This was based, however, on a

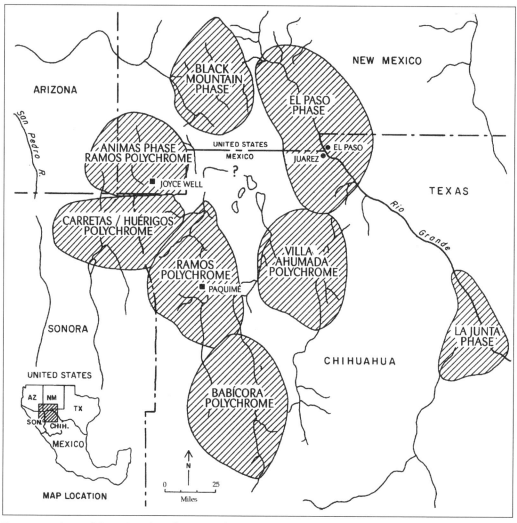

FIGURE 8.7. Areas of Casas Grandes influence, with major pottery types (after Fish and Fish, "Reflections").

misreading of the dating, and it now seems clear that the Animas region collapsed in the same general time period as the rest of the Casas Grandes world. A Casas Grandes political hegemony that extended to this region seems very unlikely for logistic reasons. There were likely commercial ties, the Animas towns perhaps acting as middlemen in the serpentine or even the turquoise trade to Paquimé. Or there may have been religious factors involved.[40]

To the east and north of the Animas region lay the important El Paso phase of Jornada Mogollon and the Postclassic, Black Mountain, and Cliff phases in the Mimbres area, all of which fall fairly tightly into the Medio period.

Clearly both the Animas and the Casas Grandes heartland had some sort of relationship with the Jornada people, and quite possibly the Black Mountain and Cliff phase populations also had a part, however peripheral it might have been, in the "Casas Grandes Interaction Sphere." Given the popularity of Gila Polychrome in Casas Grandes and the areas to the north, it would seem that the Salado area also had a part in this interaction.

One interesting thing vis-à-vis the Pueblo world is that there do not seem to be kivas in the Casas Grandes Interaction Sphere. It is true that Stephen Lekson has made the argument that at Paquimé itself, Room 38, part of the

FIGURE 8.8. Corralitos Polychrome double pot. El Paso Museum of Archaeology.

House of the Serpent complex, could be compared to twelfth through fourteenth century Mogollon Great Kivas.[41] However, other archaeologists are reluctant to use the term *kiva* for enclosed spaces outside the Pueblo and Mogollon areas that may or may not have ceremonial import of some sort. Di Peso himself simply called Room 38 a "ceremonial room."[42] Not only does the heartland lack kivas; they are absent in the Animas region, in the Jornada Mogollon, and, as far as we know, in the southern and western extensions of Casas Grandes. For example the cave sites southwest of Paquimé have extremely well-preserved villages with walls largely intact. Kivas do not occur.[43]

The great center of Casas Grandes was the city of Paquimé (Figure 8.9). Although several of the other sites are impressive by southwestern standards, Paquimé simply represents a different scale. It was not actually the largest southwestern site, for, as Di Peso points out, the Arizona Classic Hohokam site of Los Muertos is more than twice the size of Paquimé (ca. 9.5 million square feet to 4 million square feet).[44] Nor did it necessarily have the largest

population. Certain Classic Hohokam/Salado towns, as well as the largest sites in the Galisteo Basin and other parts of the upper Rio Grande Valley, plus one or two of the Sonora River settlements (see chapter 9), may have rivaled Paquimé in this regard. In one crucial aspect, however, Paquimé is impressive beyond all others. It is surely the most *Mesoamerican-looking* site in Aztlan.[45] One might go farther and say that it is the only southwestern town that would not seem too much out of place if found along the northern or western frontiers of Mesoamerica proper.

One of the very Mesoamerican aspects of Paquimé is the ball court. Ball courts are found in various parts of the Southwest, not only in Casas Grandes but also in the Hohokam-Sinagua area (a large number of courts), in southwest New Mexico, and, probably, in northeastern Sonora. As I said earlier, the most Mesoamerican-looking ball courts in the Paquimé region are the I- or double-T-shaped courts. In these are two side walls, formed by low mounds with additional mounds at either end. The courts may be closed, or there may be openings at the corners. The I-shaped court

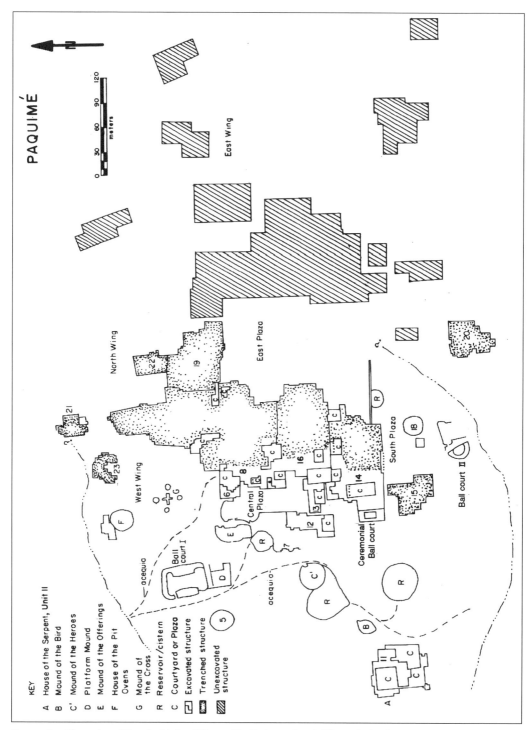

FIGURE 8.9. Floor plan of Paquimé (after Wilcox, "Preliminary Graph-Theoretic Analysis").

FIGURE 8.10. I-shaped ball court at Paquimé. Amerind Foundation, Dragoon, AZ.

is a classic Mesoamerican form and is found as far south and east as the Maya area (see Figure 8.10). There are two of those in Paquimé itself (one is much eroded), as well as one T-shaped, where only one end of the court is enclosed. Whalen and Minnis reported eleven additional courts in the valley area around Paquimé and one in the sierra southwest of the city. Two of these were I-shaped courts, two were T-shaped courts, and the remainder were a third category, a simple playing field demarcated with parallel rows of stones without clear end-field structures. In addition to these fifteen sites, seven courts, all of the simple playing field variety, have been reported. Of these, four are from extreme northeastern Sonora and three from the Animas region of New Mexico. Courts are found in Joyce Well and nearby Timberlake and Culberson in the New Mexico boot heel on the eastern edge of the Animas Mountains (Culberson is about four miles southeast of Joyce Well, and Timberlake lies some seven miles to the northeast). In all probability other courts exist or did exist in the past. These ball courts (from Chihuahua, Sonora, and New Mexico) all seem to be Medio period.[46]

The Casas Grandes courts are quite different from the oval Hohokam courts, first identified as such by Emil W. Haury in the 1930s, which, in any case, were generally earlier in time. The Hohokam ball courts appear in early Colonial times, probably sometime around AD 700 and last through the Sedentary and early Classic periods, the fashion ending by AD 1200 to 1250.[47] Another hypothesis, that the courts were dance floors, analogous to the historic Papago *wiikita* dance platforms, was popular for a time.[48] The consensus today, however, is that the courts actually were used for playing ball. David R. Wilcox has suggested that the ball game itself diffused northward to the Hohokam country, where it was taken up as a mechanism for regional integration. The Hohokam then independently invented their own particular kind of ball court.[49] Apropos of this, it should be pointed out that a ritual ball game, probably played in an open field, was reported in northwest Mexico during early conquest times.[50]

Casas Grandes was a "ball court culture," the general view being that the ball game had some sort of integrative ceremonial function. An analogy might perhaps be to the Pueblo region, with its "kiva culture." Again let me stress that the courts at Paquimé are clearly Mesoamerican and not closely related to Hohokam courts. Paquimé and its environs represent the most northerly distribution of the I-shaped court, the probable nearest neighbor to the south being the I-court at the great "fortress" site of La Quemada in the Malpaso region of southern Zacatecas, about 675 crow-fly miles from Paquimé. There is, however, a possible I-shaped court at Alta Vista, in the Chalchihuites area, a hundred miles or so northwest of La Quemada and therefore that much nearer Paquimé. The major distribution of the I-shaped court is in the Mesoamerican heartland. Other ball courts in the Durango and Zacatecas areas, reported by J. Charles Kelley, suggest the simple rectangular courts in the Casas Grandes region, though they may have somewhat more elaborate side structures.[51]

Another way the Casas Grandes ball courts may differ from those of the Hohokam was discussed by Di Peso. In Mesoamerica the ball game was often linked with human sacrifice, including sacrifice of the ball players themselves, and Di Peso found evidence for this kind of ritual at the small T-shaped court at Paquimé:

> The center marker, an unshaped stone, was found embedded in the paved playing floor and covered a "spirit hole," or symbolic entrance to the underworld. This, in turn, led down to the head of an adult male who was seated upon a flexed male, after the fashion of the Veracruz palma design, wherein Death sits on his victim while cornstalks issue upward from the scene, supporting the theory that fertility was a considerable measure of the game's religious symbolism....
>
> The south end, which lacked a surface marker, involved another subfloor burial cache, that of a pregnant adult female overlying another woman, whose severed right arm was draped over her shoulders. The north goal, marked by an upright wooden standard, had a third burial group, which consisted of a disjointed adult female, whose severed feet were articulated, and an odd adult male skull complete with mandible scattered above an articulated adult female. These implied that ceremonial dismember-

ment of humans was associated with this northern ceremonial ball court cult, even as it was in Mesoamerica.[52]

Though alternative explanations have been made for these remains—for example, that they may represent a series of burials at different times—the clear parallels with Mesoamerican practices suggest that we do have ritual sacrifice at Paquimé. In particular, severed heads and skulls were important in the Mesoamerican ball game complex.[53] In any case no such associations appear with ball courts anywhere else in the Southwest.

In addition to the I-shaped and T-shaped ball courts, other architectural features at Paquimé have a Mesoamerican flavor. Clustered on the western part of the site, these include platform mounds, some with structures on them, others in effigy form. One of the most noticeable of these mounds is what is now known as the Mound of the Cross, a structure formed by four projecting arms, oriented to the cardinal directions (Figure 8.11). Off the end of each arm is an ovoid mound. These mounds, 20 to 25 feet across, are separated from the cross arms, which extend roughly 45 feet east-west and north-south. The east and

FIGURE 8.11. Mound of the Cross. Paquimé, Amerind Foundation, Dragoon, AZ.

west mounds are each a little less than 10 feet off the tips of the cross, while the north and south ones are about 14.5 and 13.5 feet respectively. The equinox sunrise falls directly across the east mound to the center of the cross, and Polaris lines up across the center of the cross and of the south mound, being slightly offset when sighted across the north mound. The meaning of these alignments is not known, but presumably they served some ceremonial purpose. Di Peso suggested that the Mound of the Cross reflected Mesoamerican usage, where such architectural features honored the sun in his calendar aspect.[54] This seems likely but also may be the widespread southwestern symbol of the four-pointed star, representing the planet Venus and the god Quetzalcoatl. Indeed, in Mesoamerica there were equinoctial associations with the god, Quetzalcoatl. As archaeologists J. Charles Kelley and Ellen A. Kelley have pointed out, equinox alignments were important at the Chalchihuites city of Alta Vista in Zacatecas,[55] and Di Peso (see below) points to probable equinox sacrifice of scarlet macaws in Casas Grandes. A primary association of Quetzalcoatl is with the feathered serpent, which certainly appears in Casas Grandes art. In fact, some of the figures appearing on pot-

tery vessels that Di Peso identified as macaws are pretty clearly horned or feathered serpents.[56]

At Paquimé there are enclosed plazas with colonnaded porches or galleries, complex structures, some of several stories with massive adobe walls and complex interlocking rooms. A truncated pyramidal structure, what is today called Mound of the Heroes (Figure 8.12) has a stone and stucco facade rising some 12 feet from its pediment.[57] Another building, Mound of the Offerings, has two major terrace levels, one about 150 feet in north-south extent and some 95 feet east and west. This terrace is about 5 feet above ground level at the highest point, slanting downward from north to south, and sits on a larger, lower platform. On the terrace is a roughly circular mound about 16.5 feet by 12.5 feet at the summit and rising to 2.5 feet above the lower terrace. Directly south and actually merging with the terrace is a series of unroofed rooms of adobe that Di Peso considered to have been used as a religious sanctuary. These rooms contained, in Di Peso's words, "a number of altar stones, statues, secondary urn burials in tombs, and the lack of household artifacts and architectural features."[58] Another mound, southwest of the

FIGURE 8.12. Mound of the Heroes. Amerind Foundation, Dragoon, AZ.

marketplace, is the effigy Mound of the Bird, about 70 feet in its long axis and rising some 6 feet above ground level. Di Peso believed that it represented a mantling bird, that is one with wings spread covering the legs. In his reconstruction the bird is clearly a raptor.[59] What Di Peso thought to be a central marketplace, similar to the great Aztec market at Tenochtitlan, lies south of the Mound of the Cross, southeast of Mound of the Offerings, and northeast of Mound of the Heroes, with sales booths and small "guest houses" (or perhaps chapels for foreign visitors).[60] The marketplace forms the southern part of a central plaza area and is flanked on the south by a maze of rooms that collectively have been called House of the Skulls, the name indicating the discovery of a number of trophy skulls along with long bones of bears in one of the rooms.[61]

Di Peso's interpretation of the marketplace has been challenged by Whalen and Minnis, who think that it may have had a more generalized usage:

The listing of artifacts from the plaza includes chipped stone implements, debitage, ground stone, pottery, animal bone of a number of species, shell tinklers, and beads of shell, copper, and stone. Neither the Central Plaza's features nor the materials found in it are unique to any particular activity. Market activities *could* have taken place there, but there seems to be nothing in the archaeological record to argue for so specific a function. Rather, the most parsimonious interpretation is that the plaza was the scene of many activities, from domestic to ceremonial. We note that this is usually the case in the Pueblo plazas of the southwestern United States.[62]

Actually, it seems to me that although such debris is something one would perhaps find in a general work area, the extraordinary wealth and diversity of material suggest a marketplace on the Mexican model.

I am not attempting here to describe the full panoply of Paquimé architecture. Let me just

say that the variety of what seem clearly to be ceremonial buildings, the proliferation of structures (Figure 8.13), many multistoried (Figure 8.14), and the water and drainage system do suggest a level of wealth and complexity that we really do not see in other regions of the Southwest. Pueblo and Salado/Classic Hohokam structures are sometimes impressive, but they tend to have a monotony about them, a limitation of form and function that one does not find at Paquimé.

There is considerable disagreement as to the extent that elite groups in other parts of the Southwest wielded economic and political power. As we have seen, there likely were such elites, especially in the Pueblo world, but evidence of them is not always clear-cut. What, then, was the situation in the Casas Grandes area, at least at Paquimé? Maria Sprehn believes that the latter part of the Medio period saw the development of what she calls an incipient elite at Paquimé and in the surrounding area.[63] A detailed analysis of mortuary practices at Paquimé was made by John C. Ravesloot. He concluded:

A system of social ranking based on inheritance probably integrated Casas Grandes society during the Medio period. Positions of authority and power within Casas Grandes society were most likely based on the control of the distribution of agricultural goods and products obtained through exchange. Vertical social distinctions were marked by qualitative differences in mortuary treatment such as special burial locations, expensive grave facility constructions, variability in postmortem processing of the body, and the relative cost of grave accompaniments as measured in terms of procurement and production.[64]

There were several modes of burial in the Paquimé area. Burials were both flexed and extended, often in the plazas or under the floors of living rooms and in burial vaults or sealed pits. About a quarter of the Medio period burials were in a sitting position. Both articulated and disarticulated or secondary skeletons were

FIGURE 8.13. Architectural feature in excavation, Paquimé. Amerind Foundation, Dragoon, AZ.

FIGURE 8.14. Construction features, Paquimé. Amerind Foundation, Dragoon, AZ.

135

found. About half of burials in the Medio period were multiple; that is, a number of bodies were interred together. Di Peso believed that in certain multiple burials of children, ritual sacrifice was involved, perhaps to the fertility god Xipe (see below), although there is very little iconographic evidence for this deity. Di Peso also considered that a number of dismemberments of young adult females represented some sort of sacrifice. Elite forms of burial, from the Mound of the Offerings, were secondary interment in large burial urns, one elaborately marked with macaw designs. Grave offerings in Paquimé burials varied considerably but included pottery and utilitarian objects such as awls, knives, hammerstones, mauls, pestles, and projectile points. There was worked copper, including copper bells, jewelry made from shell, and various semiprecious stones, such as turquoise, azurite, malachite, quartz, and mica. Perishable materials included food offerings, matting, textiles, and fragments of worked wood. A number of the Medio period graves had mineral deposits in four colors: white, blue/green, black, and yellow. Di Peso thought that these may have had some symbolic religious meaning. To me they suggest perhaps color-directional symbolism, which was widespread throughout the Southwest. The four colors found at Paquimé most resemble those directional colors of the Pima and of the Navajo-Apache in the historic Southwest.[65] What this means—if, indeed, it means anything at all—is not clear. In any case there was body decoration, perhaps both painting and tattooing, at Paquimé, utilizing at least six colors. There are no actual examples from burials but many examples from modeled or painted faces in the Casas Grandes pottery.[66]

If there was any significant contact between Paquimé and the upper Rio Grande region, one would expect to see large amounts of Cerrillos turquoise in the former site. There was, in fact, relatively little turquoise at Paquimé. In Di Peso's excavations there appeared 5,895 items, making up about 2.6 pounds, most of it in a few caches. The difficulties in identifying turquoise sources has been discussed in earlier chapters, and we cannot say with certainty that any of the turquoise was from the Cerrillos mines. There are a number of other turquoise sources both north and south of the Casas Grandes region, including the relatively nearby Burro Mountains in Grant County of extreme southwestern New Mexico. Much more common was serpentine, over 250 pounds total, which has also been traced to Grant County. This material, a green hydrous magnesium silicate with admixtures of other minerals, takes a high polish and was widely used in a variety of jewelry—beads, pendants, rings,bracelets—as well as in effigies and pipes and such mundane objects as axes, mauls, rubbing stones, and plumb bobs. Again, it shows the high degree of interaction of Paquimé with the regions to the north and west.

One oddity is a bifacial knife of the beautiful banded alibates, a silicified dolomite found in quarries north of present-day Amarillo in the Texas Panhandle. Alibates was a much valued commodity, and alibates trade goes back perhaps 10,000 years in the Southwest. This surface find from the central plaza at Paquimé is, as far as I know, the only alibates from the area around Paquimé.[67]

One striking aspect of Paquimé life was the care and breeding of macaws and turkeys. The latter, three varieties of *Meleagris gallopavo*, numbering 344 birds, were apparently not eaten with any regularity but rather domesticated for their feathers and as grave goods. Turkeys, especially heads and blood, were also utilized as part of ceremonies. The majority of turkeys were probably kept in the vicinity of the House of the Dead, south of the marketplace, where roosting pens and eggshells have been found.[68]

Just to the southwest of the House of the Dead is the House of the Macaws, which was a major focus of the raising of macaws. There was clearly bird breeding going on, as evidenced by eggs, remains of nestlings, and the finds of birds of all ages. There were adobe nesting boxes with removable roofs, as well as stone ring entrances and elongated stone plugs, both usually of felsite. Stone feeding bowls were also of felsite. A modern experiment was made by the Di Peso group, using such a bowl in daily feedings of a scarlet macaw. The bowl withstood the constant biting and was unmarked after years of use.[69]

Food remains in the nesting boxes suggested that the bird handlers experimented with various foods for the macaws. They were not entirely successful, however; examination of macaw bones suggest calcium deficiencies. In any case roasted agave hearts, cornmeal mush, amaranth, and squash were primary bird feeds.[70]

The macaws bred at Paquimé were for the most part the scarlet macaw *(Ara macao)*, whose natural habitat lay far to the south and east, in the lowland country of northern Veracruz. The military macaw *(Ara militaris)*, whose terrain ranges into northwest Mexico, was far less popular at Paquimé. One reason for this may have been the exigencies of trade. In the upper Southwest the scarlet macaw was much more in demand (if the archaeological finds of birds is any guide). More than a hundred scarlet macaws have been found in the upper Southwest, dating from AD 1100 (or shortly before) through Aztlan times. Only one military macaw was found, this at the Mimbres Gatlin site, with a date probably circa AD 1100–1150, corresponding to the terminal Viejo period at Casas Grandes. Of course, it is also clear that the scarlet macaw was the more important bird for ceremonial purposes in the Casas Grandes region itself. This probably had to do with its role in Quetzalcoatl worship (see below).[71]

It is generally assumed that Casas Grandes was the supplier of macaws to other areas in the Southwest, but evidence for macaws in Paquimé came primarily from the Medio period. How earlier macaws reached the upper Southwest is still somewhat of a mystery. The trade may well have gone through the Viejo period Casas Grandes area but perhaps was organized and directed from farther south, as might be indicated by the Tejo story told below.

Di Peso discovered 322 examples of *Ara macao* in his excavations. There were 81 birds definitely identified as the military macaw and 100 specimens that could only be identified as to the genus *Ara*. Of the macaws to which species could be definitely assigned, about 80 percent are scarlet and 20 percent military. If we assign the same ratio to the hundred birds whose species is uncertain, we will arrive at something on the order of 400 *Ara macao* and about 100 *Ara militaris*. The age groupings were roughly the same. In both cases there were a few nestlings and adult birds, but the great majority were immature birds.[72] It should be stressed that most of these birds are found in sacramental or ceremonial burial contexts. Many of the birds seemed to have been sacrificed at about the age of eleven and a half months. Since macaws breed in March, this would suggest bird sacrifice of both scarlet and military macaws at or around the vernal equinox.[73]

It is a reasonably safe assumption that macaws served several purposes in the Casas Grandes world. They were used in various sacrificial ceremonies, were buried with important people, and were widely traded to the north and west. Although this emphasis on macaws probably really got underway in the Medio period, it may have its roots in Viejo times. The routes to the Veracruz region are not securely known, but as Di Peso points out, there may be an early historical echo of them: "The Nahuatl *alo* (macaw) hailed from the land of Cuextlan, the home of the Huaxteca, wherein Oxitipar was located in the Rio Pánuco Valley. This was the home of the father of Tejo, native informant to the first conquistadors. The former made his living as a feather merchant in the Gran Chichimeca shortly before the Spanish arrived. . . . It is not inconceivable that some of Tejo's progenitors supplied the Paquimians with their first scarlet macaws."[74]

Di Peso is discussing the information given to the early conquistador, Nuño de Guzmán, by a Huastec Indian named Tejo, whose father had followed trade routes, carrying feathers to the north and west (see the statement of Guzmán vis-à-vis Tejo in chapter 11). The father would probably have been active around the beginning of the sixteenth century, so Tejo's grandfather or great grandfather's generation may have been in contact with the last Paquimians. That routes going south and east from Paquimé were open seems beyond doubt, though beyond macaws there is little evidence of what was traded. Weigand et al. believed that a turquoise trail ran from New Mexico into the Zacatecas area and probably on to the south. Such a trail—if it were late enough in time—would probably involve the Casas Grandes region, but the relative lack of turquoise at Paquimé tells against that town being a major entrepôt for the turquoise trade.

A major part of Casas Grandes contacts was with the northwest portion of the upper Southwest, whence came the Gila Polychrome and other goods and to which Casas Grandes people exported their copper trinkets, exotic birds, and perhaps shell and other goods. It is curious that relatively few of the Chihuahuan polychromes went beyond the Animas and northern Sonoran regions. A small amount is found in the Jornada Mogollon, though, of course, El Paso Polychrome occurs throughout (see Figures 8.15 and 8.16). It has also been suggested that the Chihuahuan polychromes

FIGURE 8.16. El Paso Polychrome jar. Maxwell Museum of Anthropology, University of New Mexico, cat. no. 65.35.1.

have some sort of relationship to Mimbres Classic pottery, but John Rinaldo, in his analysis of Chihuahuan pottery, discounts that idea.[75] Very few of the Chihuahuan polychromes have been found in middle Gila and lower Salt river valleys or in the mountain Mogollon region. There are only traces in Western Pueblo; for example, a figurine found at Hawikuh in the Zuni region does look like a local copy of a Casas Grandes–type figure.[76] And, as we saw in chapter 7, the upper Rio Grande received hardly any Chihuahuan pottery.

There is a trivial amount of Casas Grandes–area pottery in central Mexico, for example a sherd of Villa Ahumada Polychrome found at the Cerro de la Estrella site, near Mexico City, and a vessel of Ramos Polychrome at Teotihuacan (temporal context unknown).[77] There were a few Chihuahuan sherds found in what are now the Mexican states of Jalisco, Nayarit, and Durango.[78]

For classificatory reasons specialists have generally concentrated on differences in ceramics, establishing separate traditions in Western Pueblo, the Salado, Casas Grandes, and so forth. That is necessary, but I have been also struck by certain broad *similarities*, in com-

FIGURE 8.15. Gila Polychrome jar. El Paso Museum of Archaeology.

plexity of layout, design elements, general ex-uberance, and "business" of the styles, form-ing a sort of Aztlan "macrotradition." Included are ceramics as diverse as the St. Johns poly-chromes and other White Mountain redwares, Gila and Tonto polychromes, the Chihuahuan polychromes, Hopi Sityatki and Jeddito wares, even certain of the Rio Grande glazes. Some of this is of course due to what seems to be the more or less independent spread of pottery styles in various parts of the Southwest.

A far more important center of contact, although not for pottery, was the west coast of Mexico, where the great mass of seashell, and probably the raw and worked copper as well, reached Paquimé. A vast amount of shell was found at Medio period Paquimé, about four million specimens (compare the 1,384 shell objects from Viejo period contexts), the pre-dominant percentage (97+) from the west coastal regions of Mexico.[79] The invertebrate zoologist Helen DuShane analyzed the Casas Grandes shell and indicated that the majority of shell came from "a coastal area bounded possibly by Tastiota Bay, Sonora, Mexico on the north to at least Banderas Bay, Jalisco on the south. The coastal distance between these points is approximately 1500 km (800 mi.)."[80]

In addition, some shell came from the Cal-ifornia or western Baja California coast. Both worked and unworked shell were found, and a vast range of artifacts, virtually every kind of artifact known in the Greater Southwest, was represented: beads, pendants, gorgets, bracelets, armlets, tinklers, finger rings, tesserae, as well as domestic-use objects such as needles, punches, and containers. Casas Grandes shell, many species of which are also found in the upper Southwest (see chapter 7), include *Nassarius, Conus, Dentalium, Glycymeris, Haliotis, Oliva, Olivella, Strombus,* and *Turritella.* It would seem likely that Casas Grandes craftsmen were involved in the retrading of worked shell to the upper Southwest, but this is difficult to demonstrate with any certainty. Most of the shell, and other exotic goods, copper for ex-ample, recovered at Paquimé came from the various multistoried rooms of Unit 8, east of

the plaza area and perhaps date from very late in the occupation of the site.[81] The coral at Casas Grandes, as is likely true throughout the prehistoric Southwest, was fashioned from the upper valve hinge area of *Chama echinata,* a bivalve not normally found north of Culiacán in Sinaloa.[82]

I briefly discussed the distribution of Casas Grandes copper in chapter 7. There was a fair amount of copper found, over 30 pounds, 688 specimens in all, in the form of nuggets and various worked pieces. These included one molded ax blade, 115 cire-perdue or lost-wax cast objects, and most of the rest sheet ham-mered. Finds included bells (also called tin-klers or crotals), beads, finger rings, tesserae, pendants, plaques, buttons, wire, needles, and worked sheet metal.

Di Peso believed that at least some of the copper finds at Paquimé were from ore sources close at hand—and were manufactured in the Casas Grandes area.[83] However, subsequent study by Victoria Vargas suggests otherwise. Reanalyzing Di Peso's data, Vargas concluded that Paquimé was primarily a consumer of cop-per products from western Mexican sources, the same sources from which other parts of the Greater Southwest received their copper goods. Vargas pointed out that other south-western sites received primarily bells, which were usually found in burials. At Paquimé, however, there was a variety of copper goods, and the focus was ritualistic but generally nonmortuary. A major conclusion of Vargas is that the relationship between Paquimé and its west-Mexican sources was quite different from that of other parts of the Southwest.[84]

The significance of this is unclear, though it does seem to underscore the importance to Casas Grandes of trade routes running down the west coast of Mexico, routes that survived the collapse of the Casas Grandes world. It is certainly possible that some copper was worked at Casas Grandes, as Di Peso thought, although there seems to be no clear evidence for special metal workshops. Perhaps only certain west coast copper objects were reworked in various ways.

In religion and general ceremonial life Casas Grandes clearly reflected the ideology of Mesoamerica. As I discussed in previous chapters, some of these religious ideas were transmitted to the upper Southwest at the beginning of the Aztlan period, and Casas Grandes was very likely involved in this transmission. The most obvious religious transmissions were the kachina cult, with its Tlaloc manifestations, and the horned and feathered serpent, discussed in detail in chapter 7.

In chapter 2 I outlined the possible or probable appearance of Mesoamerican deities into Aztlan. Di Peso believed that a series of religious influences, in discreet waves, spread from Mesoamerica to the lower Southwest. The first of those mainly affected the Colonial and Sedentary periods of the Hohokam and involved worship of the Mesoamerican god Tezcatlipoca, the influences marked by pyrite mirrors and clay figurines, as well as city planning, irrigation systems, and ball courts. Di Peso considered that this deity was brought north by trading or conquest-oriented groups interested especially in turquoise. Casas Grandes entered the picture more directly at the beginnings of Medio period times. Another set of traders, Di Peso's *puchteca*, brought the Quetzalcoatl cult, marked by the feathered serpent complex and by the intensification of use of macaws and their plumage in ceremonials. It was also the period of urban Paquimé, with multistoried adobe buildings, T-shaped doorways, and pillars and staircases. Around the time of the collapse of Casas Grandes, which now would be dated to the early to mid-fifteenth century, came the arrival of the Central Mexican deity, the bloody war god Huitzilopochtli, who was worshipped by remnant colonies of Casas Grandes. This was Di Peso's original reconstruction, but in the multivolume Casas Grandes publication he seems to have largely lost interest in Tezcatlipoca or Huitzilopochtli as Casas Grandean deities.[85] Certainly there is little or no evidence for them at Paquimé.

To Di Peso the complex divine personage Quetzalcoatl was perhaps the most obvious of the Mesoamerican deities in Casas Grandes.

Quetzalcoatl appeared in various manifestations, including that of Ehécatl, the wind god. Representing this latter manifestation at Paquimé are a series of masks, headdresses, rasps made from human long bones, and strombus shell symbols. More generically related to Quetzalcoatl were numbers of feathered (or horned) serpent designs and perhaps the large-scale use of macaws. Di Peso believed that the ball courts in the Casas Grandes area had an association with Quetzalcoatl in his likeness as the culture hero Ce Acatl, the Toltec hero god. Di Peso saw traces of a second god, the Mesoamerican fire god, Xiuhtecutli, in the form of Xiuhcoatl (Turquoise Snake), a deity that merges with Quetzalcoatl.[86] He also believed that the god of vegetation and rebirth, Xipe Tótec, was worshiped at Paquimé. Certainly depictions on human effigy jars do have a Xipe look. Di Peso also considered the finds of decapitated heads and appearance of cannibalism to be evidence for Xipe.[87]

Subsequent work on the Chihuahuan Paquimé style of rock art by Polly Schaafsma suggests Quetzalcoatl association, especially the appearance of horned serpents and horned-serpent headdresses. The Paquimé style is related to the Jornada style in art (see chapter 7). There are a number of similarities to the Jornada style, including the delineation of horned serpents, human and animal figures pecked in outline, and cloud terraces. However, the Chihuahuan rock art also differs in certain ways. This can be seen in the extreme rarity in Paquimé–style rock art of "Tlaloc" figures, so common in the Jornada, and the prevalence in the Paquimé style of what are called *cartouches* or *cuadros,* rectangular figures often enclosing a diagonal cross or sometimes other geometric and curvilinear elements. Some cartouches may have represented masks. They are rather widespread, very similar cartouches (at a somewhat earlier date) appearing as far south as the Chalchihuites culture in the Mexican state of Durango.[88]

Design elements that are part of a Tlaloc complex in the Jornada area do appear as decorations on various of the Chihuahuan polychromes (see chapter 7). Schaafsma points out that several Paquimé rock art sites are found in box canyons near water sources, two of them at springs, reminiscent of the sacred water associations among the Pueblo Indians to the north, though their relationship in Chihuahua is with the horned/feathered serpent.[89] In addition Di Peso pointed to the "multiple groups of articulated burials of common-aged young people" at Paquimé as evidence of child sacrifice to Tlaloc.[90] If, indeed, this was a Tlaloc manifestation, and if the ceramic designs are actually Tlaloc imagery, it might link Casas Grandes to the kachina cult of the upper Southwest. However, clear kachina configurations have not been identified at Paquimé and other Casas Grandes sites. In any case what we have at Paquimé are only hints of Tlaloc. The palpable manifestations of Tlaloc that appear, for example, in the Jornada are missing in the Casas Grandes region.

Christine VanPool does suggest in her study of shamans that dancers with horned-serpent headdresses found on Ramos Polychrome pots might represent kachinas, perhaps as ancestor figures with water ritual associations.[91] Rakita sees kachina similarities in what he considers an ancestor cult at Paquimé. However, this author believes that "the primary concerns of the ancestor cult at Paquimé were not fertility and regeneration, but negotiations of power."[92]

Though Di Peso does not particularly emphasize the goddess Chalchihuitlicue (Chalchiuhtlique), who is strongly associated with water and with Tlaloc, I have an idea that she was also present. Di Peso does remark that sacrifices placed in Reservoir 2 at Paquimé were perhaps to the goddess or to her male counterpart, Tlaloc. Green is a color generally associated with Chalchihuitlicue, one translation of her name being "Lady Precious Green." Some scholars believe that, just as Quetzalcoatl is associated with the scarlet macaw, Chalchihuitlicue has a special association with the green-plumaged military macaw, of which there are considerable numbers at Paquimé.[93]

As I commented in earlier chapters, one thing to remember is that the functions and the very names of gods spreading from Mesoamerica were redefined in Aztlan. There is clear evidence for this in the Pueblo area because, as in Mesoamerica, we have actual Puebloan names for the gods and goddesses and descriptions of the ceremonies. I am sure that something of the same happened at Paquimé. That is to say Quetzalcoatl or Tlaloc in that northern center would most likely not have been called by those names. The attributes of the deities and the ceremonies relating to them would be at best distorted reflections of the gods in Mesoamerica. A hypothetical visitor from central or western Mexico might, indeed, recognize Quetzalcoatl or Tlaloc, as worshiped at Paquimé but might also be amused (or perhaps shocked and outraged) by the barbarized and countrified icons and ceremonials.

The relatively complex religion in the Casas Grandes sphere suggests some sort of priesthood. Such priestly organizations existed in the Pueblo world, and the civilizations of Mesoamerica had rich and complex priesthoods. Lacking documentary or oral records, our grasp of the situation at Casas Grandes is less clear. Still thinking in terms of named Mesoamerican deities, Di Peso says, "In view of the fact that at least four Mesoamerican religious complexes—involving the worship of Quetzalcóatl, Xiuhtecutli, Xipe, and Tláloc—were present at Casas Grandes, it can be assumed that there were also corresponding priestly orders. Leastwise, such evidence as the sacred ball court, the ceremonial mounds, and several hallowed housing areas were sufficiently supportive of this concept."[94]

Though we must understand that this is highly speculative, Di Peso believed that the Casas Grandes priesthoods may well have copied those of Mesoamerica, perhaps even including the formal religious schools that served Mesoamerican children of the nobility, some of whom entered the higher echelons of the priesthood. Di Peso also pointed out priestly accouterments, including stone altar pieces, some with cut-out T shapes; red or green felsite and ricolite stools; ceremonial stone vessels and ceremonial ax heads; elaborate stone images of human beings, bear, mountain lion, and other animals; and cult paraphernalia in shell and semiprecious stones. There are also cloud ladder headdresses of felsite, similar to the cloud symbolism of the Pueblo world and to similar figures done in the round that served as incensarios in the Chalchihuites culture (Figure 8.17). Actually various of these objects have ceremonial priestly function in Mesoamerica and the upper Southwest or, in the case of the stools, in both areas.[95] Also linked to priesthoods were the variety of animal and human sacrifices, including macaws, turkeys, and human beings of both sexes and various ages. If large-scale human sacrifice was the norm at Paquimé and other Casas Grandes centers, it does tend to link the priesthoods there more with Mesoamerica than with the upper Southwest, where such sacrifice (at least by early Spanish contact times) had disappeared except as metaphor.

VanPool, in a 2003 publication, did an extensive reanalysis of the ceremonial situation in the Casas Grandes world. She pointed out the extreme importance of both the macaw and the horned or plumed serpent in Casas Grandes art, especially in pottery decoration. She had certain doubts that these Casas Grandes depictions of serpents should be identified with Quetzalcoatl, though they represented springs and water and were a part of shamanistic magical journeys.[96] VanPool believed that the "cacique model" of Casas Grandes sociopolitical organization suggested by Schaafsma and myself was probably in operation but that the caciques were shaman priests (see Figure 8.18) who "followed a well-known American strategy to justify their power by emphasizing their unique access to supernatural forces."[97] This new elite managed at some point in the Medio period to take control of the Casas Grandean polity, developing a new level of

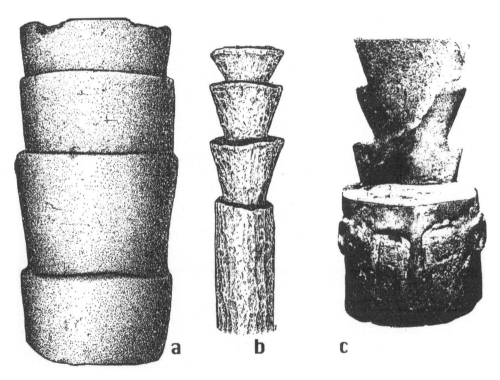

FIGURE 8.17. (a) Chalchihuites incensario, stone (after Riley and Winters, "Prehistoric Tepehuan"); (b) Tepehuan incensario, wood (after Riley and Winters, "Prehistoric Tepehuan"); (c) "Cloud ladder" from Paquimé (after Di Peso, *Casas Grandes*, Vol. 3). Amerind Foundation, Dragoon, AZ.

FIGURE 8.18. Male pottery figure, Paquimé, possibly a shaman. Amerind Foundation, Dragoon, AZ.

social hierarchy. This is reflected in strong differences in the layouts, artistic motifs, and designs of pottery and in specific icons, horned or plumed serpents, for example. VanPool sees the religion at Paquimé as developing a strong duality during Medio times. This was expressed in the juxtaposing of male/female, earth/sky, natural world/supernatural world, birds/snakes, and so forth. It also is evident in the strong tendency for pairing within a subset.[98]

VanPool's analyses certainly advance our knowledge of symbolism and religion at Casas Grandes. However, her statement that "it is difficult to accept that the horned/plumbed serpents in Casas Grandes or in the American Southwest are truly representations of 'Quetzalcoatl'" seems to me somewhat risky, considering the protean nature of Quetzalcoatl, even in the Mesoamerican heartland. The snake-bird identification with certain associated elements (twinning or pairing, and earth-sky duality, for example) is extraordinarily widespread, reaching from Yucatan to northern Arizona and

New Mexico. The particular iconic formulations differ vastly from one area to another. The most obvious symbolism of Quetzalcoatl, the horned/plumed bird-snake association appears in many different manifestations. VanPool herself pointed out that there are three structurally distinct icons of the horned or plumed serpent in the Southwest—those of Casas Grandes, the Salado, and the upper Southwest—all differing in certain key aspects.[99] Farther to the south, in the Chalchihuites region of Durango and Zacatecas, another bird-snake association appears with different iconography, serpents with star symbols and horned serpents counterpoised with roadrunners.[100]

When all the evidence is considered, it seems reasonably clear that in some generic form both Quetzalcoatl and Tlaloc (a god VanPool is less concerned with because of the greater difficulty in identifying him iconographically) were worshipped in the Casas Grandes world. There was, of course, the redefinition that I have already discussed, and, as in the upper Southwest, the names were surely different.

We have seen the comments of VanPool about the prevalence of a shaman priesthood at Paquimé, and it does not seem to me that her data *necessarily* contradict the ideas of Di Peso. The shaman or "medicine man" exists in many parts of the Americas, as well as in the Old World. These shaman figures functioned partly in conjunction with the priesthoods in the Pueblo world, something that also seems to be the case in Mesoamerica. Among various mountain peoples of historic northern Mexico the shaman was the important medico-religious practitioner and, as elsewhere, utilized tobacco and other drugs for hallucinogenic purposes. The shaman could also take an animal form while roaming the spirit world. Though we tend to think of the shaman as an individual entrepreneur, controlling medical and spiritual knowledge and functioning as intercessor between his group and the spirit world, shamans often worked together in various ways. The southern Tepehuan, a historic group who lived along the east slopes of the Sierra Madre Occidental, in modern Durango, Zacatecas, and Jalisco—and whose ancestors may have interacted with the Casas Grandes people—have shamans who are specialists in particular ceremonials.[101] In more complicated societies these congeries of shamans may have become functioning priesthoods (Figure 8.19).

In any case considerable evidence for the shaman has been found at the excavations at Paquimé. These include collections of cruciform dice, small animal effigies, quartz crystals and other exotic mineral pieces, geodes and pieces of fossil bone, red and green pigment, quartz projectile points, and tubular smoking pipes. Such objects, often found in "shamanistic bundles" are reminiscent of other such bundles found both archaeologically and in ethnographic contexts elsewhere in the Americas. Christine VanPool has pointed out elaborate pottery effigy vessels that appear to represent shamans. These figures sometimes are employing tubular pipes, which may have been used with tobacco or with some form of hallucinogen. These vessels have feathered- or horned-

serpent and macaw designs. and in some cases the shaman is shown in the throes of changing into an animal form. Shaman figures are often painted with what seem to be specific esoteric shamanistic symbols. These include circles, lozenges, and pound signs (like the pound sign on a modern telephone) often with interior dots (Figure 8.20).[102]

Accepting VanPool's ideas of a shaman priesthood, we still do not know the details of how the priestly and shamanistic components of the Casas Grandes religious organization meshed or merged. As I said above, however, in the course of group evolution, with higher population levels and greater social and technological sophistication, some priesthoods may have gradually developed from shamanistic structures. In some intermediate cases shamans continued to function but were partly incorporated into the new priestly structures. This may have been the case here.

One interesting aspect of Casas Grandes religion is its coexistence with a competing cult

FIGURE 8.19. Female and male pottery figures, possibly shamans. Amerind Foundation, Dragoon, AZ.

FIGURE 8.20. Shaman becoming macaw as part of shamanistic journey (after Di Peso, *Casas Grandes*, Vol. 3). Amerind Foundation, Dragoon, AZ.

from the Salado. As noted in chapter 6, Van-Pool et al. have pointed out the similarities and differences of these two systems:

> The Salado and Casas Grandes inhabitants must have known many details of each others' religious and ritual systems, given the groups' geographic proximity and the evidence of at least some exchange between Salado sites and Casas Grandes sites (especially at Paquimé). Still, the distinction between the systems was maintained and even reinforced through intentional differences in the presentation of concepts such as the horned/plumbed serpent. We suggest, then, that membership in one of the two systems precluded participation in the other.[103]

These writers point out that there is some spotty evidence for a transition zone, some 50 miles wide, in which the two traditions intermingled. Much more work is needed on this problem. In addition, there is one, rather uncommon, Chihuahuan polychrome type, Escondida Polychrome, which is similar to Ramos Polychrome but incorporates Salado iconography. What this means—whether it represented Salado settlers in Paquimé, local Casas Grandes individuals or families who converted to the southwestern cult, or something else quite different—is not clear at present.[104]

Thanks to the detailed and meticulous excavations at Paquimé, we have a great deal of detail on the lives of its citizens. The Casas Grandes culture was agricultural, probably with a concentration on maize. There were several varieties of corn found at Paquimé; cotton

and cottonseeds were used, both for weaving and eating, as was squash. The bottle gourd, *Lagenaria siceraria,* was probably also cultivated, and there were a number of wild plants collected. Oddly enough the common bean, valuable for its protein, does not appear in Di Peso's plant samples at Casas Grandes, but in Di Peso's time retrieval techniques were not as sophisticated as they are today. Even with modern flotation methods, beans do not show up well. It is impossible to believe that beans, ubiquitous in the Greater Southwest, were not utilized in the Casas Grandes area, and, in fact, at least one bean fragment has been recorded by Whalen and Minnis.[105]

The protein contained in beans would have been important, even though there seems to have been a considerable amount of meat consumed. Dogs were domesticated at Casas Grandes, but evidence for their contribution to the cooking pots is somewhat equivocal. The major food contributors at Paquimé seem to have been first bison then antelope, though deer (mule and white-tailed) and lagomorphs (rabbits and jackrabbits) were also important. At Villa Ahumada the various rabbits actually seem to have been the most important food animals.[106] Although the plant inventory is somewhat limited, there is no doubt that Paquimé, though with only 11 to 12 inches of precipitation annually, had an intensive agriculture. Di Peso believed there was an integrated irrigation complex, with its system of large and small canals, reservoirs, aqueducts, and urban water channels. This high degree of integration, however, has been questioned. The geographer

William E. Doolittle considers that the Casas Grandes system probably owed more to Hohokam than to Mesoamerican influences. Still, Doolittle says that irrigation in the Casas Grandes Valley was "technologically more complex than any other known in the northern part of Mexico."[107]

Pottery and other ceramic forms were important in the area. Pottery itself was made by the coiling technique, and a vast variety of pots were made, plainware, bichrome, and polychrome, in varying shapes and sizes, the largest being about 20 gallons. Collections of pottery tools, discarded coils, and lumps of clay show where the potters had their workshops.[108] There is also considerable evidence for weaving, textiles, baskets, and mats, as evidenced by spindle whorls and other spinning paraphernalia. No looms were found, but Di Peso thought that both the horizontal and backstrap looms were in use. Several kinds of raw materials were used, including cotton, apocynum, agave, yucca, and human hair. Of the spindle whorls, six examples made of fired clay can be traced to the Chalchihuites culture far to the south.[109] Workers in other media, for example stone, including lapidary stone, bone, and shell, seem to have had their own work areas in the central portion of Paquimé. There was certainly specialization; for example, Todd VanPool and Robert Leonard point out that a type of square-cornered metate there was specialist-made.[110] And Maria Sprehn has argued persuasively that specialist potters made certain of the Chihuahuan ceramics, especially Ramos Polychrome forms.[111] A study by Ann Woosley and Bart Olinger suggests that Ramos Polychrome was actually produced in the vicinity of Paquimé and a portion of it distributed to peripheral settlements (Figure 8.21).[112] Indeed, the overall problem of specialization, standardization, and distribution of various manufactured products at Paquimé needs more investigation.

As we saw in chapter 7, and will see again in chapter 9, other parts of Aztlan were extremely warlike during the Medio period at Casas Grandes. This was also true of Meso-

FIGURE 8.21. Ramos Polychrome with macaw. Amerind Foundation, Dragoon, AZ.

america to the south, the flowering time, after all, of the bellicose Aztecs. It seems very likely that the Casas Grandes area, especially the city of Paquimé, also followed this warlike tradition. Exactly how hostilities were conducted is not known. Di Peso believed that the Casas Grandes people were organized militarily much as peoples to the south, with ranked squadrons of soldiers, perhaps with specialized weapons. There is no particular evidence for this level of organization, though there may have been a military function for outlier hilltop fortresses and signal towers. These presumably sent smoke signals to other such towers in various places in the Casas Grandes and nearby valleys. To what extent such towers found in the Casas Grandes Valley itself were under the control of Paquimé is simply not known. However, an angled slit window in the Paquimé House of the Skulls has a direct line of sight to a stone signaling tower on the top of nearby Cerro de Moctezuma.[113] Swanson has recently suggested that Cerro de Moctezuma was a central point for a signaling system using fire platforms. For evidence of such systems in the Sonora region see chapter 9.[114] Other than these fortifications there is very little evidence of politico-military organization. Because of its great size Paquimé likely had some sort of control over the Casas Grandes Valley, at least for a number of miles up- and downstream from the central city. The nature of this control eludes us, nor do we know if it extended at all to adjacent valleys.

How did Paquimé relate, for example, to Galeana or Villa Ahumada, or to the towns in the Carretas Basin or those of the Animas region? In the Sonoran region, just to the west, we have documentary evidence that groups of nearby towns formed confederacies that often were hostile to each other (see chapter 9). Such confederacies also existed in the Pueblo area, at least by Spanish conquest times, and they were common in Mesoamerica. We have no evidence that this was the case with Paquimé and its neighbors, but it does seem likely that they followed this same widespread pattern. More excavation, especially in the outlying areas, and more detailed analysis of art forms could help to resolve this problem, though some details will probably never be known.

In other parts of the Southwest, weapons of hunting and of warfare tended to be the same, and this likely was the case in the Casas Grandes world. We have less evidence for such weapons at Casas Grandes than we do in the upper Southwest. One curious find was what Di Peso believed were blowgun pellets, seven finely ground stone balls of about blowgun size. These would likely not have been for warfare; the pellet blowgun would not be effective for anything as large as a human being. Because the nearest documented use of blowguns (both pellet and dart varieties) is far to the south and east, I tend to be skeptical that blowguns were in use at Paquimé. The stone balls may have been gaming pieces of some sort.[115]

The bow and arrow was certainly utilized, though exactly what type of bow is uncertain. Fragments of arrows have been found, including small ceremonial arrow shafts. Ninety-eight bifacially chipped projectile points were also found in Di Peso's excavations. These were presumably mostly arrow points, though some might have been for spears or lances.[116] However, evidence for spears in this region is lacking. I suspect that the Casas Grandes people may have used spears at least for warfare, since spears are documented for the statelet people

of northeast Sonora, an area that certainly interacted with Casas Grandes. A total of 904 ax heads were found in Medio period contexts at Paquimé, and John Rinaldo, who commented on these axes, speculated that some of them may have been war axes, one three-quarter grooved specimen being found with a cache of perforated skulls.[117]

The finds of trophy heads and of various kinds of human sacrifice suggest war. Though body armor was probably of perishable materials, one back-shield plaque plus six other fragments were found, strikingly similar to ones on the Toltec Atlantean warrior figures at the site of Tula. Di Peso believed that the two copper plates reported from Paquimé by the Ibarra 1564 expedition were also examples of such shields. The Paquimé plaque was circular, about 9 inches in diameter, and made up of eight panels, four of the panels depicting Xiuhcoatl, as Turquoise Snake, alternating with two turquoise and two hematite mosaics. The panels radiate out from a round center-piece about 4 inches in diameter, undecorated except for two perforations on each side, presumably to facilitate strapping the shield onto its wearer. The specimen looks rather like a spoked wheel with a center axle. It was a heavy object, weighing nearly a pound. These shields show something of the pageantry and glamour of Paquimian military dress and also of the influences of cultures to the south, though probably not the Toltecs per se, whose domain had largely collapsed by the Casas Grandes Medio period.[118]

The end at Paquimé (we have no such controlled information on other sites), in Di Peso's view, came around the time of the vernal equinox (based on the age of macaws found in the ruins). His date of 1340 is no longer credible, and it must have happened in the fifteenth century, a hundred years or more later. According to Di Peso several hundred men, women, and children were killed (actually the burial totals give only 126) and the city wrecked by unknown assailants, probably outside enemies. Di Peso's reconstruction has met some resistance, and it may be that at least part of the skeletal remains he describes represent later, postdestruction, interments. It does seem, however, that Paquimé came to a dramatic and tragic end, involving some sort of hostilities.[119]

The collapse of the Casas Grandes world in the fifteenth century involved not only the central region around Paquimé. In this same general period other Casas Grandes–influenced cultures—the Babícora region to the south, the Carretas Basin to the north and west, the Animas region to the north, the Santa María and Carmén drainages to the east—also ended. This period of turmoil may also have affected the Jornada Mogollon to the northeast and populations of the Cliff phase to the northwest. And we must consider the larger picture. The first half of the fifteenth century also saw the end of Salado, the mountain Mogollon, and the drastic contraction of Western Pueblo. To what extent all these events are tied together is not clear today but could be a fruitful investigation for future archaeologists.

One area that was not affected—or, if so, affected in a positive way—was northeastern Sonora. It is precisely following the time of Casas Grandes' collapse that these vigorous statelets in the Sonoran river valleys expanded their trade reach, contacting the Pueblo and Gila-Salt peoples and probably the lower Colorado groups as well. The trade routes, already flowing along well-marked trails up the west coast of Mexico, now channeled their goods into northern Sonora. There may have been some competition from remnant Casas Grandes communities. For example, both Di Peso and I have suggested that places like Marata represented such settlements (see chapter 9). If so, even these communities seemed to have died out by the time of the Spanish arrival in the early sixteenth century. But the Sonoran area may have been related to Casas Grandes by language and surely by a variety of other contacts. It may be that towns like Marata simply were absorbed in the Sonoran hegemony.

CHAPTER 9

# Sonora and the Trading Connection

By the mid-fifteenth century the Casas Grandes world, the Mountain Mogollon, and the Salado-Hohokam all had collapsed as recognizable cultures. There were descendants of the Hohokam among the sizable populations of Piman- or O'odham-speaking people in the Gila drainage, and these Indians still had a function as middlemen in the trade routes stretching from Mexico to the Pueblo towns. Nevertheless, their role in the drama of Aztlan was now a minor one. The Jornada Mogollon had dwindled, forming into those scattered Manso groups contacted by sixteenth-century explorers. The lower Colorado groups continued on, as they had for centuries, fringe peoples whose inclusion in Aztlan was primarily because of their importance on the Pacific trade routes. The La Junta populations were at a low ebb. In a few decades they would reestablish towns and some trade contacts with the Pueblo area and perhaps even with Sonora. But after the demise of Paquimé, La Junta was an insignificant part of the greater world of Aztlan.[1]

In fact, after the middle of the fifteenth century there remained only two major players in Aztlan, two groups of people who still maintained the exchange of goods and ideas with a wider world. One of these was, of course, the Pueblos, the other a collection of town-dwelling Indians in northeastern Sonora. These were groups for which I suggested in the mid 1970s the name *Sonoran statelets*. Whereas the Pueblo

area was itself shrinking, the Sonoran region was reaping the benefit of newly important trade routes. The statelets may have been near a cultural climax when the first Spaniards arrived.

With the falling away of much of Aztlan, the Pueblos were increasingly important to these Sonoran people. The Sonorans in turn formed the crucial link between Pueblo lands and the shell-rich shorelines of western Mexico. Gulf of California shell, coming from the coastal areas, was now transshipped through the statelets. These well-developed lines of contact contributed to exaggerated accounts of the Pueblos—stories that drew the Spaniards onward during those heady sixteenth-century conquest years.

The statelet area is a region, partly geographical, partly cultural, called the *Serrana*, the rugged mountainous area to the west of Casas Grandes. In this chapter I use the terms *Serrana* and *Sonoran statelets* more or less interchangeably. I have an idea that these Serrana people were molded by their environment even more than other parts of Aztlan, hence the more detailed description of material features given below. The Serrana includes the northernmost expanse of the Sierra Madre Occidental, a mountain chain that begins around the international Mexican-American border and stretches on into west-central Mexico (see Figure 9.1). Unfortunately we have relatively little prehispanic paleoenvironmental

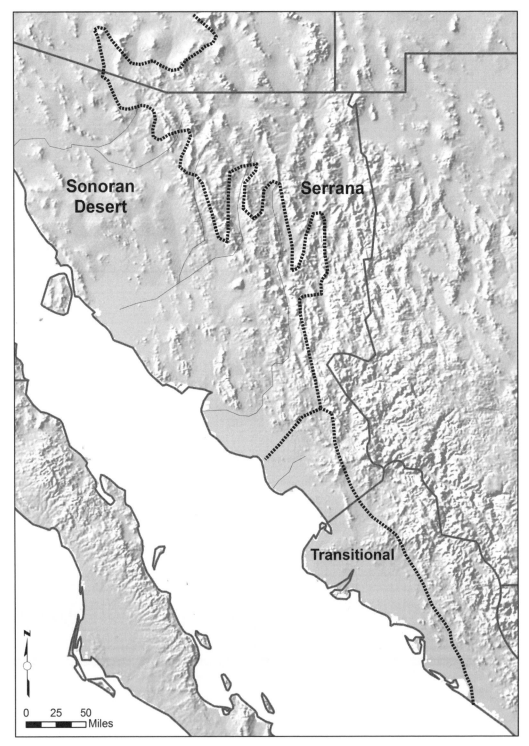

FIGURE 9.1. Sonora, showing the Serrana region (after Braniff, "Preliminary Interpretations"). Earth Analytic, Santa Fe, NM.

data for the Serrana. Here I will discuss the biota, the climate, and the general geography mainly as it exists in the modern period, with the caution that there does seem to have been some environmental deterioration since the time of first Spanish contact.[2]

Most of the major streams of the area drain southwestward, catching the seasonally heavy rains that fall in the upper reaches of the mountains. Because of the rugged nature of the terrain, many of these streams have cut deep canyons as they flow to the Gulf of California and the Pacific Ocean. This is an area of wild scenery, with grand vistas of rugged mountains and twisted canyons. These canyons, or barrancas as they are called in the Sierra Madre, vary from narrow declivities only a few tens of feet deep to such giants as the Barranca del Cobre (to the south of the Serrana proper) deeper and wider than the Grand Canyon. In the upper reaches of the mountains the topography flattens out in broad rolling grassland, called *llanos* or *vegas*, interspersed with heavy conifer growth that even today has ample animal life.

Through the canyons flow small streams, bordered with narrow strips of rich riverine land, and this has been the focus of human settlement for many centuries. The natural flow of human activities in earlier days tended to be along the rivers, with only rough tracks across the intervening mountain ranges. Although this is changing with modern highways, there are still quite remote areas in northeastern Sonora and adjacent Chihuahua. The river valleys are relatively low in elevation; for example, the Ures Basin, drained by the Sonora River, is only about 1,400 feet above sea level, whereas Arizpe, in the upper valley, is more than 2,500 feet. As one goes eastward into the northern part of the Yaqui drainage, the elevation increases. Bavispe on the eastern loop of the Bavispe River, a tributary of the Yaqui, is about 3,600 feet. The highest country is along the Sonoran-Chihuahuan border, with the highest point in this part of the Sierra Madre Occidental more than 9,000 feet.

The area is reasonably well watered. Most of the rain falls from late June through September, with a minor wet season from December through February. The greatest rainfall, that in the high mountain area of the Sonora-Chihuahua border, may exceed 39 inches annually, though it drops off as one goes westward to lower elevations. At Bavispe it is around 16 inches per year, 70 percent or more falling in the summer, and at Ures about 19 inches, three-quarters of it in the summer months. Between the sierra and the Gulf of California is a broad band of desert lowland, the southern extension of the Sonoran Desert. It is generally warm in the lower elevations; for example, at Ures, site of one of the Sonoran statelets, the January mean temperature is about 59°F, and the July mean is some 86°F.[3]

Vegetation varies considerably with altitude. In the middle portions of the river valleys, where most of the population clustered, the vegetation is semidesert, with mesquite, creosote bush, and varieties of cacti, including the cholla that grows profusely on disturbed areas such as archaeological sites. There are acacias, and a scatter of other trees and bushes including guisache, ocotillo, pochote, various palo verdes, yucca, and opuntia. As one ascends the mountains, this vegetation changes to groves of oak and the various conifers, interspersed, as said above, by areas of grassland. The animal life is much like that of Casas Grandes to the east, lagomorphs, white-tailed and mule deer, antelope, mountain sheep, and a few large carnivores, including mountain lions, bears, wolves, foxes, and an occasional jaguar. One difference between the Serrana and Casas Grandes is the utilization of bison in the latter area. The Serrana people did not seem to have much access to the bison. A trade—at least some sort of exchange—in bison hides was reported by early Spaniards, but this trade came from the Pueblo country to the north and east.[4]

The Serrana region was contacted very early in the Spanish exploration of the New World. In 1536, only 44 years after Columbus's first voyage, three Europeans and one African, victims of a shipwreck on the Texas-Louisiana coast several years earlier, reached the Sonora

River valley and stayed a time in a series of towns that they collectively called *Corazones* (Hearts). The name was given because the indigenes had supplied them with several hundred deer hearts. The leader of this little party was Alvar Nuñez Cabeza de Vaca.[5] The African slave member of the party, Esteban de Dorantes, later served as a guide for Fr. Marcos de Niza, who visited the Serrana, or at least the edge of it, in 1539.[6] Melchior Díaz arrived that same year and Coronado and his party in the period 1540–1542.[7] These expeditions gave a considerable amount of information on the area and its people, but the real mass of information came when, after a hiatus of more than 20 years, Francisco de Ibarra explored the area in the period around 1563 or 1564. It was on this far northwest trip that Ibarra crossed the inhospitable sierra to reach Paquimé.[8]

Thus, we have certain kinds of data on the Sonoran area that we cannot obtain for Casas Grandes, ethnohistoric information on the political and religious structure and warfare, for example. The general picture is that of small energetic polities, each with a primate town and satellite villages along the streams (the Sonora River, the Moctezuma, the Bavispe, and other parts of the Yaqui River system). Their citizens were heavily involved in warfare, and they were avid traders. These statelets, at least by Spanish contact times, had formed two major confederacies.[9]

After the Ibarra expedition this portion of northeastern Sonora was left alone for the better part of a century. Missionization was inevitable, however, as the Jesuits gradually pushed farther and farther up the west coast of New Spain and, from about 1615, extended into Sonoran territory with missionization of the Lower Pima area of the middle Yaqui Valley. By the late 1620s the missionaries had reached the edge of Opata territory and in the late 1630s were moving into the Sonora River area, although that region was not fully missionized until the latter part of the 1640s, more than a century after Coronado.

The Jesuits in the seventeenth century found a very different situation from that of Coronado and Ibarra. Gone were the belligerent and vital towns, the warlike federations. The people were thinly spread over the valleys in scattered rancherías. Unlike their predecessors of the previous century they seem to have welcomed the Spaniards and soon became relatively docile converts to Catholicism. There are only hints in the Jesuit documents of a more glorious and independent past. These data about impoverished people, though factual for the century, led to a misunderstanding of the prehistoric and earliest historic situation in Sonora that persists to this day.

This misunderstanding was inadvertently aided by a mind-set about the Southwest, discussed earlier in this book, that the upper Southwest and Mesoamerica were distinct entities—with no real contact beyond certain basic items, mostly relating to agriculture. Although holistically inclined early scholars, like the nineteenth-century archaeologist and historian Adolph F. Bandelier, had pointed out that the Sonoran-Chihuahuan area was rich in archaeological sites, the concept of a "cultural sink" a sort of no-man's-land between the cultural peaks of the Southwest and of Mesoamerica grew until it became an article of faith among many American specialists on the Southwest. Mexican scholars of the time, who might have addressed this problem, had a feast of archaeological riches nearer at hand and were generally indifferent to this rude northwestern frontier of Mexico.[10]

This did not begin to significantly change until the work of geographers Carl Sauer and Donald Brand and the anthropologist Ralph Beals in the late 1920s and 1930s in various parts of the west coast of Mexico. More recently there has been a new concentration on the lower Southwest and the frontiers of Mesoamerica generally. In chapter 8 I discussed the new approaches to Casas Grandes, leading to Di Peso's seminal work in the period beginning around 1958 and of the whorl of activity produced by reactions to Di Peso's ideas. This sort of thing happened, though in a much more muted way, in Sonora. Unfortunately, there was no one great magnet site such as

Paquimé to stimulate the imagination. Nevertheless, work by the Hermosillo office of Mexico's Instituto Nacional de Antropología e Historia (INAH), led by Beatríz Braniff, Arturo Oliveros, and Cynthia Radding, began to fill in some of the spaces in our knowledge, as did work by Americans Roger Dunbier and Richard Felger. About the same time, Richard Pailes and his associates, especially Daniel Reff, William Doolittle, and Virginia Durst, excavated in the Sonora River valley north of the Ures Basin. Since the 1970s there has been a slackening of work in the main statelet area, although Randall McGuire, María Villalpando, and Paul and Suzanne Fish, among others, have surveyed and excavated in peripheral areas such as Trincheras and the Altar region. At present there is new and significant work in the Bavispe area by archaeologists Elizabeth A. Bagwell, John E. Douglas, and Cesar A. Quijada that will surely lead to additional insights.

Still, Sonora remains to some degree an archaeological frontier. One great problem is that the valleys of the major rivers were foci of Spanish settlement, especially after the mission period. Modern towns, some of which can be arguably traced back to aboriginal settlements, now fill the valleys and modern fields, and irrigation systems overlie those of prehispanic times. Pailes has suggested, and I think it probable, that the major statelet centers are underneath modern town centers.[11]

From the work of archaeologists, geographers, and historians over the past three quarters of a century, a picture of the prehistoric situation in northeastern Sonora has gradually evolved, though with much disagreement as to details. Originally the region seems to have been the habitat of the Mogollon-like Rio Sonora culture identified by Monroe Amsden in 1928, originally in the Sonora and Moctezuma valleys but later found to extend throughout much of eastern Sonora. Dating of the culture is not secure, but it probably goes back to the early AD centuries. Elsewhere I have suggested that Rio Sonora, along with early Casas Grandes, Loma San Gabriel in Durango, and Tacuichamona in northern Sinaloa, formed a part of that generalized Mogollon that seems to underlie much of the later cultural activity of this part of the Southwest.[12]

A more or less connected sequence of settlement can be described for the Sonora River valley, beginning around AD 1000, defining what has been called the Serrana culture, presumably the outgrowth of the Rio Sonora culture in northeastern Sonora. At that time the population lived in pithouses (or more correctly, houses-in-pits, since the walls were structurally separate). This Early phase merged into a transitional period sometime before AD 1200 and lasted for a century or century and a half, thus overlapping the Casas Grandes Medio period. It saw an increase in surface adobe structures. The Late phase, extending from the mid-1300s, saw the augmented building of surface adobe houses both single and multistoried. The pithouse drops out as a construction feature, but existing pithouses sometimes continued to be used even into historic times.[13]

Because of the relatively limited archaeological work in the area, the kind of analyses that were conducted for the Casas Grandes area and for much of the upper Southwest cannot be done here. Specialists, however, are fortunate to have considerable historical data from the very earliest Spanish period, something essentially denied for Casas Grandes, whose first visit by literate observers came a century after its demise and the occupation of the region by nomadic peoples.

Although the archaeology to date has concerned itself with what Richard Pailes considers "second tier" or smaller sites, certain of these are reasonably impressive. The San José site (Figure 9.2), just north of present-day Baviácora, and the Las Delicias del Sur and Ojo de Agua sites, near Banámichi, farther north along the Sonora River, were partially excavated, and a large stretch of the Sonora River north of the Ures region was surveyed. In the Late phase William Doolittle, who directed this survey, noted 162 settlements, an increase of some 150 percent over the Early phase. A later report by Pailes gave the number of sites for

FIGURE 9.2. Excavation at the San José site, near Baviácora. Photo by the author.

all periods as 279, of which 253 were in the upper Sonora Valley, the focus of survey of Pailes and his associates.[14] According to Pailes:

> For the Late phase, the San Jose Site has 50 clearly identifiable surface structures, and wall segments indicating at least another 50 structures for which there is surface evidence.... In the Banamichi segment, two very large sites appear as counterparts of the San Jose site in the Baviacora segment. The site of Las Delicias del Sur, dominating the northern half of the Banamichi segment, has at least 200 visible structures, and the Ojo de Agua Site, dominating the southern half of the Banamichi segment, has 85 identifiable structures and numerous wall segments. The latter site has undergone severe erosion, which has seriously reduced the number of houses that can be identified.[15]

Remember that in the excavator's opinion these are second-tier sites. There is considerable public architecture, appearing around the beginning of the Late phase. At San José this includes what Pailes considered to be a ball court, "two parallel, elongated, platforms of stone with a rubble fill."[16] As we have seen in earlier chapters, ball courts in the Greater Southwest, though they may have had sociopolitical functions, seem to be, as they were in Mesoamerica, primarily religious in nature. Therefore, these Sonoran courts will be discussed below in the section on religion. In any case, near the ball court at San José there was a plaza area and beyond that some sort of building complex.

Other features of the Sonoran area are structures that Doolittle believed to be signal emplacements. These were located on heights above the valley floors, each with a panoramic view of the valley, and consisted of circles of rubble, nine to ten feet across raised to the height of a foot or so. Inside them was found burned earth.[17] Such signal sites were described by the earliest Spanish explorers and were used to communicate from one political entity to another. Also found were a series of trincheras, or terraced hills. Trincheras in the Serrana may have been used as settlements, like those in the more western areas, but perhaps had a military purpose as well, as gathering places in war times. This would fit with the ethnohistorical data.[18]

From historical evidence it seems clear that the Serrana people used irrigation systems, probably fairly elaborate ones. Not enough archaeological work has been done to trace the prehistoric systems, but it has been hypothesized that many of the historic and modern irrigation canals were laid down in prehistoric times. A few miles north of Banámichi in the Sonora Valley, carved on the flat side of a large boulder (about 3 feet by 4 feet), is what Doolittle believes to be a map of the local area, giving irrigation ditches, fields, and nearby habitation sites. The majority of information about agriculture in this region comes from historical sources.[19]

The Serrana area produced a considerable amount of pottery—in the excavations by Pailes, about 750,000 sherds. Most of this is plainware and, to the best of my knowledge, has not yet been analyzed in detail. However, about 30,000 of the sherds were decorated, almost all of them a locally made incised ware, sometimes with the addition of polished red paint zones. Some incised pottery, either with or without the red paint, had additional punctated areas. These ceramics were essentially locally produced examples of Playas Red Incised (see Figure 9.3) or Playas Red Punctate, related to Casas Grandes pottery. There were slightly fewer than 800 sherds of various Casas Grandes polychromes, including Ramos, Carretas, Huerigos, Dublán, Babícora, and Villa Ahumada. Other trade ware included a small amount of Gila and Santa Cruz polychromes and a few other sherds of pottery from the upper Southwest. There was also a small amount of ceramics from the Sinaloa region.[20]

At the site of Ojo de Agua de Santa Rosa Corodehuachi, near the loop of the Bavispe River, east of the Sonora River area, Beatríz Braniff of the INAH found a considerable amount of Chihuahuan polychromes (about 375 sherds), as well as more than 500 sherds of Playas Red and a very small amount of Gila Polychrome (see Figure 9.4). This is from a sherd total of approximately 12,900, five-sixths of it plainware. As Braniff has pointed out, there is a considerable distribution of Chihuahuan polychromes in Sonora, extending from the upper Yaqui drainage to the Sonora valley and beyond.[21]

Cave sites in the Sonoran sections of the upper Bavispe drainage explored by Elizabeth Bagwell have Casas Grandes Medio period pottery (see chapter 8). Recent and ongoing work by Douglas and Quijada in the Río Bavispe and a tributary, the Río Huachinera, indicate a long-term occupation in that region. One problem in this area, which needs additional study, is the question of continuity between the late prehistoric materials and the early historic populations of the Bavispe area, known from Jesuit times. During what Douglas and Quijada call the Tardio or Late period (AD 1200–1500), they found considerable populations and a large amount of the Chihuahuan polychromes, especially Carretas and Huerigos varieties. There was a certain amount

FIGURE 9.3. Playas Red Incised pottery. El Paso Museum of Archaeology.

FIGURE 9.4. Gila Polychrome bowl. El Paso Museum of Archaeology.

of construction, as yet undefined, that may be some sort of public architecture although not in clear association with the largest sites, as occurs in the Sonora River region. As Douglas and Quijada say:

It is rarely acknowledged that the geographical extensive reconstruction created by Riley (1987, 1999) has been subject to archaeological testing in only a very small area of northeastern Sonora (Doolittle 1984, 1988). The Bavispe Valley provides a new location to examine the standard model. Unlike the Sonora Valley, there is a lack of correlation between the largest sites and public architecture, settlements show a more continuous scale of size ranking, and the two sites with public architecture are close together rather than dispersed along the drainage. In contrast to past work in northeastern Sonora, the data at hand suggest a more dynamic settlement system with greater competition between settlements. While this result is not completely unanticipated (Douglas 1995) the evidence from our study suggests that Riley's (1987, 1999) model of sizable structurally similar, pre-Hispanic "statelets" may need to be modified to account for more variability in the pre-Hispanic settlement systems in the area.[22]

Figure 9.5 is a statelet map that I drew in the 1980s, when our only detailed data were from the Sonora Valley for the "standard model" position at that time. As I pointed out then, the statelet locations (at least for the eastern group) were "highly conjectural." I imagine that a clearer picture about statelets, their meaning, and distribution will emerge within the next decade or two as additional archaeological work is done not only in the Bavispe area but also in other regions of the Moctezuma and other upper Yaqui drainages.

In the Sonora River excavations 22 stone spindle whorls were uncovered, as well as a number of ceramic whorls. No cotton has yet been found archaeologically, but the earliest Spanish accounts make it clear that cotton was grown. With three of the stone whorls at the San José site is pollen evidence for *rumex,* a plant used for dyeing cotton.[23]

Pailes has suggested that the region might well have been an exporter of cotton products. Certainly, luxury goods were *imported*. These imports included turquoise beads, shell, copper tinklers, and the Chihuahuan polychromes. Four fragments of figurines and one fragment of an effigy vessel represent pieces that Pailes believes might have come from Mesoamerica or, at the very least, represented Mesoamerican concepts. The effigy fragment that I have seen illustrated, however, does not look particularly Mesoamerican.

Though limited, the archaeological evidence suggests good-sized towns. Exactly how large the major centers were is not known, but the San José site, probably a second-level town, seems to have covered some 60 acres, though probably not all built-up. Certain of the real primary centers, still undiscovered, may have been quite large indeed. There was a decided gradation of sites, from ones like San José and Las Delicias, to intermediate villages like La Mora (which was still large enough to have public architecture), down to tiny hamlets and homesteads.[24]

Looking at the Serrana as a whole, it seems clear, even from the limited demographic data, that the area expanded, population-wise, over time and may have been nearing capacity when the Spaniards arrived. Doolittle believes that there was an annual growth rate of 0.5 percent and perhaps higher. Whether or not the collapse of the Casas Grandes system augmented the population in Sonora (whether the Serrana region became a refuge area for Casas Grandes populations) is uncertain, though Doolittle feels that the Serrana growth could have been generated internally. Whatever the sources of growth, he believes that the Serrana population may have been 100,000 in the first part of the sixteenth century, with the central Sonora Valley reaching numbers of 10,000 to 15,000 individuals. For the Serrana as a whole, there are estimates of 130,000 to 140,000 acres of productive agricultural land. Irrigation was probably extensive, especially in the main valleys, and there is documentary evidence for double cropping.[25]

Daniel Reff, looking at the population estimates from an epidemiological point of view, believes that the Opata portion of the Serrana alone had 70,000 people in late prehispanic times, dropping disastrously to 40,000 by the time of the Jesuit entradas in the 1630s. I have

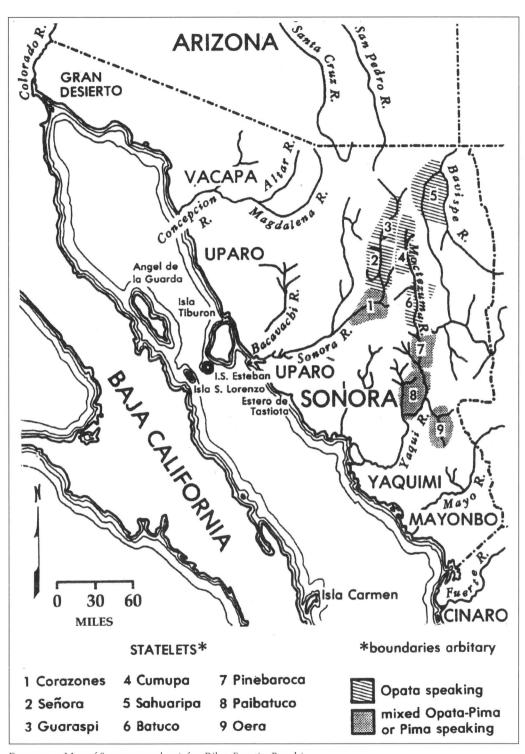

FIGURE 9.5. Map of Sonoran statelets (after Riley, *Frontier People*).

elsewhere estimated the total Serrana population to have been perhaps 90,000, including both Opata and town-dwelling Pima who lived in the southern and southwestern part of the region. This figure fits reasonably well with the calculations of both Doolittle and Reff.

If Reff's figures are reasonably correct (and they involve the best evidence available), some sort of demographic disaster overtook the Serrana area between the mid-sixteenth and early seventeenth centuries. It would certainly account for the huge disparity in the descriptions of the Coronado and Ibarra parties and the first Jesuit missionaries.[26] I made this point in an earlier publication:

> A 40 percent rapid decline in the population must have created a cultural and social crisis of giant proportions. Such catastrophes have been studied in other parts of the world. A very well-documented one is the bubonic plague that struck western Europe from 1348 to 1350. This "black death" caused the death of perhaps 20 percent of the population of England in those years and a decline of 40 percent to 50 percent over the next quarter century. . . . Although the national government maintained itself, local towns and farming villages were devastated, and the wholesale loss of life produced massive changes that greatly modified the social landscape of the country. What the Jesuits found was an analogous situation, Opata and Southern Pima groups reeling from the demographic blows of introduced European disease.[27]

On their march up the west coast of Mexico, beginning in the late 1520s, the Spaniards overran a series of rich cultures, creating havoc and devastation as they went. Citizens of these areas felt the first shock waves of Spanish disease and the disruption by Spanish contacts farther south even before 1530. They took the brunt of the brutal conquest of Nuño Beltrán de Guzmán in the early 1530s. By the end of that decade their populations could still put up a token resistance, but shortly afterward they disappeared, victims of Spanish disease,

slave raiding, and general brutality. By the late 1530s the Spaniards had basically destroyed the cultures of Nayarit and southern and central Sinaloa. In the coastal areas of Nayarit and Sinaloa, extending to the Culiacán area, were a series of entities, which are now known collectively as the *Pequeños Estados* or "Small States."[28] If we only knew more of these little states, we might be able to draw parallels with the Sonoran situation. That we know anything at all is, curiously enough, a sort of offshoot of their destruction. Carl Sauer and Donald Brand made this point three quarters of a century ago:

> Our area was almost completely destroyed because it was overrun in 1530 and 1531 by about as hard a gang of killers as Spain let loose anywhere in the New World and because in those days there was no stay upon the killing propensities of conquerors. The very ferocity of Nuño de Guzmán's entrada, however, led later to a series of depositions and relations which give a fair insight, for the time, into the conditions of native life at the moment of the conquest.[29]

Sauer and Brand were perhaps a bit optimistic about the amount of usable information that can be derived from these accounts. We do know, however, that there were large populations, good-sized towns, a fairly sophisticated political structure, and extensive agriculture.[30] I suspect that they were organized somewhat as were the Sonoran statelets, with which they were almost certainly in communication, at least by way of trade, and perhaps other forms of contact, political or religious, as well.

But this west-Mexican region belongs to the Mesoamerican world rather than to that of Aztlan. Between the Pequeños Estados and the Sonoran statelet area lay a series of Cahitan-speaking peoples (Mayo and Yaqui among other groups) where there were also large populations but which do not seem to have quite the level of political organization of those groups that lay both to the south and to the north.[31] My impression is that the peoples of the lower Fuerte, Mayo, and Yaqui valleys were organized like the lower Colorado people (see chapter 6). I freely grant that more work needs to be done on this region, especially archaeological work, but we also need reanalysis of the historical sources. For example, it seems clear that the ravages of disease in the latter part of the sixteenth century and early part of the seventeenth greatly changed the cultural picture in those regions, as it did throughout the Mexican west coast.

For the Yaqui area alone Reff estimated a decline from about 60,000 Indians found in the aboriginal population in 1533 to half that number by 1617. Some of the depredations may have been caused by the Spanish frontier captain Diego Martínez de Hurdaide, whose unrelenting wars against the Yaqui began shortly after 1600. However, Martínez de Hurdaide was trying to further the mission program and would hardly have indulged in the ruthless behavior of the kind that took place in southern and central Sinaloa during the Guzmán years. One must logically look at disease as the major causative factor in Yaqui population decline. The figures for the Yaqui are typical of the Mayo and other groups in that region.[32]

As I said above, the Serrana area initially escaped the fate suffered by groups to the south. It seems that the Coronado entrada of 1539–1542 did introduce disease. In fact, it is really not credible that an army of 1,500 or more people could have marched back and forth through the area, occupying part of it for a year or so, without putting at risk a population, unadapted to European diseases. Nevertheless, the statelet area was clearly still viable by Ibarra's time, 20 years later. The Spanish diseases may have been there, of course, for not all diseases cause an immediate decline in population. There is no evidence that Coronado's party carried either measles or smallpox, two illnesses that elsewhere in sixteenth-century New Spain caused immediate, catastrophic death tolls. Measles, for example, seems to have reached the Sinaloan area in 1533 or 1534, with devastating effect on the native population, but it does not appear to have spread northward

quite this early. Smallpox certainly contributed to population decline in the early seventeenth century but may not have reached the Serrana region during the sixteenth century.[33]

But there *is* reason to think that Coronado's people brought malaria. Children and pregnant women are especially vulnerable to malaria, with increased childhood mortality and lessened fertility. In the case of this disease full impact would not be seen for perhaps two or three generations. Cholera, typhus, typhoid, and dysentery were already in Sinaloa by Coronado's time, and it is possible that one or more of these were introduced into Sonora by his party.[34]

However that may be, the Cabeza de Vaca, Coronado, and Ibarra expeditions all give us descriptions of a particular Aztlan society in full bloom. Considering its importance, it might be well to pause a moment here and discuss the *nature* of Spanish sources for this particular area and also for the Southwest as a whole.

The early Spaniards entering the Greater Southwest, always from a Mexican base with the one exception of the very early Cabeza de Vaca party, wrote from several different perspectives, depending on the individuals involved and to some degree on the period in which they lived. Spaniards *could* be observant, as the Franciscan missionaries in central Mexico were demonstrating at this very date. Their ethnological techniques, however, did not seem to have been much utilized by the early explorers and settlers in the Southwest. A partial exception was Hernando de Alarcón, leader of a 1540 expedition to the lower Colorado River. Unfortunately, this rather observant and objective man did not get into the Serrana.

Generally speaking, these first reporters can be divided into two major groups: secular chroniclers of expeditions whose concerns were largely economic and political, and missionaries who were aiming to extend Christianity to the native peoples. These two different groups were to some degree in competition, but we should not make too much of that. The conquistadors, generally, were attuned to the needs of the religious, and the missionaries in their turn believed firmly in Spanish conquest, and economic exploitation of the region, if only as a necessary adjunct to missionization.

Still, there were different mind-sets, even within each group, and different "coloration" in the accounts given. Within the secular group the priorities and agendas of leaders like Coronado and his lieutenants, and, therefore, their view of things, did not necessarily coincide with that of writers, who were not part of the power structure, such as Castañeda and perhaps Obregón. The missionary accounts may be flavored by the utopianism and sympathy to native peoples such as those of the crusading bishop Bartolomé Las Casas or, to some degree, Marcos de Niza. Missionaries, however, could be coldly indifferent, as was Fr. Juan de Padilla, of the Coronado expedition. But however solicitous of Indian welfare certain individuals might be, *all* churchmen, whatever their missionary order, were ruthless in their destruction of native culture and values.

The very diversity of approaches to reporting on native peoples gives us several windows on native life in the Sonoran area. Cabeza de Vaca, Díaz, Castañeda, and Ibarra were interested in the technology, economics, and demography of the region and to some degree in group mores. Coronado saw the area with an administrator's eye. Unlike the run-of-the-mill missionary, Las Casas often showed a considerable interest in native religion. One problem with Las Casas is that his books ranged over the entire Spanish New World, and he usually was not an eyewitness to things he reported. There is always the worry that he may have mixed up information in inappropriate ways. As far as one can tell, however, this did not happen in the Serrana.

There was often a tendency to inflate the importance of the Indian tribes, towns, and areas for various purposes but especially to obtain more governmental backing and help for conquest or missionization. Marcos de Niza likely did this to some degree, though less so in the Serrana than at Cibola. Marcos is also probably responsible for the Las Casas material, which many scholars consider to be

exaggerated. Whether it actually was can only be tested with more archaeology.

All in all there seems to me to be less of this sort of exaggeration in Sonora than, for example, in the Pueblo Southwest, where secular captains like Antonio de Espejo and friars like Alonzo de Benavides wildly inflated population figures and where Juan de Oñate gave a grossly optimistic view of the natural wealth of the region. With the possible exception of Las Casas the demographic and town size estimates are fairly reasonable, as measured against other evidence. And even Las Casas's figures are not grossly out of line.

But perhaps the most important factor in evaluating these native data is to remember that even the most objective Spaniards saw Indians through their own Hispano-Catholic *cultural* lenses. A given chronicler might be interested in native religion, but it was judged against the one *true* religion, Catholic Christianity. All native deities were considered either false or, more commonly, manifestations of the Christian devil. Aspects of ceremonies might be reported as oddities, but no native ceremonial had any intrinsic worth. In secular matters political and social institutions were understood only in reference to European institutions. There was a bland indifference to native art. Some of the missionaries were interested in Amerind languages, although not for any comparative value but as vehicles for missionization. The upshot is that there may be considerable and varied information, but it must be evaluated very carefully.

To my mind documentary accounts, not only from the Southwest but from *anywhere,* work best when used in tandem with archaeology, comparative linguistics, biological anthropology, and ethnology, each of the various data sets supporting the others. That is not to deny that in the final analysis there are certain kinds of highly specific information that only history, or at least some sort of written documentation, can give.

For example, the historical sources suggest some tantalizing if rather vague evidence of statelet groups projected into the past. When

Marcos de Niza visited the general region in 1539, traveling north (or northeast) from the settlement of Vacapa, he heard of three rich kingdoms, Marata, Totonteac, and Acus. Exactly where Marcos was when he heard those stories is not certain. I place Vacapa in the Altar Valley, which would seem to put Marcos, as he traveled on north and east, perhaps in the extreme headwaters of either the Santa Cruz or more likely the San Pedro. However, others see Vacapa as farther south, perhaps in northern Sinaloa. If that were the case, Marcos would be somewhere in the Serrana, possibly even in the statelet area. Various attempts have been made to identify these mysterious places. The classic identification of Totonteac is the Hopi area, and, as for Acus, scholars have generally assumed it to be the Pueblo town of Acoma.[35]

Both Di Peso and I pointed out many years ago that Marata did not seem to be inhabited as of Marcos's time and perhaps dated to the previous century. Di Peso believed that Marata and Totonteac were remnant Casas Grandes colonies, formed after the breakup of Paquimé. Marata he thought to be in the Animas region of the New Mexico boot heel, Totonteac on the upper Gila. He did very tentatively accept the location of Acus as Acoma Pueblo.[36]

As I have argued elsewhere, Totonteac is certainly *not* Hopi, nor is Acus Acoma. My own identification of Marata, Totonteac, and Acus has varied over time, and perhaps we will never properly place the three sites. One clue might be in names. *Marata* is probably an Opata word, using the preposition *ma* in the sense of "with." *Totonteac* is pretty clearly a Pima word and means something like "Ant Place," while *Acus* may be also Piman, referring to a ravine or arroyo. However, except for tending to rule out the upper Southwest, this does not significantly help us with locations.[37]

More recently, Richard Flint and Shirley C. Flint have made the interesting suggestion that Marata is Casas Grandes itself and Totonteac the Hohokam area.[38] They are somewhat equivocal about Acus but have advanced the idea that it might be a folk memory of the great

towns of Chaco Canyon. Future archaeological work and possibly even new documentary sources may shed more light on these intriguing, but at present rather phantasmic, places.

What the Spaniards found were active and very warlike statelets, controlling segments of the Sonora, Moctezuma, Yaqui, and Bavispe river systems. Those of the Sonora Valley were most heavily impacted by Spanish parties, and, as we have seen, this river valley has also been the focus of the most systematic archaeology. It probably was the center of the statelet region, and three of the best reported settlements (Corazones, Señora, and Guaraspi) came from there; the fourth, Oera, was probably located on the Nuri, a north-draining tributary of the middle Yaqui. It would seem that both Opata and Pima languages were spoken, Opata in the powerful state of Señora and in Guaraspi, Cumupa, Batuco, and Sahuaripa, while Corazones may well have had a mixed-speech population. Oera and other less-known statelets on the middle Yaqui were probably Piman speaking.

As is generally true of Spanish documents of the period, the cultural information on the region is very uneven, both in detail and reliability. The data are most abundant in certain aspects of material culture, military practices, trade, and settlement size. There is less information on such things as religion, social and political organization, and arts and crafts.

The physical setup of the statelets is fairly well known, from sixteenth-century descriptions by Cabeza de Vaca and his companions and from Bartolomé de Las Casas, who seems to have had available an otherwise unknown manuscript or letter from Marcos de Niza. There is diverse information from the Coronado expedition, including the accounts of Díaz, Coronado himself, and other members of his party, some of whom testified during the Coronado *residencia* hearings. For the later Ibarra expedition we have accounts by Baltasar de Obregón and Antonio Ruiz. An interesting thing about these particular sixteenth-century documents is that in general their reports give the same overall picture of the culture, even though the two major entradas were a quarter century apart. The seventeenth century gives us less information, for by that time the statelets had collapsed, but there are certain hints of a more elaborate past in the various Jesuit documents.

The archaeological record shows graduated sites from towns of several hundred houses to tiny hamlets and homesteads, a situation that generally fits with the historic descriptions. This point was very competently made by William Doolittle a number of years ago:

> In general, it appears that the late-phase settlement pattern confirms the existence of statelets. Although the site hierarchy is more complex than that recorded in the ethnohistorical record and described by Riley, a pattern in which one site was considerably larger and more centrally and nodally located than the others did exist in late-prehistoric times. Anomalies in the settlement hierarchy seem to reflect environmental rather than cultural factors. Such an interpretation is not inconsistent with descriptions provided by the Spanish chroniclers. These early reporters were more interested in identifying sites of cultural significance than they were in asserting settlement patterns. In all likelihood they ignored many larger-than-average sites that were not distinctly centers of regional activities.[39]

The Coronado accounts talk of valleys, especially Corazones (Ures Basin) and Señora (Sonora Valley above the Ures Gorge). These areas were thickly settled with important towns, adjacent to smaller settlements with extensive planted fields extending up and down the valleys. Coronado established a way station, called San Gerónimo de los Corazones, before moving on to the upper Southwest.[40] The death of Coronado's commander in the region, Melchior Díaz, left control in the hands of Diego de Alcaráz. This brutal and incompetent captain operated from this new Spanish town where he began gold-mining operations.

The question of gold is an interesting one. Marcos de Niza, in his rapid side trip to the edge of Serrana country, reported hearing that the Indians used gold vessels, earrings, and little blades for scraping away sweat. However, there is no archaeological evidence that natives in the Serrana region ever used, much less mined, the metal. But the Spaniards under Alcaráz do seem to have discovered some gold, since the fact is mentioned by Castañeda from the Coronado expedition. This likely was a very minor operation, for it obviously failed to interest Spanish officials or settlers. Otherwise, a gold rush into northern Sonora would likely have ensued.[41]

During the Alcaráz period the Spanish settlement of Corazones was not in the same location as the native town seen by Cabeza de Vaca. It was first placed in the Señora region, then moved to an upper section of river called Suya. It was a settlement without a future. Alcaráz's brutality quickly led to a revolt in 1541, and Alcaráz and a number of other Spaniards were killed (estimates run as high as a hundred, though a dozen or so is more likely correct), the rest fleeing the area.[42] Although the sources are somewhat conflictive on this point, Coronado, on his return to Mexico in 1542, decided to bypass the hostile natives of the upper Sonora basins, probably detouring via the Moctezuma Valley, where the statelet of Batuco, being out of Alcaráz's reach, had remained friendly. Where he went from there is not clear, but the Indians of the original Corazones (Ures Basin) had also remained friendly, and he may have reached them over a trail, likely the same one that in later times ran from the Moctezuma Valley to present-day Baviácora.[43]

Confederacies in the region are suggested by the Coronado accounts, but it is from the Ibarra expedition in the early 1560s that we get most evidence. At that time there were two major federations in this area. One was under the control of Señora and probably contained towns in the Sonora, Moctezuma, and perhaps Bavispe valleys. A second was controlled by Oera and had a more southerly distribution.

There is some hint that this political split may have been along linguistic lines, Opata vs. Pima. The statelet of Batuco, in the middle Moctezuma Valley, seems to have been independent of both these groupings and may have served as a "mediating" frontier town. Where Corazones stood in all this is not clear, but if Corazones was in the Ures Basin, as seems likely, it had a certain amount of geographical isolation and may also have been aloof from political entanglements.[44]

Statelet people were subject to attack by, and conducted hostilities with, the Querecho of the old Casas Grandes area. At this early date these Querecho were probably not Apaches, though exactly *who* they were is not clear. The statelet groups also warred with the "wild Huparo" (probably ancestors of the Seri) along the Sonoran coast to the west. Oera also had hostile relationships with Cinaro on the Fuerte River, in modern-day northern Sinaloa. That the Señora group might have had more friendly relations with Cinaro is suggested by Obregón when describing a battle with the northern confederacy in the Sahuaripa region. Smoke signals form an important motif in Obregón's narrative:

> This league and alliance [liga y junta] was summoned by means of messengers and many high columns of smoke. News of the battle was spread for 300 leagues, it reached Cinaro within two days ... through the wiles of the devil or through smoke signals. This seems more likely because the natives spend hours communicating with each other, town to town, province to province. Thus, by those signals and messages the news, as I understand, reached the province of Cinaro, three hundred leagues distant from Sahuaripa, in two days.[45]

This would seem to be a historical verification of the structures, high above the Sonora River valley, that were identified as signal towers by Doolittle.

One thing that was noticed by all the early parties was the warlike nature of these statelets and their federations and the large amount of ceremonial activity related to war. It was most dramatically noted by the Ibarra party when it entered the region in the early 1560s.[46] The party arrived first at Oera, which Obregón describes as a town of a thousand houses, and perhaps 2,000 people, in a valley six miles long filled with irrigated fields. Oera was head of a confederacy that had at least 20 towns and was generally hostile to the people of the Sonora Valley. Near this first significant Serrana settlement Ibarra was met by a 20-man deputation, dressed in fine clothing, woven with cotton and white agave thread. After a gift exchange Ibarra went on, and the next day, a half-mile or so from the town, he was given an escort by another, more clearly military, party of 400 men:

> They were well dressed in blankets made of cotton and of extremely white and bright agave thread, and also elegant and showy feather plumes, beads, conches, pearl-bearing sea shells, bows, spears of brazil wood or shields and macanas. They arrived very much in order, in two squadrons, bringing quantities of maize, beans, fruits, and game, which they presented to the governor. He received them courteously and presented gifts of shirts. On this road he and the army went into the town. It is made up of good flat-roofed houses about an estado and a half in height and excellently grouped. Their fields are crossed by acequias with which they irrigate. They gather a great deal of maize, Castilian beans, melons, squash, and other vegetables.[47]

Some interpretation is needed here. One and a half estados is roughly 8.25 feet, about right for one-story houses. Doolittle, however, points out that in the Sonora River sites there are multistone footings wide enough to meet modern structural codes for multistory adobe houses. These sometimes are associated with inordinate amounts of melted adobe, again suggesting large structures. The melons were probably Spanish imports, for Obregón indicates that melon seeds brought by Coronado's party had been adopted by the Indians. Whether the Castilian beans, "frijol de Castilla," were chickpeas, as Hammond and Rey suggest, or some other kind of bean is unknown. Apropos of Spanish goods, Cabeza de Vaca in 1536 saw a metal buckle and a horseshoe nail used as decorations in the Corazones region, and Castañeda mentioned "Castilian chickens" in the same region in 1540.[48]

From Oera the Ibarra group struggled across wild terrain, meeting various of the mountain people, who were eager to trade food for glass and iron objects. Eventually the party reached the first settlements of the Señora region. It is clear that Señora *federation* to the Ibarra party referred not only to the Sonora Valley settlements but across the sierra to the Moctezuma and probably the Bavispe as well. Working their way up the Sonora Valley, Ibarra and his soldiers found a heavily settled area where the major towns each had several hundred houses and were set seven to ten miles apart. They included Guaraspi (probably modern Arizpe), which had 600 to 700 terraced houses with adobe walls, planned streets *(concertadas calles),* and irrigated fields. From Guaraspi Ibarra's army reached Batuco, a five-day march. As I said above, this town, which had been friendly to Coronado, was most likely in the Moctezuma Valley and like the other towns was very warlike, having sporadic wars with the Querechos to the east. The statelet map shown earlier (see Figure 9.5) represents my "guesstimate" of the geographical locations of these various statelets. With new research, especially in the eastern part of the Serrana, there will no doubt need to be modifications of the map.

From Batuco the Ibarra party traveled over the mountains again to Sahuaripa, a fortress town that had mustered 600 warriors, which I have very tentatively placed somewhere in the Bavispe bend area.[49] It was on the Querecho frontier and the last town of the Señora confederacy. After fighting a battle at Sahuaripa, Ibarra moved on (or was forced on) eastward, to an unnamed town probably on the present-day Sonora-Chihuahua border: "This town marked the limits of the federation and the natives lost the opportunity and hope of enjoying plunder from a victory over us (plunder they were already arguing with each other about). Here ended the lands of their friends and we encountered the territory of the Querechos, neighbors of the cattle people."[50] Ibarra was now entering the Casas Grandes Valley. Here the Spaniards were finally beyond the boundaries of the Señora federation.

The warlike nature of the statelets is obvious in all of the early accounts except perhaps for that of the Cabeza de Vaca party. Even Cabeza de Vaca mentioned that "people who were warring, immediately made friends so that they might meet us and give us gifts."[51] He also mentions the deadly tree used to make arrow poisons. But this four-man group was met with courtesy and cooperation, and likely the newcomers were taken for traders and probably also for shamans with benevolent curing skills. Other groups, beginning with Coronado, had to fight their way into or, more generally, out of the area. After Ibarra had broken through east of the Sierra Madre, winding up in the Casas Grandes Valley, he returned through nearly impassable terrain, probably in the Papigochic region, simply to avoid the hostile Señora fighting force. He swung to the south and eventually reached Cinaro without further hostilities.[52]

Because of the considerable amount of fighting done by the Spaniards in the statelet area, we know something of the weaponry and tactics of the native armies. There was a variety of weapons including spears of a hardwood that the Spaniards called brazil wood, bows, and clubs, with shields for defense. There are various mentions of the "macana" (a corruption of the Aztec word, *macuahuitl*), which in the Aztec world generally referred to a club set with obsidian teeth (see Figure 9.6). We do not know if the Serrana people utilized this refinement.[53] One thing that terrified members from Spanish expeditions throughout the period was a particular kind of arrow poison. This poison drew comments from Cabeza de Vaca,

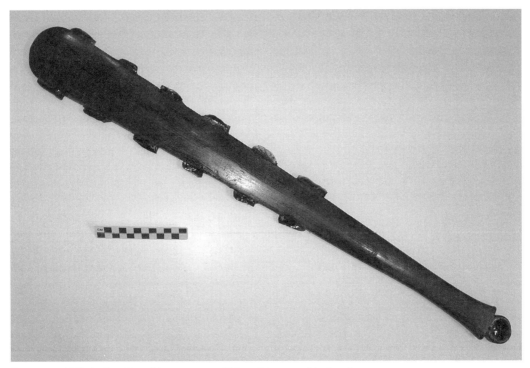

FIGURE 9.6. Full-sized replica of Aztec macana. El Paso Museum of Archaeology.

Jaramillo, Paradinas, Contreras, and Castañeda of the Coronado expedition and (with much detail) from Obregón from the Ibarra party. It is also mentioned by various of the Jesuit missionaries in the seventeenth and eighteenth centuries.

This poison came from the sap of a tree of the family Euphorbiaceae. In the general area there are a number of species of this tree, grouped into two genera, *Sebastiana* and *Sapium*, both of which were tapped in later historic times to obtain fish poison. If the frightened reactions of the Spaniards is any indication, the poison they found so troublesome came from a particularly virulent example of a Euphor, one that has not been conclusively identified today.[54]

Other documentary information dovetails with what we know archaeologically. Smoke-signal towers figure prominently in the Obregón narrative, and, as discussed above, the Ibarra party found that information on one of their battles had gone from the upper part of the statelet area to Cinaro in the Fuerte Valley of

northern Sinaloa in two days. Doolittle (see above) has demonstrated a segment of the system along the ridges overlooking the Sonora River. Other sections of the signal chain have not been found farther south in Sonora and in the north of Sinaloa, but then, to the best of my knowledge, no one has systematically searched. This might be a useful goal for future archaeologists.

The actual tactics of the statelet war parties are not discussed in any detail, but both Castañeda and Obregón talk of fortress towns that might be stocked with foodstuffs for a siege.[55] Archaeologically, such sites have been found; Adolph F. Bandelier in 1884 visited one at Baserac in the upper Yaqui drainage,[56] and Doolittle and Pailes have identified several of these sites. Obregón described Sahuaripa as such a site. It seems to have been a collecting center for the army, and according to Obregón the Señora federation was able to amass 15,000 fighting men against Ibarra at that place. Granted that these numbers are considerably exaggerated, but they still suggest a high level of political organization. Not much is known about the internal structure of these armies. Obregón does say that his "honor guard" at Oera arrived in two columns, and in the Sahuaripa night attack the Indians were organized into three columns, using spears, macanas, and clubs.[57] The ubiquitous bow was not used in this engagement, a tactic that suggested a specific night maneuver.

As late as the nineteenth century, at least in the Yaqui Valley, there were still rather widespread tales of the statelets and their wars with the inhabitants of Casas Grandes.[58] It is difficult to deny that the Serrana area was, at least in the sixteenth century, one of extreme bellicosity, a region where safety lay in alliance, military readiness, and in ever-present vigilance against all comers. The statelets, at least those of the Señora federation, had let down their guard a bit with Coronado, perhaps relying too much on their good experience with Cabeza de Vaca. They learned a bitter lesson, and Ibarra, two decades later, was met with unrelenting hostility.

If one of the hallmarks of the Aztlan period in the Southwest was warfare, another certainly was trade and a lively interchange of ideas. As shown earlier, styles of pottery making, rock art, and architecture spread widely, as did certain technologies and religious ideology. An important engine that ran this dissemination of ideas and material objects had always been trade. In that fundamental reality I do agree with Charles C. Di Peso. Here I am not endorsing Di Peso's ideas about political hegemony over large portions of the Southwest and the economic-political domination by Casas Grandes. Logistic problems alone would make it most unlikely that Casas Grandes, or any other cultural segment of Aztlan, controlled any other segment.

One especially puzzling thing is exactly where the kachina cult, its origins and dissemination, fits into the Serrana picture, an area with obvious trading connections to the upper Southwest. If the roots of the cult were in Casas Grandes, it is hard to explain why more, specifically Paquimé-derived, material culture

items did not move into the northeastern quadrant of Aztlan. There is no present evidence that the kachina cult originated in northeastern Sonora. Perhaps it came from farther south, possibly in the Sinaloa coastal region. In that case kachina ideas could have flowed along the Sonoran trade routes. However, that leaves the puzzling fact that they seem to have reached the upper Southwest a century or so before that fifteenth-century spike in trade materials to northeastern Aztlan. Indeed, the kachina cult (wherever it came from) may well have represented a true politico-religious movement into the upper part of the Southwest, not tied—or not directly tied—to exchange systems and the general economics of the greater region.

In the statelet area of Sonora, trade, like warfare, was likely in the hands of or at least much influenced by the alliances or federations. As we saw in chapter 7, federations also existed in the Pueblo area. In that part of Aztlan they seemed to fall along linguistic lines, and the same thing might have been true in the Serrana. Federations may well have existed *elsewhere* in Aztlan. Unfortunately, the archaeological evidence is not clear on this point, and our ethnohistorical information for the core area of Aztlan encompasses only the Pueblos and the Serrana.

In any case the importance of trade in the statelet region was noted by every sixteenth-century Spanish party. It is clear that this part of Sonora was now the primary entry point for goods flowing to and from Mexico and the upper Southwest. Of course, commodity exchanges were made in other parts of Aztlan. Goods from the lower Colorado and from the California coast were also important, and the eastern Pueblo world had a flourishing trade operating with the Great Plains.

Cabeza de Vaca, in 1536, was the first to note this connection between the Sonoran statelets both with the west coast of Mexico and with the upper Southwest. There were shell and corals coming into the statelets from coastal Gulf of California. He observed hides (most likely transshipped from the plains) and turquoise in quantity from the Pueblo world, described as a land of populous towns and very large houses (pueblos de mucha gente y casas muy grandes). Other interesting items of trade that Cabeza de Vaca received from the north consisted of five arrow points made of "emerald." These five stones were unfortunately lost on the trip south. I doubt if they were actually emeralds; peridots are more likely or possibly green garnets. All of these semiprecious stones are found in the Pueblo region. In this regard it might be mentioned that stone arrow points (often ones found in archaeological sites) have deep ceremonial significance for modern Pueblo Indians.[59]

Cabeza de Vaca also noted that the Pueblo Indians received in return "penachos y plumas de papagayo." This is usually translated as "plumage and feathers of parrots," but likely the most important birds were macaws. The military macaw (Ara militaris) has a habitat that extends into the Serrana, as does the similarly plumaged thick-billed parrot (Rhynchopsitta pachyrhyncha). However, if the Ara macao, or scarlet macaw, much valued in the Pueblo world, was involved, there is a serious question of how the statelet people obtained those birds. Their source would have been the lowlands of southeast Mexico, the same source used by the people of Casas Grandes. It may well be that on the collapse of Paquimé and the Casas Grandes world, the parrot and feather merchants of the Mexican east coast shifted their emphasis to the Sonoran statelets. The story that the Huaxteca Indian Tejo told Nuño de Guzmán in 1530 about such trade in his own father's time (see chapter 8) could have referred to the statelet area. Scarlet macaws did reach the Pueblos in late prehistoric and early historic times (see chapters 7 and 8), and they certainly came from somewhere.

When the Coronado party reached northeastern Sonora in the period 1539–1542, they received various kinds of information about trade and other contacts. If my routing is correct, Marcos de Niza did not actually get into the statelet area in 1539 except for a brief side expedition near the end of the journey. However, he did swing both west and north of the

region and reported much evidence of trade, including hide shields, turquoise, pottery vessels, shell, and cloth. Coronado's captain, Melchior Díaz, spent the winter of 1539–1540 in what seems to have been the statelet area and obtained very detailed and generally correct information from informants, some of whom had lived in the Western Pueblo region for 15 to 20 years. He does not discuss trade as such, though he did obtain certain semiprecious stones that had originated in the Pueblo lands. Unfortunately, our sources do not give further identification. The most dramatic thing about the Díaz account is the high level of correct information he gave about Cíbola, even though he clearly never went much beyond the statelet area.[60] Contacts between the statelets and the Pueblo Southwest certainly involved a great deal of information passing from one area to the other.

As we might expect, the Ibarra group gives the most detail in trade matters:

> They have many slaves imprisoned in wooden stocks [con armas de madera]. They barter these slaves for others and sell them for mantas, salt, feathers, and for provisions, especially salt which they do not possess. In its place they eat alum...and engage in war for it with the people of Batuco and with those who live on the coast of the South Sea [Gulf of California] even if it is over twenty-five leagues away. The Batuco people have little loaves of a pound and a half pound. There is often lives lost on both sides, those defending the goods and those trying to take them away. They have large numbers of large and small parrots and large eagles and eaglets in cages. There is all sorts of game.[61]

The salt trade continued to be important in this area and was still going on under Jesuit rule in the eighteenth century.[62] The word generally translated "alum," alumbre in the Spanish text, may have been potash (potassium aluminum sulfate), which is sometimes used in modern baking powders. Obregón remarks that the alum was not a very satisfactory substitute for salt, which would likely be the case whatever the actual compound. Going on to the Señora region, Obregón noted other evidences of trade, including trade in foodstuffs. The various statelets fought each other for salt, for female slaves, and for wives (esclavas y mujeres).[63] This mention of slaves is interesting in that the Serrana is the only area in the Greater Southwest where the Spaniards found an organized slave trade. The implication is that slaves came predominately from nearby groups, in spite of the possibilities of escape. This, perhaps, accounts for the emphasis on female slaves, who might be considered more docile and more easily assimilated into the captor group. Indeed, among groups at this organizational level around the world, female captives often do become incorporated into the society. Perhaps this accounts for the juxtaposition of the words *slaves* and *wives* in Obregón's narrative.

Another possibility is that slaves captured nearby were actually retraded over considerable distances. Di Peso believed that at least some slaves reached the settlements of the Casas Grandes.[64] This could not have been the case in Obregón's day, but it is possible that there was such a trade in the fifteenth century. Indeed, there may have been a market among the more sophisticated Pequeños Estados along the Sonoran-Sinaloan trade routes.

The political organization of the statelets is equally unsure. My own designation of "statelet" was introduced to avoid the semantic overload that scholars have put on such terms as *chiefdom* or *ranked society*. I did *not* mean to imply a belief that the groups in the Serrana had some sort of primitive state society, only that something beyond a simple band or tribal organization was involved. Archaeology has demonstrated public architecture and sizable towns, and this fits the historical accounts. From these accounts we can also see the institutionalization of war and the formation of warlike federations. The fact of federations seems secure, for several of the Spaniards noted them, and the archaeological evidence for such things

as signal-tower systems also suggests them. Federations certainly suggest a fairly sophisticated level of relationships. Exactly how they were organized, however, is still unknown.

The limited excavations certainly indicate extensive public architecture. It seems likely that there were ball courts, though they have been only tentatively identified. At San José and at La Mora, Pailes found structures 90+ feet by about 150 feet that probably served that purpose. Because the structures were in an advanced state of ruin, their features were not entirely clear, but they did have traces of some sort of transverse construction at the ends. William H. Doelle, who reexamined the Sonora Valley sites, is unconvinced that such structures were indeed ball courts. Doelle, however, was looking at the courts mainly from the perspective of the Hohokam, whereas such buildings were more likely related to Casas Grandes. Indeed, my own impression of these ruined structures, both from observation on the ground and from photographs, is that they probably were Casas Grandes–type courts.[65] Future archaeological work may shed more light on the matter.

The documentary sources are also very generalized when it comes to religious structures. Castañeda mentions temples that are in small houses in which numerous arrows are driven, "making them look like porcupines on the outside."[66] Las Casas gives considerably more information. Describing the Cabeza de Vaca journey he remarked:

It is said by other writers, although Cabeza de Vaca in his account does not mention it, that [when] they arrived at [Corazones] the inhabitants were holding a ceremony. The ceremony was celebrated in the following way. They had a great number of animals, deer, wolves, hares, and birds and carried them before a great idol which they had, accompanied by much flute music which they played and they split the animals down the middle, ripped out their hearts, and with the blood which gushed forth they bathed the idol and placed all the hearts around the idol's neck. . . . [I]t is a fact that in this region of the Valley of Señora only the hearts of animals are sacrificed, and they hold two ceremonies in which amidst great singing and music-making, they make their sacrifices with great joy, pomp and devotion. The first of these is at the time of sowing and the other at harvest time.[67]

Las Casas then describes "a very tall stone and adobe temple. And in this temple was a stone statue, filled with blood and around its neck were many animal hearts. Near the statue there were also many dead, desiccated, disemboweled human bodies leaning against the walls. They must have been the past lords of the valley and this was their sepulcher."[68]

Up and down the Sierra Madre Occidental today, Indian groups consider the deer a very important ceremonial animal. It has sun associations, and its ritual killing and use are central to certain ceremonials. Hearts, used ceremonially, suggest a connection with regions farther south, where such people as the Aztecs ceremonially plucked out hearts of both people and animals. These were offered to the gods, often ones with some solar connection.

The desiccated seated bodies of past rulers are certainly reminiscent of Casas Grandes, where seated (though not mummified) burials in the Medio period at Paquimé are common. In the Serrana the practice was still going on in the seventeenth century. As late as 1624 in the Yaqui drainage the Jesuit father Francisco Oliñano noted an "indio principal, who was buried seated and his body covered with white beads made from sea shells [*Olivella*?], blankets, colored feathers, and other things which they value." This particular leader had been killed by lightning, and there is an implication that his burial may have been special for that reason.[69] The Serrana people seem to have associated lightning and thunder with sun or sky worship. It stood the Ibarra party in good stead, for when they fired their culverins, these were thought of as thunderbolts and the Spani-

ards as "Children of the Sun." It may be significant that sun worship was also noted by Alarcón on his trip to the lower Colorado River in 1540.[70]

Unlike Casas Grandes there is as yet relatively little information on burial habits in the statelet area. In the Sonora River sites there have been found a scattering of cremations buried in pots. Two inhumation burials turned up, a bundle burial at San José and an extended burial in another site near Banámichi. Another inhumation has been reported by a local citizen in Huepac, but there is no very clear information. Richard Pailes believes that the burials (whatever the type) were on the flood plain and are now under several feet of alluvium. Daniel Reff suggests that people who were killed in the various battles may have been cremated to keep the bodies from falling into enemy hands. At least this happened in Sinaloa in Pérez de Ribas's time.[71]

There were two main ceremonies, one at planting time and the other at harvest. Since the statelet people double-cropped, it is uncertain just when these took place, but it is possible that they were equinoctial ceremonies, echoing the importance of the equinox at Paquimé. There is a hint that the number 4 had special ceremonial significance, as it did in the Pueblo world, and that both sun and moon were ceremonially important into Jesuit times. It might be pointed out that according to Las Casas both deer and hare hearts were utilized for sacrifice. Deer and rabbit symbolically represent the sun and moon, both in Mesoamerica and the Southwest.

There is no particular evidence that would indicate a priesthood, though Obregón says, "They have their preachers and persuaders [predicadores y movedores] of their idolatries and wars. They do this with such attention, fervor and shouting, that many times it happens that they fall to the ground, fainting from their zeal, concentration and shouting. This office is given to the most important captains and leaders [capitanes y mandones]."[72]

Whether these individuals represented a

priesthood or were shamans of some sort is not clear. As we have seen in the Paquimé data (chapter 8), both kinds of practitioner probably operated at Casas Grandes, and shamanistic systems certainly existed and still exist throughout the Sierra Madre Occidental.

We do not know if Sonora shared in the great pan-Aztlan religious movements centered on Tlaloc and Quetzalcoatl and perhaps Xipe Tótec and Chalchiuhtlique. I strongly suspect that these deities did appear in one guise or another in the statelet area, but proving that is impossible. As usual, the Spanish information is unbalanced and generally naive, and to date archaeology has provided very little in the way of answers. Nor is there evidence for the kachina cult in the Serrana. This may simply be due to the scarcity of archaeological work and the selective nature of historical documents. After all, the Coronado expedition did not document kachinas in the upper Southwest. Systematic rock art studies and detailed excavation will likely shed more light on this subject.

We have, therefore, a tantalizing but very incomplete picture of the Serrana area as it existed in the early sixteenth century. Such descriptions can likely be projected backward to the fifteenth century and perhaps the fourteenth (these centuries corresponding to the Late period of Doolittle and Pailes). There are hints that the breakup of the Casas Grandes world had a considerable reverberation in northeast Sonora, creating an opportunity to interdict the trading lines that ran to the Southwest. The fifteenth century was a time in which goods flowing into the upper Southwest had a dramatic increase, especially to the eastern Pueblos, and trade routes began to extend more and more into the Great Plains. These various events do seem to be linked, although our chronology is not yet firm enough to clearly establish the nature of that linkage.

The Serrana region is a frustrating place in terms of both archaeological and ethnohistorical information. Much more archaeology needs to be done, and done soon. At some point, probably in the near future, the intensive agriculture that is even today modifying the landscape of the coastal regions will spread to the river valleys, and archaeological sites will be lost or greatly disturbed. It would be well to excavate in the city centers of the larger towns. These include Arizpe, Banámichi, Baviacora, Huepac, Ures, and Moctezuma, among others. The important town of Oera, probably on the Nuri River, has to the best of my knowledge not yet been certainly located. In any case, with increasing urbanization in the area, developers will inevitably destroy a great deal of archaeological information.

The sixteenth-century documents give us a considerable amount of information of the kind denied at Paquimé and other Casas Grandes sites. It is, however, very *selective* information. As is common in Spanish sixteenth-century documentation in the Southwest, there are only generalizations about religion, no details on political structure, and generally nothing much about the arts. What the Spaniards did note is sometimes surprising; what they failed to see can sometimes be staggering.

CHAPTER 10

# A Multiplicity of Tongues

The Greater Southwest, probably for a very long time, has been a region with many languages. By the Aztlan period several major language families were represented and dozens of languages and dialects. For some of the subareas within Aztlan we are not really sure which languages were used, particularly among the Mogollon and at Casas Grandes. What, for example (in AD 1350, let us say), was the actual speech at Grasshopper or at Paquimé? We can only make more or less plausible guesses. For the Pueblo world the early Spanish parties gave a certain amount of specific information on the contemporary languages of that area. The linguistic patterns of the mid-sixteenth-century Pueblos can reasonably be extrapolated backward for a century or so, but when we get into even earlier periods—the time of the Chaco Canyon Great Houses, for example—we must again resort to guesswork. And even those sixteenth-century languages for which there is a certain amount of direct information are often not known well enough to allow us any certainty about their relationships to other languages (see Figure 10.1).[1]

As I mentioned in chapter 4, anthropologists generally agree that human beings reached the New World very late, most likely during the latter part of the Wisconsin glacial period, the last period of the Ice Age or Pleistocene epoch. We are talking about a time depth that had been measured to 11,000 or 12,000 years before the present and most likely can be extended

backward to 15,000 years or more. These were fully modern humans, members of our own species, *Homo sapiens sapiens*, for there is no credible evidence of earlier, more primitive forms of human beings. The route taken by earliest settlers, called *Paleoindians*, to reach the New World is still under contention, but traversing an ice-free corridor across the Bering area and Alaska, southward into continental America, is most widely accepted. Early migrations may also have been by some sort of primitive boats along the Pacific coast of North and South America. There have even been suggestions of boat transport across the Atlantic from Europe or Africa or across the Pacific from southeastern Asia. However, these latter routes seem unlikely at such an early date, at least on the basis of present evidence.

A number of early cultures, perhaps the best known being the Clovis tradition, extended through various parts of the New World. Dating of these cultures is still somewhat controversial, but some clearly go back to terminal Pleistocene times. Physically, early humans seem to be some sort of generalized "Mongoloid" Asiatics, though they might also resemble some of the late Pleistocene populations of Europe and the Mediterranean. Unfortunately, to date, relatively few skeletal remains of the earliest Americans have been found.[2]

As fully developed language is an attribute of our own species, and all known groups of *Homo sapiens* have such languages, it seems

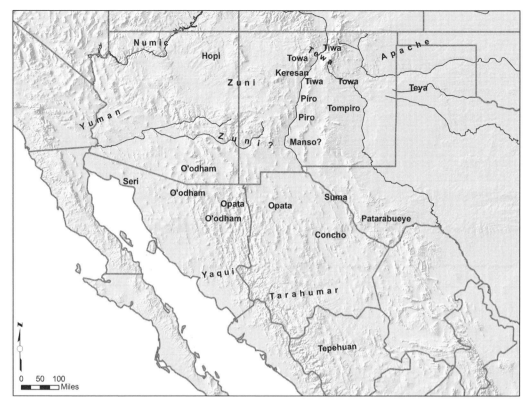

FIGURE 10.1. Southwestern languages on the eve of Spanish conquest. Earth Analytic, Santa Fe, NM.

likely that rich and versatile speech was associated with the very first men and women to reach the American continents. As early as the nineteenth century, systematized classifications of American languages began to be made, and it became obvious that there was a multiplicity of tongues. As far as I know, all modern linguists agree that there *must* be larger groupings of these American Indian languages—as, for example, English, German, French, Russian, and so forth form one branch of a larger language family known as Indo-European. A number of efforts to establish these larger groupings have been made, with varying degrees of success.

The most ambitious one to date, and one still quite controversial, is that of Joseph H. Greenberg. This classificatory system was published in 1987, though its main outline had been known for a number of years. Greenberg classifies all Native American languages into three major groups, a very widespread one called *Amerind*, dating from Paleoindian times, and two additional language families that arrived in the New World in post-Pleistocene times. Amerind extends throughout almost all the New World land mass, excepting only the very northern and northwestern regions of North America. Greenberg divided this language into six major stocks: *Northern Amerind, Central Amerind,* and four others, which fall mainly in lower Central America and South America. In Greenberg's scheme southwestern languages belong either to Northern Amerind (Zunian, Keresan, Yuman, Coahuiltecan) or to the Central Amerind (Kiowa-Tanoan and Uto-Aztecan).

The second of the three major New World groupings of American languages is the far-flung *Na-Dene* family, which extends throughout much of western North America and includes certain northwest coast languages and the more widespread northern and southern branches of *Athapaskan*. The latter branch is represented in the Southwest by the *Apachean* speakers, including the Navajo, all of whom migrated to the area in fairly recent times. The third major language grouping of Greenberg, *Eskimo-Aleut,* is limited to the northern littoral of North America and adjacent Siberia and has no representatives in the Southwest.[3]

One indication that Greenberg may be correct comes from recent DNA evidence that suggests that there was one early migration, and possibly two, to the New World, as well as two later ones, these latter two associated with the Na-Dene-speaking groups and the Eskimo-Aleut. Dental morphology patterns studied by bioanthropologist Christy Turner also seem to show certain major differentiation among Amerindians, the Na-Dene people, and Eskimos.[4]

Because of this collaborative evidence, I have tentatively accepted the Greenberg classification, but, as noted above, it is still controversial (see Figure 10.1). Some linguists, especially the more conservative students of American linguistics, remain skeptical. In any case, for the purposes of the present study one can deal with the late prehistoric and historic southwestern languages without an overriding structure—just as one can study the languages of Europe in the last two thousand years, working with accepted subfamilies such as the Germanic, Romance, and Slavic tongues, without reference to the larger Indo-European stock.

The major grouping called Uto-Aztecan has a rather extensive southwestern distribution, mostly in the western mountain reaches of North America, stretching from Idaho to Costa Rica and Panama. Its best-known language is perhaps Aztec, or Nahuatl, of central Mexico. Languages of Aztlan that are Uto-Aztecan include Hopi, one of several Uto-Aztecan languages found in the north, and several languages of what is often classified as southern Uto-Aztecan. Speakers of these languages include the Pima and related Papago, who are often referred to as O'odham, the self-designation

of both groups. Under whatever name, they are components of a subgroup called Tepiman. Another southern Uto-Aztecan group is Opata, a member of the *Taracahitan* subfamily.

In the northwestern quadrant of the Southwest is *Zunian,* now spoken only by the Zuni Indians of New Mexico. The language family Keresan is today found only in the upper Rio Grande Basin, and Tanoan is spoken in the valleys of the Rio Grande and (until recently) in the upper Pecos drainage and in the Estancia Basin to the southeast. On the margins of the Southwest, both west and east, are languages of another major family—Hokan. Still on the edges of the region when the Spaniards came were southern Athapaskans, the Apachean groups. These peoples' languages have been much studied by linguists and are widely spoken today. The Apacheans seem to be latecomers to the Southwest however, probably reaching the borders of the Southwest only two or three centuries before the Spaniards came.[5]

The field of southwestern linguistics is anything but cut and dried. Not all historic southwestern languages are classified to the satisfaction of all specialists, and there are particular problems with those languages that dropped out of use in early historic times. This is especially true in the upper Southwest, for the Franciscans, who were missionaries to the Pueblos, made few attempts to learn the languages involved or even to collect extensive word lists or other evidence. Because of this, there is real uncertainty about such languages as Manso, Concho, Suma, and Teya/Jumano. This is even true of the extinct Pueblo language Piro and its eastern dialect, Tompiro, although we do know enough about this language to say that it was almost certainly Tanoan and, within Tanoan, most likely related to the Tiwa language. The Jesuits in Sonora were better recorders of native speech, so we have considerable knowledge of certain languages that are now largely or wholly extinct (Opata, for example).

Leaving aside the early east-to-west journey of the Cabeza de Vaca party, which in any case gave very little linguistic information, the sixteenth-century Spaniards originally entered the Southwest from the south and west. They contacted first the statelet people of northeastern Sonora and reported two separate languages. These can almost certainly be identified as the Uto-Aztecan tongues Opata and Piman.[6] The very earliest expedition, that of Coronado (1539–1542), entered southern Arizona from the Opata region but gave very little information on the Indians of the Gila and Salt drainage. In fact, those groups were not clearly identified as Piman-speakers for another century and a half. Coronado's own ship captain, Hernando de Alarcón, explored the lower Colorado River and made contact with the Native American groups there.[7] The major languages that Alarcón heard in the lower Colorado are those that today are referred to as Yuman. Archaeologists and linguists are generally agreed that these speakers had been in place for a number of centuries, certainly throughout Aztlan times. Yuman is a branch of a larger stock called Hokan (but see note 8 of this chapter), which has a generally western distribution in North America. Another Hokan language, that of Seri, along the northeast coast of the Gulf of California, was also noted by a number of early Spanish parties. At least we presume that the very marginalized hunters and collectors of that region are ancestral to the historic and modern Seri Indians, though our knowledge of the actual language comes from a later time.

I discussed the Yuman region in chapters 4 and 6, and because Yuman speakers were quite marginal to Aztlan, I will not be further concerned with them here, except to say that this Hokan speech group may well have been in place for thousands of years and represented early, Archaic, adaptations in this western area. Its historic distribution includes the block of languages west of Aztlan, including the River Yumans and the Pai groups, while east of Aztlan lived the Coahuiltecans of northeastern Mexico and the Tonkawa and Karankawa of the Texas coast. It seems quite possible that these Hokan languages may at one time have

formed a continuous block across the western United States and parts of northern Mexico.[8] In the very late seventeenth century Jesuit missionaries in Sonora began to push into southern Arizona and try to missionize the large Piman-speaking populations there.[9] The Jesuits launched studies of both Opata and the various Piman languages. They had, however, only minimal contacts with Yuman speakers.

The main Coronado party in 1540 contacted the Zuni Pueblos, calling the area *Cíbola*, probably a corrupted form of the term *Ashiwi* or *Shiwi*, the Zuni name for themselves, or *Shiwana*, their name for the Zuni area. This particular name had been picked up by Spaniards far to the south, somewhere in the Pima or Opata region, and seemed in general use by the Sonoran people to refer to the Zuni. The actual name *Zuni* was given by a later Spanish party, that of Chamuscado, in 1581–1582. This explorer, entering the region from the east, used a corrupted form of the Keresan word *Sunyitsi*, which he found being used at Zia or Acoma.

The same thing was true of Hopi. Coronado's people utilized the term *Tusayan*, of uncertain origin. This term dropped out of use in the Spanish lexicon very rapidly, the expeditions of the 1580s and 1590s using a Keresan word, *Mohose*, which later became *Mohi*. The present name *Hopi* is a Hopi term for themselves *(Hopituh)* with the meaning "peaceful people."[10]

In the fall of 1540 the Spaniards first contacted Acoma, the westernmost of the Keresan-speaking Pueblos. Shortly thereafter, the town of Zia and the people called *Quirix* (a word later transformed by linguists into *Keresan*), from the upper Rio Grande and Jemez rivers, were met by Coronado's people. These Quirix villages were considered a political entity. I am not sure that there was an immediate realization that the people of Acoma, those of Zia on the Jemez River, and those of the Quirix towns spoke related languages. But the Quirix languages were clearly different from that spoken in the federation of Tiguex, in the present-day Bernalillo-Albuquerque area. They also differed from the language of the Jemez groups, those of Yuque-Yungue near the Chama River, of Taos of the Galisteo Basin, and of the large center of Cicuyé or Ciquique on the Pecos River. The Spaniards also explored southward down the Rio Grande, contacting the Piro groups and, I have suggested, went far enough (probably in the area around modern Hatch) to reach settlements of the Manso Indians.[11]

In the century following Coronado the Spaniards became more sophisticated about Indian languages in the upper portion of Aztlan. As the Franciscan missionaries spread out over this part of the Southwest, they gradually realized that the important Pecos Pueblo spoke a language similar to that of the Jemez group[12] and that the Yuque-Yungue people and those of the Galisteo Basin also spoke similar tongues. The people of the Rio Abajo region and those of the Salinas country also spoke dialects of one language.

Today we know that Zuni is a linguistic isolate, with no near linguistic relations whatsoever. The Keresan are also somewhat isolated but form several languages and dialects within the upper Rio Grande area. These are divided into a western group, including Acoma, its satellite villages, and the historic Pueblo of Laguna, and an eastern group that includes the towns along the Rio Jemez and Rio Grande. However, lexical differences in Keresan today seem more related to geographical distance, so it is possible to look on Keresan as a string of diverging dialects, with the southwestern and northeastern ends of the distribution representing distinct languages.

With the possible exception of the Manso (see below) we can classify all the non-Keresan Puebloan people of the upper Rio Grande as Tanoan speakers. The large Tiguex series of towns, first of the Rio Grande Pueblos contacted by the Coronado party, spoke what is now called the southern branch of Tiwa. A separate, northern, branch is still spoken at Taos and Picurís Pueblos. The various Indians on the upper Jemez River used what is now called Towa, as did Pecos Pueblo, isolated far

to the east. The peoples of the Rio Grande from the Española Basin and groups in the Chama drainage spoke what today is called Tewa. A related dialect, that of the Tano, was the language of the Galisteo Basin. The only Tano speakers today live in the village of Hano on Hopi First Mesa, the result of a migration in historic times.

South of this group was another Tanoan tongue in the Rio Abajo and in the Salinas Basin to the east. This was the Piro-Tompiro language, today extinct, probably most closely related to Tiwa. The Tanoan family of languages is usually linked to another language, Kiowa, that was found in later historic times in the central and western plains.[13] For the relationship of Tanoan to Kiowa see below.

One hint of wider language relationships appeared in very early Spanish days. On the lower Colorado River Alarcón, Coronado's ship captain, discovered native people who could understand his Piman-speaking interpreters. Their location was somewhere around the mouth of the Gila River. Sixty-five years later the New Mexican governor, Juan de Oñate, led an expedition to the lower Colorado River. Fr. Escobar, a Franciscan missionary with the expedition, identified a group called the Oseca, who lived around the mouth of the Gila River. I have commented elsewhere that Escobar "had probably never seen a Piman Indian but he recognized the Oseca language as similar to Tepehuan, a tongue related to Pima."[14] The Tepehuan Indians of Durango and Jalisco, as we know today, form the southern end of a distribution of the language subfamily of Uto-Aztecan called Tepiman, Piman itself being at the northern end of the distribution.

In fact, the Uto-Aztecans may have disrupted the original Hokan-speaking distribution. The more or less standard model of Uto-Aztecan has a protolanguage spreading southward out of an original homeland in the western United States sometime after 3000 BC. An alternative model presents Uto-Aztecan as originating in Mesoamerica and, reflecting the needs of early agricultural peoples for more land, slowly spreading to the north and west, finally reaching the northern limits of maize agriculture. Climatic change and the shrinkage of the limits of primitive agriculture in the western United States subsequently forced some of the very northern Uto-Aztecan groups to readapt to an Archaic, hunting/gathering mode of life.[15] For the time period discussed in this book, it would not seem to greatly matter which of these models is correct. This issue may need to be taken into account, however, when we consider the timing of the crosscutting distribution of Tepiman and Cáhitan peoples. It might also be a factor when trying to identify the language of the Hohokam.

When the first Spanish party reached the southwest portion of the Great Plains in the year 1541, they found two distinct peoples, whom they called *Querecho* and *Teya*. The Querecho spoke an Apache language and likely were in the early stages of moving into the Southwest. At the time of Coronado the Teya extended from the Llano Estacado, of modern western Texas and eastern New Mexico, through the lower Pecos Valley and to the Rio Grande in the La Junta region. In this latter place, where the Rio Grande is joined by its great tributary the Conchos, Cabeza de Vaca seems to have met the Teya in 1535. Two generations later they were being contacted by Spanish parties under the name *Jumano*.

There is still a great deal of disagreement as to just what were the language relationships on the Rio Grande and the southern plains. From the archaeological evidence and the early historical accounts, it is reasonably clear that the Teya/Jumano were not Apachean speakers. In fact, the spread of Apacheans in and around the Southwest is largely a later-sixteenth- and seventeenth-century phenomenon. And by the late seventeenth century Apachean speech was swamping earlier languages around the Southwest, one reason why we are so uncertain about the language affiliations of people like the Suma, Manso, Concho, Patarabueyes, and others.[16]

The Teya are considered by some scholars to speak Caddoan, a western extension of a language family that has a major concentration

in the central and southeastern plains and the adjacent Mississippi River valley. It seems to me, however, that an affiliation made by Nancy P. Hickerson some years ago is more logical. Hickerson believes that the Teya-Jumano, linguistically, were closely affiliated with the Tompiro-Piro-speaking branch of Tanoan. That the two groups interacted is very likely, hence the Tompiro "Pueblo of the Humanas [Jumano]," at present called Gran Quivira, mentioned in the early Spanish sources. There is also considerable indication that the Tompiro of the Estancia Basin were important trading partners of the Teya-Jumano, both aboriginally and in the sixteenth century.[17]

In the last two decades of the sixteenth century, Spaniards, moving northward down the Río Conchos, made contact with various Indians along that river. The ones they called Concho lived along the Conchos; the Patarabueyes were found at La Junta, the Jumanos north of La Junta, the Suma along the Rio Grande upstream from La Junta, and the Manso still farther upstream. How these names were derived is not clear, though *Concho* and *Manso* are probably Spanish words, and *Patarabueye* may also be a somewhat derogatory Spanish slang term.[18]

I have also suggested that, at least in the mid-sixteenth century, the Manso and Suma spoke very similar languages to Jumano and Tompiro. Since we know that the Jumano and the Patarabueye of La Junta also had a close relationship, actually living together part of each year, it seems a good possibility that the two groups employed similar languages. To take this reasoning a step further, it seems reasonable that the contiguous and interacting Teya-Jumano, Tompiro-Piro, Patarabueyes, Manso, and Suma all spoke closely related languages, possibly only dialects of the same language. However, I think that the Concho were probably not part of this linguistic grouping.[19]

Of course proximity, especially in the Southwest, does not necessarily imply linguistic relationships. Consider, for example, close neighbors such as the Tanoans and Keresans, whose languages were as different as, perhaps, English and Arabic. Indeed, alternative linguistic affiliations for various of these groups have been suggested. For example, Patrick Beckett and Terry Corbett believe that the Manso and the Jova and Jocome of the New Mexico boot heel and adjacent Chihuahua spoke the same language but that the Suma spoke a different tongue. Beckett and Corbett consider this Manso-Jova-Jocove language, and perhaps Concho as well, to be related to Tarahumar and Opata, in other words belonging to the Taracahitan branch of Uto-Aztecan.[20] Curtis Schaafsma has a somewhat similar take on this situation. He follows Beckett and Corbett in suggesting that Manso, Jova, and Jocome were related Taracahitan languages and further suggests that the Jova and Jocome may have been remnant Casas Grandes peoples. The Suma, according to Schaafsma, were likely the "Querechos" met by Ibarra near Paquimé in the early 1560s who had wandered into the region in post–Casas Grandes times.[21]

The Concho Indians are a special puzzle. Both A. L. Kroeber and Carl O. Sauer believed that the Conchos spoke a language related to Opata, and Sauer seemed to believe that they were the original inhabitants of the Casas Grandes area. William Griffen also believes that the Concho may have employed a Taracahitan language. All these individuals emphasize that the evidence, one way or the other, is rather scanty.[22]

Some years ago David Phillips suggested that the historic Opata of Sonora may be derived in part from Casas Grandes, crediting me with originating the idea.[23] At present I am somewhat two minded about the matter, though I still think the likelihood is that the Casas Grandes people spoke a Taracahitan language. It would make distributional sense if this was a dialect of, or was closely related to, Opata. Possibly a part of the Casas Grandes people drifted westward to join Opata-speaking kin in Sonora, while another part, with much cultural impoverishment, became the Concho.[24] I do not think we have enough evidence to say what the Jova and Jocome spoke, although if

they reached their seventeenth-century position from farther east, we must consider that they, too, were related to the Manso. In that case we might have a broader band of Tanoan-related languages than previously thought.

One interesting aspect of Casas Grandes populations—although at present I am not sure how it should be interpreted—is that dental crown morphology from archaeological burial populations around the Southwest show a rather close relationship between Casas Grandes and the Sinaloa region. Whether this translates into linguistic relationships is unknown, but if the Paquimé populations spoke Opata, or at least one of the Taracahitan languages, it might indicate migration and thus a mechanism for gene flow between Casas Grandes and the Cáhitan-speaking Sinaloan coastal areas. Other Casas Grandes close dental matches are with Coahuila and the Mimbres region. The Mimbres dental samples are from excavations at the NAN Ranch on the Mimbres River and represent largely Classic Mimbres populations. The Sinaloan and Coahuila samples lack good provenience.[25] In terms of Coahuila about all that can be said is that the relationship might strengthen the "Casas Grandes becoming Concho" theory. To the best of my knowledge there are no dental-comparison studies involving archaeological northeastern Sonoran populations.

Another part of the puzzle lies in the curious distribution of two Uto-Aztecan subfamilies: Taracahitan and Tepiman. Taracahitan has basically a northeast-southwest distribution, anchored on the east by Tarahumar and Opata and on the west by the Cáhitan tongues, especially Yaqui and Mayo. Crosscutting that distribution is an elongated northwest-southeast distribution of Tepiman, the northern portion taken up by the Pima languages of southern Arizona and Sonora and the southern end inhabited by northern Tepehuan and southern Tepehuan/Tepecano. The Tepiman distribution seems to have taken place rather recently, for the languages throughout are quite similar. How this interdigitation of two different branches of Uto-Aztecan occurred is not entirely clear. It might be useful if we knew whether the main thrust of Uto-Aztecan migration was south to north or north to south.

It has long been my belief that the Hohokam cultures of southern Arizona were made up of the Piman branch of Tepiman. This idea is strengthened if we accept the south-to-north spread of Uto-Aztecan, for, as linguist Jane Hill points out, it would best explain the distribution of irrigation cultures in northern Mexico and the American Southwest.[26] Of course, even if Uto-Aztecan, the Hohokam language would not necessarily have been Piman. But, considering that Piman peoples were in the area from early Hispanic times, it seems the most parsimonious explanation. There is also the possibility that more than one language was spoken by the Hohokam. This linguistic diversity could have been early, perhaps involving Hokan speakers. In later times the Salado people could have introduced another speech pattern, conceivably a northern Uto-Aztecan or perhaps Zunian language.

The question of what the Mogollon-Mimbres people spoke is also quite obscure, and, again, more than one language may have been involved. The Mimbres have a series of interesting tie-ups with Casas Grandes, including the strong affiliation in tooth crown morphology mentioned above. Whether that meant that part or all of the Mimbres shared a common tongue with Casas Grandes is unknown, but it must be taken as a possibility. It might especially apply to the boot-heel area in Postclassic Mimbres times. The Mountain branch of the Mogollon also has unknown language affiliations, but some of the Mogollon might have spoken varieties of Zunian. As of the first Spanish contact, Zuni was the language of only a handful of towns along or near the Zuni River, but there are archaeological connections to a larger region especially to the south. There is also a relatively early extension of a Chaco-like settlement, exemplified by Village of the Great Kivas, east of the modern town of Zuni, but what this might have meant linguistically is not clear. (For discussion of these western extensions of Chacoan culture see chapters 4 and 5.)

In the upper Southwest the linguistic landscape of the Aztlan period becomes increasingly vague as we go back in time. Considering the problems we have with historic languages, projecting languages into preliterate times adds special levels of difficulty. What I offer here represents mainly educated guesses, mine and others'.

A variety of Uto-Aztecan was clearly spoken at Hopi from the earliest historical times and probably from the beginning of the Hopi Pueblos. Although we have no proof (except their close affinity to Hopi itself), it seems likely that the prehistoric towns along or near the Little Colorado in the Winslow-Holbrook region also spoke the same language as Hopi. Other Uto-Aztecans, the southern Numic-speaking Utes in early historic times and the Comanches after around AD 1700, spread across the northernmost portion of the Southwest. The Comanches certainly and the Utes probably were too late to have been involved in the Aztlan mosaic of languages—although there is the *possibility* that Ute speakers may have reached the San Juan Basin in Aztlan times.

Moving eastward in the Pueblo world, we see that the speech patterns in the first part of the sixteenth century are reasonably clear (see the section on Keresan and Tanoan languages above). The farther back in time ones goes, the more chancy things become. I briefly described in chapter 5 my attempt in the mid-1990s to give what I thought was the linguistic situation in the Eastern Pueblo region at various prehistoric time levels. In my opinion an ancestral Kiowa-Tanoan language was already spoken in the Rio Grande and in the San Juan Basin in late Archaic times. Eventually these languages modified into Tiwa (or perhaps ancestral Tiwa-Piro) in the Rio Grande itself, with Tewa-Tano and Towa developing in the San Juan region. These western Tanoan speakers moved out of the San Juan at the end of P-III times, primarily during the thirteenth century, though the migrations may have begun in the twelfth century. Major groups of the Tewa moved into the Rio Grande, splitting the original Tiwa distribution, while the Towa speakers settled the Jemez Mountains area. One Tewa migration reached the Galisteo country, and a Towa contingent went as far as the upper Pecos River valley.[27] Beginning about the climax of this west-to-east *Wanderung*, but extending on into the fourteenth century, certain other Pueblo peoples, who had earlier lived on the Pecos, seem to have drifted into the plains.[28] They could have contributed to the ancestry of the Teya-Jumano.

I suggested that ancestral Keresan in the Archaic period already existed in the general region formed by the upwaters of the Little Colorado, the south watershed of the San Juan, and part of the western watershed of the Rio Grande. About the center of the large area is Chaco Canyon, which produced the Keresan-speaking Chaco culture. After the disasters of the twelfth and thirteenth centuries these Keresan speakers moved south and east, eventually, in Aztlan times, settling in the valleys of the San José, the lower Jemez, and the main Rio Grande, where they formed a further wedge, this time between the old Tiwa settlers to the south and the Tewa newcomers to the north.[29]

As I have said, this sequence is all highly speculative. Other reconstructions of various of these languages have been made. For example, David H. Snow believes that the Tanoans had a more northerly origin (see also chapter 5). He disagrees with the idea of a widespread Tanoan occupation of the San Juan region and sees the Kiowa-Tanoan ancestral group coming out of a mid to late Plains Woodland tradition on the edge of the western plains, perhaps extending along the Front Range as far south as the Canadian River drainage. This group interacted with both Plains Woodland groups from farther east and Rio Grande Puebloan peoples (whom Snow thinks might have been Keresan) as early as the tenth century AD. These Tanoan groups eventually drifted south in the Rio Grande Basin.[30]

Linguist Nancy P. Hickerson, however, suggests that the Kiowa may themselves be descended from the Teya/Jumano, contacted by the early Spaniards in the southern plains.[31] Of course it is possible that Snow and Hickerson are both right, the Teya developing from an ur-group that in prehistoric time split into ancestral Tanoan and ancestral Teya. Tanoan subsequently began that separation that produced daughter languages (northern and southern Tiwa, Tewa, Towa, and Piro/Tompiro). Possibly, that Teya-Tanoan split-off was early enough for Tanoan differentiation in the Rio Grande area, with the Tanoans learning Pueblo ways from the neighboring Keresan. Alternatively, the ancestral Teya/Tanoan may already have produced a congeries of related languages. Lacking any linguistic texts from the Teya, it is impossible to say which of these scenarios is the more plausible or, for that matter, if either of them is plausible.

It is obvious that although we have a great deal of information about the linguistic situation in Aztlan, there is a great deal more to be learned. Of course, in the absence of linguistic texts for the prehistoric and even certain historic languages many of our ideas must remain uncertain. At best we are dealing with probabilities. But it might be well to remember that each generation of archaeologists and other related specialists develop new tools and new analytical procedures that shed new and unexpected light on the past. See, for example, such radical reinterpretations of human history and prehistory made possible by tree-ring and [14]C dating; chemical analyses on soil, flesh, and bone; paleobotanical, paleozoological, and paleoclimatic studies; and DNA analyses. Perhaps we will eventually establish new methodologies to retrieve languages from nonliterate past cultures and thus provide answers undreamed of today.

CHAPTER 11

# The New Order

By the beginning of the sixteenth century the world of Aztlan had shrunk to two core areas. One of these was in the Serrana, where the energetic statelets that dominated the river basins of northeast Sonora were probably nearing their cultural peak. These tiny polities were scattered over the middle and upper Sonora Basin and parts of the Yaqui drainage areas, and their influence and connections, mainly through trade, extended in every direction.

The second core area was an elongated Pueblo world, extending like a great inverted *L*, from the remnant Western Pueblo settlements of Hopi and Zuni, eastward to a large cluster of towns in the upper Rio Grande Basin, and southward to a scatter of villages stretching down the Rio Grande. Easternmost outliers were Pecos on the upper Pecos River and the towns of the desolate and arid Estancia Basin, east of the Manzano Mountains. This was a diverse region in many ways, its inhabitants speaking dialects of several different languages drawn from several language families (see Figure 11.1). But it was united also by the widespread kachina cult and its related hierarchy of sociopolitical societies; by great similarities in material culture, perhaps most strikingly in ceramics and architecture; and by strong and economically vital trade contacts both within the Pueblo area and beyond.

Within Aztlan proper an important trend, noticeable among both Pueblos and the Serrana people, was a movement to larger towns,

many of them fortified or on easily defended locations. I take this to represent the fruits of several centuries of increased militarism, but additional factors, perhaps environmental or even social, may also have been involved.[1]

The polities in other areas, important to the earlier Aztlan, had now disappeared. In the Gila-Salt Valley that cultural florescence called the Salado, a mixture of Hohokam, and various northern and eastern elements had now ended. The related mountain Mogollon towns to the north and east no longer existed, and the late post-Mimbres Cliff phase towns of the upper Gila drainage were in ruins.

The entire Casas Grandes world had collapsed a half century or more before AD 1500. This included not only the heartland dominated by Paquimé but the outlying areas in Chihuahua, plus the Animas villages and those of the Jornada Mogollon. In fact, large portions of the Greater Southwest seem to have been deserted. When the Spaniards reached the Southwest in the first half of the sixteenth century, they found large regions that they called *despoblados*, unoccupied or barren areas. This seemed especially to be the case in the mountainous region of eastern Arizona and western New Mexico, the land of the old Mogollon. And other regions, once heavily populated, also were probably largely deserted—for example the middle Little Colorado drainage and perhaps parts of the Verde drainage, as well as large stretches of the upper and middle Pecos River.

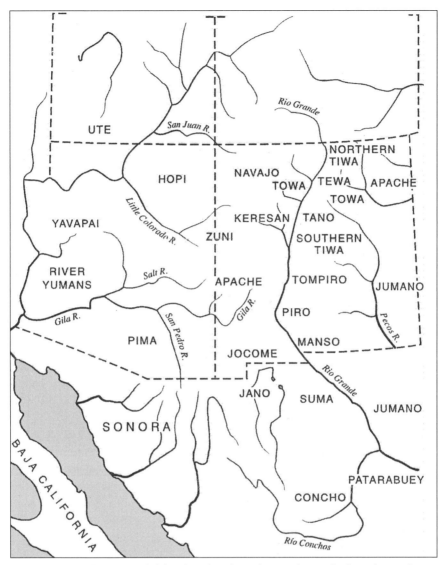

FIGURE 11.1. Southwestern tribal distribution in the early Spanish period (after Riley, *Kachina and the Cross*).

But that does not mean that all the Southwest outside the Pueblo and Serrana areas was made up of despoblados! The western periphery of Aztlan, that of the Yuman speakers of the lower Colorado River basin, continued to be linked to core lands by important ties, controlling as they did the trade in coastal California shell and perhaps other goods such as steatite. In addition, much of the Gulf of California shell, so important in Pueblo ceremonialism, may also have come from this western periphery of Aztlan—though a certain amount

likely was shipped through the Serrana. The Spaniards also found considerable "peasant" agricultural populations in the Gila-Salt region, most likely the precursors of the historic Pima-Papago groups. South of the Pueblo area, on the Rio Grande, lived the Manso people, still agricultural but without the élan of their Jornada Mogollon predecessors. And at La Junta, the easternmost fringe of the old Jornada Mogollon, native peoples were making somewhat of a comeback with crudely constructed, but still pueblo-type, towns and active social

contact with the shifting and restless bison followers to the north. The La Junta groups still
maintained a certain amount of contact, mainly
through trade, with the larger Southwest. It was
by way of such connections that the Spaniards, after the fiasco of the Coronado expedition, gradually became reacquainted with the
northern part of Aztlan.

What was missing was the ambiance that
made up Aztlan. In terms popularized by anthropologists like Redfield, no longer was
there an Aztlan "great tradition," only its shattered fragments in the Pueblo world and in the
Serrana, and a scattered series of "little traditions," now filling in the balance of the Southwest.[2] As I have pointed out in previous chapters, there was almost certainly an overall
population decline in Aztlan from the fourteenth century to the sixteenth.[3]

The series of dramatic events that so impacted the lives of southwestern Indians, as it
did those in other parts of the New World, was
the impingement of Old World Eurasia and
Africa onto the New. Although the Americas
were originally settled, almost certainly from
northern Asia, contacts between the two macro-
regions had for thousands of years been mainly
limited to the northern shorelines of the Arctic
Ocean. Major contact between the two worlds
is generally thought to have begun with the
voyages of Christopher Columbus from southern Spain, beginning in 1492. There are earlier documented voyages, for example, that of
the Vikings mentioned in chapter 2, but these
seem to have had no significant impact either
on the American Indians or on north Europeans.[4] Various suggestions of other contacts
have been made, one being a great Chinese sea
expedition that began in 1421. According to
one hypothesis it actually circumnavigated the
world, touching at many points in both North
and South America. To date the evidence for
that voyage is at best equivocal.[5]

The interest of Europeans in sea voyages of
discovery began in part because of power shifts
in the eastern Mediterranean, shifts that impacted the lucrative trade in spices and other
exotic commodities that Europeans received
from eastern and southern Asia. In part it was
because sea navigation was becoming more
sophisticated at a time when both theoretical
and practical knowledge of world geography
was suggesting the possibility of contacts of
Europe and the Orient, either around Africa
or by sailing westward. The Portuguese pio-
neered the African route, but Spaniards, beginning with Columbus, began to explore the western sea routes in the last decade of the fifteenth
century. Columbus's discovery of various Caribbean islands in 1492 opened the floodgates
of Spanish exploration. Within a few years it
was realized (though apparently not by Columbus himself) that the discovery was not East
Asia but a whole great Western Hemisphere,
a complete "New World." This great region
was soon to be called *America,* named for an
Italian mapmaker and skilled self-promoter
named Amerigo Vespucci.[6]

Contacts of Europeans with peoples of the
Caribbean and of eastern South America, the
major points of contact in the first two decades
of exploration and settlement, probably had
no effect at all on the people of Aztlan. However, beginning in 1519 a Spanish conqueror
named Cortés invaded the Aztec kingdom of
the central Mexican highlands, which was at
the time ruled by Motecuhzoma (Moctezuma
or Montezuma) II, a vacillating mystic whose
indecision greatly aided the Spaniards in their
initial thrust into the Valley of Mexico. They
entered the Aztec capital of Tenochtitlan and
seized the emperor. The Aztecs quickly repu-
diated Motecuhzoma, who was then killed,
perhaps by his captors. The European forces
were driven out of the capital with stunning
losses on the night of June 30–July 1, 1520
(the famous *noche triste* of Mexican history).
Cortés barely escaped with his life, and for a
time his efforts seemed doomed. But gaining
the aid of various Indian groups eager to challenge the overlordship of the Aztecs, Cortés re-
bounded within a few months and conquered
the Aztecs. Part of this victory was due to massive aid from Tlaxcalans and other traditional
enemies of the Aztecs, and part was attribut-
able to Cortés's superior firepower and tactics.[7]

In even larger measure, however, the Spaniards won because they (probably inadvertently) had introduced smallpox to the natives. The devastation caused by this disease was incalculable.[8] For example, the Aztec emperor, Cuitláhuac, successor to Motecuhzoma II, died of smallpox, as did huge numbers of his followers. Though his heir, Motecuhzoma's nephew Cuauhtemoc, fought on with skill and dedication, his dwindling forces eventually were defeated, and Tenochtitlan fell in August of 1521.

The Aztecs had connections to both the west and east coasts of Mexico, and it seems possible that the first news of this new order was now beginning to trickle into the Greater Southwest. In any case the Spaniards quickly expanded toward the Pacific. In 1522, the year after the fall of the Aztec kingdom, Cortés reached the Pacific coast in what is now Colima. He largely avoided the one major political entity of that region, the Tarascan state, centered around Lake Pátzcuaro in what is now the Mexican state of Michoacán. Two years later one of Cortés's captains, a man named Francisco Cortés de Buenaventura, was sent north into what is now Nayarit and the southern part of Sinaloa, penetrating to the region of the Pequeños Estados (see chapter 9). Meanwhile, during 1525 and 1526 the Franciscans had entered the Tarascan area. They found the Tarascans docile, something rather puzzling considering that they had a strongly militaristic tradition and had decisively defeated the Aztecs only a half century before. My own suspicion is that—like the Aztecs—the Tarascans had been decimated by smallpox, and their sociopolitical and military organizations were largely shattered. In any case they quickly received the attention of Nuño Beltrán de Guzmán, one of the most ruthless conquerors in the history of Spanish contact with the New World. In 1528 Guzmán moved into Tarascan territory, committing an orgy of murder and plunder. Then, two years later, drafting numbers of Tarascans to be burden bearers, or *támemes,* he made a long march up the west coast of Mexico, bringing fire and

sword to the people of the Pequeños Estados. This event, described in chapter 9, may well have given the people of Aztlan to the north their first inkling of the great new danger posed by these invaders. By 1531 Guzmán pushed into central Sinaloa and had founded a Spanish outpost at Culiacán. In the next several years small Spanish parties, mostly slave raiders, probed northward as far as the lower Yaqui River.[9]

Around this time the Spaniards in turn began to get their first information on Aztlan. They already knew the story of the mythological Aztec homeland far to the northwest and quickly began to accrue stories that seemed to give information about this fabled place.[10] One bit of information, already discussed in chapters 8 and 9, was that of Tejo. According to the Castañeda account:

In the year [one thousand] five hundred and thirty, when he was president of Nueva España, Nuño de Guzmán had in his possession an Indian [who was] a native of the valley or valleys of Oxitipar, whom the Spaniards named Tejo. This Indian said that he was the son of a merchant and that his father was dead. When he was young, however, his father used to go into the interior of the land, as a merchant, with sumptuous feathers to use as ornaments. In exchange, he brought back a great amount of gold and silver, of which there is much in that land. [Tejo also said] that once or twice he went with [his father] and saw towns so grand that he liked to compare them with [Ciudad de] México and its environs. [He said] he had seen seven very grand towns where there were streets of silver workshops. [And he said] that in order to journey to them, it took them forty days [of travel] from their land, all [across] unsettled land. The land through which they went did not have pasture grass, except some [that was] very short (one *jeme*). The course which they pursued was lengthwise through the land between the [two] seas, following the route to the north.[11]

This story, plus the information that surely was traveling up and down the trade routes, suggested a rich land somewhere off to the north or northwest, the very direction in which the Aztecs believed lay their Aztlan. This information was not immediately acted on, for in a power shift the Spanish government recalled Guzmán. There were complaints about the conquistador, and he soon faced criminal charges for his treatment of the native peoples. However, the main reason for the change was that the Spanish Crown and the powerful Council of the Indies now determined to rein in freewheeling adventurers like Cortés and Guzmán. A powerful member of the nobility, Antonio de Mendoza, was now appointed viceroy of New Spain, the recently formed viceroyalty centered in Mexico but including all the northern frontier.[12] The Church during this period in Mexico was represented mainly by members of the Franciscan order. A Franciscan bishop, Juan de Zumárraga, had taken up his duties in 1528, so he was in place when Mendoza arrived in 1535. The two men, both strongly humanist, worked well together. They had essentially the same agenda, that of advancing the power and wealth of the Spanish Crown and, at the same time, moving swiftly to convert the various Indian groups under their control.[13] This in turn was part of a Franciscan theory of history, a virtual raison d'être for New World sixteenth-century Franciscans, the idea that conversion of the American Indians would hasten the Christian millennium.[14]

Two quite separate events brought the unknown Northwest to the close attention of Mendoza and his government. First was the invasion of the central Andean region by Francisco Pizarro and his conquest of the Inca Empire. By the mid-1530s there was a flood of stories relating to the vast wealth, especially in gold, controlled by the Inca rulers. This led to a wave of interest both in Spanish America and in Europe. If the Andean area harbored such riches, why not the unknown regions beyond New Spain?[15]

The second event happened in 1536, when four stragglers—three Spaniards and a black slave—appeared at Culiacán, with an extraordinary story of years of adventure and privation in the northern Gulf of Mexico coastal region. They were shipwreck victims of a disastrous expedition to Florida led by the Spanish explorer Pánfilo de Narváez. This incompetent would-be conquistador landed in Florida in 1538 and in a series of miscalculations and misadventures succeeded in losing virtually his entire expedition to a storm in what is now coastal Louisiana or extreme eastern Texas. The few survivors dwindled over the next year or so until only four were left. Led by an officer of the expedition, Alvar Núñez Cabeza de Vaca, the four men gradually worked their way westward, reaching the edges of the Greater Southwest at La Junta de los Rios in 1535 and contacting the people of northeastern Sonora in early 1536. As described in chapter 9, primarily at a town they named *Corazones* (Hearts) Cabeza de Vaca and his companions picked up stories of rich lands even farther north. These were reasonably accurate descriptions of the Pueblo world, something the Spaniards were not to realize for several years.[16]

At about this time two additional and politically potent events impacted the regions north of New Spain and led to the pressure on Mendoza to explore the new areas. One was a decision by the still ambitious conquistador Hernán Cortés. This man, forced out of the governing power structure in New Spain but given control over parts of southern Mexico, decided to launch his own explorations of these unknown but promising new lands to the north. Cortés actually started his investigation in an attempt to counter Guzmán's thrust up the Sinaloa coast. From a new base at Acapulco Cortés, in 1532, sent ships to explore the lands to the northwest. These ships were lost, but the following year another ship sailed along the west coast of Baja California. In 1535 Cortés himself landed at the site of the future La Paz. At about this time Mendoza took over the governance of Mexico and forbade any further exploration without a specific government license. However, Cortés had already given orders to his captain, Francisco de Ulloa, who by 1540 had explored all the way to the mouth of the Colorado River. By 1540, however, Cortés himself was back in Spain beginning a lengthy litigation to protect his rights, and Mendoza had already launched the Cíbola expedition.[17] Cortés was never again to be a serious player in the geopolitics of northern New Spain.

The second event had its inception when one of Pizarro's captains, Hernando de Soto, returned to Spain and in 1537 was granted leadership of a fresh expedition to Florida. Given the fragmentary state of Spanish geographical knowledge, this seemed a direct threat to Mendoza's plans to explore the wealthy cities described by Cabeza de Vaca. Soto's large expedition reached Cuba in May of 1538, preparatory to moving north to the mainland.[18] Even so, the cautious Mendoza decided to probe the lands to the north before launching a full-fledged expedition. Mendoza had been grooming a protégé, a man still in his twenties, named Francisco Vázquez de Coronado (today, usually referred to simply as Coronado) for high political office, and Coronado was soon to be appointed governor of the new west coast province of Nueva Galicia. A small party led by a Franciscan friar, Marcos de Niza, who had been with Pizarro in Peru, was dispatched in March 1539 up the west coast of Mexico, departing from Culiacán, the northernmost regular Spanish settlement on the Sinaloan coast. With Marcos were a number of Indians from central Mexico and Piman-speaking guides and interpreters who had come south with Cabeza de Vaca three years before. A second friar, one Honorato, dropped out because of illness shortly after the beginning of the expedition. The most important member of the Marcos expedition after the leader himself, however, was the black slave from the Cabeza de Vaca party, Esteban de Dorantes, who, having been over part of the trail in 1536, was to serve as a guide. Apparently skilled at picking up the native languages, and a person with considerable charisma, Esteban soon became the de facto second leader of the party.[19]

Marcos had been directed to stay near the coast during his trip, and he apparently tried to do just that. There are various routings for the friar and his party. My own routing has him working his way up the Mariscos region of Sinaloa, into the Sonoran Desert, eventually arriving at a substantial settlement that he called Vacapa, which I place in the Altar Valley, of northern Sonora. There is no evidence that Marcos ever went into the statelet region of northeastern Sonora except for the western edge of it on his return voyage. Around this time he learned that the seven cities described by Tejo were collectively called Cíbola and obtained detailed descriptions of them. From Vacapa, Marcos reached one of the north-flowing streams of southern Arizona, most likely the San Pedro. He seems to have passed the ruin of Chichilticale, probably somewhere south of the Gila River. Meanwhile, Esteban had been sent ahead with some of the Indians.[20]

What happened in the next few weeks is unclear. Marcos claimed to have continued northeastward. At some point he was met by his native helpers, fleeing back down the trail. They had reached Cíbola, and there Esteban was murdered by the local inhabitants. Marcos now faced a dilemma. Should he follow the viceroy's orders and continue on to Cíbola, or should he retreat to Mexico? According to his own story Marcos went on and saw one of the seven cities from across a valley. If the sighting actually occurred, it was probably of the Zuni town K'iakima.[21] In any case Marcos now returned to Mexico although with another side excursion, one that I think may have involved a short trip up the Sonora River valley, perhaps as far as the Ures Gorge. There he heard of gold being used by the natives. In fact, gold was found in the Sonora Valley within a year or so in the Corazones area. It was, however, a Spanish mining discovery; as I pointed out in chapter 9, the Sonoran people do not seem to have utilized the metal. In any case this was hearsay; Marcos did not report *seeing* gold at any point in his southwestern trip.

The report of Marcos stimulated Viceroy Mendoza to move forward the plans for a major expedition, one for which he chose Vázquez de

Coronado as commander. Outfitted from private funds, including those of Coronado and Mendoza himself, this army was large for its time. Some 350 Spanish soldiers were involved, along with around 1,300 Indian auxiliaries and an unknown number of slaves and other servants, some black and others from various Indian groups. The total number of individuals could have been as high as 2,000. Three women are known to have been on the journey, and most likely there were additional females, especially servants or companions of the Indian auxiliary force, who were simply not counted. Along with the expedition were large numbers (some thousands in all) of animals, extra horses and mules, sheep, cattle, and perhaps swine.[22]

To check once more on the information about Cíbola and on the route northward, Mendoza sent one of Coronado's captains, Melchior Díaz, in that direction in November 1539, with fifteen horsemen and a contingent of Indians, the latter probably to act as guides and interpreters. Díaz spent the winter somewhere in the lower Southwest, either the Sonoran region or present-day southern Arizona. There he gained remarkably correct information on Cíbola, partly verifying Marcos's information but downplaying the size and sophistication of the seven Cíbolan towns.[23]

Still another expedition, this one by sea, was launched in 1540. With Cortés out of the way Mendoza now had control of the Gulf of California and fully intended to supply his expeditionary force from the sea. With three ships Mendoza's captain, Hernando de Alarcón, beat his way northward, reaching the mouth of the Colorado River in late August 1540.[24] Continuing upriver, Alarcón quickly learned that Coronado was now at Cíbola/Zuni, some hundreds of miles away, with no water route in between. After exploring about as far as the region of present-day Yuma, Alarcón returned to the west coast of Mexico. He planned to return the following year, but events were to make that impossible.[25]

Returning to Mexico, Díaz met the advancing Coronado army in the early spring of 1540

at the Spanish post of Culiacán. In the latter part of April Coronado set out with an advance party, approximately a hundred Spanish horsemen and foot soldiers and a number of Indian allies and servants, probably several hundred people in all. A month later Coronado was in the area of Corazones. Although the Sonoran statelets were at their height, and probably had the largest population anywhere in the Southwest, Coronado paid very little attention to this area. A certain amount of the information I presented in chapter 9 came from his party, but the leader himself was eager to continue *más allá*. He did realize the importance of the Sonoran region logistically and left orders for the main army, following slowly along behind him, to establish a way station there. But Cíbola was his goal. Coronado treated the Serrana people reasonably well, but, as said in chapter 9, he most likely contributed to the first wave of infectious disease that within another two or three generations was to destroy the Sonoran statelets.[26]

Going on to the north and east, probably with new guides from the statelet area, Coronado became increasingly disturbed that he was drawing away from the sea. This was especially worrisome because of the supplies Alarcón was carrying, including, almost certainly, winter clothing for the expedition. Like Esteban, and perhaps Marcos before him, Coronado was traveling along a well-known route northward. I believe that Coronado (and all subsequent expeditions during this period) swung eastward from the middle Gila Valley, then northward again, eventually crossing the river, probably near modern Cliff. They then followed the line of the San Francisco River and eventually devolved onto the relatively flat country near present-day Quemado. From there it was only a short distance to the Seven Cities of Cíbola.[27]

To Coronado Cíbola was a crushing disappointment. He found several relatively small Pueblo settlements, most likely six rather than seven, with a total population of only a few thousand (see Figure 11.2). As I said in chapter 10, the word *Cíbola* was perhaps an im-

FIGURE 11.2. Zuni Pueblo, around the beginning of the twentieth century. A Zuni town (but lacking the mission church) would probably have looked something like this in Coronado's day. Maxwell Museum of Anthropology, University of New Mexico, cat. no. 97.10.22.

perfect rendition of a Zuni word designating either the tribe or the homeland. The Zuni, apparently involved in important summer religious ceremonies, reacted by threatening and harassing the Spaniards.[28] Attacking the town of Hawikuh, the westernmost of the Zuni pueblos, Coronado overawed the natives and created an uneasy peace. A dominant leitmotif for the two years of Coronado's occupation of the Southwest was this alternation of sullen peace and violent outbreak of hostilities.

There followed a series of explorations that included trips to Hopi and exploration to the edge of the Grand Canyon.[29] Coronado was becoming increasingly concerned over his lack of contact with Alarcón and the sea arm of the expedition, so at some point he sent Melchior Díaz to the lower Colorado to look for the naval captain. Once he completed that task, Díaz was ordered to oversee setting up the way station at Corazones. Díaz reached the Colorado Delta only to find that Alarcón, very shortly before, had sailed back to Mexico. After briefly exploring the region and committing a few

senseless atrocities, Díaz set out across the Sonoran Desert for the Serrana. A freak accident in which the butt end of his lance was driven into his lower abdomen mortally wounded Díaz and he was buried somewhere in the desert region of southwest Arizona or northwest Sonora.[30] The control of the Corazones station passed into the hands of Diego de Alcaráz, who was killed in turn by the statelet people a year or so later.

Meanwhile, Coronado was having an interesting encounter at Zuni with a trading group from Pecos Pueblo on the edge of the Great Plains, far to the east. Whether this party simply happened to be in Zuni at this time, or whether the news of Coronado's arrival had stimulated Pueblo curiosity, is not known. In any case Coronado was soon eager to push on eastward, so in the waning months of 1540 he moved with his vanguard army to the Rio Grande area. The main army, still toiling along the trail toward Cíbola-Zuni, was given orders to rest briefly at the Zuni towns then join him in the east. The stage was set for the year-end series of events that would dictate the moves of the Spanish forces for the remainder of Coronado's stay in the Southwest.

The bellicose Tiguex confederation did not appreciate the Spanish invasion and especially the fact that Spanish soldiers took over one of their towns. This pueblo, *Ghufer* (parched corn town), called by the Spaniards *Coofor,* perhaps the later Santiago Pueblo near Bernalillo, became the headquarters for the Spanish army. Around the end of the year 1540 there were a series of revolts. A town called by the Spaniards *Arenal,* likely the Puaray Pueblo of later times, was overrun and a number of its inhabitants murdered under a flag of truce. Other towns in the Tiguex confederacy now revolted, and the Spaniards spent two or three months reducing one of them called Moho or El Cerco.[31] It was heavily fortified, but the Spaniards managed to cut off the water supply, and the town was eventually taken with great loss of life on the part of the Tiguex. By this time it was spring, and Coronado had found a new and dazzling chimera, the rich land of Quivira, supposedly somewhere in the plains to the east.[32]

The year 1541 was filled with disappointments for Coronado. Acting on information from two Pecos captives who had been tortured for information and from a Plains Indian, probably Pawnee, whom the Spaniards called "El Turco" (because they fancied he resembled a Turk), Coronado led his entire army, including the newly captive Tiguex slaves, onto the southern plains. The group probably totaled 1,500 to 2,000 people and included the remaining herds of domesticated animals. In the course of his wanderings Coronado met Indians that he called Querechos, fairly clearly early Apachean groups, and also a series of settlements of a different people, whom he named Teya. These latter people were later to be called the Jumanos, and they were in contact with the La Junta groups.

Turk, who had been some sort of captive or slave at Pecos, guided Coronado onto the flat and featureless Llano Estacado, where his army was misdirected for a time. Turk apparently had the idea, perhaps in collusion with the Pecos leadership, of losing the entire Spanish army in this vast empty land. Alerted by a traitorous Wichita Indian who had also been detained at Pecos, Coronado had Turk arrested and with 30 horsemen and an unknown number of Mexican Indian allies pushed off to the northeast in search of Quivira. They reached Quivira, the Wichita country of central Kansas, but found no cities nor riches. The Spaniards traveled on to another territory they called Harahey, probably that of a Pawnee band, and then turned back (see Figure 11.3). The unfortunate Turk, his usefulness over, was strangled.[33]

Meanwhile, the main Spanish army had returned to the Rio Grande and to towns of sullen and hostile, but for the moment quiescent, natives. Coronado's captains spent some time exploring up and down the Rio Grande while waiting for their leader to return. After Coronado's small party reached the Rio Grande in October, there was talk of returning to the plains the following spring, Coronado refusing to believe that the golden cities existed only in his imagination. However, in late December 1541, just a year after the events of Arenal, Coronado suffered a fall from his horse and received a serious head wound. While he was recovering, he had additional bad news: Diego de Alcaráz had been killed, and the entire Spanish party at the halfway station of Corazones had been slaughtered or scattered. Coronado was now determined to return to Mexico. He was doubtlessly becoming a bit concerned about his excesses in the Pueblo world and about possible accusations that he had not been involved in a "just war." At least this is a logical explanation for his order to release the captive natives (probably mostly women and children) taken at the battle of Moho and perhaps in other punitive operations. Coronado could not prevent a small party under a headstrong missionary, Juan de Padilla, returning to Quivira to continue search from the seven cities, nor another friar, Luís de Ubeda, from remaining in the Southwest to missionize. Padilla was murdered at Quivira a few months later, and Ubeda was never heard from again.[34]

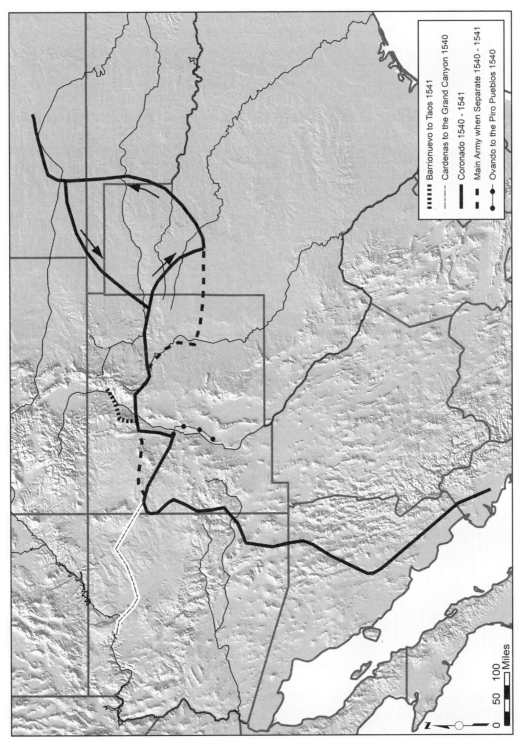

FIGURE 11.3. Coronado's exploration of the Southwest, 1540–1541. Earth Analytic, Santa Fe, NM.

Though Coronado failed to colonize any part of Aztlan, he made a certain impression on the region. Unfortunately, it was mainly through the introduction of infectious disease, which surely started with this group. Aside from this dubious gift, the Spaniards left a few plants, melons in the Sonoran region and probably also among the Pueblos. Except for possible chickens in Sonora, no domesticated animal seemed to have survived, even though Ubeda was given a flock of sheep by the departing Spaniards. As far as we know, the Aztlan Indians received no new technology of any note. They were left with a considerable knowledge of central Mexico because a number of disaffected Mexican auxiliaries, possibly a hundred or more, stayed in the Pueblo area. A few of the auxiliaries could conceivably have settled in the statelet region of Sonora, but we have no evidence for this. As discussed earlier in this book, such Mexican Indians may have contributed something to the religious and ceremonial inventory of the upper Southwest and possibly such games as patolli. They seem to have made no mark on technology, something a little surprising if they were indeed in the numbers I have suggested. However, the newcomers were most likely male, so traditional Mexican women's skills would not have been available, nor were they likely to have been specialists, except perhaps in warfare or in weapons manufacturing. In any case very little new came either to the Pueblo or to the Sonoran world.

Although we have no direct evidence, there is little doubt that the terrible cost of the Spanish invasion quickly began to tell. There was, after all, a breakup of whole pueblos and widescale looting, especially of cloth and foodstuffs, by the cold and hungry Spaniards and their Mexican allies. It seems likely that the first effects of infectious disease were now beginning to show. Exactly how this played out cannot be plotted, and the full impact was likely not felt for a number of years. The statelet people certainly were still a concern 20 years after Coronado. Even so, when the Jesuit missionaries occupied northeast Sonora in the 1630s, there had been a major collapse in that region (see chapter 9). A second wave of Spanish invasions began in the upper Southwest during the last two decades of the sixteenth century. By that time, as I discussed in chapter 7, the Pueblo numbers were entering a steep decline. My own estimate of Pueblo population is for about 60,000 Native Americans during the Coronado period and some 50,000 by Oñate's time 60 years later. If Spanish census figures are dependable, the figure had fallen to 40,000 by 1640. This is not as precipitous a drop as in the Sonoran area, but it was disruptive. By the time of the Pueblo Revolt of 1680 there were perhaps 17,000 Pueblo Indians. At least, the Pueblos still were attempting to manifest their cultural independence. The remnant populations of the old Serrana were well on their way to becoming Hispanized peasants. The fate of both these remnant Aztlan core groups is discussed in chapter 12.

My guess is that even by the mid-sixteenth century a sort of cultural malaise was beginning to engulf the entire Southwest. The advanced technology of the newcomers and the obvious fact that they now controlled the rich lands to the south and were steadily creeping northward must have had an impact on the native southwesterners. Some of the Sonorans fought valiantly against Ibarra, and the Pueblos put up some resistance to the small probing Spanish parties of the 1580s. But it was as if the people of Aztlan now knew that time had run out and that for them a cultural night was fast falling.

The Spaniards, during the Coronado period, were still driven by the dream of vast wealth in precious metals to be looted from the Indians and the parallel wealth in souls to be saved. But within a few years two other themes began to surface in the attitude of Europeans to unconquered areas in the Americas. First was the increasing realization that not loot from captured cities and kingdoms but the actual native populations and their productive and continuing labor was the real wealth of this new world. The Spanish concept of *encomienda* had been introduced into New Spain shortly after the conquest. Encomiendas were the assignment of the labor of conquered groups (in a kind of serfdom) to favored European individuals or groups. This was a way the Church and Crown could pay for the conquests, for those Spaniards assigned Indians in encomiendas were financially responsible for their conversion and general welfare. On the frontier it gradually became incumbent on the owner of an encomienda, the *encomendero*, to be involved in the defense of the encomienda as well as of any Spanish mission or secular settlements nearby. This quickly involved extending the labor burden of encomienda Indians to include military service. The importance of this varied from time to time and place to place. In the upper Southwest, as I pointed out when discussing *capitanes de guerra* in chapter 7, it was a factor of great importance from the very earliest years of Spanish permanent settlement.

The second factor, not of major importance in Coronado's time, was the discovery and exploitation of mines. This came about because, a few years after Coronado, a stunning series of metallurgical discoveries were made. Beginning in the 1540s, great silver deposits were uncovered in both North and South America. Those in New Spain were in present-day Zacatecas and along the eastern flank of the Mexican Sierra Madre Occidental, northward to Durango and Chihuahua. In South America, in the new Spanish viceroyalty of Peru, vast amounts of silver ore were found in Bolivia, especially in the vicinity of Potosí.

The discoveries in the Sierra Madre quickly changed the Spanish attitude toward the remnants of Aztlan. Although the more romantic still dreamed of golden cities and rich kingdoms, the hardheaded prospectors among the conquerors planned to open more mines. If these mines were near large native concentrations, so much the better. Mining is exacting, dangerous, and generally unpleasant work, so a large servile and docile labor force was much to be desired. These new needs for encomienda

and mines drove the Spaniards in all subsequent attempts to reach the upper Southwest. By the 1570s a string of mining settlements like irregularly spaced pearls on a string, stretched from Zacatecas to Central Chihuahua. The same mountainous landforms that produced silver in those regions seemed to also exist in the Pueblo world. This was what drove men like Chamuscado, Espejo, Castaño, and eventually Oñate.

For a decade or more before 1580 there had been some Spanish activity north of central Chihuahua. Mostly this took the form of raiding hostile Indian groups for slaves, primarily for use in the mines. Some of the raids went down the Conchos River toward the Rio Grande, where the Spaniards contacted the La Junta towns and their nomadic neighbors, the Teya-Jumano. As I said above, this area had been visited in 1535 by Cabeza de Vaca, and some bands of Teya had been contacted six years later on the western plains by Coronado. But now, because of the need for Indian slaves, Spanish contact with these borderland Southwest Indians was mostly hostile.

This hostile activity produced somewhat of a backlash from the Spanish government. By way of the Laws of Burgos (1512) the Spanish Crown had already inched toward reform in its attitude toward native peoples. Some three decades later, influenced by such reformers as Las Casas, the Spanish Crown promulgated new laws to protect the Indians. In 1573 another series of such laws attempted to stop slave raiding on Indian communities and to strengthen the hands of missionaries in their attempts to convert native groups. By 1580 Spaniards on the northern frontier were definitely receiving mixed messages. On the one hand the possibility of new riches in silver tempted every mining entrepreneur, while on the other hand, new journeys of exploration were now supposed to be guided and controlled by the Church.[35]

In 1581–1582 a "compromise" party led by Francisco Sánchez Chamuscado, and including three missionaries headed by Fray Agustín

Rodríguez, explored the Southwest, following the Conchos River northward to La Junta, then the Rio Grande north and westward into Pueblo country. The Chamuscado group reached as far west as Zuni and as far east as the Canadian River valley. When Chamuscado left the Pueblo region, the missionaries demanded to be left behind and were shortly killed by the natives, two of them at Puaray (Coronado's Arenal). Forty years, it would seem, had not been enough to erase the memory of Coronado's atrocities.[36]

Uncertainty as to the fate of the friars quickly spawned another expedition, that of Antonio de Espejo. Finding the Franciscans dead and Puaray empty of inhabitants, Espejo visited Zuni and then Hopi, where his one friar, Bernardino de Beltrán, deserted the leader, returning to Chihuahua with about half the party. Meanwhile Espejo, ever searching for mining prospects, had wandered westward as far as the Rio Verde. Returning to Hopi he had contact with a nomadic group that, like Coronado on the plains, he called the Querechos. Espejo was given, presumably by the Hopi, some Querecho female captives. When he was in the Acoma area, he met another group of Querechos, and one of the captives escaped to these ethnic kindred. In a series of skirmishes the Spaniards captured a local Querecho girl and offered to trade her for the original captive. There was another sharp battle when the trade went awry, and Espejo was left with the local girl. These Querechos, I believe, were the ancestors of the Navajo. A generation after Espejo, Oñate resettled some of his Acoma captives in a presumably nearby Querecho pueblo and that same year of 1599 described to the viceroy an "Apache" pueblo with fifteen plazas, which might well have been in the same area.[37] This town was about 50 miles from the Spanish capital of San Gabriel, located near modern Española.

Returning to the Rio Grande Valley, Espejo found that a few elderly people had moved back into Puaray. These unfortunates were murdered and the pueblo burned by the Spaniards. Like Chamuscado before him, Espejo searched the general area for mines. He returned home via the Pecos River, reaching La Junta and journeying up the Conchos to the Chihuahua mining district.[38]

Another expedition in the years 1590–1591 was led by the acting governor of the new province of Nuevo León, Gaspar Castaño de Sosa. Bringing men, women, and children, Castaño reached the Pecos area in the dying days of the year 1590, and in the next few months he explored much of the eastern Pueblo area, mainly searching for mines. He began the appointment of native officials and may have planned to divide the Pueblo world into encomiendas and to set up permanent Spanish settlements. His expedition was unauthorized, however, and in 1591 the viceroy sent a military party under Juan de Morlete to arrest Castaño and bring his expedition back to New Spain.[39] This did not discourage other bootleg entrepreneurs, and sometime around 1594 a little party under Antonio Gutiérrez de Humaña and Francisco Leyva de Bonilla trekked back to Pueblo land. After spending about a year at the Tewa pueblo of Powhoge,[40] the later San Ildefonso, where they were likely prospecting for silver, the party left for the plains. There, with the exception of one Indian servant, the group was wiped out.[41]

There was considerable competition for the honor and presumed profit of settling New Mexico, and a wealthy north Mexican settler named Juan de Oñate was eventually awarded the contract to establish a proprietary colony.[42] Oñate marched northward with a large party of men, women, and children, perhaps 560 in all, including a contingent of eight Franciscan friars and three lay brothers.[43] It was a varied party, including Europeans, Africans, various Mexican Indians, and genetic mixtures of these three macroethnic groups. Oñate had a number of wheeled vehicles and a vast amount of supplies, including mining equipment, agricultural implements, and thousands of beads and other trade materials. In the summer of 1598 Oñate, taking a leaf from Coronado, appropriated the Tewa town of Okeh. This pueblo, part of the modern San Juan, was located near the junction of the Chama and Rio Grande. Okeh was on the east side of the Rio Grande, another section of the town called Yungue being situated on the west side of the river. A few months later the Spaniards were referring to the Spanish settlement as San Gabriel del Yungue.[44]

There was trouble in this colony almost from the start. Late in the year of 1598 a Spanish party was killed in the process of taking tribute (or looting, depending on one's point of view) at Acoma Pueblo (see Figure 11.4). The Spaniards attacked the pueblo in January of 1599, killing a large number of people and taking the survivors prisoner. Assured by the Franciscans that this was a "just war," in Spanish legal parlance, Oñate held a trial for the survivors, sending the children to Mexico as wards of the missionaries, enslaving adults, and cutting off one foot from all males over 25 years of age. Two Hopi Indians found at Acoma had their right hands severed as a warning of Spanish resolve. This particular punishment has echoed down the centuries and is still the center of controversy today, some apologists for Oñate even denying that it ever happened.[45] As I have pointed out elsewhere, however, "the mutilations, no doubt chosen for their shock value, seem monstrous to the modern reader. It might be said, however, that in the context of late-sixteenth-century European penal practices and attitudes, Oñate did not inflict particularly harsh punishments. Even the enslavements were for a sharply limited period, and children were not to be punished. Of course, permanently removing children from their parents might disturb our sensibilities, but from Oñate's own point of view his actions were hardly excessive."[46]

The Acoma battle, as it turned out, was only the first of Oñate's trouble with Pueblo Indians. A year or so after Acoma the Tompiro Pueblos rose and were defeated with much bloodshed. There was also widespread dissatisfaction among the settlers, and a number deserted

FIGURE 11.4. Acoma women carrying water jars. Maxwell Museum of Anthropology, University of New Mexico, cat. no. 71.18.108.

New Mexico. In spite of these things Oñate continued to be optimistic about the possibility of silver strikes in New Mexico. He explored into the southwestern plains and as far south and west as the lower Colorado River, but his colony was dying on the vine.[47] By 1608 there was real uncertainty among the Spanish authorities as to whether a Spanish presence should be continued. Had the Spaniards decided to desert the colony, it would have had a considerable impact on the Pueblos, who already were absorbing some newcomer technology. At this point, however, the Franciscans made a stand, insisting that they had baptized thousands of Indians and requesting that New Mexico be made into a mission province. This was done within the next year or so, the capital being moved to Santa Fe.[48]

For the next 70 years New Mexico remained under joint control of the missionaries and the various governors and their encomenderos.

The search for mines continued, but no significant amount of silver or gold was exported from New Mexico during the entire seventeenth century. Although silver and gold were there, the logistics of the situation made extraction difficult or impossible. New Mexico was seriously undercapitalized throughout the century. The water resources were often inadequate, and mercury, necessary for separating silver and gold from their ores, had to be imported over the long and tortuous Camino Real.[49] The largely inbred Spanish population, scattered among the Pueblos and sharing the same water resources, grew very slowly, reaching perhaps 2,500 by 1680. By that time the Pueblo population had shrunk to perhaps 17,000.[50]

What happened in the Pueblo Southwest was one of the most intense experiments of forced acculturation in the whole New World. The missions were actually placed in the various pueblos, and the missionaries concentrated on children and young people, insisting that they learn Spanish and adhere to Spanish cultural ways. There was enforced church attendance for all Pueblo Indians and a concomitant constant war against any manifestations of the native religion, especially the hated kachina cult.[51] It is astonishing that after 70 to 80 years of this unrelenting missionization even shreds of the native religion remained. But, in fact, a strong underground faction of Pueblo religious leaders maintained themselves. At various intervals some would be caught and executed, but their places were taken by others. In 1680 these leaders allied themselves with certain *capitanes de guerra*, the Spanish-sponsored war captains, successors to the war leaders of earlier times. Together these two leadership groups, apparently with the active cooperation of the vast majority of the ordinary Pueblo Indians, drove the Spaniards out of New Mexico with considerable loss of life. The attitude of the rebels toward the Christian religion shows most clearly in the focus on missionaries. Of the 33 missionaries assigned to New Mexico in 1680, 21 were killed, almost two-thirds of the total, while Spanish losses as a whole were only about one out of six.[52]

Even during the seventeenth century, missionization of the nomadic groups had not been particularly successful. During the revolt Apacheans and the semisedentary Navajo joined the Pueblos. In the eighteenth century there was little attempt to convert such groups nor the Utes and the increasingly dangerous Comanche. Most of these nomads were somewhat outside the direct influence of Mesoamericanization and had not really partaken of Aztlan. However, the one dramatic exception was the Navajo. This western branch of the Apachean linguistic family had, I believe, already been absorbing the uses of Aztlan well before the Spaniards came. It can be seen in the rich cosmology with its Pueblo-derived deities, including the twin war gods, cloud figures, religious art, and the kachina-like masked *yeis*.[53]

As for the Pueblos themselves their determination stood them in good stead over the next two centuries. When the Spaniards returned in the period 1692–1696, the religions again went underground, but now the cautious Spaniards adopted a less draconian policy. The missionaries were instructed to ignore what were considered "harmless superstitions." In the west, among the Hopi, who remained free of Spanish control, native religions took over completely. One Hopi town, Awatovi, had a strong Christian contingent, and these converts wanted to invite the Franciscans to return. The pueblo was sacked by warriors from the other towns; some of its inhabitants were slaughtered, and others were absorbed into the other Hopi pueblos.

Perhaps J. O. Brew, in his study of Franciscan Awatovi, put it best: "The struggle, lost by the Christian God in Tusayan in 1680 stayed lost. The Kachinas won then and the Kachinas hold the field today. From that time on, Spaniards appeared on the Hopi mesas only as unwelcome visitors; except at Awatovi. And Awatovi did not live long enough to enjoy the reunion."[54] I suspect that it was the Hopi and the semi-independent Zuni that maintained the fountainhead of religious belief, rekindling the native faith in Pueblos farther east. During the late seventeenth and eighteenth centuries certain of the Tewa-Tano and Tiwa peoples, sometimes as small parties, sometimes whole pueblos, fled west. These groups, and their continuing contacts with their own peoples who remained at home in the Rio Grande Valley, were probably also vectors in the maintenance of Pueblo religion, perhaps of sociopolitical ideas and even of art. However it was done, the Pueblos did manage to salvage—and in the nineteenth and twentieth centuries recreate—certain aspects of Aztlan, with its clear afterglow of Mesoamerica.

# CHAPTER 12

# Aftermath

The invasion of the New World by Spain in 1492 had extraordinary and sometimes unintended consequences. The Spaniards, and in slightly later times the Portuguese, French, Dutch and English, had various agendas, two major ones being settlement and economic exploitation. Colonization of these vast new lands quickly brought domination over a variety of native peoples. In some portions of the New World this quickly translated into the formation of tribute and serflike populations, utilizing devices like the encomienda. However, the Indian susceptibility to Old World diseases led to dramatic depopulation in the first few generations after Columbus. This led in turn to slaving among the more disease-resistant African peoples and still another genetic influx. Opening sea routes between Mexico and East Asia after the mid-sixteenth century brought in Oriental influences both genetic and cultural.

The Spaniards made the first incursions into regions of major American populations, and within a century or so a veritable rainbow of humanity had spread through the new Spanish domain. There was massive intermixture of Spaniards and Native Americans and both of those groups with African natives, a situation that in Spanish America still exists in varying degrees today. An important factor here was the strong missionizing drive of the Spaniards. The Catholic Church and the Spanish Crown worked together to preserve native peoples but not their native cultures. The same was

more or less true of the Portuguese, whose country was under control of the Spaniards for a number of decades.

The English-occupied regions consisted mainly of what is today the eastern United States and (after the mid-eighteenth century) Canada. English settlement, beginning about a century after the Spaniards, also produced mixed populations except that, especially in the American colonies, there was much less Indian and much more African in the mixture. The Spaniards, of course, had already occupied the regions of major American civilizations with their large sedentary groups. In the English-settled areas the relatively sparse Native American populations tended to be killed off or driven away rather than assimilated. The Protestant English made sporadic and uncoordinated efforts to missionize, but for the most part the accepted way to deal with Native Americans was to drive them out or kill them.

The French made several exploratory voyages into the St. Lawrence River basin and surrounding coastal areas of Canada beginning before the mid-sixteenth century, but, like the English, their colonization was basically a seventeenth-century phenomenon. In any case the French were a somewhat special case because the Jesuit missionaries had a very powerful influence over the colonizing effort. In addition French immigrant populations remained rather small from first settlement times.

Though there was a certain amount of genetic exchange with Native Americans, the current ethnic mixtures in Canada largely date from the nineteenth and twentieth centuries.[1]

This first great European expansion into the Americas, beginning around AD 1500, also saw the beginnings of European political and commercial domination of other parts of the world. Southeast Asia passed into European control, directly or indirectly, as did the more accessible coastal regions of Africa and southern Asia. The same thing might have happened in East Asia, but large sophisticated political units such as Japan and China managed to fight off the European thrust and maintained their political independence.

Scholars have often speculated about why this did not happen in the New World. There were a number of high cultures, operating as something we might call "states." The two most powerful and impressive were, of course, the Aztec Kingdom and the Inca Empire. A number of other polities, however, were reasonably viable and reasonably highly organized. They included the Chibcha federations of Colombia, small statelets in Central America, the various Maya territories, the Tarascan Kingdom, and perhaps the Pequeños Estados of the Nayarit-Sinaloa region of Mexico. For one reason or another all of these regions collapsed under European military pressure within the first century of European rule. Why them and not the eastern Asian states? To be sure, these latter polities were somewhat more complex than their American counterparts. Another reason, however, was the differential effect of disease. Once considered of minor importance by historians, disease has in recent times been recognized as having a more important role in shaping the destiny of the Americas. Clearly, it was the great ally of the early conquistadors. Major plagues were inadvertently introduced to extremely susceptible populations in the very early years after Columbus. Europeans in eastern Asia had no such serendipitous weapon because Asia shared in the Old World pool of epidemic diseases, with its concomitant higher levels of immunity.

The two most political of the powerful civilizations in the Americas were the Aztecs and the Inca, and the former, because of specialized circumstances, probably had a greater chance of survival. However, as I argued a number of years ago:

> The Aztecs, in spite of their less sophisticated military technology, could and should have destroyed Cortés during the *noche triste1*.... [But] even had the Aztecs beaten and killed Cortés, another conqueror would surely have come along. The brittle confederation of the Aztecs, with its lunatic insistence on mass human sacrifice, probably could not have withstood the strain. In time, the Aztecs might have learned the uses of a more effective warfare, but time was the one thing they did not have.[2]

The historian Hugh Thomas offered a somewhat different analysis of the matter:

> It may be argued that if Cortés had not carried through his conquest, someone else would have done so. That cannot be proved. The conquest of 1520–1 required Cortés' capacity and determination to win over the Indians: above all the Tlaxcalans. Had it not been for their help ... the expedition would have foundered. Had that occurred, who is to say that the Mexica under Cuauhtémoc might not have acquired the use of Spanish weapons, and perhaps learned to use horses? Even allowing for the onslaught of smallpox, they might have maintained a determined opposition until Spain became weary of conquering. Perhaps they would have embarked upon their own version of the Meiji era in Japan. One Spanish proconsul in the Philippines offered to Philip II to conquer China.... The idea was turned down by the prudent king. He might have done the same in respect of a Mexico rejuvenated under a well-prepared line of emperors.[3]

Well, perhaps! In this situation the demographic is surely an important key. Was the amount of population loss at the beginning of the conquest period sufficient to seriously impact the Indian will and ability to resist? Thomas himself pointed out the great variation in estimates of central Mexican population by demographic experts.[4] But even though numbers and percentages vary, scholars generally agree that there *was* a dramatic drop in population. If we can accept a statement made in 1568 by the jurist Alonso de Zorita that the population of his day was less than a third the number of Indians at the conquest, it indicates a disaster of major proportions. The native count for Zorita's time is considered reasonably accurate. Working backwards from what he knew of the midcentury population, he estimated around eight million individuals for central Mexico at conquest times. Zorita was a cautious man, and his calculations should be taken seriously.[5]

Of course the trauma of the conquest itself was a factor in the depopulation. But even in the bloody years of the Guzmán period the Spaniards were not involved in holocaust behavior, and by the early 1530s they were taking serious steps to protect and preserve native life. In any case disease, which knows no ethnic or political boundaries, would surely have continued its rapid spread through the native population. After all, it did run ahead of the Spanish conquest in areas like the Tarascan Kingdom. Extremely favorable conditions for the spread of disease would have been created had the Spaniards been forced into a long-term struggle for control of Mexico. I find it hard to believe that they would not have done so. Regardless of what happened in Mexico, however, the conquistadors would presumably soon have expanded into the gold- and silver-rich Inca Empire. The Spanish thirst for wealth in those early years was unslakable, and Peru would hardly be secure with a viable and hostile Aztec kingdom spread across central Mexico.

The Inca Empire, consisting of much of the mountain and coastal area of Peru, plus parts of Bolivia, Ecuador, and extreme northern Chile, was America's most extensive centralized political unit. Controlled from the Peruvian highland center of Cuzco and linked by

an extensive network of roads and trails, it was a governmental tour de force, especially for a people who had no written language.[6] The Inca domain was governed by an emperor, head of a family from the southern highlands of Peru. This family for some time had held power in a semiruralized area, a cluster of villages in the Valley of Cuzco, but now exploded onto the central Andean scene with blazing rapidity. They began this expansion sometime around AD 1440, less than a century before the Spanish conquest of Peru. The Inca ruler was originally a local *sinchi,* or war chief, the head of an *ayllu,* or endogamous clan, probably with rather limited powers.[7] Under a particularly able and ambitious sinchi, who took the name Pachacuti, the Cuzco groups began a program of conquest, especially into the territory of the Chanca polity to the north and west. Under Pachacuti's successors in the next two generations, the Inca domain grew with astonishing speed. Both the northern and southern highlands and associated altiplano of Peru and Bolivia were overrun. The great coastal civilization of the Chimu Kingdom fell, as did the states of southern coastal Peru and coastal Chile. The central highlands of Ecuador became Inca territory, and there was some sort of control over the coastal lowlands. By the time of his death, in 1527 or 1528, a grandson, Huayna Capac, had established a northern frontier near the borders of modern Colombia.[8] Later Spanish and native Indian accounts describe a rigid state corporatism in which every aspect of life of the subject populations, virtually every moment of existence from birth to death, was codified and controlled. The state could be benign, creating peace and the assurance of ample food in times of famine, but its power was absolute.[9] When accounts of the Inca Empire became current in Europe, Incan society became the model for various utopias.

Huayna Capac was victim of the first wave of Spanish disease, introduced by voyagers exploring down the west coast of South America, and his brittle empire was soon wracked with civil war, two sons of the emperor, named

Atahuallpa and Huáscar, fighting for control. The country was still in considerable disarray when a Spanish adventurer and distant cousin of Hernán Cortés named Francisco Pizarro invaded the Inca domain in 1532 with around 170 soldiers, one third of them cavalry. With this small group, plus an unknown but probably considerable number of native Peruvian allies, he managed within months to overrun the Inca Empire.[10]

This has often been taken as an example of Spanish military brilliance (or, for the religious-minded, divine intervention), or it has been explained away as an artifact of rampaging disease and the weakening caused by civil war. This book is not about South America, and I hold no great expertise in Central Andean pre-history and history. But I have long believed that the whole premise of the Inca Empire is overblown. The Inca expanded over a vast area of different kinds of terrain in scarcely more than a human lifetime. They could not have done that in depth, and it is fairly clear that they simply "beheaded" the leadership of the various states and tribes, putting their own officials (or pliant locals) at the apex of the various societies. The Inca engineers and political planners did show considerable skill with roads and administrative innovations, holding the parts of the empire together. But it must have been a ramshackle edifice at best, seething with unrest on the part of the subject peoples. When the Spaniards came, they found plenty of eager native allies and simply did some "beheading" of their own.[11]

The Spanish conquest of the Inca Empire had very little effect on Aztlan, except inasmuch as the discovery of vast golden treasures inflamed the Spanish itch for more wealth and turned their eyes to the promising area north of New Spain. They would have come in any case; after all, the *real* conquest of the upper Southwest was launched primarily from the north interior of Mexico after the great silver strikes beginning in the 1540s. Even had the Coronado expedition not been undertaken, Sonora would still have been absorbed by the Jesuits as a result of their planned spread

northward along the Gulf of California. The upper Southwest would have been next in line after the discovery of rich silver mines in Zacatecas, Durango, and Chihuahua. The only thing that could have saved Aztlan would have been an Aztec victory and continued Aztec control over central and west Mexico.

Had the Aztecs won, it would have bought time, a century perhaps, for Aztlan and produced drastically different circumstances when contacts did arrive. The strong probability is that the Aztec kingdom itself would have eventually become "Europeanized," especially in technology and military organization. Very likely it would also have been forced to a less-destructive religion, perhaps based on Quetzalcoatl rather than Huitzilopochtli. To stave off the Spaniards, the Aztecs would needs adopt a great deal of European technology and would also find pressing strategic reasons to establish military and economic control over increasingly distant outlying areas. They would surely have spread into the northwestern areas of Mesoamerica and extended at least indirect influence as far as the Greater Southwest.

Such innovations would certainly change the patterns of life in Aztlan. In the first part of the sixteenth century carrying capacity of the upper Southwest was far above the actual population, operating at the technical level of the time. Only the Sonoran region was functioning at what might have been near an optimal level and even that society had ample room to expand, especially to the east. A reasonable scenario for a renewed Aztlan would have been reversal of the population decline, with the stabilization of society, and new technologies, obtained by expanding trade to the south. With superior tools, fresh societal ideas, and new lands, the population of Aztlan might have doubled or more than doubled. There would surely have been an expansion back into unoccupied or marginally occupied areas, not only the rich San Juan Valley but also the Carmén, Santa María, and Casas Grandes basins, the Rio Abajo portion of the Rio Grande, the upper Gila-Salt drainage, the Mogollon Rim country and middle Little Colorado River drainage, and the Pecos River. This new and dynamic cultural environment and the challenge of Aztec invasion from the south might have ended or curtailed internecine warfare. The fact that some of these empty areas were in the process of invasion by low-level hunters and gatherers probably would not have been an important factor. The nomads would likely have been displaced or absorbed, swamped as it were, by this expanding Aztlan. I have pointed out that even before the coming of the Spaniards the Navajo were on their way to being Pueblos. I imagine that this would have happened to a number of the hunting/gathering tribes around Aztlan—Apacheans, Uto-Aztecans, Yumans, not to mention people on the southwestern plains.

I would hazard a guess that a kachina-based religion would become very much a unifying factor, linking the Pueblos with their nomadic neighbors on the peripheries of the Southwest and spreading to Sonora and the reoccupied region of Chihuahua and the middle Rio Grande Basin. Town living would likely become more prevalent and political systems based on those loose confederacies already in place in Sonora and in the Pueblo world would gradually evolve into some sort of larger, statelike, units. This, obviously, is supposition, and perhaps events would have taken some other turn. But what we surely can say is that the Aztlan of, say, AD 1650 would already be growing in drastically different directions than what actually did take place under European conquest and control.

But of course history is immutable, and we must deal not with what might have been but with the situation that actually was. What did happen is that throughout the Spanish conquered areas native peoples gradually lost their cultural identity and became Hispanicized peasants. Their languages eroded, and their religious structures collapsed before the demands of an exclusive Catholic Christianity. Of course, this did not occur overnight, and it generally was not complete—leaving remnant languages and complicated syncretism in reli-gion, more or less tolerated by the Church. This was the case generally throughout the northern frontier of Mesoamerica, just to the south and east of Aztlan. In southern Aztlan the Sonoran and La Junta areas were shattered as both succumbed to the new order, even more completely than in many other regions of northern Mexico. Though the Piman language survived in Sonora and southern Arizona, the important Opata tongue disappeared completely.[12] The La Junta area presents even more of a puzzle, for today we cannot be certain just what languages *were* spoken there.

Only in the Pueblo world was there a sustained attempt to hold on to the several languages and something of the old life of the spirit. Among the Pueblos there was an initial attempt to maintain trade contacts with the newly conquered regions to the south, especially to continue the flow of various important ceremonial items. These included shell and bright-colored feathers traveling north and east, with turquoise and other semijeweled stones, hides, and perhaps salt moving to the south and west.

There was still evidence for this trade for a number of years into the seventeenth century,[13] but it was quickly to dwindle as the Spaniards extended and tightened their control over both Mesoamerica and Aztlan. Nevertheless, the Spaniards did find resistance. Eighty years of intense acculturation failed to eradicate Pueblo religion, and a partially successful revolt in 1680 brought the old ways back for a time. This flare-up in New Mexico was part of a wider unrest along the northern frontier of New Spain, and it took a number of years for Spanish forces to pacify the area.[14] In New Mexico itself the Spaniards returned in twelve years and after an additional four years of sporadic fighting reestablished themselves among all the Pueblos except for the Hopi. Nevertheless, in the eighteenth and nineteenth centuries they were forced to work out with the Pueblo Indians a complex accommodation that officially promoted Catholicism but tacitly allowed practice of the Indian religious ways. This state of affairs continued through the Mexican period of the early nineteenth century.

When Americans of English ancestry came in the mid-nineteenth century, their relationships with Native Americans were also originally religiously biased, though here the emphasis was on Protestant Christianity. In more recent times there has been, increasingly, a hands-off policy regarding native language, ceremonialism, and religion. Pueblo, Navajo, Apache, and Ute nativism is firmer than ever. And this is a time when Indian populations are expanding, and certain of the Indians of the Southwest and elsewhere are beginning to experiment with various types of political federation.

Outside of Aztlan, but within the domain of northern New Spain, there are, indeed, other regions where Native American groups continue to practice a certain amount of the old life. This is especially true in the remote mountainous regions of the Sierra Madre Occidental. In the Sierra Madre, groups such as the Huichol, Cora, and southern Tepehuan still have much that stems from aboriginal sources. In particular, some of the religious traditions seem to be dim reflections of Mesoamerican Great Traditions. But at least among the Tepehuan, where I have done considerable fieldwork, there is a deep sense of syncretism, and it is difficult to sort out the various elements that go into modern Tepehuan religious and ceremonial life.[15] I suspect that this is also true of Huichol, Cora, and other groups in these western mountains. And the tribes under discussion always lived in somewhat marginal areas, out of reach of strict Spanish control.

The Pueblos, however, were *from the very beginning of Spanish rule* at the very center of Hispanic life, many of them within a few miles of a provincial capital. And they have had extraordinary success in their maintenance of the great Aztlan-derived Quetzalcoatl and Tlaloc religious traditions.[16] In all of the northern portions of New Spain, as far as I know, only among the Pueblos (and in a somewhat derived way, the Navajo and certain Apache) are these religions formalized and openly practiced. Even the Nahuatl-speaking Indians of central Mexico have made a transition into a folk Christianity, flooded, of course, with native symbolism and folk beliefs but a far cry from the vibrant theology of Aztec times.[17]

This does not mean that modern Pueblo Native Americans recognize the Mesoamerican origins of major components of their religions, origins largely forgotten even in Coronado's day. Though there remain nebulous folktales of influences from the south, contemporary Pueblos (and Navajo, Apaches, and Utes) consider their religion to be autochthonous. The origins of southwesterners (and perhaps of all humanity) are generally believed by them to have taken place within the confines—or near the borders—of the Southwest and the great panoply of human events since founding times is thought to have been played out on local terrain. Mesoamerican deities such as Quetzalcoatl and Tlaloc appear under other names, and their geography is now local. But this reinterpretation should not surprise us, for it is commonplace in religions as they grow away from their founding generations. As one example, how many people, who identify themselves as Christians, really know that their religion, although developing out of a late Second Temple Judaic messianism, had other origins in the mystery- and dying-god cults of the Near East and was also leavened with early Iranian elements and a strong dollop of goddess worship from the ancient Mediterranean? These latter religions all flourished many centuries before Christianity.

Though less pervasive than religion, the political organization, especially among the Pueblos, still shows signs of the cacique structure of parts of prehispanic Mesoamerica, with its emphasis on power-conferring rituals and ritual objects. I have argued in this book that such organizational ideas were introduced in Aztlan times. The economic system, though vastly overlain with Hispanic and Anglo American technological innovation, still has at its base the cooperative agriculture, generally with some form of irrigation, and with an emphasis on certain American plants, especially maize, squash, and beans. Indeed, these domesticates had reached the Southwest well before Aztlan

FIGURE 12.1. Modern Hopi basket. El Paso Museum of Archaeology.

FIGURE 12.2. Modern Chihuahuan pottery in the Casas Grandes style. El Paso Museum of Archaeology.

times. Little in the way of new plants was added in the Aztlan era, but certain modes of organization (and perhaps advanced irrigation techniques themselves) do seem to date from that period.

Certain technologies also have at least a portion of their roots in the Aztlan period. Basketry among the Pueblo Indians and their predecessors goes back to Archaic times (see Figure 12.1). Weaving in cotton, however, owed some of its innovations to the Aztlan period. This technique was in the process of spreading to groups like the Navajo when the Spaniards came. The Spanish influence on weaving was very great, but it focused primarily on the introduction of sheep, providing a new raw material for cloth. Other technologies—ceramics, for example, and jewelry making—draw heavily from the Aztlan substratum of society, as does art generally. The great ceramic traditions of the modern Pueblos and other native southwesterners generally derive from Aztlan decorative models. An interesting example of renewal of old designs is in the pottery of Mata Ortiz, near Casas Grandes in Chihuahua.[18] Even though the people of that area are not cultural descendants of the Casas Grandes groups (though they might be to one degree or another genetically related), they have drawn on the Paquimé ceramic tradition, known to

them from archaeology (Figure 12.2). Somewhat the same thing happened in Hopi, but here the potters recognized that they were recreating the Aztlan period ceramic forms of their unquestioned ancestors.

Jewelry production also is rooted in the past, although an important new material, silver, has been added to the available raw products. There is also the occasional use of other metal or of such exotics as lapis lazuli. But the bases of decorative art—turquoise and other semi-jewel stones, shell, coral,[19] jet, and obsidian—are those of Aztlan, in raw materials, techniques of production, and form. Even such innovations as painting on canvas, introduced in recent times for the modern market, though they may employ modern or historic themes (paintings of horses, for example), also sometimes hark back inspirationally to Aztlan models. There is precedent for such paintings. In the early eighteenth century the Segesser hide paintings were probably created by a Pueblo artist, combining native and European styles.[20]

These are significant examples; nevertheless, it is in religion that the most striking relationships can be found. I talked earlier about the Mesoamerican ceremonial "flavor" of various of the societies of Aztlan. Some, like Paquimé, have vanished and are known only from archaeology. But the Pueblo world, though much diminished from the Aztlan heyday, is not gone, and the Mesoamerican infusion still permeates the native society. It is part of the being of the modern Pueblo Indian and to a considerable extent such neighbors as the Navajo with their Pueblo-inspired religious traditions and ceremonials. That such tangible remnants of Aztlan still exist in this tiny corner of the old Mesoamerican hegemony is perhaps a fortuity of history, rising from a series of discrete events not duplicated in other parts of the Hispanic-American culture world. But fortuitous or not, it does serve to enrich us all.

# Notes

*Chapter 1. Introduction*

1. A discussion of contemporary models of southwestern prehistory can be found in Schaafsma and Riley's introduction to *The Casas Grandes World*, pp. 1–6.
2. Kidder et al., *Pendleton Site*, pp. 115–116.
3. Morris, *Archaeological Studies in the La Plata District*, p. 1.
4. Ibid., p. 5 (emphasis added).
5. See Ferdon, *Trial Survey*.
6. Riley et al., *Man Across the Sea*. This book has been reprinted several times over the years and has spun off two separate Japanese-language editions.
7. For a discussion of one valuable contribution made by the processualists, Middle Range Theory (MRT), used to bring methodological sophistication to the knotty problems of ethnographic analogy, see Arnold, *Back to Basics*, pp. 55–66.
8. For comments on the New Archaeologists' dismissal of migration see Clark, *Tracking Prehistoric Migrations*, p. viii: "The early proponents of this paradigm were perhaps a bit too zealous in their desire to change the discipline, and they discarded the good with the bad of the earlier paradigm in their 'new Archaeology.' Considering its previous importance, migration was one of the casualties and, with the exception of a few torch-bearing researchers, the topic has not been discussed seriously within the discipline until recently."
9. I think that most scholars would agree with this statement, even though a few Viking specialists have argued that the Greenland contacts with the mainland of North America were more extensive than generally believed. See Ingstad and Ingstad, *Viking Discovery*, pp. 175–180.
10. I have chosen the designations *AD* and *BC* for this book rather than the relatively value-free *BCE* and *CE* because the former terms are probably more familiar to American and Mexican audiences, the majority readers of this volume. Nothing religious is implied.

*Chapter 2. Why Aztlan?*

1. See Chagoya, *Lost Continent*, p. 272. Chagoya translates it as "place of the white herons." See also Durán, *History of the Indies*, p. 21. The name *Aztlan* is often written with an accent, *Aztlán*, but the accentless form is probably a better approximation of the way the word was originally pronounced.
2. Durán, *History of the Indies*, p. 221. Technically, Colhuacan [Culhuacan] was the whole region, and Aztlan was an island, a central place, containing seven magical caves, the natal place, the womb so to speak, of the Aztec people. From 1539 to 1542 Vázquez de Coronado searched for seven cities. He was spurred on by the European legend of seven Portuguese bishops who fled the Moors, each founding a city in a new land. I suspect that the seven caves of Aztlan may have also figured into this equation.
3. For the political intricacies of the Aztec state see Brundage, *Rain of Darts*, pp. 112–157. Brundage (p. 195) believes that

Aztlan may have been situated north of Tarascan country. But really Aztlan represented a sort of land of faery, *somewhere* in the distant north and west but with no geographical parameters. The point is that the earliest Spaniards and their Aztec companions thought they would find Aztlan in the northwest of New Spain. Parenthetically, the royal name that I have rendered as *Motecuhzoma* is given variously—*Moctezuma* and *Moteuczoma* among other spellings.

4. For a discussion of the trip of Coronado and other early rainbow-chasing Spaniards see Riley, *Spaniards in Aztlan,* pp. 236–247. The story told to Coronado of wealthy trading cities to the north is in Castañeda, *Relación,* fols. 7–8. I have an idea that the informant, a man named Tejo, from the Valles area of eastern Mexico, may have echoed some folk memory of Casas Grandes (Paquimé) in Chihuahua. Tejo is further discussed in chap. 8.

5. For a discussion of the concept of the Greater Southwest of North America see Riley, *Frontier People,* pp. 1–2.

6. See, e.g., Riley and Hedrick, *Across the Chichimec Sea;* Mathien and McGuire, *Ripples in the Chichimec Sea;* Woosley and Ravesloot, *Culture and Contact: Charles C. Di Peso's Gran Chichimeca;* Reyman, *Gran Chichimeca;* and Di Peso et al., *Casas Grandes.* As well as these titles with *Chichimec* or *Chichimeca* a number of regional studies concentrate especially on the Mexican side of the Greater Southwest but also consider the upper Southwest. See, e.g., Schaafsma and Riley, *Casas Grandes World.* Another important contribution to these studies is Dahlgren and Soto de Arechavaleta, *Arqueología del norte y del occidente de México;* and Foster and Gorenstein, *Greater Mesoamerica.* The two latter collections of papers concern only the lower Southwest and adjacent northern Mesoamerica. Folan, *Contributions to the Archaeology and Ethnohistory of Greater Mesoamerica,* has papers extending from the Maya to the American Southwest. These titles hardly exhaust the list.

7. For the idea of the unity of a "greater" Greater Southwest see Strong, *Southwestern Society.*

8. See Riley, "Early Spanish-Indian Communication," pp. 304, 306, 308.

9. For a discussion of the late "Mesoamericanization" of the Southwest see Schaafsma and Riley, introduction to *The Casas Grandes World.* For the various meanings and uses of the name *Aztlan* see Riley, *Spaniards in Aztlan,* and, indeed, the whole volume from which this chapter came, Fields and Zamudio-Taylor, *Road to Aztlan.*

10. The situation in Casas Grandes is discussed in great depth in Charles C. Di Peso's great eight-volume codex *Casas Grandes: A Fallen Trading Center of the Gran Chichimeca.* Volumes 1–3 were under his sole authorship, while volumes 4–8 were published under the authorship of Di Peso, J. B. Rinaldo, and G. J. Fenner. In future I will refer to Di Peso, *Casas Grandes,* with the volume number (1–3) and to Di Peso et al., *Casas Grandes,* with the volume number (4–8).

11. Schaafsma and Riley, "Analysis and Conclusion," pp. 242–244.

12. For Chaco adobe see ibid.," p. 243. Adobe structures in the Mimbres area are discussed in Creel, "Black Mountain Phase," pp. 107–120. Also see Cosgrove and Cosgrove, *Swartz Ruin,* p. 8.

13. For house structures in Casas Grandes Viejo period see Di Peso et al., *Casas Grandes* 4:180; for the Mesoamerican origin of adobe in the Medio period see ibid., 4:198.

14. A seminal paper on diffusion of the kachina cult into the upper Southwest, one that greatly influenced my own thinking on the subject, was written by Schaafsma and Schaafsma, "Evidence for the Origins of the Pueblo Kachina Cult." Also see Adams, *Origin and Development.* I am especially indebted to Polly Schaafsma for her discussion of Tlaloc in the Greater Southwest. See P. Schaafsma, "Tlalocs, Kachinas, Sacred Bundles," pp. 165–171.

15. For ideas about the meaning of the Aztec word *Tlaloc* see Townsend, *Temple of Tlaloc,* p. 179.

16. P. Schaafsma, *Warrior, Shield, and Star,* pp. 29–30, 154–156, 179.

17. A discussion of the attributes of both Quetzalcoatl and Tezcatlipoca can be

found in Brundage, *Phoenix of the Western World*, pp. 10–16 and passim (for Quetzalcoatl), pp. 7–10 (for Tezcatlipoca). Sahagún's comments on Tezcatlipoca can be found in Sahagún, *General History*, p. 1 (Huitzilopochtli), p. 5 (Tezcatlipoca), p. 7 (Tlaloc), p. 9 (Quetzalcoatl), and pp. 21–22 (Chalchihuitlicue). For the various gods listed above see also Vaillant, *Aztecs of Mexico*, pp. 88, 172–180. Vaillant provides a useful chart listing all the principal Aztec gods and goddesses (more than 60), most of whom presumably never appeared in Aztlan (see pp. 182–184).

18. The suggestion of various Mesoamerican deities in Casas Grandes was given in an early paper by Di Peso, "Casas Grandes and the Gran Chichimeca," pp. 51–55. Di Peso gave Tezcatlipoca influence as predating Medio period Casas Grandes (p. 51) and Quetzalcoatl to the beginning of the Medio period (p. 52), the two deities perhaps representing two rival trading groups. He envisioned both Tlaloc and Huitzilopochtli as arriving in the Casas Grandes Tardio period (pp. 54–55), an epoch now generally considered not to have existed, at least not in the time frame assigned by Di Peso. See also McKusick, *Southwest Birds of Sacrifice*, pp. 18, 96. McKusick believes that Quetzalcoatl, Tezcatlipoca, and Chalchihuitlicue appeared in the Chaco, Wupatki, and Mimbres area. She associates Huitzilopochtli with the directional Tezcatlipoca of the South and its hummingbird association, hummingbirds being especially associated with Huitzilopochtli. See McKusick, *Southwest Birds of Sacrifice*, pp. 18–19, 74–75. Description of the four Tezcatlipocas is given on p. 91. For a more detailed discussion of the southwestern manifestations of Mexican deities see chaps. 7 and 8 herein.

19. This matter is discussed in Riley, "Color-Direction Symbolism."

20. Frisbie, "Hishi as Money," esp. pp. 124–129. A detailed description of the southwestern shell trade is given in Tower, *Use of Marine Mollusca*.

21. Ramusio, *Delle Navigationi et Viagii*, p. 300.

22. Weigand and García de Weigand, "Macroeconomic Study," p. 191.

23. Weigand, "Rio Grande Glaze Sherds," pp. 3–5.

24. For Fr. Marcos de Niza's identification of traded pottery, hides, and turquoise see Marcos, "Descubrimiento de las siete ciudades," pp. 336–337. It is not entirely clear if Marcos meant that his "fine pottery vessels" were traded from the upper Southwest, but from the context it would seem probable. At this point in his journey I place Marcos somewhere in or perhaps a bit north of the Magdalena-Altar region of Sonora. See Riley, *Sixteenth Century Trade*, pp. 15–16. I must say that there are almost as many opinions on Marcos's route as there are people who describe it.

25. The Guasave finds of turquoise are discussed by Carpenter, *El Ombligo*, pp. 268–269. For a detailed discussion of trade both to and from the Greater Southwest see chaps. 7 through 9 herein and specifically Figure 7.15.

26. Native alcohol in Mesoamerica is discussed in Bruman, *Alcohol in Ancient Mexico*, pp. 7–11.

27. There is a mention of chili in Sonora, presumably as a native crop, by Obregón in the 1560s. See Cuevas, *Historia*, p. 149. For the upper Southwest see Hammond and Rey, *Rediscovery of New Mexico*, p. 278.

28. Di Peso identified certain designs on Medio period Huerigos Polychrome pottery at Casas Grandes as derived from the peyote plant. See Di Peso et al., *Casas Grandes*, 6:248–249.

29. Distribution of the St. Johns redwares is charted in Carlson, *White Mountain Redware*, Figure 14. For a discussion of the widespread Pinedale style see Crown, *Ceramics and Ideology*, pp. 222–225.

30. A discussion of the general trading situation in the fourteenth to sixteenth centuries is given in Riley, *Sixteenth Century Trade*, pp. 38–45.

31. Ibid., p. 39.

32. For a map of the trade routes in and to the Southwest see ibid., Map 1; see also Riley and Manson, *Cíbola-Tiguex Route*, Figure 2. The various items traded into the upper Southwest, both east-west and north-south, are discussed in considerable

detail in Riley, *Frontier People:* see pp. 76–88 for the Sonoran middleman function, 145–152 and 190–198 for trade to and from the lower Colorado and the Zuni-Hopi area, and 236–240, 267–277, 302–304 for eastern Pueblo trade in every direction.

33. An old but serviceable definition of civilization can be found in Durant, *Our Oriental Heritage,* esp. pp. 1–4.

34. Riley, *Origins of Civilization,* pp. 125–148.

35. Tolstoy, *Mesoamerica,* pp. 29–68; and Willey, *Introduction to American Archaeology,* vol. 1, chap. 3 (Mesoamerica). See also Riley, *Rio del Norte,* pp. 135–145.

36. Willey, *Introduction to American Archaeology,* vol. 2, chap. 3 (Peru).

37. For Mesoamerican influences in the U.S. Midwest see Kehoe, *Postclassic,* pp. 201–205.

38. For the similarities and differences between the Mesoamerican and Southwestern Tlaloc cults see P. Schaafsma, "Tlalocs, Kachinas, Sacred Bundles."

## Chapter 3. Landscapes, Cultural and Natural

1. More extensive discussion of natural and cultural areas of the Greater Southwest and an expanded bibliography can be found in the various regional chapters below. For generalizations about the culture of the parts of the Greater Southwest see Riley, *Frontier People,* pp. 5–14. For Casas Grandes, the Jornada Mogollon, and Mimbres see Schaafsma and Riley, *Casas Grandes World.* For the Anasazi north see Riley, *Rio del Norte.*

2. There is what seems clearly a platform structure at Chetro Ketl in Chaco Canyon, as one of the Mesoamerican features at that site (see Ferdon, *Trial Survey;* J. C. Kelley and E. A. Kelley, *Alternative Hypothesis,* p. 204), but platforms are not really a feature of the northern Southwest.

3. The ball court appears as far north as the Verde Valley in Arizona. In New Mexico it is found in the southwestern corner but does not extend farther to the north. A large surface area has been identified as a ball court at Wupatki, but it seems to me that this may possibly have had another, albeit probably ceremonial, function. See Wilcox, *Ballgame in the American Southwest,* pp. 101–125; Gregory, *Form and Variation,* pp. 165–169. Ferdon, "Hohokam 'Ball Court,'" pp. 1–14, believed that many of the ball courts were actually dance platforms, although this idea tends to be discounted at present.

4. Aboriginal pottery in northern Sonora is discussed in Braniff, "Identification of Possible Elites." There is an extensive discussion of Casas Grandes ceramics of all types in Di Peso et al., *Casas Grandes,* 6: 1–382. For general handbooks of southwestern pottery see Hawley, *Prehistoric Southwestern Pottery Types;* and Oppelt, *Southwestern Pottery.*

5. The utilization of fish in Aztlan has not been sufficiently researched, but a recent study indicates some of the pitfalls caused by inadequate and misleading data, at least in the Pueblo area. See Snow, *Fish Tales,* pp. 119–132. According to Snow, fish had once been actively used in the Rio Grande Basin, but habitat degradation in historic times led to a sharp decline: "Where fish had once been an important source of food in the Rio Grande drainage, by the late nineteenth and early twentieth centuries, fishing was of such little importance few remembered that it had ever taken place. As a result, Puebloan informants related that fact to the early anthropologists and archaeologists working in New Mexico, and in so doing, started a now popular myth" (129).

6. For general natural features of the northern Southwest see Riley, *Frontier People,* esp. pp. 31–37, but for regional areas also see 98–102, 132–137, 169–176, 218–221, 253–256, and 286–289; see also Riley, *Rio del Norte,* 17–29. For the general features of the Chaco country see Vivian, *Chacoan Subsistence,* pp. 58–60. For the landscapes of Chihuahua see Schmidt, "Chihuahua," pp. 45–101, esp. 47–71 (land forms), 73–88 (climate), and 90–101 (vegetation).

7. For irrigation in Mesoamerica and the southern Southwest see Doolittle, *Canal Irrigation in Prehistoric Mexico;* for the Southwest regionally see Riley, *Frontier People,* pp. 59–64, 104, 106, 109–111, 114, 116, 144, 185–186, 223, 298.

## Chapter 4. Before Aztlan

1. For a discussion of the Paleoindians and the Archaic peoples see Riley, *Rio del Norte,* chaps. 3–5. A consideration of the revised dating of earlier southwestern Paleoindians is found in Fiedel, "Older Than We Thought." Fiedel believes that the calendar dates for the beginning of Clovis are ca. 13,500 years ago. See esp. the chart on page 106. Recent comparative studies of DNA on the Y chromosome of contemporary Old World and Native American populations suggest a founding date for the settlement of America at no earlier than about 18,000 years ago. This research is still in progress, however, and the results are very preliminary. See Harder, "New World Newcomers," pp. 84–85.

2. The transformation from a generalized Cochise-based Archaic culture to the Anasazi, Hohokam, and Mogollon traditions is discussed in Riley, *Rio del Norte,* pp. 63–72. The agricultural revolution increasingly influenced the peripheries. For example, Upham ("Scale, Innovation, and Change," pp. 237–239) sees vast areas of the desert West becoming sprinkled with small agricultural communities from around AD 700. Oshara Archaic is discussed by Irwin-Williams, *Oshara Tradition.* For the Archaic in the southwestern plains see Hofman, "Hunters and Gatherers," esp. pp. 45–60.

3. Riley, *Rio del Norte,* pp. 63–72.

4. For the Patayan see Riley, *Frontier People,* pp. 130–131. These prehistoric groups are sometimes called the Hakataya following Schroeder, "Hakataya Cultural Tradition." See also Schroeder, "Prehistory: Hakataya." To get an idea of the problems of synthesis in this complex area see Euler, "Ceramic Patterns." Also see Reid and Whittlesey, *Archaeology of Ancient Arizona,* pp. 111–130. The somewhat enigmatic Cohonina culture of the Coconino Plateau and the region west of Flagstaff (presumably related to or mixed with Patayan at least in the later periods) is discussed by Cartledge, "Cohonina Adaptation." On p. 299 Cartledge points up the Anasazi and Sinagua influence in Cohonina, something not surprising considering the proximity of the three traditions. For a summary of Havasupai prehistory see Schwartz, "The Havasupai."

5. Anyone wanting information on the Hohokam should consult Haury, *The Hohokam.* For Hohokam origins see Crown, "The Hohokam," 143–144; see also Haury, *The Hohokam,* pp. 351–353. Also see Gumerman and Haury, "Prehistory: Hohokam," pp. 75–90; and Fish, "The Hohokam," pp 19–63. Hohokam culture traits are covered in Haury, *The Hohokam,* esp. pp. 164–172, 380–384, an appendix on cremation by W. H. Brody, pp. 191–254 (pottery), pp. 255–272 (figurines), pp. 374–377 (an appendix on avifauna by C. R. McKusick, esp. p. 376).

6. Agriculture in the Hohokam is discussed in Haury, *The Hohokam,* pp. 117–118 and 365–366 (the appendix on corn by H. C. Cutler and L. W. Blake). For the origins of Hohokam agriculture see Huckell, *Of Marshes and Maize,* esp. pp. 1–16; and Diehl, "Three Plants," pp. 2–3. According to Michael W. Diehl (personal communication) there is evidence for considerable maize agriculture in the Tucson area in the period 1200–800 BC.

7. The independent invention of irrigation among the Hohokam is suggested by Doolittle, "Canal Irrigation at Casas Grandes," 147–148.

8. For the possible religious implications of the ball game complex see Wilcox, "Regional and Macroregional Systems," p. 377.

9. Haury, *The Hohokam,* pp. 164–166; see also Walter H. Birkby, "Cremated Human Remains," in Haury, *The Hohokam,* appendix 9.

10. Haury, *The Hohokam,* p. 116.

11. Ibid., pp. 78–79; Wilcox, "Regional and Macroregional Systems."

12. The Salado phenomenon is summarized in Reid and Whittlesey, *Archaeology of Ancient Arizona,* pp. 230–258. For changes in the basin over time see esp. pp. 243–247. Early irrigation in the Salado (Tonto Basin) area is discussed in Dean, "Introduction: The Salado Phenomenon," p. 10; and Van West et al., "Subsistence and Environmental Interactions," pp. 47–48. The Hohokam and

Mogollon are briefly but competently discussed in Lipe, "The Southwest," 344–365.

13. Hohokam Pima/Papago continuity is discussed in Riley, *Frontier People*, 102–104; also see Haury, *The Hohokam*, p. 357.

14. For the Sinagua see Pilles, "Pueblo III Period." See also Cordell, *Archaeology of the Southwest*, pp. 173–177, 209; and Colton, "Frontiers," pp. 9–16.

15. See Plog, "Sinagua," p. 285:

I see the pattern of plain ware ceramics in the Sinagua area as typical of most of the surrounding territory. Thus, plain wares provide no basis for separating Sinagua from Anasazi. The painted types found in the Sinagua area are typical Anasazi painted types. Most other material traits that one might consider I also view as having highly localized distributions. One might argue that masonry pithouses are localized, but if so, they occur over much of the area on which this discussion focuses.

Thus, if one views the question of classifying Sinagua as resolvable on the basis of patterns of interaction, the Sinagua interacted with Mogollon and Hohokam to some degree, but with other Anasazi peoples to so substantial a degree that drawing a cultural boundary between Anasazi and Sinagua is questionable.

16. For some very stimulating ideas about trade into the Sinagua see McKusick, *Southwest Birds of Sacrifice*. For McKusick's comments on macaw trade and on Quetzalcoatl worship see pp. 74–75. Within the Sinagua there are numerous macaws at Wupatki (41 specimens, of which 22 are scarlet macaws, the others not identifiable by species), and macaw remains are also found in Nalakihu, Ridge Ruin, Winona village, the Pollock site, Montezuma's Castle, Jackson Homestead, and Tuzigoot. These are documented by Hargrave, *Mexican Macaws*, pp. 36–42. Plog, "Sinagua," pp. 285–286, also sees a Casas Grandes connection in the period around AD 1270.

17. For early work on Mogollon see, among others, Haury, *Mogollon Culture*; E. K.

Reed, "Implications of the Mogollon Concept"; E. K. Reed, "Dating of the Early Mogollon"; and E. K. Reed, "Western Pueblo." The classic early synthesis of Mogollon, as noted in the text, is Wheat, *Mogollon Culture*.

18. The origins and development of Mogollon agriculture can be found in Matson, *Origins of Southwestern Agriculture*, pp. 279–303. A good concise history of Mogollon studies is given in Reid, "Concept of Mogollon," pp. 1–8. For Mogollon kivas as exemplified at the large Point of Pines site see Stone, "Kiva Diversity," esp. pp. 392, 395–397. More up-to-date information on the Mogollon can be found in Cordell, *Ancient Pueblo Peoples*, esp. pp. 60–68, and for the Mimbres subregion, pp. 68–75. For comments on Mogollon ceramics see LeBlanc, "Temporal Change in Mogollon Ceramics." Mogollon data are summarized by Martin, "Prehistory: Mogollon." For some succinct comments on Mogollon terminology see Haury, "Recent Thoughts."

19. For critical comments on the concept of Western Pueblo see Reid, "Rethinking Mogollon Pueblo." Reid says (p. 4), "Prehistoric Western Pueblo has been so misused and abused that it is not now a useful label, if, i[n]deed, it ever was."

20. Steven Leblanc suggests that there were influences in the northern Mogollon from Chaco Canyon after AD 1000. See LeBlanc, "Development of Archaeological Thought," p. 299. For Anasazi migration into and among the Mogollon in late times see Reid and Whittlesey, *Archaeology of Ancient Arizona*, pp. 151–152. For the San Simon area see Kinkade, "San Simon Mogollon."

21. For a detailed discussion of the White Mountain redwares see Carlson, *White Mountain Redware*, esp. pp. 95–115; see also Snow, "Rio Grande Glaze," pp. 243–248.

22. For the eastern Mimbres see Hegmon et al., "Abandonment and Reorganization," pp. 150–151.

23. A good overview of Mimbres, especially a summary of the Swartz ruin, is in Brody, *Mimbres Painted Pottery*, esp. pp. 37–56. The original publication of Swartz is found in Cosgrove and Cos-

grove, *Swartz Ruin.* Distribution of the Mimbres sites is discussed in Thompson, "Mimbres Iconography," pp. 16–17. For a recent survey of the Mimbres situation see Shafer, *NAN Ranch Ruin,* pp. 1–20. One unsettled economic question that concerns Mimbres is when agriculture began to become increasingly important vis-à-vis hunting. This has been thought to relate to the beginning of the Classic phase (about AD 1000), but Cannon, in a 2003 article, "Model of Central Place," pp. 20–21, argues that it took place well before that time. For Galaz see Anyon and LeBlanc, *Galaz Ruin.* See comments on palettes (pp. 269–273), shell (p. 306), turquoise (pp. 306–307), and copper (p. 307). For early Mimbres sites in the Mimbres River valley see LeBlanc, "Population Dynamics."

24. For a technical discussion of pottery making, including firing methods, see Scott, "Evolution of Mimbres Pottery," n.p. See also Erik K. Reed in an article devoted both to the Anasazi and to comparisons of Anasazi and other traditions, mainly Mogollon: Reed, "Distinctive Features and Distribution," p. 298. It has been suggested that the Classic phase of Mimbres represented the first full utilization of agriculture in Mimbres society. See Lekson, "Mangas Phase in Mimbres," p. 142. Mimbres iconography and its meaning is discussed in Thompson, "Evolution and Dissemination." For the role of decorated pottery, not only in funerary contexts but also for social-political purposes, see Shafer, *NAN Ranch Ruin,* pp. 150, 153, 158, 192–193.

25. The idea of kachinas in Mimbres was suggested by Carlson, *Mimbres Kachina Cult,* pp. 147–155. Lekson agrees with this position. See Lekson, *Chaco Meridian,* p. 55. Polly Schaafsma sees the "precursors of kachinas" in Mimbres pottery among other sources; see P. Schaafsma, "Prehistoric Kachina Cult," p. 65. However, E. Charles Adams in his studies of the development of the kachina cult points out that most authorities do not see a fully developed kachina cult in Mimbres; see Adams, *Origin and Development,* p. 28. Marc Thompson (personal correspondence) strongly discounts

any kachina cult in Mimbres though, clearly, the divine twins do appear on Mimbres pots. See also Thompson, "Mimbres Iconography," pp. 70–71; and Brody, *Mimbres Painted Pottery,* p. 206.

26. For macaws in Mimbres see McKusick, *Southwest Birds of Sacrifice,* pp. 74–75. Also for McKusick's report on one Convento site Perros Bravo phase (Viejo period) macaw bone, a skull cap of an immature individual in a child burial, see Di Peso et al., *Casas Grandes,* 8:247.

27. Anyon and LeBlanc, *Galaz Ruin,* pp. 269–273, 306. Not only shell but fish were obtained from the Gulf of California. Jett and Moyle, "Exotic Origins of Fishes," pp. 688–720, have identified some 20 fish taxa from depictions on Mimbres pots. Eighteen of these are marine forms, probably from the southern Sonoran shores of the Gulf of California.

28. Anyon and LeBlanc, *Galaz Ruin,* pp. 306–307.

29. Creel, "Black Mountain Phase in Mimbres." Information on the continuity of rock art from Classic Mimbres to the Black Mountain phase comes from Polly Schaafsma (personal communication).

30. Shafer, "Mimbres Classic and Postclassic." See also Shafer, *NAN Ranch Ruin,* pp. 7–9. The question as to the relationship of the Black Mountain phase to the preceding Mimbres Classic period is a tangled one. For further information on this period see M. Williams, "Comparison." See also Leblanc, "Cultural Dynamics."

31. For the Jornada Mogollon see Lehmer, *Jornada Branch.* For identification of the Hueco complex as Cochise see p. 90. For a brief discussion of the earlier phases, called Mesilla and Doña Ana in the south, Capitan and Three Rivers in the northern portion of the region, see pp. 10–13. A discussion of a Mesilla phase site is given on pp. 11, 13–34.

32. The Sierra Blanca region and adjacent areas (along streams draining both west and south into the Tularosa Basin and eastward to the Pecos River) are discussed in J. H. Kelley, "Capitan North Project," pp. 166–176; see also Ravesloot and Spoerl, "Jicarilla Mountains." For ceremonial structures see Wiseman, "Socioreligious

Architecture," pp. 206–209, 215–220. Wiseman also suggests (p. 206) that Glencoe phase people may have been the original inhabitants along the eastern slope of the Sierra Blanca while Lincoln phase people were intruders from the Gran Quivira area. In this brief overview I am unable to do full justice to the complexity of cultural interactions in the southeast New Mexico area. For problems involved see especially Wiseman, "Roswell South Project," pp. 11–20.

33. The Rio Abajo, with its complex Mogollon and Anasazi interconnection, is discussed in detail in Marshall and Walt, *Rio Abajo*. Anasazi intrusions into the Rio Abajo are discussed by Lekson, "Southwestern New Mexico," p. 172. Definitions of what constitutes "Rio Abajo" differ considerably. See Pearce, *New Mexico Place Names*, p. 133.

34. For the Archaic periods in Chihuahua and nearby areas see MacNeish, "Fases del Arcaico Tradición Chihuahua," esp. pp. 124–129. See also J. C. Kelley, "La Cuenca del Río Conchos"; Mallouf, "La Prehistoria"; and Beckett and MacNeish, "Archaic Chihuahua Tradition." The nature of the Chihuahuan Archaic is explored by Taylor, "Tethered Nomadism."

35. A discussion of the Mogollon-like cultures of northwest Mexico can be found in Riley, "Sonoran Statelets Revisited." See also Foster, "Loma San Gabriel-Mogollon Continuum," pp. 251–261. Foster sees a south-north movement of "Mogollon-like" traits, especially in ceramics.

36. A good overview of the prehistory of the eastern flanks of the Sierra Madre can be found in Guevara Sánchez and Phillips, "Arqueología de la Sierra Madre Occidental."

37. See Foster, "Loma San Gabriel Culture," pp. 200–202; and Riley and Winters, "Prehistoric Tepehuan," pp. 177–185. See also Willett, "Dual Festival System," p. 205, who suggests that the modern Tepehuan *xiotalh* ceremony relates to the archaeological Chalchihuites culture. She gives no evidence for this, however. In a recent book Deeds (*Defiance and Deference*, pp. 47, 220), citing work

by Marie-Areti Hers and other Mexican archaeologists, questions the Riley-Winters thesis about a Tepehuan-Loma San Gabriel connection.

38. The Viejo Casas Grandes will be discussed in greater detail in chap. 8.

39. For a succinct discussion of the Basketmaker-Pueblo see Riley, *Kachina and the Cross*, pp. 14–23. In this book I describe the origin of the somewhat imprecise (and increasingly politically incorrect) name *Anasazi* and give the reasons why I prefer to consider that name to cover only the period from Basketmaker III to the end of Pueblo III. See also Walters and Rogers, "Anasazi and 'Anaasází.'" Since the concentration in the present book is on the post–Pueblo III in the north, I will say no more about the matter. In any case I have utilized the name *Aztlan* for all of the late prehistoric and initial phases of the historic period in the Greater Southwest.

40. For the newer dating for Basketmaker II see Lipe, *Basketmaker II Period*, pp. 1–3.

41. Origins of the bow and arrow and its replacement of the atlatl or throwing stick for all but ceremonial uses is discussed in Peckham, *Prehistoric Weapons*, pp. 3–6 (atlatl) and 6–10 (bow). Material on the efficiency of the bow comes from LeBlanc, *Prehistoric Warfare*, pp. 100–101.

42. The origins of Basketmaker pottery are discussed in Martin et al., *Indians Before Columbus*, pp. 114–117. See also LeBlanc, "Temporal Change in Mogollon Ceramics," pp. 122–123; and Breternitz, "Four Corners Anasazi Ceramic Tradition," esp. pp. 130–135.

43. The sipapu as a widespread trait, originating in Mesoamerica, is discussed by E. A. Kelley and J. C. Kelley, "Sipapu and Pyramid Too," p. 77; see also Parsons, *Pueblo Indian Religion*, pp. 1012–1013.

44. For the spotty distribution of Basketmaker sites see Lyneis, "Pueblo II–Pueblo III Changes," pp. 13–15. For the Basketmaker II see Matson, *Origins of Southwestern Agriculture*, pp. 4–12, 73–124. For a discussion of the pros and cons of Fremont see Talbot, "Fremont Farmers." Early occupation in the upper Pecos area is discussed in Cordell, *Before Pecos*.

45. For discussions of "Western" versus "Eastern" Anasazi see Plog, "Prehistory: Western Anasazi," pp. 108–130; Cordell, "Prehistory: Eastern Anasazi."
46. E. K. Reed, "Distinctive Features and Distribution," p. 302.
47. Dean, "Kayenta Anasazi Settlement," pp. 29–30.
48. Lange et al. *Yellow Jacket.*
49. McKusick, *Southwest Birds of Sacrifice,* pp. 51–52.
50. McKusick, *Southwest Indian Turkeys,* pp. 4, 11.
51. Early appearance of the god Tlaloc in the extreme upper Southwest is suggested by Farmer, "Goggle Eyes and Crested Serpents." Farmer (pp. 129–132) suggests that Quetzalcoatl in his manifestation as a plumed serpent also appears in Barrier Canyon art. P. Schaafsma, *Quetzalcoatl,* p. 142, rejects the idea that early Fremont-area horned serpents are part of a southwestern distribution of this great Mesoamerican deity. However, O'Laughlin, "Dark Area Shrine," has reported a possible Tlaloc manifestation, dating perhaps between AD 700 and 900, in a cave site a few miles north of Las Cruces, NM.
52. McKusick, *Southwest Birds of Sacrifice,* p. 100.
53. For various explanations for what happened in the Chaco region see Sebastian, "Chaco Canyon."
54. For the definition of a Chaco Great House see Lekson, "Settlement Pattern and the Chaco," pp. 32–36.
55. Ibid., pp. 37–45. See also Lekson, *Chaco Meridian,* pp. 101–104, for various estimates of the extent of the Chaco regional system.
56. For the extension of Great Houses into northeastern Arizona see Gilpin, "Boundaries." A somewhat more conservative view of Great House distribution is found in Fowler and Stein, "Anasazi Great House," pp. 102–103. One interesting aspect of the Great House distribution is that associated Great Kivas are thicker on the ground as one leaves the environs of Chaco Canyon itself, with outliers lacking Great Kivas tending to be nearer the Chacoan center. It is as if people within a

near radius of the canyon found it more convenient or desirable to use the actual Chaco Canyon kivas rather than to build their own. See Van Dyke, "Chacoan Great Kiva," pp. 238–239.
57. For a discussion of Chaco as a hierarchal society see Phillips, "Rethinking Chaco." A more extended discussion of the pros and cons of Chacoan society can be found in chap. 5 below.
58. For the Chaco-Aztec connection see Lekson, *Chaco Meridian,* esp. chap. 3. A further discussion can be found in Lekson, "Landscape and Polity."
59. McKusick, *Southwest Birds of Sacrifice,* pp. 91–93.
60. Turner and Turner, *Man Corn.* See pp. 483–484, for the Turners' ideas on the Tezcatlipoca cult at Chaco. A somewhat dismissive statement on the Turner and Turner hypothesis as to the origins of cannibalism in the Southwest is made by Cordell and Judge, "Perspectives on Chaco Society," p. 3.
61. J. Miller, "Keres," p. 507. Miller considers the Keres to be direct descendants of the Chaco people. The Obi or O'pi are a society of scalp-takers found in the historic Keresan area. See also Parsons, *Pueblo Indian Religion,* p. 899.
62. A very early appearance of Quetzalcoatl is posited in Reyman, "Mexican Influence," p. 323.
63. The idea of desertion and resettlement of massive San Juan populations is an old idea, and many suggestions as to the reason or reasons had appeared by the 1960s. Then there was somewhat of a hiatus because of the New Archaeology, to whose adherents migration was deemed "not explanatory." More recently there has been a new wave of interest in the subject. For an argument that the Little Ice Age was valid for this period see Peterson, "Warm and Wet Climatic Optimum." For a discussion of various reasons for the desertion of the San Juan Basin (and a generally negative view of the Little Ice Age) see Van West and Dean, "Environmental Characteristics." For volcanic activity in the thirteenth century see Salzer, "Temperature Variability."

64. The Rio Grande in the transition period to Aztlan is discussed in Riley, *Rio del Norte,* pp. 86–92.

## Chapter 5. The Great Anasazi Migration

1. A somewhat dated but still generally valid description of Anasazi culture can be found in Martin et al., *Indians Before Columbus,* pp. 101–167.

2. In parts of the Basketmaker area clay sources with a high iron content produced a black paste. See Severance, "Cultural Dynamics," pp. 190–193.

3. For the westernmost expansion see Lyneis, "Pueblo II–Pueblo III Changes," esp. Figure 2.2. See also Lyneis, "Life at the Edge," pp. 269–271.

4. See Dean, "Kayenta Anasazi."

5. For the Cibola and White Mountain areas see Carlson, *White Mountain Redware,* pp. 95–114. For distribution of St. Johns pottery see Figure 14. Only a very small amount of St. Johns ware has been found at Mesa Verde; see Oppelt, "Pottery and Other Intrusive Materials," pp. 7–8. For comments on the Pinedale style see Crown, *Ceramics and Ideology,* pp. 211–213.

6. Crown, *Ceramics and Ideology,* p. 212.

7. Adler, "'The Great Period,'" pp. 1–10, esp. 2–3.

8. Spielmann, "Pueblo III Settlement Trends," pp. 181–183; Stuart and Gauthier, *Prehistoric New Mexico,* pp. 303–308; Cordell, *Before Pecos,* pp. 85–91.

9. The archaeology of the Rio Abajo country is dealt with in Marshall and Walt, *Rio Abajo* (for Piro see pp. 135–142). For extension of the Anasazi south along the Rio Grande to the Piro and pre-Piro areas see Davis, "The Magdalena Problem"; see also Lekson, "Archaeological Reconnaissance"; Lekson, "Southwestern New Mexico"; and Bertram et al., *Excavations.*

10. Hayes et al., "Excavation of Mound 7," p. 12. The Salinas Basin before the great Mexicanization movements is discussed in Simmons, "The Formative Period," pp. 108–109.

11. For desertion of the western expanse of Anasazi see Lyneis, "Pueblo II–Pueblo III Changes," pp. 25–26. The conditions that produced the retreat of Pueblo peoples from the Pecos and its upper tributaries are discussed in Riley, *Rio del Norte,* pp. 190–191. More information on these Apachean groups is given in Riley, "The Teya Indians," pp. 320–323. At Tecolote Pueblo on the Tecolote River, where a considerable amount of excavation has been done, the main aggregation period has been dated to ca. AD 1200 to AD 1350. See Cabebe, "Tecolote Pueblo," p. 253.

12. For comments on the physical evidence for migration from the San Juan to the Rio Grande see Schillaci et al., "Multivariate Assessment."

13. For Pueblo II population in the western Anasazi see Lyneis, "Pueblo II–Pueblo III Changes," p. 15; for depopulation of the "far west" see ibid., pp. 24–26.

14. See, e.g., Varien et al. "Southwestern Colorado and Southeastern Utah," pp. 87, 93–97. Climatic changes over time in the Anasazi area are discussed in Polyak and Asmerom, "Late Holocene Climate." See also Euler et al., "The Colorado Plateaus."

15. For the Yellow Jacket population see Lange et al., *Yellow Jacket,* pp. 14–16. The high estimate is given by Arthur Rohn; Lange (pp. 1, 16) considers it to have been somewhere in the 1,500–3,000 range.

16. Lyneis, "Pueblo II–Pueblo III Changes," pp. 25–26.

17. The importance of cotton in the Hopi area is well documented by the earliest historic times. The origin of cotton growing in the upper Southwest is still an unsolved problem. Earlier I mentioned that it was probably not grown in the Mesa Verde area, in spite of the evidence of cotton cloth. However, as Glenna Dean has pointed out, there are rare finds of pollen from prehistoric sites in the Chama Valley, an area that today has only 140 to 160 frost-free days per year and relatively little precipitation during the growing season (see Dean, "In Search of the Rare."). The Kayenta region and its final decline are discussed in Dean, "Kayenta Anasazi," esp. pp. 39–42.

18. Cordell, *Archaeology of the Southwest,* pp. 341–348.

19. The present climate of the Chaco area is discussed in Vivian, "Chaco Subsistence," pp. 58–60.
20. Roads are discussed in Cordell, *Archaeology of the Southwest*, pp. 320–324. For other consideration of Chacoan roads see Mathien, "Implications of the Chaco Road"; and Windes, "Prehistoric Road Network." The remote sensing techniques used in delineating these roads is described by Sever and Wagner, "Analysis of Prehistoric Roadways."
21. See Cordell, *Archaeology of the Southwest*, pp. 306–320, for various Chacoan house types and the number and size of the Great Houses (308, 312). See also Lekson, "Settlement Pattern," esp. pp. 37–41. The traits common to Chaco Great Houses are in part from Mahoney, "Chaco World."
22. Vivian, "Chacoan Subsistence," p. 58.
23. Judge, "Chaco," pp. 24–26.
24. For possible Chaco–Mesa Verde connections with Galisteo see Riley, "San Juan Anasazi."
25. Washburn, "Mexican Connection," pp. 79, 81–82, would add ceramic cylinder jars, a number of which were found at Pueblo Bonito but are more common at a slightly earlier period at Monte Albán in Oaxaca. This is a possibility, but given the distance between the two areas, independent development may be a better explanation. Apropos of artistic influences reaching Chaco from Mesoamerica, Polly Schaafsma (personal communication) has pointed out to me the lack of Mesoamerican influences in Chacoan rock art (see also note 32). The same seems to be true of the generally fragmentary wall decorations at Chaco. See Mathien, "Pueblo Wall Decorations," p. 112.
26. For a summary of the position of Anasazi-oriented archaeologists as it applied to the autonomy of the upper Southwest see Schaafsma and Riley, introduction to *Casas Grandes World*, pp. 3–6. A number of archaeologists have argued that Mesoamerican influences have been vastly overrated. For example, see Vivian, *Chacoan Prehistory*, pp. 416–419; and Mathien, "External Contacts," esp. pp. 223–232. Mathien does feel that some trade may have gone on, although as an incidental function of the Chaco sociopolitical organization rather than any penetration of Chaco by Mesoamerica (see pp. 232–236).
27. For populations at Chaco on the high end of the scale (ca. 3,000) see Lekson, *Chaco Meridian*, pp. 71–72; also see Hayes, "Survey of Chaco Canyon." Windes, "A New Look," sees this figure as about 1,000. The low figure of perhaps 250 people, based on distribution of hearths, was made by Bernardini, "Reassessing," esp. pp. 466–467.
28. For a description of the lumbering activity at Chaco, especially in mountains to the south and west, see English et al., "Strontium Isotopes." The large amount of timber used at Chaco is drawn from Cordell, *Archaeology of the Southwest*, p. 314. Recent analysis of corncobs at Chaco Canyon indicates that they came from the San Juan Basin, fifty miles away. This is a long way to transport foodstuffs with only human carriage, but it does point up the fact that the great ceremonial centers may not have been able to support themselves. See Benson et al., "Ancient Maize."
29. For small houses at Chaco see Vivian, *Chacoan Prehistory*, pp. 194–206; Truell, "Small Site Architecture," pp. 306–319; and Cordell, *Archaeology of the Southwest*, pp. 310–312. Recent work on skeletal populations at Chaco do suggest a considerable morphometric variability in the human populations. See Schillaci, "Population Diversity," pp. 236–240.
30. Stein and Fowler, "Looking Beyond Chaco," p. 114.
31. Sebastian, "Taking Charge at Chaco," pp. 342–343. I have not dealt in any detail with irrigation systems in the Southwest. They appear in Aztlan times but were also found in Chaco. Recent work suggests that in the Zuni area they may date to the earlier Pueblo period or before (1000–3000 years ago). See Damp et al., "Early Irrigation," p. 675.
32. Comments about the Anasazi nature of Chacoan rock art come from Polly Schaafsma (personal communication). See also P. Schaafsma, "Emblems of Power"; and note 25 of this chapter.

33. Sebastian, "Taking Charge at Chaco," pp. 342–343. For a supporting opinion to Sebastian see Phillips, "Rethinking Chaco," esp. p. 336.

34. Childe, *Man Makes Himself,* esp. pp. 106–112. Childe puts considerable emphasis on warfare, which is not a factor in Sebastian's reconstruction.

35. Wills, "Political Leadership," esp. pp. 40–42. See also Mahoney, "Monumental Architecture," p. 25.

36. Cameron, "Organization of Production," p. 9.

37. Cordell, "Society and Polity," p. 19. For various sides of this issue of complexity and of elites both for Chaco and for the Protohistoric period refer to Wills and Leonard, *Ancient Southwestern Community.* The positions taken in their volume are "right-center" in the sense that none of the contributors takes the "left" position that Mesoamerica is involved in any causative way.

38. Wiseman and Darling, "Bronze Trail Group." In Riley, *Rio del Norte,* pp. 84–85, I suggested that LA-835, north of modern Santa Fe, might be a Chaco outlier. I understand that this idea has now been generally discounted. For comments on this site—actually a group of small sites—see Wiseman, "Reassessment." See also Wiseman and Olinger, "Painted Pottery in the Rio Grande." A personal communication from archaeologist Steven A. Lakatos was also very helpful.

39. Lekson, *Chaco Meridian,* p. 96. Although Lekson talks of a meridian, Aztec is slightly off line from Chaco (measuring from Pueblo Alto), the Great North Road taking a probable dogleg down Kutz Canyon into the San Juan Valley (p. 116).

40. Though I think it unlikely, the J. C. Kelley and E. A. Kelley (*Alternative Hypothesis,* pp. 185–187, 201–205) idea that actual Mesoamerican trade groups were operating at Chaco does remain a possibility. More recently, Frisbie ("The Pochteca and Chaco," pp. 209–210) has vigorously defended the idea that the traders (pochteca), either Toltec or from some group influenced by the Toltec, were the instigators of the Chaco phenomenon.

41. Plog, "Equality and Hierarchy," p. 201.

42. Questions about the Chaco elites, especially in light of the rather equivocal evidence for "upper class" burials, come from Varien, Review of *The Chaco Meridian.* For burials in Chaco generally see Akins, "Chaco Canyon Mortuary Practices." Akin sees considerable evidence for mortuary differentiation at Chaco (pp. 184–185). The whole question of the sociopolitical system at Chaco has been very vigorously argued. The question of elites, whether they existed and, if so, what were their characteristics, is still open. For various aspects of this argument see Vivian, *Chacoan Prehistory;* Sebastian, *Chaco Anasazi;* Wilcox, "Regional and Macroregional Systems."

43. For the name *Aztec* see Pearce, *New Mexico Place Names,* p. 12. See Lekson, *Chaco Meridian,* for the dating of Aztec (p. 75) and for its size (p. 78). A discussion of Totah and its Great House ruins can be found in McKenna and Toll, "Regional Patterns," pp. 133–143. For the relatively heavy early-tenth-century settlement in the Chacoan region see Windes and Ford, "Nature of the Early Bonito Phase."

44. Check dams and reservoirs at Hovenweep are noted in Winter et al., *Hovenweep 1976,* pp. 10–62, esp. pp. 34–41, 52–60.

45. See Riley, "'Defensive' Structures."

46. A discussion of the drought-producing effects of La Niña is in Perkins, "Long Dry Spells," pp. 85–86.

47. Lipe, "Depopulation," p. 161. For comments on the probability of enemy peoples as a factor in the San Juan desertion see Lipe, "Depopulation," pp. 160–161. Ralph Linton's comments on the expectation of sizable groups in any nomadic takeover in an area are in Linton, "Nomad Raids."

48. Lipe, "Depopulation," p. 155, discussed the critical water situation, especially in the Mesa Verde during the latter decades of the thirteenth century. Peterson, *Climate and the Dolores River Anasazi,* p. 124, suggests that from Dolores River data we can deduce that growing seasons became shorter and that both summer and winter precipitation were lower in the upper San Juan area after about AD 1200. The uses of warfare in P-III times

is discussed by Haas and Creamer, *Stress and Warfare;* see also P. Schaafsma, *Warrior, Shield, and Star,* pp. 159–165.

49. For comments on early-thirteenth-century migrations from the San Juan region see Roney, "Mesa Verdean Manifestations." See also Ahlstrom et al., "Environmental and Chronological Factors." For fourteenth-century changes in northern Rio Grande society see Habicht-Mauche, "Changing Patterns," p. 187.

50. A discussion of the various modes of migration is in Howell and Howell, "Modeling Migration," pp. 215–217. For an overview of opposition to the San Juan migration hypothesis see Cameron, "Migration and Movement," pp. 109–111. Steen (*Pajarito Plateau,* pp. 39–41) makes the point that although there is considerable similarity in ceramics, Mesa Verde–type house and kiva architecture does not appear in the Rio Grande except in isolated instances. He also points to the generally nonmilitary nature of Rio Grande sites, something that might be considered surprising if large numbers of immigrants had invaded the area. Steen sees the growth in the Rio Grande as largely autochthonous, a "population explosion" brought on by a favorable environment during the fourteenth century. But for a migration, at least into the Galisteo Basin, see Dutton, "Las Madres," p. 454.

51. For an inventory of fauna at the important Anasazi sites, the Box Site (LA 16660) just south of the San Juan River east of Farmington, and Salmon Ruin just to the east also on the south side of the river, see Mick-Ohara, "Faunal Remains," pp. 133–145; for differential amounts of deer bone see pp. 151–155.

52. Health matters, especially as they affect women, are taken up by Martin, "Bodies and Lives," esp. pp. 285–286.

53. The suggested linguistic distribution of Puebloans in prehistoric times is in Riley, *Rio del Norte,* pp. 100–103. For further discussion see chap. 10 herein.

54. Specific movements of Towa speakers into the Jemez area during the migration period are discussed in Lang, "Transformation," p. 177. For the relationship of Santa Fe Black-on-white to the McElmo–

Mesa Verde pottery, and for requisite bibliography, see Lang, "Transformation," pp. 176–178. For the distribution of Santa Fe Black-on-white see Habicht-Mauche, "Changing Patterns"; see also Ruscavage-Barz, "Understanding Santa Fe Black-on-White," pp. 249–268. The situation in the Puerco Valley during the thirteenth century is discussed in Roney, "Mesa Verdean Manifestations," pp. 172, 174. For the Magdalena sites see Lekson et al., "Migrations in the Southwest," pp. 92–96.

55. For comments on the White House see F. H. Ellis, "Where Did the Pueblo People Come From?"; see also Cordell, "Tracing Migration Pathways," pp. 204–205; and Naranjo, "Thoughts on Migration," pp. 247–250. An idea of the complexity of the "abandonment" problem can be found in Kohler, "Northern American Southwest," esp. pp. 295–298.

56. The presumed movement from Aztec to Paquimé is discussed in Lekson, *Chaco Meridian,* 118–128; see also Lekson, "Landscape and Polity."

57. The last tree-ring date at Aztec is AD 1270. See Robinson and Cameron, *Directory,* p. 17. Lekson, *Chaco Meridian,* p.132, puts the end of construction at Aztec at around 1275 and adds, "Several other very interesting things coincide, approximately, with that date: the beginning of the 'Great Drought'; the depopulation of the Four Corners; and the initial construction of Paquimé, sometime after 1250 and before 1300."

58. For the suggestion of relatively late dates of the beginning Medio period Casas Grandes see Lekson, "Landscape and Polity," p. 223; and Lekson, "Chaco, Aztec, and Paquimé." In the latter publication (p. 7) Lekson seems to put the move from Aztec to Paquimé at sometime after AD 1275.

59. For the foundation of Medio period Paquimé see Di Peso, *Casas Grandes,* 2: 326–335. Di Peso saw the arrival of his donor merchant group at about AD 1060, but reevaluation of dendrochronology places the date a century and a half later.

The difficulty in Casas Grandes dating is that timbers used for tree-ring dates are dressed so that the felling dates must be estimated. Dean and Ravesloot, "Chronology of Cultural Interaction," pp. 96, 98, seem to think the likely beginning of the initial Buena Fé phase of the Medio period to be a bit after AD 1200. They do point up uncertainties in this dating (pp. 101–103). For a comparable founding date (around AD 1200) and for comments on the underlying Viejo period see Schaafsma and Riley, "Analysis and Conclusion," pp. 244–247.

Michael Whalen and Paul Minnis, who have done extensive "post–Di Peso" work in the Casas Grandes region, also accept a date of somewhere around or a little after AD 1200. See Whalen and Minnis, "Investigating the Paquimé," p. 54; see also Whalen and Minnis, *Casas Grandes and Its Hinterland*, p. 39. For the more recent work at the Tinaja site, where early Medio times seem pretty clearly to encompass much of the thirteenth century, see Whalen and Minnis, "Local and the Distant," p. 323.

60. Lekson, *Landscape and Polity*, p. 221; see also Lekson, "Was Casas a Pueblo?"

## Chapter 6. The Shaping of the Midlands

1. For a discussion of the old Anasazi area as it changes into Aztlan see chap. 7.
2. A summary of Patayan is given in Reid and Whittlesey, *Archaeology of Ancient Arizona*, pp. 111–130. For various Patayan research see McGuire, "History of Archaeological Research."
3. Riley, *Frontier People*, pp. 132–137.
4. For a discussion of Patayan trade see ibid., pp. 145–154.
5. For the Archaic background to Patayan see Schroeder, "Hakataya Cultural Tradition," p. 102; see also Irwin-Williams, "Picosa," pp. 450–453. For Patayan ceramics see Schroeder, "Hakataya Cultural Tradition," 102–104; see also Rogers, "Yuman Prehistory," pp. 187–189. For early historic burial customs see Riley, *Frontier People*, p. 154. Dating of earliest Yuman/Patayan is given in Schroeder, "Hakataya Cultural Tradition," p. 103. See also Chartkoff and Chartkoff, *Archaeology of California*, p. 162; Cordell, *Archaeology of the Southwest*, p. 212; and Rogers, "Yuman Prehistory," pp.

183, 185, 190. For agriculture (and subsistence generally) at the dawn of historic times see Riley, *Frontier People*, pp. 140–144. Agriculture among the historic Yumans is treated in Castetter and Bell, *Yuman Indian Agriculture*, pp. 115–118.

6. Riley, *Frontier People*, pp. 139–140.
7. Comments on Yuman religion and a comparison with the Sonoran area can be found in Riley, *Frontier People*, pp. 94–96, 157–159.
8. Riley, *View from the Protohistoric*, p. 236.
9. Riley, *Frontier People*, pp. 145–152.
10. Riley, *Frontier People*, p. 286.
11. For cultural development at La Junta see Mallouf, "Prehistoria del noreste de Chihuahua," pp. 149–162; see also Mallouf, "Comments on the Prehistory," pp. 64–71, 81–85. A discussion of the archaeology of the La Junta region can be found in Riley, *Frontier People*, pp. 285, 289–292. The spread of Jornada influences to La Junta is discussed in J. C. Kelley, *Jumano and Patarabueye*, pp. 130–133. (At the time of Kelley's original publication, use of the term *Jornada*, as a specific division of the Mogollon, had not been formalized.) Kelley believed that the Mogollon incomers, which he called the "El Paso phase," foreshadowing later terminology, mixed originally with people from the local Livermore focus. The trait-diffusion hypothesis and other ideas by Robert J. Mallouf, incorporated here, are the result of personal correspondence with Mallouf.
12. For descriptions of the various phases in La Junta sites see Kelley, "Architectural Sequence at La Junta"; see also J. C. Kelley, *Jumano and Patarabueye*, pp. 72–77.
13. For La Junta ceramics see J. C. Kelley, *Jumano and Patarabueye*, pp. 148–149.
14. For the Concepción phase (Kelley uses the older term, *focus*) see J. C. Kelley, *Jumano and Patarabueye*, pp. 77–84. A discussion of Concepción pottery can be found on pp. 82–83. For the Conchos phase, representing Hispanic occupation, see pp. 84–85. For Kelley's new ideas concerning the La Junta peoples see J. C. Kelley, "La Cuenca del Río Conchos," p. 136. However, see Mallouf, "Prehistoria de noreste de Chihuahua," p. 162.

15. For discussions of the Jumano consult Scholes and Mera, *Some Aspects*, p. 271. Comments on the linguistic situation of Teya/Jumano and such other languages as Patarabueyes, Manso, etc. can be found in Riley, "The Teya Indians," esp. pp. 330–335.

16. See Riley, *Rio del Norte*, pp. 64–66. A detailed discussion of the ceramic relationships up and down the Sierra Madre can be found in Foster, "Loma San Gabriel Culture."

17. Riley, "Sonoran Statelets Revisited," p. 230. Also see Pailes, *Relaciones Culturales Prehistoricas*, pp. 221–222; and Lister, *Sierra Madre Occidental*, pp. 69–77.

18. For the Jornada Mogollon see Lehmer, *Jornada Branch*. Comments on the derivation and importance of El Paso Brown can be found on pp. 27, 74–77. For a description of the El Paso phase see pp. 81–84, for the contemporary San Andres phase, pp. 86–88. Phillips and Larralde ("Archaeological Survey," pp. 10–11) have recently suggested that Mimbres sites in the Caballo and Elephant Butte basins gradually were transformed into El Paso phase Jornada Mogollon after AD 1200.

19. The position of Chupadero black-on-white pottery is discussed in Wiseman, "Origins of Chupadero Black-on-White."

20. For Feather Cave see Ellis and Hammack, "Inner Sanctum of Feather Cave." The macaw find is reported on pp. 27–28.

21. Ibid., p. 33.

22. Moore and Wheat, "Archaeological Cache."

23. Wooldridge, *Implications of Trade in the Jornada Region*.

24. For a report on the Villa Ahumada site see Cruz Antillón and Maxwell, "Villa Ahumada Site."

25. For continuity between Classic Mimbres and the Black Mountain phase see Creel, "Black Mountain Phase"; see also Creel, "End of the Mimbres Classic." Terminology is not totally standardized, examples being terms like *Postclassic* and *post-Mimbres*. See Creel, "Black Mountain Phase," pp. 110–111; see also Anyon and LeBlanc, *Galaz Ruin*, p. 143; for dating of terminal Classic Mimbres and the incipient Black Mountain see p. 118.

Ceramics are discussed on pp. 108, 114–116, lithics on p. 114, mortuary practices on p. 110, association of macaw burials with Playas Red pottery on p. 112. Also see LeBlanc, "Cultural Dynamics." For comments on architectural relationships between Casas Grandes and the Black Mountain phase see Ravesloot, "Animas Phase."

26. Hegmon et al., "Abandonment and Reorganization," pp 149–151.

27. Shafer, "Mimbres Classic and Postclassic," p. 132. For additional discussion see ibid., pp. 121, 132–133; and Shafer, *NAN Ranch Ruin*, p. 8.

28. Curtis Schaafsma and I pointed out the closeness of El Paso and Black Mountain phases several years ago. See Schaafsma and Riley, "Analysis and Conclusion," pp. 241–242.

29. Anasazi movement into the Grasshopper area is discussed in Reid and Whittlesey, *Grasshopper Pueblo*, pp. 38–44. For kivas at Grasshopper see pp. 122–125.

30. For the spread of cremation northward into Zuni and the Aztlan Pueblo world see Riley, *Frontier People*, pp. 204–205. Charles Di Peso gives extensive documentation of burials at Casas Grandes. See Di Peso et al., *Casas Grandes*, 8:325–415.

31. My information for the Sonoran statelet area comes from personal correspondence with Richard A. Pailes and Daniel T. Reff.

32. For the Trincheras region see Doyel, "Interpreting Prehistoric Cultural Diversity," pp. 53–55; Fish and Fish, "Trincheras Heartland"; McGuire and Villalpando, "Prehistory," pp. 166–168; McGuire et al., "Cerro de Trincheras"; and Villalpando, "La Tradición Trincheras," pp. 95–103. Stacy, "Cerro de Trincheras," p. xiv, points out that the Trincheras sites in Sonora seemed to have different functions from those in Arizona.

33. For Hohokam Classic traits see Haury, *The Hohokam*, pp. 48–53 (houses), pp. 132, 202–205 (pottery). See also Crown, "The Hohokam," pp. 150–153. For population shifts at the end of Sedentary times see Crown, "The Hohokam," pp. 150–151, The use of comales, beginning in Classic times, is discussed in Beck, "Archaeological Signatures," pp. 204–205, 211. For changing ideas about

Hohokam chronology see Dean, "Thoughts on Hohokam Chronology," esp. the comparative chart on p. 91.

34. Crown, "The Hohokam," pp. 153–154.

35. Riley, *Frontier People*, pp. 104–106. For additional discussion (or lack thereof) of the continuum from the prehistoric to the historic see Doelle and Wallace, "Transition to History," esp. pp. 254–257.

36. For the history of Salado research I am indebted to Lincoln, "Brief History." The original Gladwin monograph was Gladwin and Gladwin, *Southwestern Pottery Types*. The Salado polychromes (Pinto, Gila, and Tonto) are all decorated with white, black, and red. They differ in design layout and in the arrangement of colors. Pinto Polychrome occurs in bowls, Gila Polychrome and Tonto Polychrome in bowls and jars. See Simon, "Salado Decorated Ceramics," pp. 78, 80–81. For possible Salado-Hopi connections see Lyons, *Ancestral Hopi Migrations*, esp. chaps. 4 and 5.

37. Crown, *Ceramics and Ideology*, p. 212. For the southwestern cult see ibid., pp. 211–225. A comparison of the southwestern cult with Casas Grandes religion is given by VanPool et al., "Casas Grandes and Salado Phenomena."

38. See Crown, *Ceramics and Ideology*. A discussion of regional cults appears on pp. 213–217 and 223–225; for precursors of the cult see p. 221; for the kachina cult tie-up see pp. 117–121; and for the comparison with Mimbres see pp. 221–222. For a description of horned serpents see pp. 134, 214. A comparison of Salado and Casas Grandes horned serpents is in VanPool et al., "Evolution of the Horned Serpent." Thompson and Brown, "Scarlet Macaws," p. 6, point out a clear association in Mimbres art with macaws and the twin war gods. Adams, "Salado," p. 271, sees a divergence by the early 1300s between the southwestern cult and the kachina cult: "The Katsina Cult is associated with large pueblos having enclosed plazas, kivas, death/ancestor worship, and new modes of food processing, especially piki. . . . Its iconography includes rock art, ceramics, and kiva murals. . . . Although it shares its roots in the Pinedale style with the Southwestern Cult,

it clearly diverges in its expression of anthropomorphs, or katcinas, in all of these media from the Southwestern Cult." For an opposed view of the ubiquity of the Pinedale style see Duff, *Western Pueblo Identities*, pp. 58–59.

39. For "proto-glazing" and local Rio Grande manufacture of St. Johns pottery see Peckham, *From This Earth*, p. 82.

## Chapter 7. Building Aztlan in the North

1. For desertion of the Kayenta region see Dean, "Kayenta Anasazi," p. 39.

2. For the Chaco extension into the Zuni region see Kintigh, "Cibola Region," pp. 131–134.

3. For the physical description of the Rio Grande country see Riley, *Rio del Norte*, pp. 21–23.

4. Fortified towns in the Southwest after about AD 1300 are discussed in LeBlanc, *Prehistoric Warfare*, pp. 219–221. See also E. K. Reed, "Village-Plan Layouts," esp. pp. 11–16. Not all sites were defensive. Adams, *Homol'ovi*, pp. 255–256, points out that Homol'ovi II, occupied during this period, does not seem to have been built with a particular eye to defense. For Spanish problems with southwestern fortified towns see Riley, *Rio del Norte*. esp. chaps. 11–14, 16.

5. For warfare among the Aztecs and on the Mexican central plateau generally see Riley, *Rio del Norte*, pp. 138–141.

6. Beals, *Acaxee*, pp. 14–18, 33–34; see also Beals, *Comparative Ethnology*, pp. 115–116. For the west coast of Mexico see Sauer and Brand, *Aztatlán*, though these authors do point out (p. 15) that sites in the lowlands normally did not show a defensive character.

7. For the military attributes of La Quemada see Trombold, "Causeways," pp. 148–150; see also Jiménez Betts and Darling, "Archaeology of Southern Zacatecas," pp. 163–167. For Chalchihuites see J. C. Kelley, "Archaeology of the Northern Frontier," esp. pp. 778–783. The northeast Sonoran area and its warlike proclivities are discussed in Riley, "Sonoran Statelets," 197–198. Casas Grandes is discussed in Bradley, "Advances in Chihuahuan Archaeology," p. 239; see also Ravesloot and Spoerl, "Role of Warfare."

8. LeBlanc, *Prehistoric Warfare*, pp. 197–198. Huntley ("Interaction, Boundaries, and Identities," pp. 238–240), though not questioning the warlike propensities of Pueblo IV peoples, suggests that the nucleation of pueblos may have not been the result of aggression but a *cause* for it. Nucleation itself may have created considerable social tension. For further documentation of protohistoric warfare see LeBlanc, "Regional Interaction and Warfare"; LeBlanc, "Settlement Consequences"; Adams, "Case for Conflict"; and Upham and Reed, "Structure of Anasazi Warfare."

   For a contrary view see Rohn, "War and Violence," esp. p. 151. Rohn believes that the Pueblos "would appear to represent one of the less warlike and less violent societies in the world." However, Woodbury, *Reconsideration of Pueblo Warfare*, p. 131, noted a half century ago "considerable evidence, much of which archeologists have overlooked or given too little consideration to, indicating that warfare was a regular part of Pueblo life prior to the last couple of centuries, and that the peacefulness [often] attributed to the Puebloan groups is illusory." See also Jonathan Haas's review of LeBlanc's *Prehistoric Warfare*. The question of Mesoamerican stimulus to southwestern war is complex. See Nelson, "Aggregation," pp. 317–329.

9. The disturbed climatic rhythms during this period are discussed in Lekson, "War in the Southwest," pp. 611–613. Also see Dean, "Reconstruction on Colorado Plateaus"; and Dean, "Demography, Environment, and Subsistence Stress." Dean, however, cautions that more work is needed on these problems.

10. For the hostilities at Burnt Corn Pueblo see Munson, "Excavations at Burnt Corn Pueblo"; and Snead, "Ancestral Pueblo Settlement," pp. 246–251.

11. For Quetzalcoatl and his many manifestations see Brundage, *Phoenix of the Western World*, 169–170.

12. For the war and fertility aspects of Tlaloc see P. Schaafsma, *Warrior, Shield, and Star*, p. 177.

13. Riley, *Rio del Norte*, p. 110. Indications of a former child sacrifice with parallels to the water goddess, Chalchihuitlicue, the female embodiment of Tlaloc, can be found in the Hopi late-winter ceremony of Ponsu. See James, "Mimetic Rituals," p. 354.

14. Various aspects of the historic kachina cult are given in Ladd, "Zuni Ceremonial System"; Hieb, "Meaning of Katsina"; and Adams, "Katsina Cult."

15. P. Schaafsma, "Tlalocs, Kachinas, Sacred Bundles," p. 173.

16. Reyman, "Mexican Influence," pp. 130–131. For a consideration of southwestern astronomy from at least Chacoan times see Malville and Putnam, *Prehistoric Astronomy*.

17. Reyman, "Mexican Influence," p. 130. Williamson, "Light and Shadow," p. 114, has pointed out that at least in historic Zuni the supernatural twins are associated with the morning and evening star. This is a complex linkage, delineating Quetzalcoatl in his star and twin manifestations. It also involves the divine twins, who may originally have represented the sun and moon and perhaps antedate Quetzalcoatl in Mesoamerica, although absorbed by him probably sometime in the first millennium AD. For a discussion of these twins see Thompson, "Evolution and Dissemination," esp. pp. 98–101. Young, "Puebloan and Mesoamerican Ideology," p. 114, points out that "in his manifestation as Venus, as well as in his aspect as sun, Quetzalcóatl is strikingly parallel to the Zuni and Hopi Twin War Gods."

18. Riley, "Color-Direction Symbolism." Color-direction symbolic involvement in the kachina cult is discussed in Parson, *Pueblo Indian Religion*, pp. 173, 228–230, 366.

19. A discussion of patolli can be found in Riley, *Rio del Norte*, p. 217.

20. Adams, *Origin and Development*, p. 4. Ware and Blinman, "Origin of Ritual Sodalities," p. 392, doubt the importance of the prehistoric and early historic kachina cult among the eastern Pueblos. However, the rich seventeenth-century Spanish documentation of the cult along the Rio Grande would seem to argue otherwise. See Riley, *Kachina and the Cross*, pp. 173–178.

21. For Tlaloc and kachinas see Parsons, *Pueblo Indian Religion*, pp. 1015–1025; see also Parsons, "Aztec Pueblo Parallels," p. 132.

22. Brew, "Katchina-Tlaloc Relations," pp. 244–245; and Beals, "Meso America and the Southwest," p. 246. For the importance of Tlaloc and Quetzalcoatl in post-1300 sites in the southwest see J. C. Kelley, "Mesoamerica," pp. 108–109.

23. For the attributes of rock figures in Jornada art see P. Schaafsma, "Prehistoric Kachina Cult," pp. 65–69. See also Slifer, *Signs of Life*, p. 39, for descriptions of Jornada Tlaloc and Quetzalcoatl figures.

24. P. Schaafsma, *Rock Art in New Mexico*, pp. 60–61.

25. Early spread to Cerro Indio is discussed in P. Schaafsma, "Prehistoric Kachina Cult," p. 64.

26. Adams, *Origin and Development*, p. 120. Adams discusses the inception of the cult on pp. 92–99. For the idea that the kachina cult appears first in the west see ibid., p. 136.

27. Ibid., p. 120.

28. Adams, "Katsina Cult," p. 46.

29. Ibid., pp. 38–39; see also Hays, "Kachina Depictions on Prehistoric Pueblo Pottery," pp. 54–61; Hays, "Shalako Depictions," pp. 73–81; and Hays, "Katsina Depictions on Homol'ovi Ceramics." For possible kachina use of an aggregating Pueblo near Taos see Crown and Kohler, "Community Dynamics," p. 113. For dates on the arrival of the kachina cult into the upper Southwest see Adams, *Origin and Development*, 185–191; P. Schaafsma and C. F. Schaafsma, "Origins of the Pueblo Kachina Cult"; and P. Schaafsma, "The Prehistoric Kachina Cult," pp. 63–64. Earlier kachinas are suggested for the Hovenweep area by Olsen, *Hovenweep Rock Art*, pp. 135–137; and at Chetro Ketl at Chaco by Vivian et al., *Wooden Ritual Artifacts*, 45–48; but for reasons discussed earlier I think that these occurrences are very unlikely.

30. Kiva murals are discussed in Adams, *Origin and Development*, pp. 29–38. See also Smith, *Kiva Mural Decorations*, pp. 29–38, 296–298, for kiva murals at Awatovi and Kawaika-a. See Hayes, *Excavation of Mound 7*, pp. 48–49, 51, for

murals at Gran Quivira; P. Schaafsma, "Kiva Murals," for those at Pueblo del Encierro; and Dutton, *Sun Father's Way*, for the Kuaua murals.

31. A discussion of Kokopelli can be found in Slifer, *Serpent and the Sacred Fire*, pp. 100–101, 103–104, 107. Polly Schaafsma (*Indian Rock Art*, pp. 122, 125) has identified earlier nonhumped players who date back to Basketmaker III, perhaps AD 700. Dockstader, *Kachina and the White Man*, p. 28, suggests that the Kokopelli kachina (with its "koko" element in the name) may be Zuni in origin. This kachina in Hopi has fertility implications, with its prominent erect penis, and simulated intercourse during the ceremonies (pp. 50–51).

32. For kachina dolls see Adams, "Katsina Cult," p. 39. For a certain fluidity in kachinas see Wright, "Changing Kachina." See also Dockstader, *Kachina and the White Man*, pp. 95–106.

33. See Adams, *Origin and Development*, pp. 101–108.

34. See ibid., p. 82, for the ritual importance of piki bread. For comales in the Rio Grande area and for bibliographic references to various finds see Snow, "Tener Comal y Metate," pp. 292–294. Snow makes the point that this new tortilla technology may have been a factor in population increase (p. 292).

35. A discussion of shoe-shaped pots can be found in Adams, *Origin and Development*, pp. 79–80. For the "duck effigies" at Casas Grandes, perhaps the same type of vessel, see Di Peso et al., *Casas Grandes*, 6:91. What are perhaps duck-effigy pots are illustrated in Haury, *The Hohokam*, pp. 217, 219.

36. For an alternative opinion to Mesoamerican influence on kachinas see Crotty, "Anasazi Mural Art." The idea of kachinas originating from Casas Grandes is not new; for example, it was suggested in 1983 by Griffith, *Kachinas and Masking*, pp. 764–765.

37. P. Schaafsma, "Tlalocs, Kachinas, Sacred Bundles," p. 184.

38. Ibid., pp. 184–192.

39. See P. Schaafsma, *Rock Art Sites in Chihuahua*, pp. 21–22, for Tlaloc images in rock art. Swanson, "Prehistoric Commu-

nication Networks," pp. 763–764, points out that an *atalaya*, or lookout tower, on Cerro Moctezuma, near Paquimé, has the appearance of a stepped-cloud motif, which in Mesoamerica is associated with Tlaloc. See also P. Schaafsma, "Emblems of Power"; and P. Schaafsma, "Quetzalcoatl." For possible Tlaloc or Tlaloc-related images on Chihuahuan pottery see Di Peso et al., *Casas Grandes*, 6:175–176 (Figure 202-6, subfigures 3, 4, 6–8), p. 236 (Figure 269-6, subfigures 23–25), pp. 274, 276 (Figure 290-6, subfigures 62, 65, 71, 73), p. 307 (Figure 345-6, subfigure 18). Compare these with Tlaloc rock depictions in P. Schaafsma, "Tlalocs, Kachinas, Sacred Bundles," pp. 176–181. Also compare Sutherland, "Mesoamerican Ceremony," pp. 72, 80. Whalen and Minnis, *Casas Grandes and Its Hinterland*, p. 187, speak of "what may be Tlaloc symbols on Ramos Polychrome vessels," but as far as I can tell, they give no examples of these.

40. For the southwestern cult see Crown, *Ceramics and Ideology*, pp. 221–225. For questions of the meaning of *cult* see Cordell, *Archaeology of the Southwest*, p. 419. A discussion of the Uto-Aztecan flower associations is given in Hill, "Flower World," pp. 117, 136–139. Something that might strengthen the flower-association idea comes in a more recent study by Hill, "Proto-Uto-Aztecan," a suggestion that the proto-Uto-Aztecan speakers might actually have originated in central Mexico. Hays-Gilpin and Hill, "Flower World in Prehistoric Southwest," pp. 413–414, propose that a "Flower World system of images originated as a recruitment of the flower, a symbol of feminine power... to masculine ritual practice. This recruitment may have happened independently in Mesoamerica and the Southwest." The Flower World complex appeared in the southwestern and kachina cults and in the Mimbres mortuary complex.

41. Parsons, *Pueblo Indian Religion*, p. 134. For details on the Hunt society see ibid., pp. 114–115, 127, 134, 243–246.

42. Gutiérrez, *When Jesus Came*, p. 143.

43. For a rich discussion of the war symbolism on post-1325 rock art and kiva murals in the Anasazi Southwest see P. Schaafsma, *Warrior, Shield, and Star*, pp. 29–105. Depictions and descriptions of weapons, and scenes of warriors and weapons, can be found on pp. 32–49. For various animals in war settings see Plate 11 and pp. 63–69. Specifically for bear and star associations see pp. 66–67. For jaguars see Plate 11 and p. 143; see also Hibben, *Kiva Art of the Anasazi*. For bears, curing societies, and shamanism see Parsons, *Pueblo Indian Religion*, pp. 189–190; for association of Morning Star with war see ibid., pp. 181, 213.

44. A discussion of the recurved bow is in LeBlanc, *Prehistoric Warfare*, 99–104. LeBlanc says that in the Southwest recurved bows are almost always sinew backed. His discussion on the origin of both the simple or self-bow and the compound bow can be found on pp. 101–102. For speeds at which various weapons can throw darts or arrows see p. 100. Distribution of complex bows in North America is given in Driver and Massey, *Comparative Studies*, p. 352. These double-curved bows are illustrated in Awatovi (Hopi) kiva murals, as shown in Peckham, *Prehistoric Weapons*, Figure 6. P. Schaafsma, *Warrior, Shield, and Star*, p. 48, comments that there is no evidence that simple bows among the Pueblos ever had sinew backing.

45. The *capitanes de guerra* and Indian contingents with Spanish war parties are discussed in Riley, *Kachina and the Cross*, pp. 218–219.

46. For figures on Indian allies with Spanish war parties in the early eighteenth century see Hendricks and Wilson, *Navajos in 1705*, pp. 3–4. See also Hendricks, "Pueblo-Spanish Warfare," p. 185. Hendricks (p. 183) makes the point that the sinew-backed bow of the Pueblos did not have sufficient penetrating power to seriously threaten Spaniards with metal or even leather armor. A discussion of the Indian allies in the later eighteenth century can be found in Jones, "Pueblo Indian Auxiliaries."

47. Descriptions of Indian warfare appear in Riley, *Frontier People*, pp. 200–201, 241–242. For the struggles during the Coronado period see Riley, *Rio del Norte*,

pp. 161–162 (Zuni), 162–163 (Hopi), 176–180 (Tiwa), 180 (Keresan allies), 194 (Tewa). For ethnographic accounts of war see also Haas and Creamer, "Warfare Among the Pueblos." I have emphasized the defensive nature of Pueblo towns attacked by Coronado, but Potter, "Structure of Open Space," p. 150, doubts that defense was necessarily a factor in town construction in late prehistoric times—but see LeBlanc, "Settlement Consequences," p. 128. Creamer, "Regional Interaction," p. 111, doubts that language was the unifying military-political factor in Pueblo organization that I am suggesting here. To me, however, the early Spanish accounts of basically linguistic alliances, especially at Zuni, Hopi, and Tiguex, seem quite incontrovertible.

48. Eggan, *Social Organization,* pp. 61–64, 89–106.

49. Ibid., pp. 198–210.

50. Ibid., pp. 224, 240–252.

51. Ibid., p. 316.

52. Gutiérrez, *When Jesus Came,* p. 79.

53. Descriptions of the Eastern Pueblo socioreligious and political organizations are drawn from a number of sources. See Dozier, *Pueblo Indians,* pp. 150–162 (Keresan), and 162–176 (Tanoan); and Dutton, *American Indians,* 19–24 (Tiwa), 24–27 (Tewa), 27–28 (Towa), 29–31 (Keresan). Ware and Blinman ("Cultural Collapse and Reorganization," 384–385) have pointed out the strong political control of the Medicine Societies in eastern Keresan life. See also various sections of Ortiz, *Southwest,* for the several Eastern Pueblos. In particular see Bodine, "Taos Pueblo"; Ortiz, "San Juan Pueblo"; Arnon and Hill, "Santa Clara Pueblo"; Ellis, "Isleta Pueblo"; Lange, "Cochiti Pueblo"; Lange, "Santo Domingo Pueblo"; Strong, "Santa Ana Pueblo"; Sando, "Jemez Pueblo"; and Hoebel, "Zia Pueblo." For Towa see Dozier, *Pueblo Indians,* p. 165; and Sandos, "Jemez Pueblo," pp. 423, 425–426. For the specific situation at Taos see Parsons, *Taos Pueblo,* pp. 71–72, 77–80. For Isleta see also Parsons, "Introduction," pp. 4–8.

54. For the idea of a *Cacique Model* see Schaafsma and Riley, "Analysis and Con-

clusion," p. 248. See also Furst, "Lords of Place," pp. 57–68.

55. Apropos of the Zuni towns, the Spaniards spoke of the "Seven Cities of Cibola," and though they listed only six, it is conceivable that there were seven or even eight. Future archaeology may shed light on this question. For early historic populations in the Pueblo world see Riley, *Kachina and the Cross,* pp. 52, 201–203. Population is also documented by Zubrow, *Population, Contact, and Climate,* Figure 5. Zubrow also sees a secondary peak around the time of the Pueblo Revolt, but I believe this to be extremely unlikely.

56. For the heavy Western Pueblo population in the fourteenth century see Upham, *Politics and Power,* pp. 60–62, 64–73, 106–107. For pottery exchange see pp. 125–133; for other goods see pp. 196–197. See also Urban, "Shell," p. 112; and Bernardini and Brown, "Settlement Clusters," pp. 115–117. Cotton trade between the middle Little Colorado River towns and Hopi is discussed in Adams, "Homol'ovi: A 13th–14th-Century Settlement," pp. 122, 124–125. The Zuni area is discussed in detail in Kintigh, *Settlement, Subsistence, and Society,* pp. 115–117 (see also the extended site descriptions in Kintigh's chap. 4). Also see Huntley and Kintigh, "Archaeological Patterning." For fifteenth-century developments at Zuni, particularly in ceramics, see Mills, "Protohistoric Zuni Ceramic Production." For the Chavez Pass pueblos see Brown, "Nuvakwewtaqa."

57. Upham, *Politics and Power,* p. 201.

58. For discussion of the ceramics of Homol'ovi see Hays, "Ceramics," pp. 23–24. See also Lange, *Prehistoric Land-Use,* pp. 20–54; and Lange, "Survey of Homol'ovi," pp. 203–212. Use of foodstuffs in trade necessitates settlements that are fairly near because of the calorie budget involved in human haulage. About 30 miles is generally considered the maximum distance ordinary food can be traded, according to Lightfoot, "Food Redistribution." Of course special kinds of food supplies, salt, for example, or condiments, can be traded over much greater distances. And, indeed,

special circumstances may alter this distribution pattern. Chaco Canyon, for example, may have depended on maize from 50 miles away. See Benson et al., "Ancient Maize." For Hopi ties with Homol'ovi II see Adams, "Late Prehistory," pp. 56–57.

59. Kintigh, *Settlement, Subsistence, and Society*, p. 1. Kintigh points out that during this period 28 large villages, with more than 13,000 rooms, were built and abandoned (p. 115).

60. The terminal dates for various Pueblos are given in Adler and Johnson, *Mapping the Puebloan Southwest*, pp. 257–262, 266. Also see Adams, *Homol'ovi*, Table 8.1. For the foundation of historic Western Pueblo by about AD 1400 see Duff, *Scale, Interaction, and Regional Analysis*, p. 81. For the foundations of Zuni see Ferguson, "Emergence of Modern Zuni," pp. 337–338; for Hopi see Adams, "View from the Hopi Mesas," pp. 322–324. On some problems of deriving southwestern populations from archaeological data see Powell, "Anasazi Demographic Patterns." A discussion of various demographic studies is made by Gumerman, "Historical Perspective," pp. 17–22.

61. Spread of the White Mountain and glaze wares is discussed in Snow, "Rio Grande Glaze," pp. 243–252. Sources for ores that were used in the prototype western areas are discussed in Huntley, "Interaction, Boundaries, and Identities," pp. 126–157. For the utilization of glaze wares for storage and trade see Habicht-Mauche, *Pottery from Arroyo Hondo*, p. 47; for the ritual use of glazed pottery see Spielmann, "Ritual Influences," p. 254; and Chamberlin, "Technology, Performance, and Intended Use," p. 270.

62. See Riley, *Frontier People*, pp. 204–205 (Zuni), 246–248 (Pottery Mound, Salinas pueblos).

63. Distribution of Gila Polychrome is given by Crown and Bishop, "Manufacture of Gila Polychrome," p. 50. For cremations in association with Gila Polychrome at Kechipawan see Bushnell, "Some Pueblo IV Pottery Types," p. 662; for Hawikuh see Smith et al., *Excavation of Hawikuh*, pp. 203–205.

64. Distribution of prehistoric irrigation systems in the Greater Southwest during the Aztlan period is discussed in Greiser and Moore, "Case for Prehistoric Irrigation," 190–192. For irrigation specifically in the Taos area see Greiser and Greiser, "Prehistoric Irrigation in the Taos Valley," pp. 224–225. Use of grids for irrigation is discussed by Dominguez, "Optimal Gardening Strategies," pp. 156–157. For the development of large towns in the Rio Grande region see P. F. Reed, "Spatial Analysis," pp. 1–2, 20.

65. P. F. Reed's count of large pueblos is given in "Spatial Analysis," pp. 28–33. See also Riley, *Rio del Norte*, p. 95. Collapse of pueblos in post-Spanish times is discussed in Schroeder, "Pueblos Abandoned in Historic Times."

66. Counts of pueblos in 1540 are given by Castañeda, *Relación*, fols. 115–116. For the Chamuscado party the count of Martín de Pedrosa is given in Hammond and Rey, *Rediscovery of New Mexico*, pp. 115–119.

67. Discussion of the alliances in De Vargas's time can be found in Riley, *Kachina and the Cross*, 245–246.

68. Population declines in the post-1300 Southwest are charted in Dean et al., "Adaptive Stress," pp. 64, 69–70. However, Wiseman, "Hinterlands," pp. 174–176, points out that at least in the lower Jemez Valley conditions were favorable for dry farming in the period ca. 1325 up to conquest times. Polyak and Asmerom, "Late Holocene Climate," however, see this as a generally dry period in the upper Southwest. Climate as a variable in the dynamics of southwestern population will probably prove to be a rather complex matter.

69. Riley, *Frontier People*, pp. 36–37.

70. Riley, *Sixteenth Century Trade*, pp. 38–44. There is a very considerable literature on trade in the Southwest, much of which I have considered in previous publications. Cabeza de Vaca's comments on semiprecious stones in Sonora can be found in Hedrick and Riley, *Journey*, pp. 63, 147; Cabeza de Vaca, *Naufragios*, p. 62. Exchange of turquoise for bright-plumaged parrots or macaws (*Naufragios* reads "papaguayos") is discussed on

p. 62. For coral in Sonora, the lower Colorado region, and the upper Southwest see Riley, *Frontier People*, pp. 78, 121, 130–131, 145–152, 304. Also see Hodge, "Coral."

71. For southwestern pottery in California see Ruby and Blackburn, "Southwestern Pottery"; see also Farmer, *Mojave Trade Route*, pp. 155–157.

72. See Riley, *Frontier People*, pp. 145–152, for a discussion of trade from the lower Colorado area both to the upper Southwest and to coastal California.

73. Ibid., p. 151. For the comment about soapstone at Pecos see Kidder, *Artifacts of Pecos*, p. 92.

74. Riley, *Frontier People*, p. 149.

75. Ball, *Mining of Gems*, pp. 17, 26–27.

76. Pogue, *The Turquoise*, p. 96. Pogue considers it "almost certain" that part of the turquoise used in central Mexican prehispanic mosaics came from the Cerrillos area. The widespread availability of turquoise in southwestern states (not just from the Cerrillos area) is attested by Northrop, *Turquoise*, pp. 3–22; and Snow, "Prehistoric Southwestern Turquoise." See especially Snow's map of sources (p. 39).

77. Weigand and Weigand, "Macroeconomic Study," p. 191.

78. Presumed southwestern turquoise found in Chalchihuites sites is discussed by Weigand et al., "Turquoise Sources," pp. 30–31. These authors state (p. 31) that "our results are certainly consistent with the idea that the 80-odd artifacts from the two Alta Vista sites [El Vesuvio and Cerro de Moctezuma] originated from turquoise mined in New Mexico, perhaps at Cerrillos." They also believe (p. 31) that these two sites were "closely athwart the turquoise trade route from the southwestern United States into Mesoamerica." For discussion of the Chalchihuites culture see Jiménez Betts and Darling, "Archaeology of Southern Zacatecas," pp. 155–180; and Foster, "Archaeology of Durango," pp. 197–219. For the west Mexican coast connection see Meighan, "Archaeology of Sinaloa"; and J. C. Kelley, "Aztatlán Mercantile System."

79. The turquoise finds at Guasave are discussed in Carpenter, "El Ombligo,"

pp. 268–269; see also Weigand and Harbottle, "Role of Turquoises."

80. See Brand, "Aboriginal Trade Routes," esp. pp. 94–96, for the species and places of origin for shell traded to the Southwest. In the 1890s Fewkes, "Pacific Coast Shells," described shell, both Gulf of California and California coast, from Homol'ovi, Chevron, Chavez Pass, Awatovi, Sityatki, and other sites in the Hopi area.

81. Hargrave, *Mexican Macaws*, pp. 28–52, has a comprehensive listing of all macaw discoveries in the Greater Southwest.

82. The argument for meat trade into the Salinas region comes from Spielmann and Angstadt-Leto, "Hunting, Gathering, and Health," p. 100.

83. Manson, "Transmississippi Trade and Travel," pp. 386–391; see also Riley, *Frontier People*, pp. 267–270. For a description of the goods brought to Zuni from Pecos see Castañeda, *Relación*, fol. 49.

84. The finds of western *Olivella* shells at Spiro are discussed in Kozuch, *Olivella Beads from Spiro*, pp. 701–702.

85. Manson, "Transmississippi Trade and Travel," pp. 386–391. See also Riley, *Frontier People*; for the Missouri and Mississippi finds of southwestern artifacts see p. 270; for trade to Pecos from the plains, pp. 269–272. The Pueblo pottery in Missouri, however, may be intrusive. Trade into the Great Lakes area is given by Ball, *Mining of Gems*, p. 26. Habicht-Mauche, "Pottery, Food, Hides, and Women," p. 219, suggests that the locally made Puebloan wares might have come from the labor of Pueblo women who married into plains groups or who were brought as captives, or as a result of actual migrations of Pueblo households or kin groups, to the plains.

86. The Tonque-Pecos trade is discussed by Shepard, "Rio Grande Glaze-Paint Pottery," pp. 69–81. For the linguistic affiliations of Tonque see Schroeder, "Tunque Pueblo," p. 262.

87. Riley, *Frontier People*, pp. 268–271.

88. Frisbie, "Hishi as Money," esp. pp. 126–131, discussed the use of that commodity as a sort of primitive currency.

89. Teague, *Textiles*, p. 483. One can speculate on the possibility that the kilt spread

to the upper Southwest as part of some ceremonial complex, perhaps the kachina cult. The possibility that embroidery was aboriginal in the Southwest is discussed in Mera, *Pueblo Embroidery,* pp. 2–7.

90. The spread of cotton to the Southwest is considered in Kent, *Textiles of the Prehistoric Southwest,* pp. 27–29; see also Ford, "Gardening and Farming," p. 18. For the development of the southwestern loom see Kent, *Textiles of the Prehistoric Southwest,* pp. 123–125. See also Teague, *Textiles,* p. 112.

91. Hammond and Rey, *Rediscovery of New Mexico,* pp. 226–227.

92. Ibid., pp. 190–193.

93. Distribution of shell is discussed by Bradley, *Shell Exchange,* p. 224.

94. For Chihuahua polychromes in general Western Pueblo and in the Gila-Southeast Arizona area see Di Peso et al., *Casas Grandes,* 8:142–144. A map on p. 144 seems to claim Ramos and Carretas polychromes at Hawikuh and Kechipawan, but I can find no other data on these. Keith Kintigh, Barbara Mills, and Deborah Huntley (personal communications) have all indicated to me the lack of Chihuahuan ceramics in the Zuni area. The find of possible Ramos Polychrome at Site 34 at the head of Little Soda Canyon in Mesa Verde is reported in O'Bryan, *Excavations in Mesa Verde,* pp. 63, 98, and Plate L. For identification of Ramos Polychrome at Pottery Mound see Hibben, *Possible Pyramidal Structure,* p. 525. I am indebted to Polly Schaafsma for pointing out the similarities of horned serpents on the Pottery Mound murals and on Ramos Polychrome vessels. Schaafsma says that they are nearly identical "in regard to the specific complexes of horn, snout, and feathers." Mesa Verde–like sites in the Magdalena-Socorro area are reported by Lekson et al., "Migrations in the Southwest" (for pottery see pp. 87–88); Wilson, "Prehistory of the Gallinas Mountains," 197–204; and Stuart and Gauthier, *Prehistoric New Mexico,* pp. 63–73.

95. For possible Playas wares influencing Potsuwi'i Incised pottery from the Tewa area see Peckham, *From This Earth,* pp. 116–119. Wendorf, *Salvage Archaeology,* p. 98, also sees a possible diffusion from the south. Lang, "White Ware Pottery," p. 182, thinks that a Playas origin for Potsuwi'i Incised is possible but is troubled by the chronological difficulties. He suggests Great Plains pottery influences as an alternative. More decisively, David Snow (personal communication) believes that Potsuwi'i Incised pottery is of Caddoan and/or Late Plains Woodland derivation.

96. Worked copper is discussed by Vargas, *Copper Bell Trade* [1995], pp. 69–71; also Vargas, "Copper Bell Trade" [1994], pp. 90–94; see also Sprague and Signori, *Southwestern Copper Bells.*

97. For my discussion about Espejo and the Navajo see Riley, *Kachina and the Cross,* p. 73. A good summary of the Navajo situation can be found in Brugge, "Navajo Prehistory." For possible early Navajo occupation in the San Juan drainage see A. D. Reed and Horn, "Early Navajo Occupation," p. 297; see also Brown, "Protohistoric Transition," p. 68; and P. F. Reed and L. S. Reed, "Reexamining Gobernador Polychrome," p. 83. Curtis Schaafsma, "Ethnic Identity," pp. 43–44, does not believe that the Navajo had shifted west of the Continental Divide before the seventeenth century. See also C. F. Schaafsma, *Apaches de Navajo,* p. 220. Brugge and Gilpin, "Navajo Ritual Histories," p. 365, believe that the "Pueblization" of the Navajo may have taken place around the period of the Pueblo Revolt (1680). For various aspects of the Navajo problem see the perceptive paper by Brugge, "Navajo Archaeology."

## Chapter 8. The Casas Grandes World

1. Ball courts in Paquimé are discussed in Whalen and Minnis, "Ball Courts and Political Centralization."

2. Description of the site of Paquimé comes from Di Peso, *Casas Grandes,* 2:407–415 (Mound of the Cross and the ball courts), 344–346 (acequia), 351 (sewer system), 352 (drains), 370 (town size), 370–375, 394–399 (living areas), and 400–401 (marketplace). See also Di Peso et al., *Casas Grandes,* 5:613, 680–681, 709, 722–723, 817.

3. Cuevas, *Historia,* pp. 184–185.

4. It is not entirely clear whether or not the town name was originally pronounced paquiME. The Cuevas edition of Obregón does not use the accent mark, though the Hammond and Rey English translation does. The original manuscript document does not contain the accent, but, as Di Peso has pointed out (*Casas Grandes*, 2:653–654), there is a general lack of accents in this document.

5. The meaning of the word *Paquimé* is discussed in Di Peso, *Casas Grandes*, 2:295, 653–654.

6. For a discussion of the Suma see Beckett, "Historic Relationships"; Naylor, "Extinct Suma"; Naylor, "Athapaskans They Weren't," p. 276; and C. F. Schaafsma, "Ethnohistoric Groups," pp. 90–91.

7. Cuevas, *Historia*, p. 186.

8. For Bandelier's trip see Lange and Riley, *Southwestern Journals*, pp. 291–326.

9. Comments on hostilities between the Opata and Casas Grandes people can be found in Bandelier, *Final Report . . . Part 1*, p. 91.

10. Lumholtz, *Unknown Mexico*, 1:87.

11. A discussion of the history of Casas Grandes research can be found in Whalen and Minnis, *Casas Grandes and Its Hinterland*, pp. 27–32. See also Lekson, "Was Casas a Pueblo?" For a somewhat different view of Casas Grandes see Carey, "Analysis." For distribution of sites in the vicinity of Casas Grandes see Di Peso et al., *Casas Grandes*, 4:6–7.

12. For the Plainware period see Di Peso, *Casas Grandes*, 1:86–93. The Viejo period is discussed on pp. 95–198.

13. VanPool et al., "Evolution of the Horned Serpent."

14. For trade pottery see Di Peso, *Casas Grandes*, 2:622–627, 745; see also Di Peso et al., *Casas Grandes*, 4:77–78, and 8:141–160. For percentages of trade ware see Douglas, "Distant Sources," pp. 14, 18.

15. Wilcox, "Historical Analysis," p. 28, points out that very few Salado Polychrome sherds (514 out of 26,585) have been found in "pure Buena Fé" contexts and thinks the association of Salado wares and Buena Fé phase may be spurious.

16. For the idea that the Salado polychromes may have evolved in the south at a relatively early date see Di Peso et al., *Casas Grandes*, 4:29; and Di Peso, "Gila Polychrome." For an opposing opinion see Ravesloot et al., "A Reanalysis," 329–330. Other views of Salado polychromes are given by Lekson, "Salado in Chihuahua," pp. 282–283; and Dean, "Introduction," pp. 13–14. Both Dean and Lekson in these separate papers of the Salado volume use a metaphor, the oversized gorilla, to describe the vexed problem of Casas Grandes Salado wares. In Dean it is six hundred pounds. Lekson is more expansive, making the animal an eight-hundred pounder.

17. The revised tree-ring dating of Casas Grandes is discussed by Dean and Ravesloot, "Chronology," pp. 91–93. For use of trade ceramics to establish the beginning of the Medio period see Phillips and Carpenter, "Robles Phase," p. 80.

18. For difficulties in determining phases within the Casas Grandes Medio period see Whalen and Minnis, *Casas Grandes and Its Hinterland*, p. 42. There is some disinclination to use Di Peso's subdivisions of the Medio. Schaafsma and Riley ("Introduction," Table 1) make the point that "there is no longer justification for dividing the Medio period into phases." More recently, however, Rakita, "Temporal Sensitivity," pp. 178–180, has suggested that it may be possible in the future to establish temporal values for Paquimé ceramics. Sprehn, "Specialist Potters of Casas Grandes," p. 241, citing a paper by G. F. M. Rakita and G. R. Raymond delivered at the 2000 Annual Meeting of the SAA in Philadelphia, suggests that the chronological order of the main polychrome pottery types at Paquimé is (early to late) Babícora, Villa Ahumada, and Ramos (see also note 33 of this chap.).

19. Schaafsma and Riley, "Analysis and Conclusion," pp. 239–241.

20. For a discussion of Di Peso's contributions to the field of Casas Grande studies see Riley, "Charles C. Di Peso."

21. For the Casas Grandes Interaction Sphere of Schaafsma and Riley see Schaafsma and Riley, "Introduction," Figure 1. Also see Phillips, "Areas arqueológicas," pp. 11–12. Phillips includes the Animas Pueb-

los to the north, the Bavispe River to the west, the Santa María and Carmén valleys to the east, and the Babícora area to the south. J. Charles Kelley's speculation regarding trade into the Casas Grandes area from La Junta is in J. C. Kelley, "La Cuenca del Río Conchos," p. 136. However, Mallouf, "Comments on the Prehistory," p. 84, believes there were trade connections, but he doubts that La Junta was ever an "ethnic satellite of Casas Grandes or the Jornada Mogollon and having the primary purpose of supplying raw materials to the parent redistribution center in northwestern Chihuahua" (84). Mallouf sees, instead, a more informal symbiotic relationship.

22. The various estimates of size of the "Casas Grandes World" can be found in Whalen and Minnis, *Casas Grandes and Its Hinterland*, pp. 52–55. See also Wilcox, "Processual Model," pp. 287–292.

23. For Viejo period site sizes see Whalen and Minnis, *Casas Grandes and Its Hinterland*, pp. 100–101; see also Whalen and Minnis, "Investigating the Paquimé Regional System," pp. 57–58.

24. Architecture is discussed in Di Peso et al., *Casas Grandes,* 4:146–157 (Convento phase), 157–177 (Pilón phase), and 178–195 (Perros Bravos phase).

25. A discussion of trade pottery in the Viejo period can be found in Di Peso et al., *Casas Grandes,* 6:21–22, ceramics in general, pp. 21–25. Di Peso et al., *Casas Grandes,* 4:194–195, list a sherd of Galisteo Black-on-white in fill in the north plaza and one on the west plaza at the Convento site. For Mata Polychrome see Schaafsma and Riley, "Analysis and Conclusion," p. 245; for Dublán Polychrome see VanPool, "Symbolism of Casas Grandes," p. 103. Larkin et al., "Ceramics," pp. 188–191, have recently suggested another polychrome type, Santa Ana Polychrome, as transitional Viejo to Medio in the Santa Maria region, south of Paquimé. See also Steward et al., "Archaeological Chronology," p. 237.

26. Whalen and Minnis, *Casas Grandes and Its Hinterland*, p. 43; for the idea of a large Viejo presence in the Medio period see also pp. 43–44. More recently, Whalen and Minnis, *Local and Distant*, pp. 318–

321 again emphasize the "homegrown" nature of the Casas Grandes Medio period.

27. Whalen and Minnis, *Casas Grandes and Its Hinterland*, pp. 43–44.

28. Comments on the "quickening" in Perros Bravos times can be found in Schaafsma and Riley, "Analysis and Conclusion," pp. 245–246, where Schaafsma and I cited various examples of this increased complexity. For a further view see C. F. Schaafsma, Review of *Casas Grandes and Its Hinterland*. Rakita, "Social Complexity," p. 272, has pointed out the increase of exotic grave goods in Perros Bravos times, foreshadowing the richer grave-good complexes of the Medio period.

29. In a recent paper Leonard et al. ("Casas Grandes Intellectual Traditions") had suggested that at least some of the ancestry of the Medio period Casas Grandes may have come from Classic Mimbres and some from the Comala phase of western Mexico. For sizes of Medio period sites in the Casas Grandes Valley see Whalen and Minnis, *Casas Grandes and Its Hinterland*, pp. 109, 124.

30. Maxwell, *Casas Grandes Region,* 16–17. T-shaped doors have a wide distribution, being found as far north as Mesa Verde. See Love, "Survey."

31. Cruz Antillón and Maxwell, "Villa Ahumada." The pottery types that Brand considered markers for his Chihuahuan complex included Dublán, Corralitos, Ramos, Babícora, Carretas, Huérigos, and Villa Ahumada polychromes, as well as Madera Red-on-black, Médanos Red-on-brown, Playas Red, and Ramos Black. See Brand, "Chihuahua Culture Area," pp. 155–156; and Cruz and Maxwell, "Villa Ahumada," pp. 44–46. Also see Cruz, "Recientes Investigaciones"; and Cruz et al., "Galeana, Villa Ahumada, and Casa Chica."

32. Whalen and Minnis, "Local and the Distant," pp. 322–324.

33. Hendrickson, "Lost Pots," pp. 49–50, has suggested that based on design elements Babícora Polychrome may be a somewhat earlier type and Ramos Polychrome a more fully developed one. What this means in terms of spatial distribution (Ramos in the core area, Babícora with

a more southerly distribution) is unclear. See also note 18 above.

34. J. H. Kelley et al., "West Central Chihuahuan Perspective."

35. MacWilliams, "Beyond the Reach," p. 60.

36. Lazcano Sahagún, *Explorando un mundo olvidado,* pp. 149–155. See also plates on pages 72–74, 82, 85–90, 92–93, 98–101, 104–105, 109–114, 126, 130–131, 136, 138–139, 148. For sites that extend into northeastern Sonora see Bagwell, *Production,* esp. pp. 2, 10–26.

37. Kidder et al., *Pendleton Ruin,* p. 135.

38. Walker and Skibo, "Joyce Well and the Casas Grandes Religious Interaction Sphere." For ceramic distribution at Joyce Well see Carpenter, "Animas Phase and Paquimé," 157–161; and McCluney, "1963 Excavation," pp. 35–37, 42–45. It would seem that Ramos Polychrome was the most common of the Chihuahuan polychromes at the Pendleton Ruin.

39. For a possible Casas Grandes move to the New Mexico boot heel see Di Peso, *Casas Grandes,* 3:836, 844.

40. Dating in the Animas sites is discussed in C. F. Schaafsma et al., *Archaeomagnetic Dating,* pp. 134–136. See also DeAtley, *Regional Integration,* p. 73. DeAtley's dates for the Animas phase (1200–1425) are considered reliable.

41. For discussion of possible kivas at Paquimé see Lekson, "Was Casas a Pueblo?" pp. 87–88.

42. For Di Peso's comments on Room 38 see Di Peso et al., *Casas Grandes, 5:* 475–478.

43. At least in Lazcano Sahagún, *Explorando un mundo olvidado,* they are not illustrated in the various plates and plans. Lazcano was aware of kivas, for he has a photograph of a Chaco Canyon kiva and mentions them as characteristic of the Anasazi culture (pp. 57–58). Nor do they appear in Bagwell's eastern Sonoran sites. See Bagwell, *Production.* In a personal correspondence (Oct. 11, 2003) Bagwell says that she believes some of the rooms in the Sonora sites are ceremonial but doubts that they are kivas, as the word is used in the upper Southwest.

44. The size of Paquimé compared to Los Muertos is given in Di Peso, *Casas Grandes,* 2:370–371, 674; also Di Peso et al., *Casas Grandes,* 4:198.

45. The Mesoamerican flavor of Paquimé was pointed out a number of years ago by Foster, "Casas Grandes as Mesoamerican Center," pp. 33–39. More recently Lekson et al., "Pueblo IV in the Chihuahuan Desert," p. 60, made the point that "Paquimé was almost certainly the most cosmopolitan, most spectacular city in the long history of the Southwest."

46. For Casas Grandes ball courts see Whalen and Minnis, "Ball Courts and Political Centralization," pp. 734–740. The ball courts at Joyce Well, Culberson, and Timberlake are discussed in Skibo and Walker, *Ball Courts,* pp. 107–119 (Joyce Well), 119–123 (Culberson and Timberlake).

47. Wilcox and Sternberg, *Hohokam Ballcourts,* pp. 70–75.

48. Ferdon, "Hohokam 'Ball Court.'"

49. A good discussion of the Hohokam courts is given in Wilcox, "Mesoamerican Ballgame." Dating is discussed on pp. 108–114.

50. For the historic ball game see Beals, *Comparative Ethnology,* p. 113; see also Beals, *Acaxee,* pp. 11–12.

51. For distribution and types of ball courts in interior northern Mexico see J. C. Kelley, "Known Archaeological Ballcourts"; see also Foster, "Archaeology of Durango"; and Weigand, "Western Mesoamerican Tlachco." The ball courts at Paquimé are described in Di Peso et al., *Casas Grandes,* 4:292–304; and in Di Peso, *Casas Grandes,* 2:410–415.

52. Di Peso, *Casas Grandes,* 2:414–415.

53. A possible alternative explanation to Di Peso's interpretation is given in Wilcox and Sternberg, *Hohokam Ballcourts,* p. 73. For a discussion of severed heads see Gillespie, "Ballgames and Boundaries," pp. 321–330.

54. A description of the Mound of the Cross can be found in Di Peso et al., *Casas Grandes,* 4:287–291. For the astronomical orientations see p. 288. Thompson and Brown, "Scarlet Macaws," p. 8, believe that the Mound of the Cross represents Venus imagery, also connected to the scarlet macaw.

55. J. C. Kelley and E. A. Kelley, "Archaeoastronomical System," p. 183–184. Equinox relations to Quetzalcoatl are given in Brundage, *Phoenix of the Western World*, pp. 182–183.

56. P. Schaafsma, *Rock Art Sites in Chihuahua*, p. 26. VanPool, *Birds, Burials, and Beliefs*, pp. 79–81, points out that macaws and other birds found on pottery decoration at Casas Grandes sometimes show merged features, for example macaw-turtle and macaw-serpent.

57. Di Peso, *Casas Grandes*, 2:422–423; and Di Peso et al., *Casas Grandes*, 4:465–467.

58. Di Peso et al., *Casas Grandes*, 4:305; see also Di Peso, *Casas Grandes*, 2:418–421.

59. Di Peso, *Casas Grandes*, 2:471–474.

60. For a description of the marketplace and plaza area see Di Peso, *Casas Grandes*, 2:400–406; see also end map in vol. 2; and Di Peso et al., *Casas Grandes*, 5:807–815.

61. Di Peso, *Casas Grandes*, 2:388–391.

62. Whalen and Minnis, *Casas Grandes and Its Hinterland*, p. 50.

63. Sprehn, "Specialist Potters of Casas Grandes," pp. 235–238, 243–244.

64. Ravesloot, *Mortuary Practices*, p. 68. For a discussion of grave goods see pp. 22–37, 70–73. For general comments see pp. 68–77.

65. Di Peso et al., *Casas Grandes*, 8:327–338, 364–367. See also Riley, "Color-Direction Symbolism."

66. Di Peso, *Casas Grandes*, 2:482–483. See also Malagón, "Tattoos, Women, and Rites," pp. 65, 68–70.

67. A discussion of turquoise is in Di Peso et al., *Casas Grandes*, 8:187. For alibates and serpentine see p. 188. VanPool et al., *Flaked Stone*, p. 172, analyzing the flaked stone assemblage at the site of Galeana, did not find the same range of exotic materials as at Paquimé. They suggest that while Paquimé was a consumer of exotic stone materials, it did not serve as a redistribution center, at least not into the Galeana region.

68. For the breeding and use of turkeys see Di Peso, *Casas Grandes*, 2:602, 734–735. See also the descriptions of turkey pens at the House of the Dead in Di Peso et al., *Casas Grandes*, 5:590.

69. For macaw nesting boxes see Di Peso, *Casas Grandes*, 2:599–600, 2:733–734, Di Peso et al., *Casas Grandes*, 7:219–224 (nesting box entrances), and 7:224–229 (stone entrance plugs). Use of felsite for pens and bowls is discussed in Di Peso, *Casas Grandes*, 2:734.

70. For dietary deficiencies see Di Peso, *Casas Grandes*, 2:600; for feeding habits and the food used see ibid., pp. 600, 734; see also Di Peso et al., *Casas Grandes*, 4:34–36.

71. The distribution of macaws is given in Di Peso et al., *Casas Grandes*, 8:272–279; see also Di Peso, *Casas Grandes*, 2:600. For macaw distribution see also Hargrave, *Mexican Macaws*, pp. 52–54, 57–58, and, for the Galaz site military macaw, pp. 48–49.

72. Age grouping of the macaws at Paquimé, and their breeding habits, is discussed in Di Peso, *Casas Grandes*, 2:733–734.

73. McKusick, *Southwest Birds of Sacrifice*, p. 81.

74. Di Peso, *Casas Grandes*, 2:733n9. I also discussed that presumed feather trade, "rich-colored plumes used for feather crests," in a 1976 publication and suggested that the distances given would put Tejo's trading family near the Opata country. The same, of course, could be said of nearby Paquimé. See Riley, *Sixteenth Century Trade*, pp. 13–14.

75. Di Peso et al., *Casas Grandes*, 6:251. Rinaldo quotes A. V. Kidder as saying that Mimbres pottery was "neither parent to nor derived from the more limited naturalism of Casas Grandes . . . but strongly suggest[s] intercourse between the two groups." Leonard et al., "Casas Grandes Intellectual Traditions," however, believe in a strong affinity between Casas Grandes and Classic Mimbres, though perhaps not particularly in pottery. In regard to the widespread influences of the Pinedale style see Crown, "Change in Ceramic Design," p. 241.

76. The lack of Chihuahuan pottery in the Gila-Salt region is indicated by Doyel, "On Rivers and Boundaries," pp. 458–462, 464–467; and Lekson, "Salado in Chihuahua" (see esp. p. 302). For the Zuni area see my discussion in chap. 7n94 above. For the shell trade see

Di Peso et al., *Casas Grandes*, 6:401–525. As quoted in chap. 7, Weigand et al., *Turquoise Sources*, pp. 30–31, state that two sites in the Alta Vista (Zacatecas) area were "closely athwart the turquoise trade route from the southwestern United States into Mesoamerica."

77. Griffin and Krieger, "Notes on Some Ceramic Techniques," pp. 161, 166, Plate 12.

78. Di Peso et al., *Casas Grandes*, 6:78.

79. See Di Peso et al., *Casas Grandes*, 6:401, for amounts of Medio period shell at Paquimé; descriptions of various types of shell are in subsequent pages. Di Peso's discussion of Casas Grandes interaction with the upper Southwest vis-à-vis shells is on pp. 406–408. The relatively small amount of Viejo period shell is discussed on pp. 390–400.

80. Helen DuShane quoted in Di Peso et al., *Casas Grandes*, 6:401.

81. For variety and origin of shell see Di Peso et al., *Casas Grandes*, 6:550–551. For the distribution of shell and other prestige items at the Casas Grandes site see Bradley, "Networks of Shell Exchange," p. 176.

82. Helen DuShane quoted in Di Peso et al., *Casas Grandes*, 6:401.

83. Di Peso et al., *Casas Grandes*, 7:500–532. Di Peso's ideas concerning Paquimé as a manufacturing center can be found on p. 500, the amounts of copper on pp. 500, 507.

84. Vargas, *Copper Bell Trade* [1995], pp. 69–71.

85. For a description of the various cultic waves to Casas Grandes and other parts of the Southwest see Di Peso, "Casas Grandes and Gran Chichimeca," pp. 51–55. In the Casas Grandes volumes Di Peso (*Casas Grandes*, 2:292–293) gives lip service to his earlier idea of waves of influences: "The general Gran Chichimecas continuum of events proposed herein was somehow associated with the missionary activities of certain Mesoamerican cults of the gods Tezcatlipoca, Quetzalcóatl, and Huitzilopochtli, in that order. Each appeared on the Northern Frontier with its own identifiable iconographic trait cluster." However, Di Peso does not really follow up on this. As for

the upper Southwest, Florence Hawley Ellis believed that both Tezcatlipoca and Huitzilopochtli left recognized traces in historic Pueblo Indian ceremonials. See Ellis, "Datable Ritual Components," pp. 87–91. I suspect, however, that the ceremonials she describes were more related to Quetzalcoatl and Tlaloc.

86. For the god Quetzalcoatl in a Paquimé setting see Di Peso, *Casas Grandes*, 2:548–553. For Xiuhtecutli influence see ibid., 556–559; for Xipe Tótec see ibid., 560–564, 712–713 (esp. note 79).

87. Ibid., 560–564.

88. For a discussion of the Paquimé style in rock art see P. Schaafsma, *Rock Art Sites in Chihuahua*, pp. 21–22, 25. See also P. Schaafsma, "Paquimé Rock Art Style." Schaafsma's comments on the appearance in Durango of the *cuadro* or cartouche are on p. 40.

89. For a Tlaloc effigy see also P. Schaafsma, *Rock Art Sites in Chihuahua*, p. 22.

90. For possible Tlaloc sacrifices of young people see Di Peso, *Casas Grandes*, 2:567. As I pointed out in chap. 7, Griffith ("Kachinas and Masking," pp. 764–765) suggests that the kachina cult of the upper Southwest may have originated at Casas Grandes.

91. VanPool, *Shaman-Priests*, pp. 708–709.

92. For similarities of the ancestor cult at Paquimé with the kachina cult see Rakita, "Social Complexity," pp. 314–315. The quote is on p. 315.

93. For comments on Chalchihuitlicue and the military macaw see McKusick, *Southwest Birds of Sacrifice*, pp. 81–86.

94. Di Peso, *Casas Grandes*, 2:574. For a more general discussion of priesthoods see pp. 574–576, 718–719.

95. For priestly paraphernalia see Di Peso, *Casas Grandes*, 2:576–581; see also Di Peso et al., *Casas Grandes*, 7:291–302 (human and animal effigies), 307–314 (ceremonial ax heads), 315–318 (stools), 319–324 (stone vessels), and 325–327 (altars). A Chalchihuites incense burner in cloud ladder shape (and a quite similar one from modern Tepehuan) is illustrated in Riley and Winters, "Prehistoric Tepehuan," Figure 2.

96. VanPool, "Symbolism of Casas Grandes," p. 295.

97. Ibid., p. 343.

98. Ibid., pp. 341, 348–354, 357. See also VanPool and Vanpool, "Evolution and Agency," pp. 104–113.

99. VanPool, "Symbolism of Casas Grandes," pp. 260–271, 292–293. The quote questioning the Quetzalcoatl ancestry of Casas Grandes horned serpents is on p. 280. One argument that VanPool uses ("Symbolism of Casas Grandes," p. 280) for the nonidentification of the Casas Grandes horned serpent with Quetzalcoatl is a statement by Braniff, "Paquimé," p. 82: "[I]n Paquimé we find Mesoamerican elements associated with the southern elites. These are generally of an ideological nature: the ceremonial ball-game, copper bells, and representations of deities such as Tláloc, the 'plumed serpent,' the 'turquoise serpent' or the 'fire serpent' portrayed in so-called 'back mirrors.'" It seems to me that Braniff was treating Tlaloc, the plumed serpent, and the fire and turquoise serpents as three different categories. In any case it hardly clarifies the question of Casas Grandes' religious relationship to Mesoamerican religion. The Fire Serpent, Xiuhcóatl or Turquoise Dragon, probably symbolized the sun disk in its passage through the sky. Its relationship to Quetzalcoatl is complex and in some ways represents a duality, sky water/sky fire (see Brundage, *Phoenix of the Western World*, pp. 27–29, 189). Di Peso (*Casas Grandes*, 2:498, 556–557) identifies Xiuhcóatl as the deity on the Casas Grandes copper back-shields, and as "one of the many guises of Xiuhtecutli [the old Fire God of Mesoamerica] when in affinity with Quetzalcóatl."

100. J. C. Kelley, "Archaeology of the Northern Frontier," pp. 784–785.

101. For shamans among the southern Tepehuan see Riley, "Southern Tepehuan," pp. 819–821.

102. See Di Peso, *Casas Grandes*, 2:586–589, 725–729; and C. S. VanPool, "Flight of the Shaman."

103. T. L. VanPool et al., "Casas Grandes and Salado," p. 14 (this refers to the ms. page).

104. Ibid., p. 15.

105. Agriculture in Paquimé has not undergone the intense study that other aspects of culture have been given. There were a number of varieties of corn according to the analysis of Hugh C. Cutler and Leonard W. Blake in their section of Di Peso et al., *Casas Grandes* (8:308–310). They include Chapalote, Reventador, Harinoso de Ocho, Onaveño and Maíz Blando de Sonora, among others. For cotton and squash see pp. 714–715. For use of beans I am indebted to Paul Minnis (correspondence of March 13, 2003).

106. Di Peso et al., *Casas Grandes*, 8:242–246, 248–253. For the consumption of lagomorphs at Villa Ahumada see Cruz Antillón and Maxwell, "Villa Ahumada," esp. p. 49.

107. Doolittle, *Canal Irrigation in Prehistoric Mexico*, p. 85. See also Doolittle, "Canal Irrigation at Casas Grandes," 142–145. For another approach to this irrigation problem see Schaafsma and Riley, "Analysis and Conclusion," p. 248.

108. Pottery and workshops are discussed by Di Peso et al., *Casas Grandes*, 6:77–97. See also Di Peso, *Casas Grandes*, 2:531–539.

109. For weaving see Di Peso, *Casas Grandes*, 2:540–545; for the imported whorls see 5:704. See also Mary Elizabeth King's comments in Di Peso et al., *Casas Grandes*, 8:76–79, 107–110.

110. T. L. VanPool and Leonard, "Specialized Ground Stone," pp. 725–726.

111. Sprehn, "Specialist Potters of Casas Grandes," pp. 209, 242–243.

112. Woosley and Olinger, "Casas Grandes Ceramic Tradition," 121–123.

113. For outer perimeter defenses in the Casas Grandes region see Di Peso, *Casas Grandes*, 2:360–365, 672–673. The line of sight communication with a signaling tower on Cerro Moctezuma is described in Di Peso et al., *Casas Grandes*, 4:227.

114. Swanson, "Prehistoric Communication Networks," pp. 765–766.

115. For possible blowgun pellets see Di Peso, *Casas Grandes*, 2:614; see also Riley, "South and Central American Blowgun."

116. Ceremonial arrows are described by Di Peso et al., *Casas Grandes*, 8:116–118. For projectile points see Di Peso et al., *Casas Grandes*, 7:389–398.

117. Information about axes possibly used in warfare is given in Di Peso et al., *Casas Grandes*, 7:58.

118. For the copper plaques see Di Peso et al., *Casas Grandes,* 7:517-521; see also Ravesloot and Spoerl, "Role of Warfare," p. 135.

119. Di Peso, *Casas Grandes,* 2:320-321; Di Peso et al., *Casas Grandes,* 8:355. For commentary on this destruction see Ravesloot, *Mortuary Practices,* pp. 75-76; and Ravesloot and Spoerl, "Role of Warfare," pp. 134-135.

## Chapter 9. Sonora and the Trading Connection

1. Manso "towns" in the sixteenth century are discussed by Riley, *Rio del Norte,* p. 166. For the question of what role the La Junta area actually did perform in the Casas Grandes Interaction Sphere see chap. 8 herein. I might stress that Mallouf ("Comments," p. 84) doubts that La Junta was any sort of heavy player in the Casas Grandes world.

2. For a discussion of the natural features of the Serrana country see Riley, *Frontier People,* pp. 40-47.

3. Doolittle, *Pre-Hispanic Occupance,* pp. 14-15. For agricultural potential and development see Doolittle, "Aboriginal Agricultural Development." Specific rainfall and temperature are from Dunbier, *Sonoran Desert,* appendices A-E.

4. For trade in bison hides see Riley, *Frontier People,* pp. 78, 80.

5. The two accounts of Cabeza de Vaca have been transcribed and translated a number of times. For both transcription and translation of the *Joint Report* see Hedrick and Riley, *Journey.* For the second account I mostly use the 1555 version of what today is generally called the *Naufragios* (Cabeza de Vaca, *La Relación*). For a translation of the *Naufragios* consult Hodge, *Spanish Explorers.* A recent very extensively annotated translation of *La Relación* is contained in Adorno and Pautz, *Cabeza de Vaca;* see esp. 1:228-245.

6. There are two manuscript versions of the Marcos de Niza journey. Here I use the Library of Congress copy from Patronato 20, Ramo 10, Archivos General de Indias (AGI). The standard transcription can be found in Pacheco and Cárdenas, *Colección de documentos,* 3:325-351. See also Hartmann, "Pathfinder," esp. pp. 87-101.

7. All of the major accounts from the Coronado expedition can be found in Hammond and Rey, *Narratives,* which are generally, but by no means entirely, reliable. The important Castañeda account is best drawn from the one extant manuscript copy in the New York City Library, Castañeda, *Relación de la Jornada,* or at least from the printed transcription in Winship, *Coronado Expedition,* pp. 107-185. The Coronado trial hearings, important for Sonora, have been recently republished both in a transcription and in translation. See Flint, *Great Cruelties.* More recently a new and exceptionally accurate translation of the Coronado documents, with painstaking transcriptions for the various source documents, has been made by Flint and Flint, *Documents of the Coronado Expedition.*

8. There are a number of sources relating to the Ibarra expedition. For the Obregón account see Cuevas, *Historia.* An English translation by Hammond and Rey, *Obregón's History,* is also useful. The much shorter Ruiz account has been transcribed in Sauer, *Road to Cíbola,* pp. 53-58 (taken from Ruiz, *Punctos Sacados,* Vol. 25, *Misiones,* Archivos General de Mexico). Material for Las Casas appears in O'Gorman, *Apologética historia sumaria.* For the Jesuit missionization of Sonora see Spicer, *Cycles of Conquest,* pp. 86-91 (Lower Pima), and 91-96 (Opata). The Jesuits left a series of documents, including *Anuas,* or annual reports, of various mission conditions. An extremely valuable source is that of Andrés Pérez de Ribas, at one time Jesuit Provincial, in charge of the west coast missions. His massive *History* was very competently translated in the 1990s by Daniel T. Reff et al. and extensively annotated by Reff.

9. My concept of "statelets" has been enthusiastically accepted by some scholars and rejected by others. For a discussion of this see Riley, "Sonoran Statelets," pp. 197-198. For "pro" views see Doolittle, "Development of 'Statelets,'"; and Reff, "Location of Corazones and Señora," 105-108. For "con" perspectives see McGuire and Villalpando, "Prehistory," pp. 170-171; and Fontana,

"Were There Indian Statelets?" A survey of recent research in the southwestern United States and northwestern Mexico can be found in Fish and Fish, "Southwest and Northwest"; for comments on statelets in Sonora see pp. 24–25. Recently Quijada and Douglas, "Arqueología del Alto Valle," pp. 424–425, have suggested that the statelet model may need to be modified to take into account variability between the Sonora River valley and that of the Bavispe.

10. For a brief discussion of the early history of exploration of the Sonoran area and the curious misconceptions that rose early in southwestern archaeology see Riley, "Sonoran Statelets," pp. 193–195, 197–198.

11. See Pailes, "Archaeological Perspective," pp. 186–187.

12. For the Rio Sonora culture see Amsden, *Archaeological Reconnaissance in Sonora;* see also Pailes, "Río Sonora Culture," pp. 135–137; Pailes, *Archaeological Reconnaissance;* and Pailes, "Relaciones Culturales." For the place of the Rio Sonora culture in the larger area see Riley, "Sonoran Statelets Revisited," p. 230.

13. Doolittle, *Pre-Hispanic Occupance,* pp. 36–38; and Pailes, "Agricultural Development," pp. 312–314. What Doolittle calls a "Transitional phase," Pailes refers to as the "Middle phase." As I am primarily interested in the Late period, I am not really concerned here with such terminological matters.

14. Doolittle, *Pre-Hispanic Occupance,* pp. 40–43; Pailes, "Upper Rio Sonora," p. 26. The distribution and meaning of the Sonora River sites are given in Pailes, "Upper Rio Sonora," pp. 27–33. See also Pailes, "Agricultural Development," pp. 311–315; and Dirst, "Prehistoric Frontier." Site distribution is discussed in Doolittle, *Pre-Hispanic Occupance,* pp. 63–74 (appendices A–C). Apropos of Pailes's idea that his archaeological sites were second level, Bartolomé Las Casas (O'Gorman, *Apologética historia sumaria,* 1:281), whose report is one of the earliest, notes numerous large towns in the Señora Valley, including the government center, also called Señora, with 3,000 "well appointed" houses.

15. Pailes, "Agricultural Development," p. 313.

16. Ibid., p. 314.

17. Doolittle, *Pre-Hispanic Occupance,* pp. 30–33.

18. Ibid., pp. 33–34.

19. For a discussion and photograph of the Banámichi "field map" see ibid., pp. 46–47.

20. Ibid., p. 59; Pailes, "Upper Rio Sonora," pp. 32–34.

21. Braniff, "Ojo de Agua," pp. 72–73, 78.

22. Douglas and Quijada, "Between the Casas Grandes," pp. 107–108. The recent work of Quijada and Douglas is discussed in "Arqueología del Alto Valle," 411–429; and in Douglas and Quijada, "Between the Casas Grandes." Cave sites in the upper Bavispe drainage, excavated by Bagwell (see Bagwell, *Production*), have not yet been securely dated but may have some relationship with the sites investigated by Douglas and Quijada.

23. Pailes, "Upper Rio Sonora," pp. 35–36.

24. Ibid., p. 36. For the area of San José see p. 29. The photograph of the effigy vessel appears on p. 36.

25. Ideas on population size, amount of arable land, and crop systems are discussed in Doolittle, "Land of Maize." For additional discussion of the demography and carrying capacity of the land see Riley, *Frontier People,* 51–58 (population), 59–67 (subsistence), 68–75 (settlement patterns). Double-cropping is discussed on p. 65. The availability of arable land is considered in Doolittle, "Land of Maize," p. 257, possible population on p. 258. Size of the Sonoran towns is discussed in Riley, "Sonoran Statelets," pp. 194–195. For distribution of settlements in the Sonora Valley see Doolittle, *Pre-Hispanic Occupance,* pp. 52–61, appendices A–C.

26. Reff, *Disease,* p. 226. See also Reff, "Old World Diseases," pp. 89–92. For my own estimates of Serrana population see Riley, "Sonoran Statelets," pp. 194–195.

27. Riley, "Sonoran Statelets," p. 195.

28. Mendizábal, "Influencia de la sal."

29. Sauer and Brand, *Aztatlán,* p. 41.

30. Ibid., pp. 41–62. The authors did not use the term *Pequeños Estados,* which to the best of my knowledge was coined by

Mendizábal about the time the Sauer and Brand volume went to press.

31. Sauer, *Distribution of Aboriginal Tribes*, esp. pp. 22–30. See also Kroeber, *Uto-Aztecan Languages*, pp. 10–15.

32. Reff, *Disease*, pp. 212–218. Sauer and Brand, *Aztatlán*, pp. 61–62. Also see Sauer, *Aboriginal Population*, pp. 6–11. Interestingly, Spicer, "Yaqui," p. 251, gives a precontact figure of 35,000 for the Yaqui and contrasts it with the 30,000 estimated in 1617. This would seem to almost totally discount the epidemics that ravaged the area. For a discussion see Reff, *Disease*, p. 215.

33. Reff, *Disease*, 108–134, 230–242.

34. For an excellent article on disease from the Coronado expedition see Roberts and Ahlstrom, "Mechanisms of Change," pp. 120–125. Roberts and Ahlstrom (pp. 125–129) think that malaria may have reached southern Arizona with Coronado. The Sonora and Moctezuma river areas have much the environmental conditions as the river valleys of Arizona. See also Reff, *Disease*, 108–134, 230–242.

35. See, e.g., Day, *Coronado's Quest*, p. 331.

36. For Marata and the other Marcos-named towns see Di Peso, *Casas Grandes*, 3:767, 777–778, 799, 807–808, 836.

37. Riley, "Las Casas and the Golden Cities," pp. 27–28; Riley, "Marata and Its Neighbors," pp. 216–219; Riley, "Sonoran Statelets Revisited," pp. 232–233.

38. Flint and Flint, *Documents of the Coronado Expedition*.

39. Doolittle, "Development of 'Statelets,'" p. 20. The fact that archaeological investigations tend to support the sixteenth-century historical data is discussed on pp. 13–24.

40. For descriptions of the Serrana towns see Castañeda, *Relación*, fols. 102–103; see also O'Gorman, *Apologética historia sumaria*, 1:280–281, and 2:182–183; see also Riley, "Las Casas and the Golden Cities," pp. 19–24.

41. For Marcos's comments on gold see Pacheco and Cárdenas, *Colección de documentos*, 3:349. The gold discoveries in the Serrana are discussed in Castañeda, *Relación*, fol. 134. Castañeda uses the phrase "mineros de oro," which Hammond and Rey (*Narratives*, p. 269) and Winship

(*Coronado Expedition*, p. 289) translate as "veins." Gold in the general area was mentioned by the Jesuit missionary Joseph Och in the mid-eighteenth century. According to Och the Sonoran Indians mixed "gold scales" in their pottery clay. Och was certain that this really was gold since he tested samples with quicksilver. See Smith, "Pots of Gold?" p. 41.

42. For an account of Alcaráz's death see Cuevas, *Historia*, pp. 152–153.

43. Consideration of possible sixteenth-century routes across the Serrana is made by Riley and Manson, "Sonoran Connection," pp. 138–140.

44. Riley, "Warfare," pp. 139–141. Spanish comments on federations in the statelet area come in Castañeda, *Relación*, fol. 102; Cuevas, *Historia*, pp. 171, 173.

45. Cuevas, *Historia*, pp. 171–172.

46. Concerning hostilities, Obregón (Cuevas, *Historia*, p. 146) says that the Oera people "son belicosos, guerreros y enemigos de los de las valles de Cinaro, Corazones, Guaraspias." The sentence ends with the meaningless phrase "en muca." I suspect that this is another area or valley, but it is impossible to say which one it represented.

47. Cuevas, *Historia*, p. 146.

48. Multistory houses are discussed in Doolittle, *Pre-Hispanic Occupance*, p. 26. The Spanish introduction of melons is described by Obregón in Cuevas, *Historia*, p. 149. For "chick-peas" see Hammond and Rey, *Obregón's History*, p. 160. The finding of Spanish goods in the statelet area is mentioned by Cabeza de Vaca; see Hedrick and Riley, *Journey*, pp. 64, 148. For Castañeda's Spanish chickens see Castañeda, *Relación*, fol. 103.

49. Obregón's descriptions of settlements in the area are given in Cuevas, *Historia*, pp. 145–149, 157–160, 171–174. But see Quijada and Douglas, "Arqueología del Alto Valle," pp. 424–425, which gives us new information on the Bavispe region.

50. Cuevas, *Historia*, p. 173. Here Obregón again uses the expression "liga y junta" for the Señora confederacy.

51. Cabeza de Vaca, *Relación*, fol. xlvi.

52. For Ibarra's return from the Casas Grandes area see Riley, "Warfare," p. 140.

53. Ibid., pp. 139–140.

54. For comments on the arrow poison see Riley, *Frontier People*, pp. 94, 361, which also cites the various Spanish references to the poison. Also see Flint, *Great Cruelties*, pp. 82, 87, 115. For the Jesuit period see Guitéras, *Rudo Ensayo*, p. 48; and Lombardo, "Arte," fol. 7.

55. For fortress sites see Obregón, in Cuevas, *Historia*, pp. 160–164; Doolittle, *Pre-Hispanic Occupance*, pp. 64–67.

56. For Bandelier's comments see Lange and Riley, *Journals*, pp. 277–278; see also Bandelier, *Final Report*, 1:59.

57. Cuevas, *Historia*, pp. 168–169.

58. For war between the statelet peoples and those of Casas Grandes see Lange and Riley, *Journals*, pp. 273–274, 276, 278–280.

59. Cabeza de Vaca, *Relación*, fols. xlv–xlvi. A useful modern transcription of the report is Cabeza de Vaca, *Naufragios*, pp. 62–63. See also Hedrick and Riley, *Journey*, pp. 62–64 (English text) and 146–147 (Spanish text).

60. For the Marcos and Díaz trips see Hammond and Rey, *Narratives*, esp. Marcos's account, pp. 67–71, and Mendoza's letter to King Carlos, pp. 157–159. Hammond and Rey use the Spanish transcription of the Mendoza letter contained in Pacheco and Cárdenas, *Colección de documentos*, 2:356–362.

61. Cuevas, *Historia*, pp. 146–147.

62. For the long involvement in the salt trade consult Riley, *Sixteenth Century Trade*, p. 32.

63. Slaves in the Señora region are discussed in Obregón, *Historia*, p. 149.

64. Di Peso, *Casas Grandes*, 3:851.

65. Public architecture is described by Pailes, "Upper Rio Sonora," pp. 26–29; and by Doolittle, *Pre-Hispanic Occupance*, 29–34. A photograph of what is perhaps a ball court can be found on p. 30 of Doolittle. However, for reservations on the question of ball courts see Doelle, Review of *Frontier People*, pp. 166–167.

66. Castañeda, *Relación*, fol. 102.

67. O'Gorman, *Apologética historia sumaria*, 2:182–183.

68. Ibid., 183.

69. The observations of Jesuit Father Oliñano are taken from Reff et al., *History*, p. 404.

70. Alarcón's mention of sun worship in the lower Colorado is in Hammond and Rey, *Narratives*, pp. 131, 135–136. For sun worship in the statelet area see Cuevas, *Historia*, p. 146.

71. Burial patterns are discussed by Richard A. Pailes and Daniel T. Reff in correspondence dated May 1, 2002, and May 7, 2002, respectively. For burning of bodies to prevent their falling into enemy hands see Pérez de Ribas in Reff et al., *History*, p. 243.

72. Cuevas, *Historia*, pp. 146, 174. For more on religion in the Serrana see Riley, *Frontier People*, pp. 94–96.

## Chapter 10. A Multiplicity of Tongues

1. For a discussion of southwestern languages see Riley, *Rio del Norte*, 95–104.

2. Ibid., pp. 32–47.

3. For Greenberg's classification see Greenberg, *Language in the Americas*, appendix D. As even conservative linguists accept the idea that there are larger groupings of American languages, the main controversy is in the methodologies involved in finding them. See Campbell, Comments, p. 488.

4. Ideas concerning the parallelism of the linguistic, dental, and genetic evidence, with various critical commentaries, are given in Greenberg et al., "Settlement of the Americas."

5. Hale and Harris, "Historical Linguistics"; see also Goddard, "Classification," pp. 316–317, 321–323. For the Apachean arrival times in the Southwest see Riley, *Rio del Norte*, pp. 103–105. For additional points of view consult various papers in Towner, *Navajo Origins;* also see C. F. Schaafsma, *Apaches de Navajo*, esp. pp. 208–214.

6. For the two languages of the Sonoran area see Cuevas, *Historia*, p. 173. *Opata* was a term used for two closely related languages, Teguima and Eudeva, and a third, Jova, whose position is less certain. The designation Opata itself is perhaps from the Piman language. The name *Piman* was given by the Spaniards, probably from the Piman word meaning "nothing" or "absence." The modern Pima and Papago Indians prefer the name *O'odham*, which means "person" in

Pima. See Fontana, "Pima and Papago," p. 134; and Hinton, "Southern Periphery: West," pp. 320–321; see also Pennington, *Arte y Vocabulario,* which gives Eudeva grammar and vocabulary collected by an unknown seventeenth-century Jesuit missionary. Pennington (pp. 16–17, 39) is uncertain as to the closeness of Opata proper and Eudeva.

7. Kroeber, *Handbook,* p. 803.

8. A discussion of Hokan languages, including the Yuman-Seri languages, can be found in Jacobsen, "Hokan Inter-Branch Comparisons," pp. 545–547. See also Langdon, "Some Thoughts on Hokan"; and Kendall, "Yuman Languages." However, Goddard, "Classification," p. 320, has called for "extensive reexamination and evaluation" of the core Hokan complex. See also Campbell and Mithun, introduction to *The Languages of Native America,* p. 42.

9. Bannon, *Spanish Borderlands Frontier,* pp. 57–62.

10. Riley, *Frontier People,* pp. 137–138. The variations of Zuni and Hopi names can be found in ibid., pp. 182–183.

11. For a discussion of various Pueblo group designations see Castañeda, *Relación,* fols. 115–116. For an indication that Spaniards under Coronado had actually reached the Manso area see Riley, *Rio del Norte,* p. 166.

12. In 1630 Benavides goes further, stating that the Pecos Indians were "part of the Hemes [Jemez] nation, and even though they speak the same language, they are considered a distinct people" (Forrestal and Lynch, *Benavides' Memorial,* p. 23).

13. Hale and Harris, "Historical Linguistics," pp. 170–173. See also Davis, "Kiowa-Tanoan, Keresan, and Zuni," esp. pp. 400–412. The Kiowa-Tanoan link was first suggested in 1910 by Harrington, "Phonetic and Lexical Resemblances." See also Miller, "Note on Kiowa."

14. Riley, *Frontier People,* p. 138. Two decades after Escobar, the missionary Zárate Salmerón contributed a variant name, *Ozara,* and stated that the group extended throughout the whole Gila Valley. For these group names see Hammond and Rey, *Oñate,* 2:1020 (Escobar); and Riley, *Frontier People,* p. 138 (Zárate Salmerón).

15. Consideration of the two major models of Uto-Aztecan can be found in Hill, "Proto-Uto-Aztecan." Hill favors the south-to-north model. For a good general summary of this important language family see Miller, "Uto-Aztecan Languages."

16. For Apachean linguistics see Young, "Apachean Languages."

17. The situation with the early plains groups is discussed in Riley, "Teya Indians," pp. 320–323 (Querecho), 324–332 (Teya-Jumano). For the latter language group see also Hickerson, "Jumano: The Missing Link," p. 12; and Hickerson, *The Jumano,* p. 221.

18. For languages in the general Conchos area and the Rio Grande drainage from Piro country to La Junta see Griffen, "Southern Periphery: East"; and Campbell, "Coahuiltecans." I have suggested elsewhere that *Patarabueye* perhaps meant "ox footed" (Riley, *Frontier People,* p. 294). David Snow (personal communication) thinks that it might be from "patear a bueyes," meaning something like "ox kickers."

19. My ideas about the linguistic affiliations of Jumano, Manso, Suma, and Tompiro are discussed in Riley, "Teya Indians," pp. 333–334; see also Riley, *Rio del Norte,* pp. 191–192.

20. Beckett and Corbett, *Manso Indians,* pp. 32–37. Also see Troike, "Amotomanco," p. 240; and Beckett, "Historic Relationships," pp. 163–165.

21. C. F. Schaafsma, "Ethnohistoric Groups," pp. 89–93. For my own suggestions about Casas Grandes see Schaafsma and Riley, "Analysis and Conclusion," p. 246.

22. Kroeber, *Uto-Aztecan Languages,* p. 14 says, "It can be inferred that Concho was a distinct language within the Co-Op-Tar group, [most] closely related to Opata and perhaps most different from Tarahumar." See Sauer, *Aboriginal Tribes and Languages,* pp. 59–62. For the idea that Concho may have been the original Casas Grandes peoples see p. 62. See also Griffen, "Southern Periphery: East," p. 330; and Griffen, *Indian Assimilation,* pp. 133–134.

23. See Phillips, "Prehistory of Chihuahua," pp. 389–390.

24. See additional discussion of this problem in chap. 9 herein.

25. Turner, *Dentition of Casas Grandes,* pp. 229–233. Additional information about provenience comes in a personal communication from Christy Turner. Also see C. F. Schaafsma, "Ethnohistoric Groups," p. 92.
26. Hill, "Proto Uto-Aztecan," pp. 925–926.
27. Riley, *Rio del Norte,* pp. 99–103.
28. Jelinek, *Prehistoric Sequence,* pp. 159–164.
29. Riley, *Rio del Norte,* pp. 101–103.
30. Snow, personal communication; and Snow, "Transition from History to Prehistory." See also Snow, "Prologue," pp. 126–129; and Snow, "Upland Prehistoric Maize Agriculture," pp. 74–75.
31. Hickerson, "Ethnogenesis," pp. 76–82; and Hickerson, "Kiowa," pp. 158–160.

## Chapter 11. The New Order

1. I am indebted to conversations with David Wilcox, who is quantifying these changes as part of his important ongoing work on major demographic trends in the Greater Southwest. See also Duff, "Process of Migration," pp. 41–43.
2. See Redfield, *Peasant Society,* chap. 3.
3. For decline in the Pueblo Southwest see Upham, *Politics and Power,* pp. 199–202; and Dean et al., "Adaptive Stress," pp. 64, 69–70. Of all the subregions of Aztlan only the Serrana was likely to have been increasing in population (see Doolittle, *Pre-Hispanic Occupance,* pp. 36–43). The lower Colorado River region was also heavily populated at first Spanish contact, but we simply do not have sufficient demographic data from archaeology to say what were the population trends.
4. For a discussion of Viking contacts see Morison, *European Discovery of America,* 1:32–78.
5. See Menzies, *1421.* There are many other theories of contact, and a vast literature on the subject has developed. See, e.g., Riley et al. *Man Across the Sea;* and Sorenson and Raish, *Pre-Columbian Contact.*
6. For early Spanish contact with the New World see Riley, *Kachina and the Cross,* pp. 2–8.
7. There are many good accounts of the conquest of Mexico by Cortés. One of the more readable and detailed accounts

is Thomas, *Conquest.* The personality of Motecuhzoma II is discussed in Brundage, *Rain of Darts,* pp. 253–263, the events surrounding Motecuhzoma's death on pp. 274–276. Brundage considers it probable that the Spaniards murdered Motecuhzoma (see. pp. 275–276).

8. For discussion of the smallpox epidemic and its demographic effects, as it reached the Aztecs and other central Mexican groups, see Thomas, *Conquest,* pp. 443–446, 451, 592–593. For further comments on the ravages of smallpox among the Aztecs and other parts of native America see Diamond, *Guns, Germs, and Steel,* pp. 210–212.
9. Riley, *Rio del Norte,* pp. 149–150.
10. For a discussion of the Spaniards' first reports on the Southwest and the mythology they built around this information see Riley, "Spaniards in Aztlan," pp. 236–237.
11. See Flint and Flint, *Documents of the Coronado Expedition,* pt. 1, chap. 1; see also Castañeda, *Relación,* fols. 7–8.
12. For an idealized picture of Mendoza's mission see Von Habsburg, *Charles V,* pp. 188–189.
13. For a discussion of Zumárraga see Padden, *Hummingbird and the Hawk,* pp. 242–245.
14. Lafaye, *Quetzalcoatl and Guadalupe,* pp. 30–37.
15. The classic account in English is Prescott, *Conquest of Peru,* first published in 1847, with many editions since that time.
16. As pointed out in chap. 9n5, there are two major accounts of the Cabeza de Vaca expedition, the *Relación* (sometimes called *Naufragios*) and the *Joint Report,* compiled jointly by the three Spanish members of the party. *Relación* was published in 1542 and 1555, and a number of newer Spanish language transcriptions have appeared. For an English translation see Hodge, *Spanish Explorers,* the portion that deals with Sonora appearing on pp. 105–126. The *Joint Report* is known only from its inclusion of the massive work by Gonzalo Fernández de Oviedo y Valdes, *Historia general.* For both an English translation and the original Spanish text see Hedrick and Riley, *Journey.* The Sonoran portions are included on

pp. 59–80 (English text) and pp. 143–163 (Spanish text).

17. For Cortés's activity in the Pacific see Morison, *European Discovery of America*, 2:617–624.

18. For Soto's expedition see Riley, *Rio del Norte*, p. 151, and Ewen, "Coronado's Contemporary," pp. 117–120. Kessell, *Spain in the Southwest*, pp. 22–23, points out that Cabeza de Vaca, recently returned to Spain, had bid for leadership of the Florida expedition, suggesting that kindness and good treatment be the conquest tactics employed. This novel approach to Indians was not well received, and in any case Soto had already been given the coveted position.

19. See Hartmann, "Pathfinder"; and Hartmann and Flint, "Before the Coronado Expedition."

20. Riley, *Rio del Norte*, pp 152–154. The route of Marcos de Niza is much disputed. Historians Richard and Shirley Cushing Flint (personal communication), as a result of their extensive scholarly reexamination of the various Coronado documents, think that a Sonora Valley route for Marcos better fits the interspacing of despoblados with other features as described in the documents. I remain unconvinced of this. The Sonoran landscape is exceedingly various, and the descriptions have a low level of specificity. To my mind, they could fit any one of several alternate routes.

21. Rodeck, "Cíbola," pp. 106–107, argues vigorously for K'aikima as the "city" seen by Marcos.

22. Flint, "What's Missing," pp. 57–80. For a count of animals see Riley, introduction to *Coronado Expedition*, p. 6.

23. For Díaz's account see Hammond and Rey, *Narratives*, pp. 157–161.

24. For most of the sixteenth century, dates given are in the Julian calendar, which at that time ran about 10 days behind the actual seasons of the sidereal year. Alarcón's late August would be early September in the corrected Gregorian calendar, but this calendar was not introduced until the 1580s.

25. See Flint and Flint, *Documents of the Coronado Expedition,* for translation and transcription of the Italian version of the

Alarcón account (the Spanish original has been lost). A savage rebellion in the Guadalajara region (the Mixtón War) broke out in 1541, and all Spanish attention was directed to that region. It probably would not have mattered, for a return to the lower Colorado River by Alarcón could not have helped Coronado.

26. For a discussion of Coronado's relationship to the Sonoran area see Riley, *Rio del Norte*, pp. 156–158, 206–207.

27. For the route of Coronado from Sonora to Zuni see Riley, "Coronado in the Southwest," pp. 148, 150–151. Richard and Shirley C. Flint have informed me of a recent discovery of a horseshoe with attached nails, characteristic of the Coronado period. This shoe, possibly still on the horse when the animal was killed, was found in the area near Douglas, Arizona, east of the upper San Pedro Valley. It could have been lost by the Díaz party, by Coronado's vanguard, or by his main party, either coming to the upper Southwest or returning. Alternatively, it was perhaps associated with Spaniards fleeing the fiasco at Corazones, or with a small group led by Juan Gallego, men who were pushing northward to meet Coronado in 1542, when he met the commander somewhere in southern Arizona. Alternatively, the attribution may be in error, the shoe possibly belonging to a later Spanish period.

28. The Zuni anthropologist Edmund Ladd believed that the Zuni people were involved in the eight-day solstice ceremony celebrated at Ko:thluwala:wa, the sacred lake near the junction of the Zuni and Little Colorado rivers. At this time of year no one was supposed to cross the path of the pilgrims going to and from the lake. Part of the hostilities (of course totally misunderstood by the Spaniards) was triggered by a Zuni attempt to scare the newcomers off the trail. See Ladd, "Zuni on the Day," pp. 230–231.

29. Riley, *Rio del Norte*, pp. 162–163.

30. The Díaz story is told in Riley, *Rio del Norte*, p. 162.

31. For identifications of Arenal, Coofor, and Moho see Riley, "Puaray and Coronado's Tiguex," pp. 203–210. See also Riley, *Rio del Norte*, p. 170.

32. Riley, *Rio del Norte*, pp. 173–181.

33. For an indication of the high drama of these events see ibid., chap. 13, "Turk and the Pecos Plot."

34. See ibid., pp. 199–207, 212–215.

35. Ibid., pp. 226–227.

36. Actually, one of the three missionaries, Juan de Santa María, had attempted to leave the region while the Chamuscado party was exploring the edge of the Great Plains and was killed probably by the Piro. The two other missionaries, Rodríguez and Francisco López, chose to remain at Puaray in spite of Chamuscado's doubts as to the wisdom of such a move. See Riley, *Rio del Norte*, pp. 231–233. For identification of Puaray with Arenal, and a suggestion that the missionaries may have chosen this site because it was the scene of a massacre, see Riley, "Puaray and Coronado's Tiguex," pp. 209–210. A discussion of the Chamuscado expedition can be found in Riley, *Rio del Norte*, 227–233.

37. For the Espejo expedition see Riley, *Rio del Norte*, pp. 233–239. Later contact with the Querechos is discussed by Riley, *Kachina and the Cross*, p. 81; for the suggestion that the town with 15 plazas was a Navajo town perhaps somewhere north of Acoma see p. 82. However, C. F. Schaafsma, *Apaches de Navajo*, p. 222, doubts that any such town ever existed.

38. A description of Espejo's return voyage is given in Hammond and Rey, *Rediscovery of New Mexico*, pp. 206–212 (Luxán), pp. 229–231 (Espejo).

39. For an account of Castaño de Sosa see the highly annotated publication by Schroeder and Matson, *Colony on the Move*. See also Riley, *Rio del Norte*, pp. 242–244.

40. This is an approximation of the word *poxwoge*, as given by Edelman, "San Ildefonso Pueblo," p. 315. In the Oñate period the native Pueblo name was rendered as *Bove*, a word of uncertain derivation. See F. W. Hodge, "Pueblo Names in the Oñate Documents," 1:364.

41. The Gutiérrez de Humaña and Leyva de Bonilla expedition is discussed in Riley, *Rio del Norte*, pp. 245–246. The brief account is contained in Hammond and Rey, *Rediscovery of New Mexico*, pp. 323–326.

42. For the Oñate expedition see Riley, *Kachina and the Cross*, pp. 37–49, 75–88. Most of the extant Oñate documents have been translated and published in the two volumes of Hammond and Rey, *Oñate*.

43. Even this may have been an incomplete count. See Snow, "New Mexico's First Colonists," p. 3.

44. Riley, *Kachina and the Cross*, p. 75.

45. For the attack on Acoma see ibid., pp. 79–81. Salaz Marquez, *New Mexico*, pp. 27–28, suggests that "puntas de pie," which he translates as "toes," were the actual appendages removed. However, the two separate documents in the case are quite unequivocal that feet were cut off (nor do the words "puntas de pie" appear). I suppose that it is possible, as John Kessell, *Spain in the Southwest*, p. 84, has suggested, that this was a case where a harsh punishment was ordered by the civil authority, who then allowed the missionaries to override the order. Such a charade was performed by Chamuscado 18 years before Oñate. But Chamuscado fully documented this "missionization" strategy, whereas the rather detailed Oñate documents on the Acoma affair say nothing whatsoever about it. One also wonders why it did not become a factor in Oñate's later trial. After all, he was accused and convicted of excessive severity to Indians taken alive at Acoma.

46. Riley, *Kachina and the Cross*, p. 81.

47. Ibid., pp. 83–88.

48. For the various documents on the end of the Oñate regime and the founding of Santa Fe by his successor, Pedro de Peralta, see Hammond and Rey, *Oñate*, 2: 1056–1108; see also Simmons, *Last Conquistador*, pp. 178–195; and Riley, *Kachina and the Cross*, pp. 92–95.

49. Riley, *Kachina and the Cross*, pp. 142–143.

50. Ibid., p. 201.

51. See Riley, *Rio del Norte*, pp. 261–265; and Knaut, *Pueblo Revolt of 1680*, pp. 72–87.

52. For Spanish casualties see Riley, *Kachina and the Cross*, pp. 115, 224, 252. For

other views of the revolt see the various papers in Preucel, *Archaeologies*.

53. Underhill, *The Navajos*, pp. 41–57. As was fashionable a half century ago, Ruth Underhill thought in terms of post-Spanish Navajo-Pueblo interaction. In my opinion, as argued in this book, much of this borrowing came in prehistoric times.

54. Brew, "History of Awatovi," p. 18.

## Chapter 12. Aftermath

1. For a discussion of the early period of exploration, perhaps the classic source is Morison, *European Discovery of America*.

2. Riley, *Rio del Norte*, p. 148. Clendinnen, "Cortés and Conquest," pp. 78–79, points to the Aztec desire to capture rather than to kill their Spanish enemies as a severe tactical disadvantage in the struggle for Tenochtitlan.

3. Thomas, *Conquest*, p. 601.

4. Ibid., appendix I.

5. Zurita [Zorita], *Relación*, p. 162. Zurita's estimate falls in a kind of midrange between those of the extremes of modern demographic minimalists and maximalists.

6. They did, of course, have the *quipu*, a complicated calculating device with various colored strings projecting from a central rod. Its computational use is still not fully understood, but the quipu could be used for keeping track of land, people and animals, produce, trade items, etc. in quite complicated ways.

7. See Stern, *Peru's Indian Peoples*, p. 10.

8. Métraux, *History*, p. 52.

9. An excellent description of Inca life and society is given in Rowe, "Inca Culture." For political organization see specifically pp. 257–274. Rowe very competently summarizes early writers such as Bernabé Cobo, Pedro Cieza de León, and "El Inca," Garcilaso de la Vega.

10. Rowe, "Inca Culture," p. 209, comments that "if Pizarro had arrived a year later, he would have found Atahuallpa in full possession of all of Huayna Capac's power, Huascar's cause forgotten, and a political situation much less favorable to outside interference than he found in 1532." For a detailed discussion of the political situation and Spanish-Inca military maneuvers in 1532 see Prescott, *Conquest of Peru*, 1:245–299. For a very

readable unfolding of the Pizarro story, somewhat simplified and for a younger audience, see Marrin, *Inca and Spaniard*, esp. chaps. 3 and 4. However, these authors and virtually every other expert on the Spanish conquest of Peru ignore or vastly underplay the role of Indian allies. Modeling his conquest on that of his cousin, Hernán Cortés, Pizarro utilized Indians from the beginning. He had collected native boys to serve as interpreters several years before the major attack on the Peruvian highlands. During the conquest native peoples served in several capacities, including that of warrior. See Cieza de León, *Conquest of Peru*, pp. 126, 128, 153–154, 176–177, 181, 198, 271–273, 298–299, 399–402.

11. See Stern, *Peru's Indian Peoples*, pp. 20–26, 28–35. It is clear that many of the subordinate peoples in the Inca Empire were restless and dissatisfied. Even in the Inca stronghold of Cuzco there was a very large exploited "plebeian" population of conquered peoples. They could not be expected to fight enthusiastically for the Inca. See Katz, "Comparison," pp. 206–207.

12. Charles Di Peso once told me that at some point in his Casas Grandes research he had run across an old Opata woman who still spoke the language. However, that would have been in the mid-twentieth century, and I imagine that the language is now extinct. Miller, "Uto-Aztecan Languages," p. 121, considers Opata to have become extinct by the 1960s.

13. Riley, "Pre-Spanish Camino Real," p. 19.

14. Deeds, *Defiance and Deference*, pp. 86–87.

15. See Riley, "Southern Tepehuan."

16. Of course, this success varies, with the Eastern Pueblos maintaining a peasant and much-adulterated Christianity, alongside of and to some extent interdigitated with the "old religion." This is far less true in the west, especially at Hopi, where the mission period, with its enforced Christianity, lasted for only about a half century. However, see Suina, "Persistence of the Corn Mothers," 214–215. Suina, who is a Cochiti native, seems to think that Christianity in the Eastern Pueblos was mainly a pretense, adapting the new ceremonial calendar to fit the native reli-

gion. The Eastern Pueblos were, then, "Christian" to the Franciscans but in their own minds believers in the Puebloan deities and rituals.

17. Carrasco, "Central Mexican Highlands," pp. 598–600, points out that a number of the old gods, Quetzalcoatl, Tezcatlipoca, Tonantzin, among them, have been identified with saints or with the Virgin Mary. See also Madsen, "The Nahua," pp. 627–628, for the Tonantzin identification with the Virgin of Guadalupe. This is basically the same sort of syncretism that took place in northern Europe when Christianity first penetrated there and for which there are many examples, especially in the "traditional saints."

18. For a modern revival of Casas Grandes pottery see Johnson, *From Paquimé to Mata Ortiz,* 37–54.

19. Although it is similar in form and function to aboriginal coral, the coral used by modern Indian jewelers, as I understand it, is generally some variety of "true" Mediterranean coral. Prehistoric southwestern coral was from *Chama echinata,* a Sinaloan coastal bivalve.

20. Hotz, *Indian Skin Paintings,* p. 27.

# References

Adams, E. C.

1981 "The View from the Hopi Mesas." In *The Protohistoric Period in the North American Southwest, AD 1450–1700*, ed. D. R. Wilcox and W. B. Masse, pp. 321–335. Anthropological Research Papers No. 24. Arizona State University, Tempe.

1989 "The Case for Conflict During the Late Prehistoric and Protohistoric Periods in the Western Pueblo Area of the American Southwest." In *Cultures in Conflict: Current Archaeological Perspectives: Proceedings of the 20th Annual Conference of the Chacmool Archaeological Association*, ed. D. C. Tkaczuk and B. C. Vivian, pp. 103–111. University of Calgary, Calgary, Alberta.

1991 "Homol'ovi II in the 14th Century." In *Homol'ovi II: Archaeology of an Ancestral Hopi Village, Arizona*, ed. E. C. Adams and K. A. Hays, pp. 116–121. University of Arizona Press, Tucson.

1991 *The Origin and Development of the Pueblo Katsina Cult.* University of Arizona Press, Tucson.

1994 "The Katsina Cult: A Western Pueblo Perspective." In *Kachinas in the Pueblo World*, ed. P. Schaafsma, pp. 35–46. University of New Mexico Press, Albuquerque.

1998 "Late Prehistory in the Middle Little Colorado River Area: A Regional Perspective." In *Migration and Reorganization: The Pueblo IV Period in the American Southwest*, ed. K. A. Spielmann, pp. 53–63. Anthropological

Research Papers No. 51. Arizona State University, Tempe.

2000 "Salado: The View from the Colorado Plateau." In *Salado*, ed. J. S. Dean, pp. 263–274. Amerind Foundation, Dragoon, AZ, and University of New Mexico Press, Albuquerque.

2002 *Homol'ovi: An Ancient Hopi Settlement Cluster.* University of Arizona Press, Tucson.

2004 "Homol'ovi: A 13th–14th-Century Settlement Cluster in Northeastern Arizona." In *The Protohistoric Pueblo World, A.D. 1275–1600*, ed. E. C. Adams and A. I. Duff, pp. 119–127. University of Arizona Press, Tucson.

Adler, M. A.

1996 "'The Great Period': The Pueblo World During the Pueblo III Period, A.D. 1150–1350." In *The Prehistoric Pueblo World, A.D. 1150–1350*, ed. M. A. Adler, pp. 1–10. University of Arizona Press, Tucson.

Adler, M. A., and A. Johnson, comps.

1996 "Mapping the Puebloan Southwest." In *The Prehistoric Pueblo World, A.D. 1150–1350*, ed. M. A. Adler, pp. 255–272. University of Arizona Press, Tucson.

Adorno, R., and P. C. Pautz

1999 *Álvar Núñez Cabeza de Vaca.* 3 vols. University of Nebraska Press, Lincoln.

Ahlstrom, R. V. N., C. R. Van West, and J. S. Dean

1995 "Environmental and Chronological Factors in the Mesa Verde–Northern Rio

Grande Migration." *Journal of Anthropological Archaeology,* Vol. 14, no. 2, pp. 125–142.

Akins, N. J.

2001   "Chaco Canyon Mortuary Practices: Archaeological Correlates of Complexity." In *Ancient Burial Practices in the American Southwest,* ed. D. R. Mitchell and J. L. Brunson-Hadley, pp. 167–190. University of New Mexico Press, Albuquerque.

Amsden, M.

1928   *Archaeological Reconnaissance in Sonora.* Southwest Museum Papers No. 1. Southwest Museum, Los Angeles.

Anyon, R., and S. A. LeBlanc

1984   *The Galaz Ruin: A Prehistoric Mimbres Village in Southwestern New Mexico.* Maxwell Museum of Anthropology and University of New Mexico Press, Albuquerque.

Arnold, P. J., III

2003   "Back to Basics: The Middle Range Program as Pragmatic Archaeology." In *Essential Tensions in Archaeological Method and Theory,* ed. T. L. VanPool and C. S. VanPool, pp. 55–66. University of Utah Press, Salt Lake City.

Arnon, N. S., and W. W. Hill

1979   "Santa Clara Pueblo." In *Southwest,* ed. A. Ortiz, pp. 296–307. Handbook of North American Indians, Vol. 9, William C. Sturtevant, general editor, Smithsonian Institution, Washington, DC.

Bagwell, E. A.

2003   *The Production of Architectural Artifacts: An Analysis of Cliff-Dwellings in the Northern Sierra Occidental, Sonora, Mexico.* Informe al Consejo de Arqueología Instituto Nacional de Antropología e Historia, México, DF.

Ball, S. H.

1941   *The Mining of Gems and Ornamental Stones by American Indians.* Bureau of American Ethnology Bull. No. 128, Anthropological Papers 13. Smithsonian Institution, Washington, DC.

Bandelier, A. F.

1990   *Final Report of Investigations Among the Indians of the Southwestern United States, Part I.* Papers of the Archaeological Institute of America, American Series III, Cambridge, MA.

1992   *Final Report of Investigations Among the Indians of the Southwestern United States, Part II.* Papers of the Archaeological Institute of America, American Series IV, Cambridge, MA.

Bannon, J. F.

1970   *The Spanish Borderlands Frontier, 1513–1821.* Holt, Rinehart, and Winston, New York.

Beals, R. L.

1932   *The Comparative Ethnology of Northern Mexico Before 1750.* University of California Press, Berkeley.

1933   *The Acaxee, a Mountain Tribe of Durango and Sinaloa.* University of California Press, Berkeley.

1943   "Relations Between Meso America and the Southwest." In *El norte de Mexico y el sur de Estados Unitos,* pp. 245–252. Tercera Reunión de Mesa Redonda, Sociedad Mexicana de Antropología, Castillo de Chapultepec, México.

Beck, M.

2001   "Archaeological Signatures of Corn Preparation in the U.S. Southwest." *Kiva,* Vol. 67, no. 2, pp. 187–218.

Beckett, P. H.

1994   "Historic Relationships to Prehistoric Populations." In *Mogollon VII: The Collected Papers of the 1992 Mogollon Conference Held in Las Cruces, New Mexico,* ed. P. H. Beckett, pp. 163–165. COAS Publishing and Research, Las Cruces, NM.

Beckett, P. H., and T. L. Corbett

1992   *The Manso Indians.* COAS Publishing and Research, Las Cruces, NM.

Beckett, P. H., and R. S. MacNeish

1994   "The Archaic Chihuahua Tradition of South-Central New Mexico and Chihuahua, Mexico." In *Archaic Hunter-Gatherer Archaeology in the American Southwest,* ed. B. J. Vierra, pp. 335–371. Contributions in Anthropology, Vol. 13, no. 1, Eastern New Mexico University, Portales.

Benson, L., L. Cordell, K. Vincent, H. Taylor, J. Stein, G. L. Farmer, and K. Futa

2003   "Ancient Maize from Chacoan Great Houses: Where Was It Grown?"

*Proceedings of the National Academy of Sciences,* Vol. 100, no. 22, Oct., pp. 13,111–13,115.

Bernardini, W.
1999 "Reassessing the Scale of Social Action at Pueblo Bonito, Chaco Canyon, New Mexico." *Kiva,* Vol. 64, no. 4, pp. 447–470.

Bernardini, W., and G. M. Brown
2004 "The Formation of Settlement Clusters on Anderson Mesa." In *The Protohistoric Pueblo World, A.D. 1275–1600,* ed. E. C. Adams and A. I. Duff, pp. 108–118. University of Arizona Press, Tucson.

Bertram, J. B., A. R. Gomolak, S. R. Hoaglund, T. L. Knight, E. Garber, and K. L. Ford
1990 *Excavations in the South Room Block of Gallinas Springs Ruin (LA1178).* Submitted to USDA Forest Service, Cibola National Forest, Chambers Group, Albuquerque.

Blakeslee, D. L., D. K. Boyd, R. Flint, J. Habicht-Mauche, N. P. Hickerson, J. T. Hughes, and C. L. Riley
2003 "Bison Hunters of the Llano in 1541: A Panel Discussion." In *The Coronado Expedition: From the Distance of 460 Years,* ed. R. Flint and S. C. Flint, pp. 164–186. University of New Mexico Press, Albuquerque.

Bodine, J. J.
1979 "Taos Pueblo." In *Southwest,* ed. A. Ortiz, pp. 255–267. Handbook of North American Indians, Vol. 9, William C. Sturtevant, general editor, Smithsonian Institution, Washington, DC.

Bradley, R. J.
1999 "Shell Exchange Within the Southwest." In *The Casas Grandes World,* ed. C. F. Schaafsma and C. L. Riley, pp. 213–228. University of Utah Press, Salt Lake City.
2000 "Networks of Shell Ornament Exchange: A Critical Assessment of Prestige Economies in the North American Southwest." In *The Archaeology of Regional Interaction: Religion, Warfare, and Exchange Across the American Southwest and Beyond,* ed. M. Hegmon, pp. 167–187. University Press of Colorado, Boulder.
2000 "Recent Advances in Chihuahuan Archaeology." In *Greater Mesoamerica:*

*The Archaeology of West and Northwest Mexico,* ed. M. S. Foster and S. Gorenstein, pp. 221–239. University of Utah Press, Salt Lake City.

Brand, D. D.
1943 "The Chihuahua Culture Area." *New Mexico Anthropologist,* Vol. 6–7, no. 3, pp. 115–158. Department of Anthropology, University of New Mexico, Albuquerque.
1973 "Aboriginal Trade Routes for Sea Shells in the Southwest." In *The Classic Southwest,* ed. B. C. Hedrick, J. C. Kelley, and C. L. Riley, pp. 92–101 [corrected by Brand from his original 1938 publication], Southern Illinois University Press, Carbondale.

Braniff, C., B.
1978 "Preliminary Interpretations Regarding the Role of the San Miguel River, Sonora, Mexico." In *Across the Chichimec Sea: Papers in Honor of J. Charles Kelley,* ed. C. L. Riley and B. C. Hedrick, pp. 67–82. Southern Illinois University Press, Carbondale.
1986 "Ojo de Agua, Sonora, and Casas Grandes, Chihuahua: A Suggested Chronology." In *Ripples in the Chichimec Sea,* ed. F. J. Mathien and R. H. McGuire, pp. 70–80 Southern Illinois University Press, Carbondale.
1990 "The Identification of Possible Elites in Prehispanic Sonora." In *Perspectives on Southwestern History,* ed. P. E. Minnis and C. L. Redman, pp. 173–183. Westview Press, Boulder, CO.
1994 "The Opata-Pima Frontier: Preliminary Notes and Comments." In *The Gran Chichimeca: Essays on the Archaeology and Ethnohistory of Northern Mesoamerica,* ed. J. E. Reyman, pp. 252–268. Avebury, Ashgate Publishing, Aldershot, UK.
1999 "Paquimé: The Roots of a New Ceramic Tradition." *Ceramica de Mata Ortiz,* Artes de Mexico, Vol. 45, pp. 82–83.

Breternitz, D. A.
1982 "The Four Corners Anasazi Ceramic Tradition." In *Southwestern Ceramics: A Comparative Review,* ed. A. H. Schroeder, pp. 129–148. Arizona Archaeologist No. 15. Arizona Archaeological Society, Phoenix.

Brew, J. O.

1943 "On the Pueblo IV and on the Katchina-Tlaloc Relations." In *El norte de Mexico y el sur de Estados Unitos*, pp. 241–245. Tercera Reunión de Mesa Redonda, Castillo de Chapultepec, México.

1949 "The History of Awatovi." In *Franciscan Awatovi*, by R. G. Montgomery, W. Smith, and J. O. Brew, pp. 1–43. Papers of the Peabody Museum of American Archaeology and Ethnology Vol. 36. Harvard University, Cambridge, MA.

Brody, J. J.

1977 *Mimbres Painted Pottery.* School of American Research, Santa Fe, and University of New Mexico Press, Albuquerque.

Brown, G. M.

1990 "Nuvakwewtaqa and the Chavez Pass Region: An Overview." In *Technological Change in the Chavez Pass Region, North-Central Arizona*, ed. G. M. Brown, pp. 5–19. Anthropological Research Papers No. 41. Arizona State University, Tempe.

1996 "The Protohistoric Transition in the Northern San Juan Region." In *The Archaeology of Navajo Origins*, ed. R. H. Towner, pp. 47–69. University of Utah Press, Salt Lake City.

Brugge, D. M.

1983 "Navajo Prehistory and History to 1850." In *Southwest*, ed. A. Ortiz, pp. 489–501. Handbook of North American Indians, Vol. 10, William C. Sturtevant, general editor, Smithsonian Institution, Washington, DC.

1996 "Navajo Archaeology: A Promising Past." In *The Archaeology of Navajo Origins*, ed. R. H. Towner, pp. 255–271. University of Utah Press, Salt Lake City.

Brugge, D. M., and D. Gilpin

2000 "Navajo Ritual Histories, Organization, and Architecture." In *The Archaeology of Regional Interaction: Religion, Warfare, and Exchange Across the American Southwest and Beyond*, ed. M. Hegmon, pp. 361–379. University Press of Colorado, Boulder.

Bruman, H. J.

2000 *Alcohol in Ancient Mexico.* University of Utah Press, Salt Lake City.

Brundage, B. C.

1972 *A Rain of Darts: The Mexica Aztecs.* University of Texas Press, Austin.

1982 *The Phoenix of the Western World.* University of Oklahoma Press, Norman.

Bushnell, G. H. S.

1955 "Some Pueblo IV Pottery Types from Kechipaun, New Mexico, U.S.A." *31st Congreso Internacional de Americanistas*, 2:657–665. São Paulo, Brazil.

Cabebe, T. E.

2002 "Site Aggregation and the Archaeological Record of Tecolote Pueblo (LA 296), 1917–2000." Unpublished master's thesis, Department of Anthropology, New Mexico Highlands University, Las Vegas.

Cabeza de Vaca, A. N.

1555 *La Relación y comentarios.* Published in Valladolid, Spain. Modern editions of this work normally call it *Naufragios* [see next entry].

1944 *Naufragios . . . y Relación de la Jornada que Hizo a la Florida.* Editorial Layac, México, DF.

Cameron, C. M.

1995 "Migration and the Movement of Southwestern Peoples." *Journal of Anthropological Archaeology*, Vol. 14, no. 2, pp. 104–124.

2000 "Organization of Production, Chaco Synthesis Project." *Archaeology Southwest*, Vol. 14, no. 1, pp. 8–11.

Campbell, L.

1986 Comments on *The Settlement of the Americas*, by J. H. Greenberg, C. G. Turner II, and S. L. Zegura. *Current Anthropology*, Vol. 27, no. 5, pp. 477–497.

Campbell, L., and M. Mithun

1979 Introduction to *The Languages of Native America*, ed. L. Campbell and M. Mithun, pp. 3–69. University of Texas Press, Austin.

Campbell, T. N.

1983 "Coahuiltecans and Their Neighbors." In *Southwest*, ed. A. Ortiz, pp. 343–358. Handbook of North American Indians, Vol. 10, William C. Sturtevant, general editor, Smithsonian Institution, Washington, DC.

Cannon, M. D.

2003 "A Model of Central Place Forager Prey Choice and an Application to Faunal Remains from the Mimbres Valley, New Mexico." *Journal of Anthropological Archaeology,* Vol. 22, pp. 1–25.

Carey, H. A.

1931 "An Analysis of the Northwestern Chihuahua Culture." *American Anthropologist,* Vol. 33, no. 3, pp. 325–374.

Carlson, R. L.

1970 *White Mountain Redware: A Pottery Tradition of East-Central Arizona and Western New Mexico.* University of Arizona Press, Tucson.

1982 "The Mimbres Kachina Cult." In *Mogollon Archaeology: Proceedings of the 1980 Mogollon Conference,* ed. P. H. Beckett and K. Silverbird, pp. 147–155. Acoma Books, Ramona, CA.

Carpenter, J. P.

1996 "El Ombligo en la Labor: Differentiation, Interaction, and Integration in Prehispanic Sinaloa, Mexico." Unpublished PhD dissertation, Department of Anthropology, University of Arizona, Tucson.

2002 "The Animas Phase and Paquimé." In *The Joyce Well Site: On the Frontier of the Casas Grandes World,* ed. J. M. Skibo, E. B. McCluney, and W. H. Walker, pp. 149–166. University of Utah Press, Salt Lake City.

Carpenter, J. P., and G. Sanchez, eds.

1997 *Prehistory of the Borderlands: Recent Research in the Archaeology of Northern Mexico and the Southern Southwest.* Arizona State Museum, University of Arizona, Tucson.

Carrasco, P.

1969 "Central Mexican Highlands: Introduction." In *Ethnology, Part 2,* ed. E. Z. Vogt, pp. 579–601. Handbook of Middle American Indians, Vol. 8, Robert Wauchope, general editor, University of Texas Press, Austin.

Cartledge, T. R.

1979 "Cohonina Adaptation to the Coconino Plateau: A Reevaluation." *Kiva,* Vol. 44, no. 4, pp. 297–317.

Castañeda de Nagera [Najera], P. de

1598 Relación de la jornada de Cibola, donde se trata de aquellos poblados y ritos y costumbres, la qual fué el año de 1540. Manuscript on file, New York Public Library.

Castetter, E. F., and W. H. Bell

1951 *Yuman Indian Agriculture: Primitive Subsistence on the Lower Colorado and Gila Rivers.* University of New Mexico Press, Albuquerque.

Chagoya, E.

2001 "A Lost Continent: Writings Without an Alphabet." In *The Road to Aztlan: Art from a Mythic Homeland,* ed. V. M. Fields and V. Zamudio-Taylor, pp. 262–273. Los Angeles County Museum of Art, Los Angeles, CA.

Chamberlin, M. A.

2002 "Technology, Performance, and Intended Use: Glaze Ware Jars in the Pueblo IV Rio Grande." *Kiva,* Vol. 67, no. 3, pp. 269–296.

Chartkoff, J. L., and K. K. Chartkoff

1984 *The Archaeology of California.* Stanford University Press, Stanford, CA.

Childe, V. G.

1951 *Man Makes Himself.* New American Library, New York.

Cieza de León, P. de

1998 *The Discovery and Conquest of Peru.* Ed. and trans. A. P. Cook and N. D. Cook. Duke University Press, Durham, NC.

Clark, J. J.

2001 *Tracking Prehistoric Migrations: Pueblo Settlers Among the Tonto Basin Hohokam.* University of Arizona Press, Tuson.

Clendinnen, I.

1991 "'Fierce and Unnatural Cruelty': Cortés and the Conquest of Mexico." *Representations,* no. 33, pp. 65–100.

Colton, H. S.

1968 "Frontiers of the Sinagua." *Collected Papers in Honor of Lyndon Lane Hargrave,* ed. A. H. Schroeder, pp. 9–16. Papers of the Archaeological Society of New Mexico No. 1. Museum of New Mexico Press, Santa Fe.

Cordell, L. S.

1979 "Prehistory: Eastern Anasazi." In *Southwest,* ed. A. Ortiz, pp. 131–151. Handbook of North American Indians, Vol. 9, William C. Sturtevant, general editor, Smithsonian Institution, Washington, DC.

1994   *Ancient Pueblo Peoples.* St. Remy Press, Montreal.

1995   "Tracing Migration Pathways from the Receiving End." *Journal of Anthropological Archaeology,* Vol. 14, no. 2, pp. 203–211.

1997   *Archaeology of the Southwest.* 2nd ed. Academic Press, San Diego.

1998   *Before Pecos: Settlement Aggregation at Rowe, New Mexico.* Maxwell Museum of Anthropology Anthropological Papers No. 6. University of New Mexico, Albuquerque.

2000   "Society and Polity, Chaco Synthesis Project." *Archaeology Southwest,* Vol. 14, no. 1, pp. 18–19.

Cordell, L. S., and W. J. Judge

2001   "Perspectives on Chaco Society and Polity." In *Chaco Society and Polity: Papers from the 1999 Conference,* ed. L. S. Cordell, W. J. Judge, and J. Piper, pp. 1–12. New Mexico Archeological Council, Special Pub. 4.

Cosgrove, H. S., and C. B. Cosgrove

1932   *The Swartz Ruin: A Typical Mimbres Site in Southwestern New Mexico.* Papers of the Peabody Museum of American Archaeology and Ethnology Vol. 15, No. 1. Harvard University, Cambridge, MA.

Craddock, J. R.

2002   "La Guerra Justa en Nuevo México en 1598–1599." In *Initium: Revista Catalana D'Història del Dret,* no. 7, pp. 331–359.

Creamer, W.

2000   "Regional Interactions and Regional Systems in the Protohistoric Rio Grande." In *The Archaeology of Regional Interaction: Religion, Warfare, and Exchange Across the American Southwest and Beyond,* ed. M. Hegmon, pp. 99–118. University Press of Colorado, Boulder.

Creel, D. G.

1997   "Interpreting the End of the Mimbres Classic." In *Prehistory of the Borderlands: Recent Research in the Archaeology of Northern Mexico and the Southern Southwest,* ed. J. Carpenter and G. Sanchez, pp. 25–31. Arizona State Museum, University of Arizona, Tucson.

1999   "The Black Mountain Phase in the Mimbres Area." In *The Casas Grandes World,* ed. C. F. Schaafsma and C. L. Riley, pp. 107–120. University of Utah Press, Salt Lake City.

Crotty, H. K.

1995   "Anasazi Mural Art of the Pueblo IV Period, AD 1300–1600." Unpublished PhD dissertation, Department of Art History, University of California, Los Angeles.

Crown, P. L.

1991   "The Hohokam: Current Views of Prehistory and the Regional System." In *Chaco and Hohokam,* ed. P. L. Crown and W. J. Judge, pp. 135–157. School of American Research Press, Santa Fe, NM.

1994   *Ceramics and Ideology: Salado Polychrome Pottery.* University of New Mexico Press, Albuquerque.

1996   "Change in Ceramic Design Style and Technology in the Thirteenth- to Fourteenth-Century Southwest." In *Interpreting Southwestern Diversity,* ed. P. R. Fish and J. J. Reid, pp. 241–247. Anthropological Research Papers No. 48. Arizona State University, Tempe.

Crown, P. L., and R. L. Bishop

1991   "Manufacture of Gila Polychrome in the Greater American Southwest: An Instrumental Neutron Activation Analysis." In *Homol'ovi II: Archaeology of an Ancestral Hopi Village, Arizona,* ed. E. C. Adams and K. A. Hays, pp. 49–56. University of Arizona Press, Tucson.

Crown, P. L., and W. J. Judge, eds.

1991   *Chaco and Hohokam.* School of American Research Press, Santa Fe, NM.

Crown, P. L., and T. A Kohler

1994   "Community Dynamics, Site Structure, and Aggregation in the Northern Rio Grande." In *The Ancient Southwestern Community,* ed. W. H. Wills and R. D. Leonard, pp. 103–117. University of New Mexico Press, Albuquerque.

Cruz Antillón, R.

1997   "Recientes Investigaciones Arqueológicas en Villa Ahumada, Chihuahua." In *Prehistory of the Borderlands: Recent Research in the Archaeology of Northern Mexico and the Southern Southwest,* ed. J. Carpenter and G. Sanchez, pp. 1–9. Arizona State Museum, University of Arizona, Tucson.

Cruz Antillón, R., R. D. Leonard,
T. D. Maxwell, T. L. VanPool, M. J. Harmon,
C. S. VanPool, D. A. Hyndman, and
S. S. Brandwein
2004 "Galeana, Villa Ahumada, and Casa Chica: Diverse Sites in the Casas Grandes Region." In *Surveying the Archaeology of Northwest Mexico*, ed. G. E. Newell and E. Gallaga, pp. 149–175. University of Utah Press, Salt Lake City.

Cruz Antillón, R., and T. D. Maxwell
1999 "The Villa Ahumada Site: Archaeological Investigations East of Paquimé." In *The Casas Grandes World*, ed. C. F. Schaafsma and C. L. Riley, pp. 43–53. University of Utah Press, Salt Lake City.

Cuevas, M., ed.
1924 *Historia de los descubrimientos antiguos y modernos de la Nueva España, escrita por el conquistador Baltasar de Obregón, año de 1584*, Departamento Editorial de la Sría, de Educación Pública, México, DF.

Dahlgren, B., and M. D. Soto de Arechavaleta, eds.
1995 *Arqueología del norte y del occidente de México. Homenaje al Doctor J. Charles Kelley*, Universidad Nacional Autónoma de Mexico, México, DF.

Damp, J. E., S. A. Hall, and S. J. Smith
2002 "Early Irrigation on the Colorado Plateau Near Zuni Pueblo, New Mexico." *American Antiquity*, Vol. 67, no. 4, pp. 665–676.

Davis, E. L.
1964 "The Magdalena Problem." Manuscript on file, Laboratory of Anthropology, Santa Fe.

Davis, I.
1979 "The Kiowa-Tanoan, Keresan, and Zuni Languages." In *The Languages of Native America*, ed. L. Campbell and M. Mithun, pp. 390–443. University of Texas Press, Austin.

Day, A. G.
1964 *Coronado's Quest*. University of California Press, Berkeley.

Dean, G.
1995 "In Search of the Rare: Pollen Evidence of Prehistoric Agriculture." In *Soil, Water, Biology, and Belief in Prehistoric and Traditional Southwestern Agriculture*, ed. H. W. Toll, pp. 353–359.

New Mexico Archaeological Council, Special Pub. 2.

Dean, J. S.
1988 "Dendrochronology and Paleoenvironmental Reconstruction on the Colorado Plateaus." In *The Anasazi in a Changing Environment*, ed. G. J. Gumerman, pp. 119–167. Cambridge University Press, Cambridge, UK.

1991 "Thoughts on Hohokam Chronology." In *Exploring the Hohokam: Prehistoric Desert Peoples of the American Southwest*, ed. G. J. Gumerman, pp. 61–149. Amerind Foundation, Dragoon, AZ, and University of New Mexico Press, Albuquerque.

1996 "Demography, Environment, and Subsistence Stress." In *Evolving Complexity and Environmental Risk in the Prehistoric Southwest*, ed. J. A. Tainter and B. B. Tainter, pp. 25–59. Addison-Wesley, Reading, MA.

1996 "Kayenta Anasazi Settlement Transformations in Northeastern Arizona, AD 1150 to 1350." In *The Prehistoric Pueblo World, AD 1150–1350*, ed. M. A. Adler, pp. 29–47. University of Arizona Press, Tucson.

2000 "Introduction: The Salado Phenomenon." In *Salado*, ed. J. S. Dean, pp. 3–16. Amerind Foundation, Dragoon, AZ, and University of New Mexico Press, Albuquerque.

Dean, J. S., W. H. Doelle, and J. D. Orcutt
1994 "Adaptive Stress, Environment, and Demography." In *Themes in Southwestern Prehistory*, ed. G. J. Gumerman, pp. 53–86. School of American Research Press, Santa Fe, NM.

Dean, J. S., and J. C. Ravesloot
1993 "The Chronology of Cultural Interaction in the Gran Chichimeca." In *Culture and Contact: Charles C. Di Peso's Gran Chichimeca*, ed. A. I. Woosley and J. C. Ravesloot, pp. 83–103. Amerind Foundation, Dragoon, AZ, and the University of New Mexico Press, Albuquerque.

DeAtley, S. P.
1980 *Regional Integration on the Northern Casas Grandes Frontier*. University Microfilms, Ann Arbor, MI.

Deeds, S. M.

2003 *Defiance and Deference in Mexico's Colonial North.* University of Texas Press, Austin.

Diamond, J. M.

1999 *Guns, Germs, and Steel: The Fates of Human Societies.* Norton, New York.

Diehl, M. W.

2003 "Three Plants for Three Cultures Through Three Millennia." In *Old Pueblo Archaeology*, pp. 1–5. Bull. No. 32. Old Pueblo Archaeology Center, Tucson, AZ.

Di Peso, C. C.

1968 "Casas Grandes and the Gran Chichimeca." *El Palacio*, Vol. 75, no. 4, pp. 47–61.

1974 *Casas Grandes: A Fallen Trading Center of the Gran Chichimeca.* Vols. 1–3. Amerind Foundation, Dragoon, AZ, and Northland Press, Flagstaff, AZ.

1976 "Gila Polychrome in the Casas Grandes Region." *Kiva*, Vol. 42, no. 1, pp. 57–63.

Di Peso, C. C., J. B. Rinaldo, and G. J. Fenner

1974 *Casas Grandes: A Fallen Trading Center of the Gran Chichimeca.* Vols. 4–8. Amerind Foundation, Dragoon, AZ, and Northland Press, Flagstaff, AZ.

Dirst, V. A.

1979 "The Prehistoric Frontier in Sonora." Unpublished PhD dissertation, Department of Anthropology, University of Arizona, Tucson.

Dockstader, F. J.

1985 *The Kachina and the White Man.* Rev. ed. University of New Mexico Press, Albuquerque. Originally published 1954, Cranbrook Institute of Science, Bloomfield Hills, MI.

Doelle, W. H.

1989 Review of *The Frontier People*, by C. L. Riley, *Kiva*, Vol. 54, no. 2, pp. 165–168.

Doelle, W. H., and H. D. Wallace

1990 "The Transition to History in Pimeria Alta." In *Perspectives on Southwestern Prehistory*, ed. P. E. Minnis and C. L. Redman, pp. 239–257. Westview Press, Boulder, CO.

Dominguez, S.

2002 "Optimal Gardening Strategies: Maximizing the Input and Retention of Water in Prehistoric Gridded Fields in North Central New Mexico." *World Archaeology*, Vol. 34, no. 1, pp. 131–163.

Doolittle, W. E.

1980 "Aboriginal Agricultural Development in the Valley of Sonora, Mexico." *Geographical Review*, Vol. 70, no. 3, pp. 328–342.

1984 "Cabeza de Vaca's Land of Maize: An Assessment of Its Agriculture." *Journal of Historical Geography*, Vol. 10, no. 3, pp. 246–262.

1984 "Settlements and the Development of 'Statelets' in Sonora, Mexico." *Journal of Field Archaeology*, Vol. 11, pp. 13–24.

1988 *Pre-Hispanic Occupance in the Valley of Sonora, Mexico.* University of Arizona Press, Tucson.

1990 *Canal Irrigation in Prehistoric Mexico.* University of Texas Press, Austin.

1993 "Canal Irrigation at Casas Grandes: A Technological and Developmental Assessment of Its Origins." In *Culture and Contact: Charles C. Di Peso's Gran Chichimeca*, ed. A. I. Woosley and J. C. Ravesloot, pp. 133–151. Amerind Foundation, Dragoon, AZ, and University of New Mexico Press, Albuquerque.

Douglas, J. E.

1992 "Distant Sources, Local Contexts: Interpreting Nonlocal Ceramics at Paquimé (Casas Grandes), Chihuahua." *Journal of Anthropological Research*, Vol. 48, no. 1, pp. 1–24.

2000 "Exchanges, Assumptions, and Mortuary Goods in Pre-Paquimé, Chihuahua, Mexico." In *The Archaeology of Regional Interaction: Religion, Warfare, and Exchange Across the American Southwest and Beyond*, ed. M. Hegmon, pp. 189–208. University Press of Colorado, Boulder.

Douglas, J. E., and C. A. Quijada

2004 "Between the Casas Grandes and the Río Sonora Valleys: Chronology and Settlement in the Upper Bavispe Drainage." In *Surveying the Archaeology of Northwest Mexico*, ed. G. E. Newell and E. Gallaga, pp. 93–109. University of Utah Press, Salt Lake City.

Doyel, D. E.

1993 "Interpreting Prehistoric Cultural Diversity in the Arizona Desert." In *Culture and Contact: Charles C. Di Peso's Gran*

*Chichimeca*, ed. A. I. Woosley and J. C. Ravesloot, pp. 39–64. Amerind Foundation, Dragoon, AZ, and University of New Mexico Press, Albuquerque.

1993    "On Rivers and Boundaries in the Phoenix Basin." *Kiva*, Vol. 58, no. 4, pp. 455–474.

Dozier, E. P.
1970    *The Pueblo Indians of North America*. Holt, Rinehart, and Winston, New York.

Driver, H. E., and W. C. Massey
1957    *Comparative Studies of North American Indians*. American Philosophical Society, Philadelphia, PA.

Duff, A. I.
1998    "The Process of Migration in the Late Prehistoric Southwest." In *Migration and Reorganization: The Pueblo IV Period in the American Southwest*, ed. K. A. Spielmann, pp. 31–52. Anthropological Research Papers No. 51. Arizona State University, Tempe.

2000    "Scale, Interaction, and Regional Analysis in Late Pueblo Prehistory." In *The Archaeology of Regional Interaction: Religion, Warfare, and Exchange Across the American Southwest and Beyond*, ed. M. Hegmon, pp. 71–98. University Press of Colorado, Boulder.

2002    *Western Pueblo Identities: Regional Interaction, Migration, and Transformation*. University of Arizona Press, Tucson.

Dunbier, R.
1968    *The Sonoran Desert*. University of Arizona Press, Tucson.

Durán, Fr. D.
1994    *The History of the Indies of New Spain*. Trans. and annot. D. Heyden. University of Oklahoma Press, Norman.

Durant, W.
1954    *Our Oriental Heritage*. Vol. 1 of *The Story of Civilization*. Simon and Schuster, New York.

Dutton, B. P.
1963    *Sun Father's Way*. University of New Mexico Press, Albuquerque.

1964    "Las Madres in the Light of Anasazi Migrations." *American Antiquity*, Vol. 29, no. 4, pp. 449–454.

1983    *American Indians of the Southwest*. University of New Mexico Press, Albuquerque.

Edelman, S. A.
1979    "San Ildefonso Pueblo." In *Southwest*, ed. A. Ortiz, pp. 308–316. Handbook of North American Indians, Vol. 9, William C. Sturtevant, general editor, Smithsonian Institution, Washington, DC.

Eggan, F.
1950    *Social Organization of the Western Pueblos*. University of Chicago Press, Chicago, IL.

Ellis, F. H.
1967    "Where Did the Pueblo People Come From?" *El Palacio*, Vol. 74, no. 3, pp. 35–43.

1976    "Datable Ritual Components Proclaiming Mexican Influence in the Upper Rio Grande of New Mexico." In *Collected Papers in Honor of Marjorie Ferguson Lambert*, ed. A. H. Schroeder, pp. 85–108. Archaeological Society of New Mexico, Albuquerque.

1979    "Isleta Pueblo." In *Southwest*, ed. A. Ortiz, pp. 351–365. Handbook of North American Indians, Vol. 9, William C. Sturtevant, general editor, Smithsonian Institution, Washington, DC.

Ellis, F. H., and L. Hammack
1968    "The Inner Sanctum of Feather Cave." *American Antiquity*, Vol. 33, no. 1, pp. 25–44.

English, N. B., J. L. Betancourt, J. S. Dean, and J. Quade
2001    "Strontium Isotopes Reveal Distant Sources of Architectural Timber in Chaco Canyon, New Mexico." In *Proceedings of the National Academy of Sciences, USA*, Vol. 98, no. 21, 11,891–11,896, Sept. 25, PNAS Online, 11 pp. http://www.pnas.org/cgi/content/full/98/21/11891 (accessed Jan. 7, 2005).

Euler, R. C.
1982    "Ceramic Patterns of the Hakataya Tradition." In *Southwestern Ceramics: A Comparative Review*, ed. A. H. Schroeder, pp. 53–69. Arizona Archaeologist No. 15. Arizona Archaeological Society, Phoenix.

Euler, R. C., G. J. Gumerman, T. N. V. Karlstrom, J. S. Dean, and R. H. Hevly
1979    "The Colorado Plateaus: Cultural Dynamics and Paleoenvironment." *Science*, Vol. 205, pp. 1089–1101.

Ewen, C. R.
1997 "The Search for Coronado's Contemporary: The Discovery, Excavation, and Interpretation of Hernando de Soto's First Winter Encampment." In *The Coronado Expedition to Tierra Nueva*, ed. R. Flint and S. C. Flint, pp. 116–134. University Press of Colorado, Niwot.

Farmer, J. D.
2001 "Goggle Eyes and Crested Serpents of Barrier Canyon." In *The Road to Aztlan: Art from a Mythic Homeland*, ed. V. M. Fields and V. Zamudio-Taylor, pp. 124–137. Los Angeles County Museum of Art, Los Angeles, CA.

Farmer, M. F.
1935 "The Mojave Trade Route." *Masterkey*, Vol. 9, no. 5, pp. 154–157.

Ferdon, E. N., Jr.
1955 *A Trial Survey of Mexican-Southwestern Architectural Parallels*. School of American Research Press, Santa Fe, NM.
1967 "The Hohokam 'Ball Court': An Alternative View of Its Function." *Kiva*, Vol. 33, no. 1, pp. 1–14.

Ferguson, T. J.
1981 "The Emergence of Modern Zuni Culture and Society." In *The Protohistoric Period in the North American Southwest, AD 1450–1700*, ed. D. R. Wilcox and W. B. Masse, pp. 336–353. Anthropological Research Papers No. 24. Arizona State University, Tempe.

Fewkes, J. W.
1896 "Pacific Coast Shell from Prehistoric Tusayan Pueblos." *American Anthropologist*, o.s., Vol. 9, no. 11, pp. 359–367.
1919 "Designs on Prehistoric Hopi Pottery." In *33rd. Annual Report for the Bureau of American Ethnology for the Years 1911–1912*, pp. 207–284, Washington, DC.

Fiedel, S. J.
1999 "Older Than We Thought: Implications of Corrected Dates for Paleoindians." *American Antiquity*, Vol. 64, no. 1, pp. 95–115.

Fields, V. M., and V. Zamudio-Taylor, eds.
2001 *The Road to Aztlan: Art from a Mythic Homeland*. Los Angeles County Museum of Art, Los Angeles, CA.

Fish, P. R.
1989 "The Hohokam: 1,000 Years of Prehistory in the Sonoran Desert." In *Dynamics of Southwest Prehistory*, ed. L. S. Cordell and G. J. Gumerman, pp. 19–63. Smithsonian Institution Press, Washington, DC.

Fish, P. R., and S. K. Fish
1994 "Southwest and Northwest: Recent Research at the Juncture of the United States and Mexico." *Journal of Archaeological Research*, Vol. 2, no. 1, pp. 3–44.
1999 "Reflections on the Casas Grandes Regional System from the Northwestern Periphery." In *The Casas Grandes World*, ed. C. F. Schaafsma and C. L. Riley, pp. 27–42. University of Utah Press, Salt Lake City.

Fish, S. K., and P. R. Fish
2004 "In the Trincheras Heartland: Initial Insights from Full-Coverage Survey." In *Surveying the Archaeology of Northwest Mexico*, ed. G. E. Newell and E. Gallaga, pp. 47–63. University of Utah Press, Salt Lake City.

Flint, R.
2002 *Great Cruelties Have Been Reported*. Southern Methodist University Press, Dallas, TX.
2003 "What's Missing from This Picture? The *Alarde*, or Muster Roll, of the Coronado Expedition." In *The Coronado Expedition: From the Distance of 460 Years*, ed. R. Flint and S. C. Flint, pp. 57–80. University of New Mexico Press, Albuquerque.

Flint, R., and S. C. Flint
2005 *Documents of the Coronado Expedition, 1539–1542: "They Were Not Familiar with His Majesty, nor Did They Wish to Be His Subjects."* Southern Methodist University Press, Dallas, TX.

Flint, R., and S. C. Flint, eds.
1997 *The Coronado Expedition to Tierra Nueva*. University Press of Colorado, Niwot.
2003 *The Coronado Expedition: From the Distance of 460 Years*. University of New Mexico Press, Albuquerque.

Folan, W. J., ed.
1985 *Contributions to the Archaeology and Ethnohistory of Greater Mesoamerica:*

*Essays in Honor of Carroll L. Riley.* Southern Illinois University Press, Carbondale.

Fontana, B. L.
1983 "Pima and Papago: Introduction." In *Southwest,* ed. A. Ortiz, pp. 125–136. Handbook of North American Indians, Vol. 10, William C. Sturtevant, general editor, Smithsonian Institution, Washington, DC.
1989 "Were There Indian Statelets in the Sonora Valley?" *Southwestern Mission Research Center Newsletter,* Vol. 23, p. 8.

Ford, R. I.
1981 "Gardening and Farming Before A.D. 1000: Patterns of Prehistoric Cultivation North of Mexico." *Journal of Ethnobotany,* Vol. 1, no. 1, pp. 6–27.

Forrestal, P. P., and C. J. Lynch, trans. and eds.
1954 *Benavides' Memorial of 1630.* Academy of American Franciscan History, Washington, DC.

Foster, M. S.
1982 "The Loma San Gabriel–Mogollon Continuum." In *Mogollon Archaeology: Proceedings of the 1980 Mogollon Conference,* ed. P. H. Beckett and K. Silverbird, pp. 251–261. Acoma Books, Ramona, CA.
1990 "Casas Grandes as a Mesoamerican Center and Culture." In *Actas del Primer Congreso de Historia Regional Comparada, 1989,* pp. 33–39. Universidad Autónoma de Ciudad Juárez, Chihuahua.
1994 "The Loma San Gabriel Culture and Its Suggested Relationships to Other Early Plainware Cultures of Northwest Mesoamerica." In *The Gran Chichimeca: Essays on the Archaeology and Ethnohistory of Northern Mesoamerica,* ed. J. E. Reyman, pp. 179–207. Avebury, Ashgate Publishing, Aldershot, UK.
2000 "The Archaeology of Durango." In *Greater Mesoamerica: The Archaeology of West and Northwest Mexico,* ed. M. S. Foster and S. Gorenstein, pp. 197–219. University of Utah Press, Salt Lake City.

Foster, M. S., and S. Gorenstein, eds.
2000 *Greater Mesoamerica: The Archaeology of West and Northwest Mexico.* University of Utah Press, Salt Lake City.

Fowler, A. P., and J. R. Stein
1992 "The Anasazi Great House in Space, Time, and Paradigm." In *Anasazi Regional Organization and the Chaco System,* ed. D. E. Doyel, pp. 101–122. Maxwell Museum of Anthropology, University of New Mexico, Albuquerque.

Frisbie, T. R.
1975 "Hishi as Money in the Pueblo Southwest." In *Collected Papers in Honor of Florence Hawley Ellis,* ed. T. R. Frisbie, pp. 120–142. Papers of the Archaeological Society of New Mexico No. 2. Hooper Publishing, Norman, OK.
2003 "The Pochteca and Chaco." In *Anasazi Archaeology at the Millennium,* ed. P. F. Reed, pp. 209–211. Proceedings of the Sixth Occasional Anasazi Symposium, Center for Desert Archaeology, Tucson, AZ.

Furst, J. L.
1986 "The Lords of Place of the Ascending Serpent." In *Symbol and Meaning Beyond the Closed Community: Essays in Mesoamerican Ideas,* ed. G. H. Gossen, pp. 57–68. Institute for Mesoamerican Studies, State University of New York, Albany.

Gillespie, S. D.
1991 "Ballgames and Boundaries." In *The Mesoamerican Ballgame,* ed. V. L. Scarborough and D. R. Wilcox, pp. 317–345. University of Arizona Press, Tucson.

Gilpin, D.
2001 "Boundaries of Tsegi Phase Architecture in Northeastern Arizona." In *The Archaeology of Ancient Tactical Sites,* ed. J. R. Welch and T. W. Bostwick, pp. 7–19. Arizona Archaeologist No. 32. Arizona Archaeological Society, Phoenix.

Gladwin, W., and H. S. Gladwin
1930 *Some Southwestern Pottery Types.* Medallion Papers No. 8. Gila Pueblo, Globe, AZ.

Goddard, I.
1996 "The Classification of the Native Languages of North America." In *Languages,* ed. I. Goddard, pp. 290–323. Handbook of North American Indians, Vol. 17, William C. Sturtevant, general editor, Smithsonian Institution, Washington, DC.

González Arratia, L.

1992 "La población prehispánica cazadora-recolectora y el Desierto de Chihuahua." In *Historia General de Chihuahua I, Geología Geografía y Arqueología,* coord. A. Márquez-Alameda, pp. 163–185. Universidad Autónoma de Ciudad Juárez, Chihuahua.

Greenberg, J. H.

1987 *Language in the Americas.* Stanford University Press, Stanford, CA.

Greenberg, J. H., C. G. Turner II, and S. L. Zegura

1986 "The Settlement of the Americas: A Comparison of the Linguistic, Dental, and Genetic Evidence." *Current Anthropology,* Vol. 27, no. 5, pp. 477–497.

Gregory, D. A.

1991 "Form and Variation in Hohokam Settlement Patterns." In *Chaco and Hohokam,* ed. P. L. Crown and W. J. Judge, pp. 159–193. School of American Research Press, Santa Fe, NM.

Greiser, S. T., and T. W. Greiser

1995 "Prehistoric Irrigation in the Taos Valley." In *Soil, Water, Biology, and Belief in Prehistoric and Traditional Southwestern Agriculture,* ed. H. W. Toll, pp. 221–237. New Mexico Archaeological Council, Special Pub. 2.

Greiser, S. T., and J. L. Moore

1995 "The Case for Prehistoric Irrigation in the Northern Southwest." In *Soil, Water, Biology, and Belief in Prehistoric and Traditional Southwestern Agriculture,* ed. H. W. Toll, pp. 189–195. New Mexico Archaeological Council, Special Pub. 2.

Griffen, W. B.

1979 *Indian Assimilation in the Franciscan Area of Nueva Vizcaya.* University of Arizona Press, Tucson.

1983 "Southern Periphery: East." In *Southwest,* ed. A. Ortiz, pp. 329–342. Handbook of North American Indians, Vol. 10, William C. Sturtevant, general editor, Smithsonian Institution, Washington, DC.

Griffin, J. B., and A. D. Krieger

1947 "Notes on Some Ceramic Techniques and Intrusions in Central Mexico." *American Antiquity,* Vol. 12, no. 3, pp. 156–173.

Griffith, J. S.

1983 "Kachinas and Masking." In *Southwest,* ed. A. Ortiz, pp. 764–777. Handbook of North American Indians, Vol. 10, William C. Sturtevant, general editor, Smithsonian Institution, Washington, DC.

Guevara Sánchez, A., and D. A. Phillips Jr.

1992 "Arqueología de la Sierra Madre Occidental en Chihuahua." In *Historia General de Chihuahua I, Geología Geografía y Arqueología,* coord. A. Márquez-Alameda, pp. 187–213. Universidad Autónoma de Ciudad Juárez, Chihuahua.

Guitéras, E., trans.

1951 *Rudo Ensayo by an Unknown Jesuit Padre, 1763.* Originally published 1894 as Vol. 2, no. 2, *Records of the American Catholic Historical Society of Philadelphia.* Repr., Arizona Silhouettes, Tucson, AZ.

Gumerman, G. J.

1988 "A Historical Perspective on Environment and Culture in Anasazi Country." In *The Anasazi in a Changing Environment,* ed. G. J. Gumerman, pp. 1–24. Cambridge University Press, Cambridge, UK.

Gumerman, G. J., and E. W. Haury

1979 "Prehistory: Hohokam." In *Southwest,* ed. A. Ortiz, pp. 75–90. Handbook of North American Indians, Vol. 9, William C. Sturtevant, general editor, Smithsonian Institution, Washington, DC.

Gutiérrez, R. A.

1991 *When Jesus Came, the Corn Mothers Went Away.* Stanford University Press, Stanford, CA.

Haas, J.

2000 Review of *Prehistoric Warfare in the American Southwest,* by S. A. LeBlanc. *Journal of Field Archaeology,* Vol. 27, no. 4, pp. 483–485.

Haas, J., and W. Creamer

1993 *Stress and Warfare Among the Kayenta Anasazi of the Thirteenth Century A.D.* Field Museum of Natural History, Chicago, IL.

1997 "Warfare Among the Pueblos: Myth, History, and Ethnography." *Ethnohistory,* Vol. 44, no. 2, pp. 235–261.

Habicht-Mauche, J. A.

1993    *The Pottery from Arroyo Hondo Pueblo New Mexico.* School of American Research Press, Santa Fe, NM.

1995    "Changing Patterns of Pottery Manufacture and Trade in the Northern Rio Grande Region." In *Ceramic Production in the American Southwest,* ed. B. J. Mills and P. L. Crown, pp. 167–199. University of Arizona Press, Tucson.

2000    "Pottery, Food, Hides, and Women: Labor, Production, and Exchange Across the Protohistoric Plains-Pueblo Frontier." In *The Archaeology of Regional Interaction: Religion, Warfare, and Exchange Across the American Southwest and Beyond,* ed. M. Hegmon, pp. 209–231. University Press of Colorado, Boulder.

Hale, K., and D. Harris

1979    "Historical Linguistics and Archeology." In *Southwest,* ed. A. Ortiz, pp. 170–177. Handbook of North American Indians, Vol. 9, William C. Sturtevant, general editor, Smithsonian Institution, Washington, DC.

Hammond, G. P., and A. Rey, trans. and eds.

1928    *Obregón's History.* Wetzel Publishing, Los Angeles, CA.

1940    *Narratives of the Coronado Expedition, 1540–1542.* University of New Mexico Press, Albuquerque.

1953    *Don Juan de Oñate, Colonizer of New Mexico, 1595–1628.* 2 vols. (paged consecutively). University of New Mexico Press, Albuquerque.

1966    *The Rediscovery of New Mexico: 1580–1594.* University of New Mexico Press, Albuquerque.

Harder, B.

2003    "New World Newcomers." *Science News,* Vol. 164, no. 6, Aug. 9, pp. 84–85.

Hargrave, L. L.

1970    *Mexican Macaws: Comparative Osteology and Survey of Remains from the Southwest.* University of Arizona Press, Tucson.

Harrington, J. P.

1910    "On Phonetic and Lexical Resemblances Between Kiowa and Tanoan." *American Anthropologist,* Vol. 12, no, 1, pp. 119–123.

Hartmann, W. K.

1997    "Pathfinder for Coronado: Reevaluating the Mysterious Journey of Marcos de Niza." In *The Coronado Expedition to Tierra Nueva,* ed. R. Flint and S. C. Flint, pp. 73–101. University Press of Colorado, Niwot.

Hartmann, W. K., and R. Flint

2003    "Before the Coronado Expedition: Who Knew What and When Did They Know It?" In *The Coronado Expedition: From the Distance of 460 Years,* ed. R. Flint and S. C. Flint, pp. 20–41. University of New Mexico Press, Albuquerque.

Haury, E. W.

1936    *The Mogollon Culture of Southwestern New Mexico.* Medallion Papers No. 20. Gila Pueblo, Globe, AZ.

1976    *The Hohokam: Desert Farmers and Craftsmen.* University of Arizona Press, Tucson.

1988    "Recent Thoughts on the Mogollon." *Kiva,* Vol. 53, no. 2, pp. 195–196.

Hawley, F. M.

1936    *Field Manual of Prehistoric Southwestern Pottery Types.* University of New Mexico Bulletin, Anthropological Series, Vol. 1, no. 4.

Hayes, A. C.

1981    "A Survey of Chaco Canyon Archaeology." In *Archaeological Surveys of Chaco Canyon, New Mexico,* ed. A. C. Hayes, D. M. Brugge, and W. J. Judge, pp. 1–68. Publications in Archeology 18A, Chaco Canyon Studies, National Park Service, Washington, DC.

Hayes, A. C., D. M. Brugge, and W. J. Judge

1981    *Archaeological Surveys of Chaco Canyon, New Mexico.* Publications in Archeology 18A, Chaco Canyon Studies, National Park Service, Washington, DC.

Hayes, A. C., J. N. Young, and A. H. Warren

1981    *Excavation of Mound 7: Gran Quivira National Monument.* National Park Service, Washington, DC.

Hays, K. A.

1989    "Katsina Depictions on Homol'ovi Ceramics." *Kiva,* Vol. 54, no. 3, pp. 297–311.

1991    "Ceramics." In *Homol'ovi II: Archaeology of an Ancestral Hopi Village,* ed.

E. C. Adams and K. A. Hays, pp. 23–48. University of Arizona Press, Tucson.

1992 "Shalako Depictions on Prehistoric Hopi Pottery." In *Archaeology, Art, and Anthropology: Papers in Honor of J. J. Brody,* ed. M. S. Duran and D. T. Kirkpatrick, pp. 73–83. Archaeological Society of New Mexico, Albuquerque.

1994 "Kachina Depictions on Prehistoric Pueblo Pottery." In *Kachinas in the Pueblo World,* ed. P. Schaafsma, pp. 47–62. University of New Mexico Press, Albuquerque.

Hays, K. A., E. C. Adams, and R. C. Lange

1991 "Regional Prehistory and Research." In *Homol'ovi II: Archaeology of an Ancestral Hopi Village,* ed. E. C. Adams and K. A. Hays, pp. 1–9. University of Arizona Press, Tucson.

Hays-Gilpin, K., and J. H. Hill

2000 "The Flower World in Prehistoric Southwest Material Culture." In *The Archaeology of Regional Interaction: Religion, Warfare, and Exchange Across the American Southwest and Beyond,* ed. M. Hegmon, pp. 411–428. University Press of Colorado, Boulder.

Hedrick, B. C., and C. L. Riley, eds. and trans.

1974 *The Journey of the Vaca Party.* University Museum Studies No. 2. Southern Illinois University, Carbondale.

Hegmon, M., M. C. Nelson, and S. M. Ruth

1998 "Abandonment and Reorganization in the Mimbres Region of the American Southwest." *American Anthropologist,* Vol. 100, no. 1, pp. 148–162.

Hendricks, R.

2002 "Pueblo-Spanish Warfare in Seventeenth-Century New Mexico." In *Archaeologies of the Pueblo Revolt: Identity, Meaning, and Renewal in the Pueblo World,* ed. R. W. Preucel, pp. 180–197. University of New Mexico Press, Albuquerque.

Hendricks, R., and J. P. Wilson, eds. and trans.

1996 *The Navajos in 1705: Roque Madrid's Campaign Journal.* University of New Mexico Press, Albuquerque.

Hendrickson, M.

2001 "Lost Pots and Untold Tales: Design Analysis of Chihuahuan Medio Period Polychrome Jars from Museum Collections." In *From Paquimé to Mata Ortiz:*

*The Legacy of Ancient Casas Grandes,* ed. G. Johnson, pp. 37–54. Museum of Man, San Diego, CA.

Hibben, F. C.

1966 "A Possible Pyramidal Structure and Other Mexican Influences at Pottery Mound, New Mexico." *American Antiquity,* Vol. 31, no. 4, pp. 522–529.

1975 *Kiva Art of the Anasazi at Pottery Mound.* KC Publications, Las Vegas, NV.

Hickerson, N. P.

1990 "Jumano: The Missing Link in South Plains Prehistory." *Journal of the West,* Vol. 29, no. 4, pp. 5–12.

1994 *The Jumano: Hunters and Traders of the South Plains.* University of Texas Press, Austin.

1996 "Ethnogenesis in the South Plains." In *History, Power, and Identity: Ethnogenesis in the Americas, 1492–1992,* ed. J. D. Hill, pp. 70–89. University of Iowa Press, Iowa City.

1997 "Kiowa: An Emergent People." In *Ethnographic Originals: Portraits of Culture,* Vol. 1, *North America,* ed. M. Ember, C. R. Ember, and D. Levinson, pp. 155–182. Prentice-Hall, New York.

Hieb, L. A.

1994 "The Meaning of Katsina." In *Kachinas in the Pueblo World,* ed. P. Schaafsma, pp. 23–33. University of New Mexico Press, Albuquerque.

Hill, J. H.

1992 "The Flower World of Old Uto-Aztecan." *Journal of Anthropological Research,* Vol. 48, no. 2, pp. 117–144.

2001 "Proto-Uto-Aztecan: A Community of Cultivators in Central Mexico?" *American Anthropologist,* Vol. 103, no. 4, pp. 913–934.

Hinton, T. B.

1983 "Southern Periphery: West." In *Southwest,* ed. A. Ortiz, pp. 315–328. Handbook of North American Indians, Vol. 10, William C. Sturtevant, general editor, Smithsonian Institution, Washington, DC.

Hodge, F. W., ed.

1907 *Spanish Explorers in the Southern United States, 1528–1543: The Narrative of Alvar Nuñez Cabeça de Vaca.* Charles Scribner's Sons, New York.

1935    "Coral Among Early Southwestern Indians." *Masterkey,* Vol. 9, no. 5, pp. 157–159.

1953    "Pueblo Names in the Oñate Documents." In *Don Juan de Oñate, Colonizer of New Mexico, 1595–1628,* ed. and trans. G. P. Hammond and A. Rey, Vol. 1, pp. 363–374. University of New Mexico Press, Albuquerque.

Hoebel, E. A.

1979    "Zia Pueblo." In *Southwest,* ed. A. Ortiz, pp. 407–417. Handbook of North American Indians, Vol. 9, William C. Sturtevant, general editor, Smithsonian Institution, Washington, DC.

Hofman, J. L.

1989    "Prehistoric Culture History—Hunters and Gatherers in the Southern Great Plains." In *From Clovis to Comanchero: Archeological Overview of the Southern Great Plains,* ed. J. L. Hofman, R. L. Brooks, J. S. Hays, D. W. Owsley, R. L. Jantz, M. K. Marks, and M. H. Manhein, pp. 25–60. Arkansas Archeological Survey Research Series No. 35. Arkansas Archeological Survey, Fayetteville, AR.

Hogan, P., and L. Sebastian, eds.

1991    *Archeology of the San Juan Breaks: The Anasazi Occupation.* Office of Contract Archeology, University of New Mexico, Prepared for the Bureau of Land Management, Farmington Research Area, New Mexico.

Hotz, G.

1970    *Indian Skin Paintings from the American Southwest.* University of Oklahoma Press, Norman.

Howell, T. L., and K. D. K. Howell

2003    "Modeling Migration." In *Anasazi Archaeology at the Millennium,* ed. P. F. Reed, pp. 215–218. Proceedings of the 6th Occasional Anasazi Symposium, Center for Desert Archaeology, Tucson, AZ.

Huckell, B. B.

1995    *Of Marshes and Maize: Preceramic Agricultural Settlements in the Cienega Valley, Southeastern Arizona.* University of Arizona Press, Tucson.

Huntley, D. L.

2004    "Interaction, Boundaries, and Identities: A Multiscalar Approach to the Organizational Scale of Pueblo IV Zuni Society." Unpublished PhD dissertation, Department of Anthropology, Arizona State University, Tempe.

Huntley, D. L., and K. W. Kintigh

2004    "Archaeological Patterning and Organizational Scale of Late Prehistoric Settlement Clusters in the Zuni Region of New Mexico." In *The Protohistoric World, A.D. 1275–1600,* ed. E. C. Adams and A. I. Duff, pp. 62–74. University of Arizona Press, Tucson.

Ingstad, H., and A. S. Ingstad

2001    *The Viking Discovery of America.* Checkmark Books, New York.

Irwin-Williams, C.

1967    "Picosa: The Elementary Southwestern Culture" *American Antiquity,* Vol. 32, no. 4, pp. 441–457.

1973    *The Oshara Tradition: Origins of Anasazi Culture.* Contributions in Anthropology, Vol. 5, no. 1., Eastern New Mexico University, Portales.

Jacobsen, W. H., Jr.

1979    "Hokan Inter-Branch Comparisons." In *The Languages of Native America,* ed. L. Campbell and M. Mithun, pp. 545–591. University of Texas Press, Austin.

James, S. E.

2002    "Mimetic Rituals of Child Sacrifice in the Hopi Kachina Cult." *Journal of the Southwest,* Vol. 44, no. 3, pp. 337–356.

Jelinek, A. J.

1967    *A Prehistoric Sequence in the Middle Pecos Valley, New Mexico.* Anthropological Papers No. 31. Museum of Anthropology, University of Michigan, Ann Arbor.

Jett, S. C., and P. B. Moyle

1986    "The Exotic Origins of Fishes Depicted on Prehistoric Mimbres Pottery from New Mexico." *American Antiquity,* Vol. 51, no. 4, pp. 688–720.

Jiménez Betts, P. F., and J. A. Darling

2000    "Archaeology of Southern Zacatecas." In *Greater Mesoamerica: The Archaeology of West and Northwest Mexico,* ed. M. S. Foster and S. Gorenstein, pp. 155–180. University of Utah Press, Salt Lake City.

Johnson, G., ed.
2001 *From Paquimé to Mata Ortiz: The Legacy of Ancient Casas Grandes.* Museum of Man, San Diego, CA.

Jones, O. L., Jr.
1962 "Pueblo Indian Auxiliaries in New Mexico, 1763–1821." *New Mexico Historical Review,* Vol. 37, no. 2, pp. 81–109.

Judge, W. J.
1991 "Chaco: Current Views of Prehistory and the Regional System." In *Chaco and Hohokam,* ed. P. L. Crown and W. J. Judge, pp. 11–30. School of American Research Press, Santa Fe, NM.

Katz, F.
1978 "A Comparison of Some Aspects of the Evolution of Cuzco and Tenochtitlán." In *Urbanization in the Americas from Its Beginnings to the Present,* ed. R. P. Schaedel, J. E. Hardoy, and N. S. Kinzer, pp. 203–214. Mouton Publishers, The Hague.

Kehoe, A. B.
1999 "The Postclassic Along the Northern Frontiers of Mesoamerica." *The Casas Grandes World,* ed. C. F. Schaafsma and C. L. Riley, pp. 201–205. University of Utah Press, Salt Lake City.

Kelley, E. A., and J. C. Kelley
1980 "Sipapu and Pyramid Too: The Temple of the Crypt at Alta Vista, Chalchihuites." *Transactions of the Illinois State Academy of Science,* Vol. 73, no. 2, pp. 62–79.

Kelley, J. C.
1966 "Mesoamerica and the Southwestern United States." In *Archaeological Frontiers and External Connections,* ed. G. F. Ekholm and G. R. Willey, pp. 95–110. Handbook of Middle American Indians, Vol. 4, Robert Wauchope, general editor, University of Texas Press, Austin.
1971 "Archaeology of the Northern Frontier: Zacatecas and Durango." In *Archaeology of Northern Mesoamerica, Part 2,* ed. G. F. Ekholm and G. R. Willey, pp. 768–801. Handbook of Middle American Indians, Vol. 11, Robert Wauchope, general editor, University of Texas Press, Austin.
1986 *Jumano and Patarabueye: Relations at La Junta de los Rios.* Anthropological Papers No. 77. Museum of Anthropology, University of Michigan, Ann Arbor.
1991 "The Known Archaeological Ballcourts of Durango and Zacatecas, Mexico." In *The Mesoamerican Ballgame,* ed. V. L. Scarborough and D. R. Wilcox, pp. 87–100. University of Arizona Press, Tucson.
1992 "La Cuenca del Río Conchos." In *Historia General de Chihuahua I: Geología, Geografíay Arqueología,* coord. A. Márquez-Alameda, pp. 131–136. Universidad Autónoma de Ciudad Juárez, Gobierno del Estado de Chihuahua.
2000 "The Aztatlán Mercantile System." In *Greater Mesoamerica: The Archaeology of West and Northwest Mexico,* ed. M. S. Foster and S. Gorenstein, pp. 137–154. University of Utah Press, Salt Lake City.
n.d. "A Review of the Architectural Sequence at La Junta de los Rios." Manuscript in author's possession.

Kelley, J. C., and E. A. Kelley
1975 "An Alternative Hypothesis for the Explanation of Anasazi Culture History." In *Collected Papers in Honor of Florence Hawley Ellis,* ed. T. R. Frisbie, pp. 178–223. Papers of the Archaeological Society of New Mexico No. 2. Hooper Publishing, Norman, OK.
2000 "The Archaeoastronomical System in the Río Colorado Chalchihuites Polity, Zacatecas." In *Greater Mesoamerica: The Archaeology of West and Northwest Mexico,* ed. M. S. Foster and S. Gorenstein, pp. 181–195. University of Utah Press, Salt Lake City.

Kelley, J. H.
1991 "An Overview of the Capitan North Project." In *Mogollon V,* comp. P. H. Beckett, pp. 166–176. COAS Publishing and Research, Las Cruces, NM.

Kelley, J. H., J. D. Stewart, A. C. MacWilliams, and L. C. Neff
1999 "A West Central Chihuahuan Perspective on Chihuahuan Culture." In *The Casas Grandes World,* ed. C. F. Schaafsma and C. L. Riley, pp. 63–77. University of Utah Press, Salt Lake City.

Kendall, M. B.
1983 "Yuman Languages." In *Southwest,* ed. A. Ortiz, pp. 4–12. Handbook of North American Indians, Vol. 10, William C.

Sturtevant, general editor, Smithsonian Institution, Washington, DC.

Kent, K. P.
1983 *Textiles of the Prehistoric Southwest.* School of American Research Press and University of New Mexico Press, Santa Fe.

Kessell, J. L.
2002 *Spain in the Southwest.* University of Oklahoma Press, Norman.

Kidder, A. V.
1932 *The Artifacts of Pecos.* Yale University Press, New Haven, CT.

Kidder, A. V., H. S. Cosgrove, and C. B. Cosgrove
1949 *The Pendleton Ruin, Hidalgo County, New Mexico.* Contributions to American Anthropology and History Vol. 10, no. 50., pp. 107–152, Carnegie Institution of Washington, Pub. 585, Washington, DC.

Kinkade, G. M.
1986 "The San Simon Mogollon." In *Mogollon Variability,* ed. C. Benson and S. Upham, pp. 211–217. University Museum Occasional Papers 15, New Mexico State University, Las Cruces, NM.

Kintigh, K. W.
1985 *Settlement, Subsistence, and Society in Late Zuni Prehistory.* University of Arizona Press, Tucson.
1996 "The Cibola Region in the Post-Chacoan Era." In *The Prehistoric Pueblo World, AD 1150–1350,* ed. M. A. Adler, pp. 131–144. University of Arizona Press, Tucson.

Knaut, A. L.
1995 *The Pueblo Revolt of 1680.* University of Oklahoma Press, Norman.

Kohler, T. A.
1993 "News from the Northern American Southwest: Prehistory on the Edge of Chaos." *Journal of Archaeological Research,* Vol. 1, no. 4, pp. 267–321.

Kozuch, L.
2002 "Olivella Beads from Spiro and the Plains." *American Antiquity,* Vol. 67, no. 4, pp. 697–709.

Kroeber, A. L.
1925 *Handbook of the Indians of California.* Bureau of American Ethnology, Bull. 78. Repr. 1976, Dover Publications, New York.

1934 *Uto-Aztecan Languages of Mexico.* University of California Press, Berkeley.

Ladd, E. J.
1994 "The Zuni Ceremonial System: The Kiva." In *Kachinas in the Pueblo World,* ed. P. Schaafsma, pp. 17–21. University of New Mexico Press, Albuquerque.
1997 "Zuni on the Day the Men in Metal Arrived." In *The Coronado Expedition to Tierra Nueva,* ed. R. Flint and S. C. Flint, pp. 225–233. University Press of Colorado, Niwot, CO.

Lafaye, J.
1976 *Quetzalcóatl and Guadalupe.* Trans. B. Keen. University of Chicago Press, Chicago, IL.

Lang, R. W.
1982 "Transformation in White Ware Pottery of the Northern Rio Grande." In *Southwestern Ceramics: A Comparative Review,* ed. A. W. Schroeder, pp. 153–200. Arizona Archaeologist No. 15. Arizona Archaeological Society, Phoenix.

Langdon, M.
1979 "Some Thoughts on Hokan with Particular Reference to Pomoan and Yuman." In *The Languages of Native America,* ed. L. Campbell and M. Mithun, pp. 592–649. University of Texas Press, Austin.

Lange, C. H.
1979 "Cochiti Pueblo." In *Southwest,* ed. A. Ortiz, pp. 366–378. Handbook of North American Indians, Vol. 9, William C. Sturtevant, general editor, Smithsonian Institution, Washington, DC.
1979 "Santo Domingo Pueblo." In *Southwest,* ed. A. Ortiz, pp. 379–389. Handbook of North American Indians, Vol. 9, William C. Sturtevant, general editor, Smithsonian Institution, Washington, DC.

Lange, C. H., and C. L. Riley, eds.
1970 *The Southwestern Journals of Adolph F. Bandelier, 1883–1884.* Vol. 2. University of New Mexico Press, Albuquerque.

Lange, F., N. Mahaney, J. B. Wheat, M. L. Chenault, and J. Cater
1988 *Yellow Jacket: A Four Corners Anasazi Ceremonial Center.* 2nd ed. Johnson Books, Boulder, CO.

Lange, R. C.
1989 "The Survey of Homol'ovi Ruins State Park." *Kiva*, Vol. 54, no. 3, pp. 195–216.
1998 *Prehistoric Land-Use and Settlement of the Middle Little Colorado River Valley.* Arizona State Museum/University of Arizona Press, Tucson.

Larkin, K. B., J. H. Kelley, and M. J. Hendrickson
2004 "Ceramics as Temporal and Spatial Indicators in Chihuahua Culture." In *Surveying the Archaeology of Northwest Mexico,* ed. G. E. Newell and E. Gallaga, pp. 177–204. University of Utah Press, Salt Lake City.

Lazcano Sahagún, C.
1998 *Explorando un mundo olvidado: Sitios perdidos de la cultura Paquimé.* Grupo Cementos de Chihuahua, México, DF.

LeBlanc, S. A.
1982 "Temporal Change in Mogollon Ceramics." In *Southwestern Ceramics: A Comparative Review,* ed. A. H. Schroeder, pp. 107–127. Arizona Archaeological Society, Phoenix.
1986 "Development of Archaeological Thought on the Mimbres Mogollon." In *Emil W. Haury's Prehistory of the American Southwest,* ed. J. J. Reid and D. E. Doyel, pp. 297–304. University of Arizona Press, Tucson.
1989 "Cultural Dynamics in the Southern Mogollon Area." In *Dynamics of Southwest Prehistory,* ed. L. S. Cordell and G. J. Gumerman, pp. 197–207. Smithsonian Institution Press, Washington, DC.
1998 "Settlement Consequences of Warfare During the Late Pueblo III and Pueblo IV Periods." In *Migration and Reorganization: The Pueblo IV Period in the American Southwest,* ed. K. A. Spielmann, pp. 115–135. Anthropological Research Papers No. 51. Arizona State University, Tempe.
1999 *Prehistoric Warfare in the American Southwest.* University of Utah Press, Salt Lake City.
2000 "Regional Interaction and Warfare in the Late Prehistoric Southwest." *The Archaeology of Regional Interaction: Religion, Warfare, and Exchange Across the American Southwest and Beyond,* ed. M. Hegmon, pp. 41–70. University Press of Colorado, Boulder.

2001 "Population Dynamics at the McAnally and Thompson Sites and Their Valley-wide Context." In *Early Pithouse Villages of the Mimbres Valley and Beyond,* by M. W. Diehl and S. A. LeBlanc, pp. 115–119. Papers of the Peabody Museum of American Archaeology and Ethnology Vol. 83. Harvard University, Cambridge, MA.

Lehmer, D. J.
1948 *The Jornada Branch of the Mogollon.* University of Arizona Bulletin, Vol. 19, no. 2.

Lekson, S. H.
1988 "The Mangas Phase in Mimbres Archaeology." *Kiva,* Vol. 53, no. 2, pp. 129–145.
1989 "An Archaeological Reconnaissance of the Rio Grande Valley in Sierra County, New Mexico." *Artifact,* Vol. 27, no. 2, pp. 1–102.
1991 "Settlement Pattern and the Chaco Region." In *Chaco and Hohokam,* ed. P. L. Crown and W. J. Judge, pp. 31–55. School of American Research Press, Santa Fe, NM.
1996 "Southwestern New Mexico and Southeastern Arizona, AD 900 to 1300." In *The Prehistoric Pueblo World, AD 1150–1350,* ed. M. A. Adler, pp. 170–176. University of Arizona Press, Tucson.
1999 *The Chaco Meridian.* AltaMira Press, Walnut Creek, CA.
1999 "Was Casas a Pueblo?" In *The Casas Grandes World,* ed. C. F. Schaafsma and C. L. Riley, pp. 84–92. University of Utah Press, Salt Lake City.
2000 "Salado in Chihuahua." In *Salado,* ed. J. S. Dean, pp. 275–294. Amerind Foundation, Dragoon, AZ, and University of New Mexico Press, Albuquerque.
2001 "Chaco, Aztec, and Paquimé." In *From Paquimé to Mata Ortiz: The Legacy of Ancient Casas Grandes,* ed. G. Johnson, pp. 1–10. Museum of Man, San Diego, CA.
2001 "Landscape and Polity: The Interplay of Land, History, and Power in the Ancient Southwest." In *The Road to Aztlan: Art from a Mythic Homeland,* ed. V. M. Fields and V. Zamudio-Taylor, pp. 212–229. Los Angeles County Museum of Art, Los Angeles, CA.

2002 "War in the Southwest, War in the World." *American Antiquity*, Vol. 67, no. 4, pp. 607–624.

Lekson, S. H., M. Bletzer, and
A. C. MacWilliams
2004 "Pueblo IV in the Chihuahuan Desert." In *The Protohistoric World, A.D. 1275–1600*, ed. E. C. Adams and A. I. Duff, pp. 53–61. University of Arizona Press, Tucson.

Lekson, S. H., C. P. Nepstad-Thornberry,
B. E. Yunker, T. S. Laumbach, D. P. Cain, and
K. W. Laumbach
2002 "Migrations in the Southwest: Pinnacle Ruin, Southwestern New Mexico." *Kiva*, Vol. 68, no. 2, pp. 73–101.

Leonard, R. D., T. L. VanPool, C. S. VanPool,
M. J. Harmon, G. F. M. Rakita, T. Maxwell,
R. Cruz Antillón, and L. A. Salter
2002 "Casas Grandes Intellectual Traditions: Implications for Prehistoric West Mexico, Northern Mexico, the American Southwest, and South America." Paper presented at the Southwest Symposium, Tucson, AZ.

Lightfoot, K. G.
1979 "Food Redistribution Among Prehistoric Pueblo Groups." *Kiva*, Vol. 44, no. 4, pp. 319–339.

Lincoln, T. R.
2000 "A Brief History of Salado Archaeology." In *Salado*, ed. J. S. Dean, pp. 17–25. Amerind Foundation, Dragoon, AZ, and University of New Mexico Press, Albuquerque.

Lindsay, A. J., Jr.
1987 "Anasazi Population Movements to Southeastern Arizona." *American Archaeology*, Vol. 6, no. 3, pp. 190–198.

Linton, R.
1944 "Nomad Raids and Fortified Pueblos." *American Antiquity*, Vol. 10, no. 1, pp. 28–32.

Lipe, W. D.
1978 "The Southwest." In *Ancient Native Americans*, ed. J. D. Jennings, pp. 327–401. W. H. Freeman, San Francisco.

1993 "The Basketmaker II Period in the Four Corners Area." *Anasazi-Basketmaker: Papers from the 1990 Wetherill-Grand Gulch Symposium*, ed. V. M. Atkins, pp. 1–10. Cultural Resource Series No.

24. Bureau of Land Management, Salt Lake City, Utah.

1995 "The Depopulation of the Northern San Juan: Conditions in the Turbulent 1200s." *Journal of Anthropological Archaeology*, Vol. 14, no. 2, pp. 143–169.

Lister, R. H.
1958 *Archaeological Excavations in the Northern Sierra Madre Occidental, Chihuahua, and Sonora, Mexico*. University of Colorado Press, Boulder.

Lombardo, N.
1702 "Arte de la lengua Teguima." Bancroft Library ms. copy no. 150601.3, Berkeley, CA.

Love, M. F.
1975 "A Survey of the Distribution of T-shaped Doorways in the Greater Southwest." In *Collected Papers in Honor of Florence Hawley Ellis*, ed. T. R. Frisbie, pp. 296–311. Papers of the Archaeological Society of New Mexico No. 2. Hooper Publishing, Norman, OK.

Lumholtz, C.
1973 *Unknown Mexico*. 2 Vols. Rio Grande Press, Glorieta, NM. Originally published 1902, C. Scribner's Sons, New York.

Lyneis, M. M.
1996 "Pueblo II–Pueblo III Changes in Southwestern Utah, the Arizona Strip, and Southern Nevada." In *The Prehistoric Pueblo World, AD 1150–1350*, ed. M. A. Adler, pp. 11–28. University of Arizona Press, Tucson.

2000 "Life at the Edge: Pueblo Settlements in Southern Nevada." In *The Archaeology of Regional Interaction: Religion, Warfare, and Exchange Across the American Southwest and Beyond*, ed. M. Hegmon, pp. 257–274. University Press of Colorado, Boulder.

Lyons, P. D.
2003 *Ancestral Hopi Migrations*. University of Arizona Press, Tucson.

MacNeish, R. S.
1992 "Fases del Arcaico Tradición Chihuahua." In *Síntesis, Historia General de Chihuahua I: Geología, Geografía y Arqueología*, coord. A. Márquez-Alameda, pp. 121–129. Universidad Autónoma de Ciudad

Juárez, Gobierno del Estado de
Chihuahua.

MacWilliams, A. C.

2001 "Beyond the Reach of Casas Grandes:
Archaeology in Central Chihuahua."
In *From Paquimé to Mata Ortiz: The
Legacy of Ancient Casas Grandes,* ed.
G. Johnson, pp. 55–64. Museum of
Man, San Diego, CA.

Madsen, W.

1969 "The Nahua." In *Ethnology, Part 2,* ed.
E. Z. Vogt, pp. 602–637. Handbook of
Middle American Indians, Vol. 8, Robert
Wauchope, general editor, University of
Texas Press, Austin.

Mahoney, N.

2000 "Chaco World, Chaco Synthesis Project." *Archaeology Southwest,* Vol. 14,
no. 1, pp. 15–17.

2001 "Monumental Architecture as Conspicu-
ous Display in Chaco Canyon." In
*Chaco Society and Polity: Papers from
the 1999 Conference,* ed. L. S. Cordell,
W. J. Judge, and J. Piper, pp. 13–29.
New Mexico Archeological Council,
Special Pub. 4.

Malagón, M. S.

2001 "Tattoos, Women, and Rites of Passage:
Body Art in the Casas Grandes World."
In *From Paquimé to Mata Ortiz: The
Legacy of Ancient Casas Grandes,* ed.
G. Johnson, pp. 65–72. Museum of
Man, San Diego, CA.

Mallouf, R. J.

1992 "La Prehistoria del noreste de Chihuahua: Complejo Cielo y distrito La
Junta." In *Historia General de Chihuahua I: Geología, Geografía y Arqueología,* coord. A. Márquez-Alameda,
pp. 137–162. Universidad Autónoma de
Ciudad Juárez, Gobierno del Estado de
Chihuahua.

1999 "Comments on the Prehistory of Far
Northeastern Chihuahua, the La Junta
District, and the Cielo Complex." *Journal of Big Bend Studies,* Vol. 11, pp.
49–92.

Malville, J. M., and C. Putnam

1989 *Prehistoric Astronomy in the Southwest.*
Johnson Publishing, Boulder, CO.

Manson, J. L.

1998 "Transmississippi Trade and Travel: The
Buffalo Plains and Beyond." *Plains
Anthropologist,* Vol. 43, no. 166, pp.
385–400.

Marcos de Niza, Fr.

1865 "Descubrimiento de las siete ciudades."
In *Colección de Documentos Inéditos,*
Vol. 3, ed. J. F. Pacheco and F. de Cárde-
nas, pp. 325–351. Madrid, Imprenta de
Manuel B. de Quirós.

Márquez-Alameda, A.

1992 "Sobre los pobladores más antiguos del
actual estado de Chihuahua." In *Historia General de Chihuahua I, Geología,
Geografía y Arqueología,* coord. A.
Márquez-Alameda, pp. 105–120. Universidad Autónoma de Ciudad Juárez,
Chihuahua.

Marrin, A.

1989 *Inca and Spaniard: Pizarro and the Conquest of Peru.* Atheneum, New York.

Marshall, M. P., and H. J. Walt

1984 *Rio Abajo: Prehistory and History of a
Rio Grande Province.* New Mexico His-
toric Preservation Program, Historic
Preservation Division, Santa Fe.

Martin, D. L.

2000 "Bodies and Lives." In *Women and Men
in the Prehispanic Southwest,* ed. P. L.
Crown, pp. 267–300. School of American Research Press, Santa Fe, NM.

Martin, P. S.

1979 "Prehistory: Mogollon." In *Southwest,*
ed. A. Ortiz, pp. 61–74. Handbook of
North American Indians, Vol. 9, William
C. Sturtevant, general editor, Smithsonian Institution, Washington, DC.

Martin, P. S., G. I. Quimby, and D. Collier

1947 *Indians Before Columbus.* University of
Chicago Press, Chicago, IL.

Mathien, F. J.

1986 "External Contacts and the Chaco Anasazi." In *Ripples in the Chichimec Sea,*
ed. F. J. Mathien and R. H. McGuire,
pp. 220–242. Southern Illinois University Press, Carbondale.

1991 "Political, Economic, and Demographic
Implications of the Chaco Road Net-
work." In *Ancient Road Networks and
Settlement Hierarchies in the New
World,* ed. C. D. Trombold, pp. 99–110.

Cambridge University Press, Cambridge, UK.

2003 "Pueblo Wall Decorations: Examples from Chaco Canyon." In *Climbing the Rocks: Papers in Honor of Helen and Jay Crotty,* ed. R. N. Wiseman, T. C. O'Laughlin, and C. T. Snow, pp. 111–126. Archaeological Society of New Mexico, Albuquerque.

Mathien, F. J., and R. H. McGuire, eds.
1986 *Ripples in the Chichimec Sea.* Southern Illinois University Press, Carbondale.

Matson, R. G.
1991 *The Origins of Southwestern Agriculture.* University of Arizona Press, Tucson.

Maxwell, T. D.
2002 "Casas Grandes Region: Prehistoric Life in the Chihuahuan Desert." *El Palacio,* Vol. 107, no. 3, pp. 12–19.

McCluney, E. B.
2002 "The 1963 Excavation." In *The Joyce Well Site: On the Frontier of the Casas Grandes World,* ed. J. M. Skibo, E. B. McCluney, and W. H. Walker, pp. 11–96. University of Utah Press, Salt Lake City.

McGuire, R. H.
1982 "A History of Archaeological Research." In *Hohokam and Patayan: Prehistory of Southwestern Arizona,* ed. R. H. McGuire and M. B. Schiffer, pp. 101–152. Academic Press, New York.

McGuire, R. H., and M. E. Villalpando
1989 "Prehistory and Making of History in Sonora." In *Columbian Consequences,* Vol. 1, ed. D. H. Thomas, pp. 159–177. Smithsonian Institution Press, Washington, DC.

McGuire, R. H., M. E. Villalpando C., V. D. Vargas, and E. Gallaga M.
1999 "Cerro de Trincheras and the Casas Grandes World." In *The Casas Grandes World,* ed. C. F. Schaafsma and C. L. Riley, pp. 134–146. University of Utah Press, Salt Lake City.

McKenna, P. J., and H. W. Toll
1992 "Regional Patterns of Great House Development Among the Totah Anasazi, New Mexico." In *Anasazi Regional Organization and the Chaco System,* ed. D. E. Doyel, pp. 133–143. Maxwell

Museum of Anthropology, University of New Mexico, Albuquerque.

McKusick, C. R.
1986 *Southwest Indian Turkeys: Prehistory and Comparative Osteology.* Southwest Bird Laboratory, Globe, AZ.
2001 *Southwest Birds of Sacrifice.* Arizona Archaeologist No. 31. Arizona Archaeological Society, Phoenix.

Meighan, C. W.
1971 "Archaeology of Sinaloa." In *Archaeology of Northern Mesoamerica,* ed. G. F. Ekholm and I. Bernal, pp. 754–767. Handbook of Middle American Indians, Vol. 11, Robert Wauchope, general editor, University of Texas Press, Austin.

Mendizábal, M. A. de
1930 "Influencia de la sal en la distribución geográfica de los grupos indígenas de México." In *Proceedings of the 23rd International Congress of Americanists,* pp. 93–100. Science Press, Lancaster, PA.

Menzies, G.
2003 *1421: The Year China Discovered America.* William Morrow, New York.

Mera, H. P.
1943 *Pueblo Indian Embroidery.* University of New Mexico Press, Santa Fe.

Métraux, A.
1969 *A History of the Incas.* Random House, New York.

Mick-Ohara, L.
1991 "Identification and Analysis of Faunal Remains." In *Archaeology of the San Juan Breaks: The Anasazi Occupation,* ed. P. Hogan and L. Sebastian, pp. 129–155. Office of Contract Archaeology, University of New Mexico, prepared for the Bureau of Land Management, Farmington Research Area, New Mexico.

Miller, J.
2001 "Keres: Engendered Key to the Pueblo Puzzle." *Ethnohistory,* Vol. 48, no. 3, pp. 495–514.

Miller, W. R.
1959 "A Note on Kiowa Linguistic Affiliations." *American Anthropologist,* Vol. 61, no. 1, pp. 102–105.
1983 "Uto-Aztecan Languages." In *Southwest,* ed. A. Ortiz, pp. 113–124. Handbook of North American Indians, Vol.

10, William C. Sturtevant, general editor, Smithsonian Institution, Washington, DC.

Mills, B. J.
1995 "The Organization of Protohistoric Zuni Ceramic Production." In *Ceramic Production in the American Southwest*, ed. B. J. Mills and P. L. Crown, pp. 200–230. University of Arizona Press, Tucson.

Minnis, P. E., M. E. Whalen, J. H. Kelley, and J. D. Stewart
1993 "Prehistoric Macaw Breeding in the North American Southwest." *American Antiquity*, Vol. 58, no. 2, pp. 270–276.

Moore, Mrs. G. E., and Mrs. J. B. Wheat
1951 "An Archaeological Cache from the Hueco Basin, Texas." *Bulletin of the Texas Archaeological and Paleontological Society*, Vol. 22, pp. 144–163.

Morison, S. E.
1971 *The European Discovery of America*, Vol. 1, *The Northern Voyages, A.D. 500–1600*. Oxford University Press, New York.
1974 *The European Discovery of America*, Vol. 2, *The Southern Voyages, A.D. 1492–1616*. Oxford University Press, New York.

Morris, E. H.
1939 *Archaeological Studies in the La Plata District*. Pub. 519. Carnegie Institution of Washington, Washington, DC.

Munson, M.
2002 "Excavations at Burnt Corn Pueblo, Galisteo Basin." Paper presented at the 2002 Pecos Conference, Pecos National Historical Park, NM.

Myers, H. C.
2003 "The Mystery of Coronado's Route from the Pecos River to the Llano Estacado." *The Coronado Expedition: From the Distance of 460 Years*, ed. R. Flint and S. C. Flint, pp. 140–150. University of New Mexico Press, Albuquerque.

Naranjo, T.
1995 "Thoughts on Migration by Santa Clara Pueblo." *Journal of Anthropological Archaeology*, Vol. 14, no. 2, pp. 247–250.

Naylor, T. H.
1969 "The Extinct Suma of Northern Chihuahua." *Artifact*, Vol. 7, no. 4, pp. 1–14.

1981 "Athapaskans They Weren't: The Suma Rebels Executed at Casas Grandes in 1685." In *The Protohistoric Period in the North American Southwest, AD 1450–1700*, ed. D. R. Wilcox and W. B. Masse, pp. 275–281. Anthropological Research Papers No. 24. Arizona State University, Tempe.

Nelson, B. A.
2000 "Aggregation, Warfare, and the Spread of the Mesoamerican Tradition." In *The Archaeology of Regional Interaction: Religion, Warfare, and Exchange Across the American Southwest and Beyond*, ed. M. Hegmon, pp. 317–337. University Press of Colorado, Boulder.

Nordenskiöld, G.
1893 *The Cliff Dwellers of the Mesa Verde*. Trans. D. L. Morgan. Norstedt and Söner, Stockholm, Sweden.

Northrop, S. A.
1973 "Turquoise." *El Palacio*, Vol. 79, no. 1, pp. 3–22.

O'Bryan, D.
1950 *Excavations in Mesa Verde National Park, 1947–1948*. Medallion Papers No. 39. Gila Pueblo, Globe, AZ.

O'Gorman, E., ed.
1967 *Apologética historia sumaria*. 2 vols. Universidad Nacional Autónoma de México, Instituto de Investigaciones Históricos, México.

O'Laughlin, T. C.
2003 "A Possible Dark Area Shrine in Chavez Cave, Doña Ana County, New Mexico." In *Climbing the Rocks: Papers in Honor of Helen and Jay Crotty*, ed. R. N. Wiseman, T. C. O'Laughlin, and C. T. Snow, pp. 137–146. Archaeological Society of New Mexico, Albuquerque.

Olsen, N. H.
1985 *Hovenweep Rock Art: An Anasazi Visual Communication System*. Institute of Archaeology, University of California, Los Angeles.

Oppelt, N. T.
1988 *Southwestern Pottery: An Annotated Bibliography and List of Types and Wares*. 2nd ed. Scarecrow Press, Metuchen, NJ.

2002    *List of Southwestern Pottery Types and Wares.* Oppelt Publications, Greeley, CO.

2002    "Pottery and Other Intrusive Materials in Mesa Verde National Park." *Southwestern Lore,* Vol. 68, no. 4, pp. 1–10.

Ortiz, A.

1979    "San Juan Pueblo." In *Southwest,* ed. A. Ortiz, pp. 278–295. Handbook of North American Indians, Vol. 9, William C. Sturtevant, general editor, Smithsonian Institution, Washington, DC.

Ortiz, A., ed.

1979    *Southwest.* Handbook of North American Indians, Vol. 9, Smithsonian Institution, Washington, DC.

Oviedo y Valdés, G. F. de

1959    *Historia general y natural de las Indias.* Biblioteca de Autores Españoles, Vols. 67–71. Ediciones Atlas, Madrid.

Pacheco, J., and F. de Cárdenas

1864–1884    *Colección de documentos inéditos relativos al descubrimiento, conquista y organización de las antiguas posesiones españolas en América y Oceania.* 42 vols. M. G. Hernández, Madrid.

Padden, R. C.

1970    *The Hummingbird and the Hawk: Conquest and Sovereignty in the Valley of Mexico, 1503–1541.* Harper Colophon Books, New York.

Pailes, R. A.

1973    *An Archaeological Reconnaissance of Southern Sonora and Reconsideration of the Rio Sonora Culture.* PhD dissertation, Southern Illinois University, Carbondale. University Microfilms, Ann Arbor, MI.

1976    "Relaciones Culturales Prehistóricas en el Noreste de Sonora." In *Sonora: Antropología del Desierto,* coord. B. Braniff C. and R. S. Felger, pp. 213–228. Colección Científica Diversa 27, Centro Regional del Noroeste, Instituto Nacional de Antropología e Historia, México.

1978    "The Río Sonora Culture in Prehistoric Trade Systems." In *Across the Chichimec Sea: Papers in Honor of J. Charles Kelley,* ed. C. L. Riley and B. C. Hedrick, pp. 134–143. Southern Illinois University Press, Carbondale.

1979    "The Upper Rio Sonora Valley in Prehistoric Trade." *Transactions of the Illinois State Academy of Science,* Vol. 72, no. 4, pp. 20–39.

1984    "Agricultural Development and Trade in the Rio Sonora." In *Prehistoric Agricultural Strategies in the Southwest,* ed. S. K. Fish and P. R. Fish, pp. 309–325. Anthropological Research Papers No. 33. Arizona State University, Tempe.

1997    "An Archaeological Perspective on the Sonoran Entrada." In *The Coronado Expedition to Tierra Nueva,* ed. R. Flint and S. C. Flint, pp. 177–189. University Press of Colorado, Niwot.

Parsons, E. C.

1936    *Taos Pueblo.* George Banta Publishing, Menasha, WI.

1939    *Pueblo Indian Religion.* 2 vols. (paged consecutively). University of Chicago Press, Chicago, IL.

1962    Introduction to *Isleta Paintings,* ed. E. S. Goldfrank, pp. 1–12. Bureau of American Ethnology, Bull. 181, Washington, DC.

1974    "Some Aztec and Pueblo Parallels." In *The Mesoamerican Southwest,* ed. B. C. Hedrick, J. C. Kelley, and C. L. Riley, pp. 128–146. Southern Illinois University Press, Carbondale.

Pearce, T. M.

1965    *New Mexico Place Names: A Geographical Dictionary.* University of New Mexico Press, Albuquerque.

Peckham, S.

1965    *Prehistoric Weapons in the Southwest.* Museum of New Mexico Press, Santa Fe.

1990    *From This Earth.* Museum of New Mexico Press, Santa Fe.

Pennington, C. W., ed.

1981    *Arte y Vocabulario de la Lengua Dohema. Heve o Eudeva,* Instituto de Investigaciones Filológicas, Universidad Nacional Autónoma de México, México, DF.

Perkins, S.

2002    "Long Dry Spells: Lengthy Droughts Tied to Long-lived La Niñas." *Science News,* Vol. 162, no. 6, Aug., pp. 85–86.

Peterson, K. L.

1988    *Climate and the Dolores River Anasazi.* University of Utah Press, Salt Lake City.

1994 "A Warm and Wet Climatic Optimum and a Cold and Dry Little Ice Age in the Southern Rocky Mountains." In *The Medieval Warm Period*, ed. M. K. Hughes and H. F. Diaz, pp. 243–269. Kluwer Academic Publishers, Dordrecht, The Netherlands.

Phillips, D. A., Jr.
1989 "Prehistory of Chihuahua and Sonora." *Journal of World Prehistory*, Vol. 3, no. 4, pp. 373–401.
1990 "Areas arqueológicas de Chihuahua." In *Actas del Primer Congreso de Historia Regional Comparada, 1989*, pp. 11–21. Universidad Autónoma de Ciudad Juárez, Chihuahua.
1996 "Rethinking Chaco." In *Debating Complexity: Proceedings of the 26th Annual Chacmool Conference*, ed. D. A. Meyer, P. C. Dawson, and D. T. Hanna, pp. 333–338. Archaeological Society of the University of Calgary, Calgary, Alberta.

Phillips, D. A., Jr., and J. P. Carpenter
1999 "The Robles Phase of the Casa Grandes Culture." In *The Casas Grandes World*, ed. C. F. Schaafsma and C. L. Riley, pp. 78–83. University of Utah Press, Salt Lake City.

Phillips, D. A., Jr., and S. Larralde
2003 "Archaeological Survey of Elephant Butte and Caballo Reservoirs: Preliminary Results." Paper given at the 68th Annual Meeting of the Society for American Archaeology, Milwaukee, WI.

Pilles, P. J., Jr.
1996 "The Pueblo III Period Along the Mogollon Rim: The Honanki, Elden, and Turkey Hill Phases of the Sinagua." In *The Prehistoric Pueblo World, A.D. 1150–1350*, ed. M. A. Adler, pp. 59–72. University of Arizona Press, Tucson.

Plog, F.
1979 "Prehistory: Western Anasazi." In *Southwest*, ed. A. Ortiz, pp. 108–130. Handbook of North American Indians, Vol. 9, William C. Sturtevant, general editor, Smithsonian Institution, Washington, DC.
1989 "The Sinagua and Their Relations." In *Dynamics of Southwest Prehistory*, ed. L. S. Cordell and G. J. Gumerman, pp. 263–291. Smithsonian Institution Press, Washington DC.

Plog, S.
1995 "Equality and Hierarchy: Holistic Approaches to Understanding Social Dynamics in the Pueblo Southwest." In *Foundations of Social Inequality*, ed. T. D. Price and G. M. Feinman, pp. 189–206. Plenum Press, New York.

Plog, S., and J. Solometo
1996 "Alternative Pathways in the Evolution of Western Pueblo Ritual." In *Debating Complexity: Proceedings of the 26th Annual Chacmool Conference*, ed. D. A. Meyer, P. C. Dawson, and D. T. Hanna, pp. 326–332. Archaeological Association of the University of Calgary, Calgary, Alberta.

Pogue, J. E.
1975 *The Turquoise*. Rio Grande Press, Glorieta, NM.

Polyak, V. J., and Y. Asmerom
2001 "Late Holocene Climate and Cultural Changes in the Southwestern United States." *Science*, Vol. 294, pp. 148–151.

Potter, J. M.
1998 "The Structure of Open Space in Late Prehistoric Settlements in the Southwest." In *Migration and Reorganization: The Pueblo IV Period in the American Southwest*, ed. K. A. Spielmann, pp. 137–163. Anthropological Research Papers No. 51. Arizona State University, Tempe.

Powell, S.
1988 "Anasazi Demographic Patterns and Organizational Responses." In *The Anasazi in a Changing Environment*, ed. G. J. Gumerman, pp. 168–191. Cambridge University Press, Cambridge, UK.

Prescott, W. H.
1890 *History of the Conquest of Peru*. 2 vols. John B. Alden, New York. Originally published 1847, Baudry's European Library, Paris.

Preucel, R. W., ed.
2002 *Archaeologies of the Pueblo Revolt: Identity, Meaning, and Renewal in the Pueblo World*. University of New Mexico Press, Albuquerque.

Quijada, C. A., and J. E. Douglas
2001 "Arqueología del alto valle Bavispe, Sonora." In *Memoria del XXV Simposio de Historia y Antropología de Sonora*, pp. 411–429. Universidad de Sonora, Hermosillo, Son.

Rakita, G. F. M.
2001 "Social Complexity, Religious Organization, and Mortuary Ritual in the Casas Grandes Region of Chihuahua, Mexico." Unpublished PhD dissertation, Department of Anthropology, University of New Mexico, Albuquerque.

Rakita, G. F. M., and G. R. Raymond
2003 "The Temporal Sensitivity of Casas Grandes Polychrome Ceramics." *Kiva*, Vol. 68, no. 3, pp. 153–184.

Ramusio, G. B.
1556 *Delle Navigationi et Viagii...* Volume Terzo. In Venetia appressi i. Guinti.

Ravesloot, J. C.
1979 "The Animas Phase: Post Classic Mimbres Occupation of the Mimbres Valley, New Mexico." Unpublished master's thesis, Department of Anthropology, Southern Illinois University, Carbondale.

1988 *Mortuary Practices and Social Differentiation at Casas Grandes, Chihuahua, Mexico*. University of Arizona Press, Tucson.

Ravesloot, J. C., J. S. Dean, and M. S. Foster
1995 "A Reanalysis of the Casas Grandes Tree-Ring Dates: A Preliminary Discussion." In *Arqueología del norte y del occidente de México*, ed. J. Charles Kelley, B. Dahlgren, and M. D. Soto de Arechavaleta, pp. 325–332. Universidad Nacional Autónoma de Mexico, México, DF.

Ravesloot, J. C., and P. M. Spoerl
1984 "The Jicarilla Mountains: Pre-Lincoln Phase Settlement in the Northern Jornada Mogollon Periphery." In *Recent Research in Mogollon Archaeology*, ed. S. Upham, F. Plog, D. G. Batcho, and B. Kauffman, pp. 179–187. Occasional Papers No. 10. New Mexico State University, Las Cruces.

1989 "The Role of Warfare in the Development of Status Hierarchies at Casas Grandes, Chihuahua, Mexico." In *Cultures in Conflict: Current Archaeological*

*Perspectives: Proceedings of the 20th Annual Conference of the Chacmool Archaeological Association*, ed. D. C. Tkaczuk and B. C. Vivian, pp. 130–137. University of Calgary, Calgary, Alberta.

Redfield, R.
1956 *Peasant Society and Culture*. University of Chicago Press, Chicago, IL.

Reed, A. D., and J. C. Horn
1990 "Early Navajo Occupation of the American Southwest: Reexamination of the Dinetah Phase." *Kiva*, Vol. 55, no. 4, pp. 283–300.

Reed, E. K.
1942 "Implications of the Mogollon Concept." *American Antiquity*, Vol. 8, no. 1, pp. 27–32.

1946 "The Distinctive Features and Distribution of the San Juan Anasazi Culture." *Southwestern Journal of Anthropology*, Vol. 2, no. 3, pp. 295–305.

1948 "The Dating of the Early Mogollon Horizons." *El Palacio*, Vol. 55, no. 12, pp. 382–386.

1948 "The Western Pueblo Archaeological Complex." *El Palacio*, Vol. 55, no. 1, pp. 9–15.

1956 "Types of Village-Plan Layouts in the Southwest." In *Prehistoric Settlement Patterns in the New World*, ed. G. R. Willey, pp. 11–17. Viking Fund Publications in Anthropology No. 23. Wenner-Gren Foundation for Anthropological Research, New York.

Reed, P. F.
1990 "A Spatial Analysis of the Northern Rio Grande Region." In *Economy and Polity in Late Rio Grande Prehistory*, ed. S. Upham and B. D. Staley, pp. 1–89. University Museum Occasional Papers No. 16. New Mexico State University, Las Cruces.

Reed, P. F., and L. S. Reed
1996 "Reexamining Gobernador Polychrome." In *The Archaeology of Navajo Origins*, ed. R. H. Towner, pp. 83–108. University of Utah Press, Salt Lake City.

Reff, D. T.
1981 "The Location of Corazones and Señora: Archaeological Evidence from the Rio Sonora Valley, Mexico." In *The Protohistoric Period in the North American*

*Southwest, AD 1450–1700*, ed. D. R. Wilcox and W. B. Masse, pp. 94–112. Anthropological Research Papers No. 24. Arizona State University, Tempe.

1987  "Old World Diseases and the Dynamics of Indian and Jesuit Relations in Northwestern New Spain, 1520–1660." In *Ejidos and Regions of Refuge in Northwestern Mexico,* ed. N. R. Crumrine and P. C. Weigand, pp. 85–94. University of Arizona Press, Tucson.

1991  *Disease, Depopulation, and Culture Change in Northwestern New Spain.* University of Utah Press, Salt Lake City.

1997  "The Relevance of Ethnology to the Routing of the Coronado Expedition in Sonora." In *The Coronado Expedition to Tierra Nueva,* ed. R. Flint and S. C. Flint, pp. 165–176. University Press of Colorado, Niwot.

Reff, D. T., M. Ahern, and R. K. Danford, trans.

1999  *History of the Triumphs of our Holy Faith,* by Andrés Pérez de Ribas [1645]. University of Arizona Press, Tucson.

Reid, J. J.

1986  "Historical Perspective on the Concept of Mogollon." In *Mogollon Variability,* ed. C. Benson and S. Upham, pp. 1–8. University Museum Occasional Papers 15, New Mexico State University, Las Cruces.

1994  "Rethinking Mogollon Pueblo." In *Mogollon VII: The Collected Papers of the 1992 Mogollon Conference Held in Las Cruces, New Mexico,* ed. P. H. Beckett, pp. 3–7. COAS Publishing and Research, Las Cruces, NM.

Reid, J. J., and S. Whittlesey

1997  *The Archaeology of Ancient Arizona.* University of Arizona Press, Tucson.

1999  *Grasshopper Pueblo.* University of Arizona Press, Tucson.

Reyman, J. E.

1971  "Mexican Influence on Southwestern Ceremonialism." Unpublished PhD dissertation, Department of Anthropology, Southern Illinois University, Carbondale.

Reyman, J. E., ed.

1994  *The Gran Chichimeca.* Avebury, Aldershot, Hampshire, UK.

Riley, C. L.

1950  "'Defensive' Structures in the Hovenweep Monument." *El Palacio,* Vol. 57, no. 11, 339–344.

1952  "San Juan Anasazi and the Galisteo Basin." *El Palacio,* Vol. 59, no. 3, pp. 77–82.

1954  "Early Accounts of the South and Central American Blowgun." University of Colorado Studies, Series in Anthropology, no. 4, pp. 78–89.

1963  "Color-Direction Symbolism: An Example of Mexican-Southwestern Contacts." *América Indígena,* Vol. 23, no. 1, pp. 49–60.

1969  *The Origins of Civilization.* Southern Illinois University Press, Carbondale.

1969  "The Southern Tepehuan and Tepecano." In *Ethnology, Part 2,* ed. E. Z. Vogt, pp. 814–821. Handbook of Middle American Indians, Vol. 8, Robert Wauchope, general editor, University of Texas Press, Austin.

1971  "Early Spanish-Indian Communication in the Greater Southwest." *New Mexico Historical Review,* Vol. 46, no. 3, pp. 285–314.

1976  "Las Casas and the Golden Cities." *Ethnohistory,* Vol. 23, no. 1, pp. 19–30.

1976  *Sixteenth Century Trade in the Greater Southwest.* Mesoamerican Studies No. 10. Southern Illinois University Museum, Carbondale.

1981  "Puaray and Coronado's Tiguex." In *Collected Papers in Honor of Erik Kellerman Reed,* ed. A. H. Schroeder, pp. 197–213. Archaeological Society of New Mexico, Albuquerque.

1987  *The Frontier People: The Greater Southwest in the Protohistoric Period.* University of New Mexico Press, Albuquerque. Originally published 1982, Center for Archaeological Investigations, Southern Illinois University, Carbondale.

1989  "Warfare in the Protohistoric Southwest: An Overview." In *Cultures in Conflict: Current Archaeological Perspectives: Proceedings of the 20th Annual Conference of the Chacmool Archaeological Association,* ed. D. C. Tkaczuk and B. C. Vivian, pp. 138–146. University of Calgary, Calgary, Alberta.

1990  "The Sonoran Statelets Revisited: Urbanism in the Serrana Province of Northeastern Sonora." In *Clues to the Past: Papers in Honor of William M. Sundt,* ed. M. S. Duran and D. T. Kirkpatrick, pp. 229–238. Archaeological Society of New Mexico, Albuquerque.

1990 "A View from the Protohistoric." In *Perspectives on Southwestern Prehistory,* ed. P. E. Minnis and C. L. Redman, pp. 228–238. Westview Press, Boulder, CO.

1992 "Coronado in the Southwest." In *Archaeology, Art, and Anthropology: Papers in Honor of J. J. Brody,* ed. M. S. Duran and D. T. Kirkpatrick, pp. 147–156. Archaeological Society of New Mexico, Albuquerque.

1993 "Charles C. Di Peso: An Intellectual Biography." In *Culture and Contact: Charles C. Di Peso's Gran Chichimeca,* ed. A. I. Woosley and J. C. Ravesloot, pp. 11–22. Amerind Foundation, Dragoon, AZ, and University of New Mexico Press, Albuquerque.

1993 "The Pre-Spanish Camino Real." In *El Camino Real de Tierra Adentro,* ed. G. G. Palmer, pp. 13–19. Bureau of Land Management, New Mexico State Office, Santa Fe.

1994 "Marata and Its Neighbors." In *The Gran Chichimeca: Essays on the Archaeology and Ethnohistory of Northern Mesoamerica,* ed. J. E. Reyman, pp. 208–223. Avebury, Ashgate Publishing, Aldershot, Hampshire, UK.

1995 *Rio del Norte: People of the Upper Rio Grandes from Earliest Times to the Pueblo Revolt.* University of Utah Press, Salt Lake City.

1997 Introduction to *The Coronado Expedition to Tierra Nueva,* ed. R. Flint and S. C. Flint, pp. 1–28. University Press of Colorado, Niwot.

1997 "The Teya Indians of the Southwestern Plains." In *The Coronado Expedition to Tierra Nueva,* ed. R. Flint and S. C. Flint, pp. 320–343. University Press of Colorado, Niwot.

1999 *The Kachina and the Cross: Indians and Spaniards in the Early Southwest.* University of Utah Press, Salt Lake City.

1999 "The Sonoran Statelets and Casas Grandes." In *The Casas Grandes World,* ed. C. F. Schaafsma and C. L. Riley, pp. 193–200. University of Utah Press, Salt Lake City.

2001 "Spaniards in Aztlan." In *The Road to Aztlan: Art from a Mythic Homeland,* ed. V. M. Fields and V. Zamudio-Taylor, pp. 236–247. Los Angeles County Museum of Art, Los Angeles, CA.

Riley, C. L., and B. C. Hedrick
1978 *Across the Chichimec Sea.* Southern Illinois University Press, Carbondale.

Riley, C. L., J. C. Kelley, C. W. Pennington, and R. L. Rands
1971 *Man Across the Sea.* University of Texas Press, Austin.

Riley, C. L., and J. L. Manson
1983 "The Cíbola-Tiguex Route: Continuity and Change in the Southwest." *New Mexico Historical Review,* Vol. 58, no. 4, pp. 347–367.

1991 "The Sonoran Connection: Exchange Networks in the Protohistoric Period." In *Ancient Road Networks and Settlement Hierarchies in the New World,* ed. C. D. Trombold, pp. 132–144. Cambridge University Press, Cambridge, UK.

Riley, C. L., and H. D. Winters
1963 "The Prehistoric Tepehuan of Northern Mexico." *Southwestern Journal of Anthropology,* Vol. 19, no. 2, pp. 177–185.

Roberts, H., and R. V. N. Ahlstrom
1997 "Malaria, Microbes, and Mechanisms of Change." *Kiva,* Vol. 63, no. 2, pp. 117–135.

Robinson, W. J., and C. M. Cameron
1991 *A Directory of Tree-Ring Dated Prehistoric Sites in the American Southwest.* Laboratory of Tree-Ring Research, University of Arizona, Tucson.

Rodeck, M. T.
1997 "Cíbola, from Fray Marcos to Coronado." In *The Coronado Expedition to Tierra Nueva,* ed. R. Flint and S. C. Flint, pp. 102–115. University Press of Colorado, Niwot.

Rogers, M. J.
1945 "An Outline of Yuman Prehistory." *Southwestern Journal of Anthropology,* Vol. 1, no. 2, pp. 167–198.

Rohn, A. H.
1989 "War and Violence Among Southwestern Pueblos." In *Cultures in Conflict: Current Archaeological Perspectives: Proceedings*

of the 20th Annual Conference of the
Chacmool Archaeological Association,
ed. D. C. Tkaczuk and B. C. Vivian,
pp. 147–152. University of Calgary,
Calgary, Alberta.

Roney, J. R.
1995 "Mesa Verdean Manifestations South of
the San Juan River." *Journal of Anthropological Archaeology,* Vol. 14, no. 2,
pp. 170–183.

Rowe, J. H.
1946 "Inca Culture at the Time of the Spanish
Conquest." In *Handbook of South Amer-
ican Indians,* ed. J. H. Steward, Vol. 2,
*The Andean Civilizations,* pp. 183–330.
Smithsonian Institution, Bureau of
American Ethnology, Bull. 143, Wash-
ington, DC.

Ruby, J., and T. Blackburn
1964 "Occurrence of Southwestern Pottery
in Los Angeles County, California."
*American Antiquity,* Vol. 30, no. 2,
pp. 209–210.

Ruiz, Antonio
[1932] *Punctos Sacados,* Vol. 25, *Misiones,*
Archivo General de México. [In Sauer,
*Road to Cíbola,* pp. 53–58.]

Ruscavage-Barz, S. M.
2002 "Understanding Santa Fe Black-on-
White Style and Technology." *Kiva,*
Vol. 67, no. 3, pp. 249–268.

Sahagún, Fr. B. de
1970 *General History of Things in New Spain:
Book I, The Gods,* ed. and trans. A. J. O.
Anderson and C. E. Dibble [contains
English and Aztec texts]. Monographs
of the School of American Research No.
14, pt. 2. School of American Research,
Santa Fe, and University of Utah, Salt
Lake City.

Salaz Marquez, R.
1999 *New Mexico: A Brief Multi-History.*
Cosmic House, Albuquerque, NM.

Salzer, M. W.
2000 "Temperature Variability and the Northern Anasazi: Possible Implications for
Regional Abandonment." *Kiva,* Vol. 65,
no. 4, pp. 295–318.

Sando, J. S.
1979 "Jemez Pueblo." In *Southwest,* ed. A.
Ortiz, pp. 418–429. Handbook of North

American Indians, Vol. 9, William C.
Sturtevant, general editor, Smithsonian
Institution, Washington, DC.

Sauer, C. O.
1932 *The Road to Cíbola.* University of California Press, Berkeley.
1934 *The Distribution of Aboriginal Tribes
and Languages in Northwestern Mexico.*
University of California Press, Berkeley.
1935 *Aboriginal Population of Northwestern
Mexico.* University of California Press,
Berkeley.

Sauer, C. O., and D. B. Brand
1932 *Aztatlán: Prehistoric Mexican Frontier
on the Pacific Coast.* University of California Press, Berkeley.

Schaafsma, C. F.
1996 "Ethnic Identity and Protohistoric Archae-
ological Sites in Northwestern New Mex-
ico." In *The Archaeology of Navajo
Origins,* ed. R. H. Towner, pp. 19–46.
University of Utah Press, Salt Lake City.
1997 "Ethnohistoric Groups in the Casas
Grandes Region, Circa A.D. 1500–
1700." In *Layers of Time: Papers in
Honor of Robert H. Weber,* ed. M. S.
Duran and D. T. Kirkpatrick, pp. 85–98.
Archaeological Society of New Mexico,
Albuquerque.
2002 *Apaches de Navajo: Seventeenth-Century
Navajos in the Chama Valley of New
Mexico.* University of Utah Press, Salt
Lake City.
2002 Review of *Casas Grandes and Its Hinter-
land,* by M. E. Whalen and P. E. Minnis.
*American Anthropologist,* Vol. 104, no.
3, pp. 1006–1007.

Schaafsma, C. F., J. R. Cox, and D. Wolfman
2002 "Archaeomagnetic Dating at the Joyce
Well Site." In *The Joyce Well Site: On
the Frontier of the Casas Grandes World,*
ed. J. M. Skibo, E. B. McCluney, and
W. H. Walker, pp. 129–148. University
of Utah Press, Salt Lake City.

Schaafsma, C. F., and C. L. Riley
1999 "The Casas Grandes World: Analysis
and Conclusion." In *The Casas Grandes
World,* ed. C. F. Schaafsma and C. L.
Riley, pp. 237–249. University of Utah
Press, Salt Lake City.
1999 Introduction to *The Casas Grandes
World,* ed. C. F. Schaafsma and C. L.

Riley, pp. 1–11. University of Utah Press, Salt Lake City.

Schaafsma, C. F., and C. L. Riley, eds.
1999 *The Casas Grandes World.* University of Utah Press, Salt Lake City.

Schaafsma, P.
1965 "Kiva Murals from Pueblo del Encierro (LA 70)." *El Palacio,* Vol. 72, pp. 6–16.
1980 *Indian Rock Art of the Southwest.* School of American Research Press, Santa Fe, and University of New Mexico Press, Albuquerque.
1992 *Rock Art in New Mexico.* Museum of New Mexico Press, Santa Fe.
1994 "The Prehistoric Kachina Cult and Its Origins as Suggested by Southwestern Rock Art." In *Kachinas in the Pueblo World,* ed. P. Schaafsma, pp. 63–79. University of New Mexico Press, Albuquerque.
1997 *Rock Art Sites in Chihuahua, Mexico.* Museum of New Mexico, Santa Fe.
1998 "The Paquimé Rock Art Style, Chihuahua, Mexico." In *Rock Art of the Chihuahuan Desert Borderlands,* ed. S. Smith-Savage and R. J. Mallouf, pp. 33–44. Center for Big Bend Studies, Occasional Papers No. 3. Sul Ross State University, Alpine, Texas.
1999 "Tlalocs, Kachinas, Sacred Bundles, and Related Symbolism in the Southwest and Mesoamerica." In *The Casas Grandes World,* ed. C. F. Schaafsma and C. L. Riley, pp. 164–192. University of Utah Press, Salt Lake City.
2000 "Emblems of Power: Visual Symbols as a Means of Social Identity and the Role of Rock Art in the Chaco System and in the Casas Grandes Region." Paper given at the 65th Annual Meeting of the Society for American Archaeology, Philadelphia, PA.
2000 *Warrior, Shield, and Star: Imagery and Ideology of Pueblo Warfare.* Western Edge Press, Santa Fe, NM.
2001 "Quetzalcoatl and the Horned and Feathered Serpent of the Southwest." In *The Road to Aztlan: Art from a Mythic Homeland,* ed. V. M. Fields and V. Zamudio-Taylor, pp. 138–149. Los Angeles County Museum of Art, Los Angeles, CA.

Schaafsma, P., and C. F. Schaafsma
1974 "Evidence for the Origins of the Pueblo Kachina Cult as Suggested by Southwestern Rock Art." *American Antiquity,* Vol. 39, no. 4, pp. 535–545.

Schillaci, M. A.
2003 "The Development of Population Diversity at Chaco Canyon." *Kiva,* Vol. 68, no. 3, pp. 221–245.

Schillaci, M. A., E. G. Ozolins, and T. C. Windes
2001 "Multivariate Assessment of Biological Relationships Among Prehistoric Southwest Amerindian Populations." In *Following Through: Papers in Honor of Phyllis S. Davis,* ed. R. N. Wiseman, T. C. O'Laughlin, and C. T. Snow, pp. 133–149. Archaeological Society of New Mexico, Albuquerque.

Schmidt, R.
1992 "Chihuahua, tierra de contrastes geográficos." In *Historia General de Chihuahua I: Geología, Geografía y Arqueología,* coord. A. Márquez-Alameda, pp. 45–101. Universidad Autónoma de Ciudad Juárez, Gobierno del Estado de Chihuahua.

Scholes, F. V., and H. P. Mera
1940 *Some Aspects of the Jumano Problem.* Carnegie Institution of Washington Contributions to American Anthropology and History, Vol. 6, no. 34 (Pub. 523), pp. 271–299.

Schroeder, A. H.
1957 "The Hakataya Cultural Tradition." *American Antiquity,* Vol. 23, no. 2,, pp. 176–178.
1979 "Prehistory: Hakataya." In *Southwest,* ed. A. Ortiz, pp. 100–107. Handbook of North American Indians, Vol. 9, William C. Sturtevant, general editor, Smithsonian Institution, Washington, DC.
1979 "Pueblos Abandoned in Historic Times." In *Southwest,* ed. A. Ortiz, pp. 236–254. Handbook of North American Indians, Vol. 9, William C. Sturtevant, general editor, Smithsonian Institution, Washington, DC.
1990 "Tunque Pueblo—Who Lived There?" In *Clues to the Past: Papers in Honor of William M. Sundt,* ed. M. S. Duran and D. T. Kirkpatrick, pp. 259–264.

Archaeological Society of New Mexico, Albuquerque.

Schroeder, A. H., and D. S. Matson
1965   *A Colony on the Move: Gaspar Castaño de Sosa's Journal, 1590–1591.* School of American Research Press, Santa Fe, NM.

Schwartz, D. W.
1956   "The Havasupai, 600 A.D.–1955 A.D.: A Short Culture History." *Plateau*, Vol. 28, no. 4, pp. 77–85.

Scott, C. J.
1983   "The Evolution of Mimbres Pottery." In *Mimbres Pottery: Ancient Art of the American Southwest*, by J. J. Brody, C. J. Scott, and S. A. LeBlanc, not paged. Hudson Hills Press, in association with The American Federation of Arts and Viking Press, New York.

Sebastian, L.
1992   *The Chaco Anasazi.* Cambridge University Press, Cambridge, UK.
1992   "Chaco Canyon and the Anasazi Southwest: Changing Views of Sociopolitical Organization." In *Anasazi Regional Organization and the Chaco System*, ed. D. E. Doyel, pp. 23–31. Maxwell Museum of Anthropology, University of New Mexico, Albuquerque.
1996   "Taking Charge in Chaco: The Evolution of Political Structure." In *Debating Complexity: Proceedings of the 26th Annual Chacmool Conference*, ed. D. A. Meyer, P. C. Dawson, and D. T. Hanna, pp. 339–344. Archaeological Association of the University of Calgary, Calgary, Alberta.

Sever, T. L., and D. W. Wagner
1991   "Analysis of Prehistoric Roadways in Chaco Canyon Using Remotely Sensed Digital Data." In *Ancient Road Networks and Settlement Hierarchies in the New World*, ed. C. D. Trombold, pp. 42–52. Cambridge University Press, Cambridge, UK.

Severance, O.
2003   "Cultural Dynamics in Southeastern Utah: Basketmaker III Through Pueblo III." In *Climbing the Rocks: Papers in Honor of Helen and Jay Crotty*, ed. R. N. Wiseman, T. C. O'Laughlin, and C. T. Snow, pp. 189–203. Archaeological Society of New Mexico, Albuquerque.

Shafer, H. J.
1999   "The Mimbres Classic and Postclassic: A Case for Discontinuity." In *The Casas Grandes World*, ed. C. F. Schaafsma and C. L. Riley, pp. 121–133. University of Utah Press, Salt Lake City.
2003   *Mimbres Archaeology at the NAN Ranch Ruin.* University of New Mexico Press, Albuquerque.

Shepard, A. O.
1965   "Rio Grande Glaze-Paint Pottery: A Test of Petrographic Analysis." In *Ceramics and Man*, ed. F. R. Matson, pp. 62–87. Viking Fund publications in Anthropology No. 41. Aldine, Chicago, IL.

Simmons, A. H. (with D. D. Dykeman and P. A. Hicks)
1989   "The Formative Period—Neolithic Archeology in the Southwest." In *Human Adaptations and Cultural Change in the Greater Southwest*, ed. A. H. Simmons, A. L. W. Stodder, D. D. Dykeman, and P. A. Hicks, pp. 75–118. Arkansas Archeological Survey Research Series No. 32. Arkansas Archeological Survey, Fayetteville, AR.

Simmons, M.
1991   *The Last Conquistador.* University of Oklahoma Press, Norman.

Simon, A. W.
1998   "Salado Decorated Ceramics: Paint, Pigment, and Style." In *Salado Ceramics and Social Organization: Prehistoric Interactions in Tonto Basin*, ed. A. W. Simon, with J. H. Burton, J.-C. Komorowski, and O. Lindauer, pp. 69–92. Roosevelt Monograph Series 11, Anthropological Field Studies 40, Arizona State University, Tempe.

Skibo, J. M., E. B. McCluney, and W. H. Walker, eds.
2002   *The Joyce Well Site: On the Frontier of the Casas Grandes World.* University of Utah Press, Salt Lake City.

Skibo, J. M., and W. H. Walker
2002   "Ball Courts and Ritual Performance." In *The Joyce Well Site: On the Frontier of the Casas Grandes World*, ed. J. M. Skibo, E. B. McCluney, and W. H. Walker, pp. 107–128. University of Utah Press, Salt Lake City.

Slifer, D.

1998 *Signs of Life: Rock Art of the Upper Rio Grande.* Ancient City Press, Santa Fe, NM.

2000 *The Serpent and the Sacred Fire: Fertility Images in Southwest Rock Art.* Museum of New Mexico Press, Santa Fe.

Smith, W.

1952 *Kiva Mural Decorations at Awatovi and Kawaika-a, with a Survey of Other Wall Paintings in the Pueblo Southwest.* Papers of the Peabody Museum of American Archaeology and Ethnology Vol. 37. Harvard University, Cambridge, MA.

1970 "Pots of Gold?" *Kiva,* Vol. 36, no. 1, 39–43.

1980 "Mural Decoration from Ancient Hopi Kivas." In *Hopi Kachina: Spirit of Life,* ed. D. K. Washburn, pp. 29–38. California Academy of Sciences, San Francisco, and University of Washington Press, Seattle.

Smith, W., R. B. Woodbury, and N. F. S. Woodbury

1966 *The Excavation of Hawikuh by Frederick Webb Hodge.* Museum of the American Indian, Heye Foundation, New York.

Snead, J. E.

2004 "Ancestral Pueblo Settlement Dynamics: Landscape, Scale, and Context in the Burnt Corn Community." *Kiva,* Vol. 69, no. 3, pp. 243–269.

Snow, C. T.

2002 "Fish Tales: The Use of Freshwater Fish in New Mexico from A.D. 1000 to 1900." In *Forward into the Past: Papers in Honor of Teddy Lou and Francis Stickney,* ed. R. N. Wiseman, T. C. O'Laughlin, and C. T. Snow, pp. 119–132. Archaeological Society of New Mexico, Albuquerque.

Snow, D. H.

1973 "Prehistoric Southwestern Turquoise Industry." *El Palacio,* Vol. 79, no. 1, pp. 33–51.

1982 "The Rio Grande Glaze, Matte-Paint, and Plainware Tradition." In *Southwestern Ceramics: A Comparative Review,* ed. A. H. Schroeder, pp. 235–278. Arizona Archaeologist No. 15. Arizona Archaeological Society, Phoenix.

1984 "Prologue to Rio Grande Protohistory." In *Collected Papers in Honor of Harry L. Hadlock,* ed. N. L. Fox, pp. 125–132. Archaeological Society of New Mexico, Albuquerque.

1990 "Tener Comal y Metate: Protohistoric Rio Grande Maize Use and Diet." In *Perspectives on Southwestern History,* ed. P. E. Minnis and C. L. Redman, pp. 289–300. Westview Press, Boulder, CO.

1991 "Upland Prehistoric Maize Agriculture in the Eastern Rio Grande and Its Peripheries." In *Farmers, Hunters, and Colonists,* ed. K. A. Spielmann, pp. 71–88. University of Arizona Press, Tucson.

1998 "The Transition from History to Prehistory: Archaeology and Ethnohistory in the Eastern Pueblo Provinces." Paper prepared for a conference entitled The Transition from Prehistory to History in the Southwest, Albuquerque, Feb. 27–March 1, Library, MIAC/LabAnth, Museum of New Mexico, Santa Fe.

Snow, D. H., comp.

1998 "New Mexico's First Colonists." In *The 1597–1600 Enlistments for New Mexico Under Juan de Oñate, Adelante and Governor.* Hispanic Genealogical Research Center of New Mexico, Albuquerque.

Sorenson, J. L., and M. H. Raish

1996 *Pre-Columbian Contact with the Americas Across the Oceans: An Annotated Bibliography.* 2 Vols. 2nd rev. ed. Foundation for Ancient Research and Mormon Studies, Provo, Utah.

Spicer, E. H.

1962 *Cycles of Conquest.* University of Arizona Press, Tucson.

1983 "Yaqui." In *Southwest,* ed. A. Ortiz, pp. 250–263. Handbook of North American Indians, Vol. 10, William C. Sturtevant, general editor, Smithsonian Institution, Washington, DC.

Spielmann, K. A.

1994 "Clustered Confederacies: Sociopolitical Organization in the Protohistoric Río Grande." In *The Ancient Southwestern Community,* ed. W. H. Wills and R. D. Leonard, pp. 45–54. University of New Mexico Press, Albuquerque.

1996 "Impressions of Pueblo III Settlement Trends Among the Rio Abajo and Eastern Border Pueblos." In *The Prehistoric*

*Pueblo World, A.D. 1150–1350,* ed. M. A. Adler, pp. 177–187. University of Arizona Press, Tucson.

1998 "Ritual Influences on the Development of Rio Grande Glaze A Ceramics." In *Migration and Reorganization: The Pueblo IV Period in the American Southwest,* ed. K. A. Spielmann, pp. 253–261. Anthropological Research Papers No. 51. Arizona State University, Tempe.

Spielmann, K. A., and E. A. Angstadt-Leto

1996 "Hunting, Gathering, and Health in the Prehistoric Southwest." In *Evolving Complexity and Environmental Risk in the Prehistoric Southwest,* ed. J. A. Tainter and B. B. Tainter, pp. 79–106. Addison-Wesley, Reading, MA.

Sprague, R., and A. Signori

1963 "Inventory of Prehistoric Southwestern Copper Bells." *Kiva,* Vol. 28, no. 4, pp. 1–20.

Sprehn, M. S.

2003 "Social Complexity and the Specialist Potters of Casas Grandes in Northern Mexico." Unpublished PhD dissertation, Department of Anthropology, University of New Mexico, Albuquerque.

Stacy, V. K. P.

1974 "Cerro de Trincheras in the Arizona Papagueria." Unpublished PhD dissertation, Department of Anthropology, University of Arizona, Tucson.

Steen, C. R.

1977 *Pajarito Plateau Archaeological Survey and Excavations.* Los Alamos Scientific Laboratories, pub. 77-4.

Stein, J. R., and A. P. Fowler

1996 "Looking Beyond Chaco in the San Juan Basin and Its Peripheries." *The Prehistoric Pueblo World, A.D. 1150–1350,* ed. M. A. Adler, pp. 114–130. University of Arizona Press, Tucson.

Stern, S. J.

1982 *Peru's Indian Peoples and the Challenge of Spanish Conquest.* University of Wisconsin Press, Madison.

Steward, J. D., J. H. Kelley, A. C. MacWilliams, and P. J. Reimer

2004 "Archaeological Chronology in West-Central Chihuahua." In *Surveying the Archaeology of Northwest Mexico,* ed. G. E. Newell and E. Gallaga, pp.

205–264. University of Utah Press, Salt Lake City.

Stone, T.

2002 "Kiva Diversity in the Point of Pines Region of Arizona." *Kiva,* Vol. 67, no. 4, pp. 385–411.

Strong, P. T.

1979 "Santa Ana Pueblo." In *Southwest,* ed. A. Ortiz, pp. 398–406. Handbook of North American Indians, Vol. 9, William C. Sturtevant, general editor, Smithsonian Institution, Washington, DC.

Strong, W. D.

1973 "An Analysis of Southwestern Society." In *The Classic Southwest,* ed. B. C. Hedrick, J. C. Kelley, and C. L. Riley, pp. 110–152. Southern Illinois University Press, Carbondale.

Stuart, D. E., and R. P. Gauthier

1981 *Prehistoric New Mexico.* University of New Mexico Press, Albuquerque.

Suina, J. H.

2002 "The Persistence of the Corn Mothers." In *Archaeologies of the Pueblo Revolt: Identity, Meaning, and Renewal in the Pueblo World,* ed. R. W. Preucel, pp. 212–216. University of New Mexico Press, Albuquerque.

Sutherland, K.

1998 "Mesoamerican Ceremony Among the Prehistoric Jornada Mogollon." In *Rock Art of the Chihuahuan Desert Borderlands,* ed. S. Smith-Savage and R. J. Mallouf, pp. 61–87. Center for Big Bend Studies, Occasional Papers No. 3. Sul Ross State University, Alpine, Texas.

Swanson, S.

2003 "Documenting Prehistoric Communication Networks: A Case Study in the Paquimé Polity." *American Antiquity,* Vol. 68, no. 4, pp. 753–767.

Talbot, R. K.

2000 "Fremont Farmers: The Search for Context." *The Archaeology of Regional Interaction: Religion, Warfare, and Exchange Across the American Southwest and Beyond,* ed. M. Hegmon, pp. 275–293. University Press of Colorado, Boulder.

Taylor, W. W.
1964 "Tethered Nomadism and Water Territoriality: An Hypothesis." *35th Congreso Internacional de Americanistas, Actos y Memorias:* 2, pp. 197–203. Editorial Libros de México, México, DF.

Teague, L. S.
1998 *Textiles in Southwestern Prehistory.* University of New Mexico Press, Albuquerque.
2000 "Outward and Visible Signs: Textiles in Ceremonial Contexts." In *The Archaeology of Regional Interaction: Religion, Warfare, and Exchange Across the American Southwest and Beyond,* ed. M. Hegmon, pp. 429–447. University Press of Colorado, Boulder.

Thomas, H.
1993 *Conquest: Montezuma, Cortés, and the Fall of Old Mexico.* Simon and Schuster, New York.

Thompson, M.
1994 "The Evolution and Dissemination of Mimbres Iconography." In *Kachinas in the Pueblo World,* ed. P. Schaafsma, pp. 93–105. University of New Mexico Press, Albuquerque.
1999 "Mimbres Iconography: Analysis and Interpretation of Figurative Motifs." Unpublished PhD dissertation, Department of Archaeology, University of Calgary, Alberta.

Thompson, M., and R. B. Brown
2004 "Scarlet Macaws: Sunbirds of the Southwest." Paper given at the 13th Mogollon Archaeology Conference, Silver City, NM, Sep. 30–Oct. 2.

Tolstoy, P.
1974 "Mesoamerica." In *Prehispanic America,* ed. S. Gorenstein, R. G. Forbis, P. Tolstoy, and E. P. Lanning, pp. 29–64. St. Martin's, New York.

Toulouse, J. H., Jr., and R. L. Stephenson
1960 *Excavations at Pueblo Pardo.* Museum of New Mexico, Santa Fe.

Tower, D. B.
1945 *The Use of Marine Mollusca and Their Value in Reconstructing Prehistoric Trade Routes in the American Southwest.* Excavators' Club, Cambridge, MA.

Towner, R. H., ed.
1996 *The Archaeology of Navajo Origins.* University of Utah Press, Salt Lake City.

Townsend, R. F.
1992 "The Renewal of Nature at the Temple of Tlaloc." In *The Ancient Americas: Art from Sacred Landscapes,* ed. R. F. Townsend, pp. 171–186. Art Institute of Chicago.

Troike, R.
1988 "Amotomanco (Otomoaco) and Tanpachoa as Uto-Aztecan Languages, and the Jumano Problem Once More." *International Journal of American Linguistics,* Vol. 54, no. 2, pp. 235–241.

Trombold, C. D.
1991 "Causeways in the La Quemada Region." In *Ancient Road Networks and Settlement Hierarchies in the New World,* ed. C. D. Trombold, pp. 145–168. Cambridge University Press, Cambridge, UK.

Truell, M. L.
1986 "A Summary of Small Site Architecture in Chaco Canyon, New Mexico." In *Small Site Architecture of Chaco Canyon,* ed. P. J. McKenna and M. L. Truell, pp. 115–502. Publications in Archaeology no. 18D, Chaco Canyon Studies, National Park Service, Santa Fe, NM.

Turner, C. G., II
1999 "The Dentition of Casas Grandes with Suggestions on Epigenetic Relationships Among Mexican and Southwestern U.S. Populations." In *The Casas Grandes World,* ed. C. F. Schaafsma and C. L. Riley, pp. 229–233. University of Utah Press, Salt Lake City.

Turner, C. G., II, and J. A. Turner
1999 *Man Corn: Cannibalism and Violence in the Prehistoric American Southwest.* University of Utah Press, Salt Lake City.

Underhill, R. M.
1956 *The Navajos.* University of Oklahoma Press, Norman.

Upham, S.
1982 *Politics and Power.* Academic Press, New York.
2000 "Scale, Innovation, and Change in the Desert West: A Macroregional Approach." In *The Archaeology of Regional Interaction: Religion, Warfare,*

*and Exchange Across the American Southwest and Beyond,* ed. M. Hegmon, pp. 235–256. University Press of Colorado, Boulder.

Upham, S., and P. F. Reed
1989 "Inferring the Structure of Anasazi Warfare." In *Cultures in Conflict: Current Archaeological Perspectives: Proceedings of the 20th Annual Conference of the Chacmool Archaeological Association,* ed. D. C. Tkaczuk and B. C. Vivian, pp. 153–162. University of Calgary, Calgary, Alberta.

Urban, S.
1991 "Shell." In *Homol'ovi II: Archaeology of an Ancestral Hopi Village, Arizona,* ed. E. C. Adams and K. A. Hays, pp. 112–115. University of Arizona Press, Tucson.

Vaillant, G. C.
1941 *Aztecs of Mexico.* Doubleday, Doran, Garden City, NY.

Van Dyke, R. M.
2002 "The Chacoan Great Kiva in Outlier Communities." *Kiva,* Vol. 67, no. 3, pp. 231–247.

VanPool, C. S.
2001 "Birds, Burials, and Beliefs at Paquimé, Chihuahua, Mexico." In *From Paquimé to Mata Ortiz: The Legacy of Ancient Casas Grandes,* ed. G. Johnson, pp. 73–88. Museum of Man, San Diego, CA.
2002 "Flight of the Shaman." *Archaeology,* Vol. 55, no. 1, pp. 40–43.
2003 "The Shaman-Priests of the Casas Grandes Region, Chihuahua, Mexico." *American Antiquity,* Vol. 68, no. 4, pp. 696–717.
2003 "The Symbolism of Casas Grandes." Unpublished PhD dissertation, Department of Anthropology, University of New Mexico, Albuquerque.

VanPool, T. L., and R. D. Leonard
2002 "Specialized Ground Stone Production in the Casas Grandes Region of Northern Chihuahua, Mexico." *American Antiquity,* Vol. 67, no. 4, pp. 710–730.

VanPool, T. L., R. D. Leonard, M. J. Harmon, C. S. VanPool, and D. A. Phillips Jr.
2004 "The Evolution of the Horned Serpent." Paper presented at the 69th Annual Meetings of the Society for American Archaeology, Montreal.

VanPool, T. L., and C. S. VanPool
2003 "Evolution and Agency: The Role of Intended and Unintended Action." In *Essential Tensions in Archaeological Method and Theory,* ed. T. L. VanPool and C. S. VanPool, pp. 89–113. University of Utah Press, Salt Lake City.

VanPool, T. L., C. S. VanPool, R. Cruz Antillón, R. D. Leonard, and M. J. Harmon
2000 "Flaked Stone and Social Interaction in the Casas Grandes Region, Chihuahua, Mexico." *Latin American Antiquity,* Vol. 11, no. 2, pp. 163–174.

VanPool, T. L., C. S. VanPool, and D. A. Phillips Jr.
n.d. "The Casas Grandes and Salado Phenomena." In *Religion of the Prehispanic Southwest,* ed. C. S. VanPool, T. L. VanPool, and D. A. Phillips, chap. 13. Archaeology of Religion Series, D. S. Whitley, general editor, AltaMira, Walnut Creek, CA.

Van West, C. R., R. S. Ciolek-Torrello, J. R. Welch, J. H. Altschul, K. R. Adams, S. D. Shelley, and J. A. Homburg
2000 "Subsistence and Environmental Interactions." In *Salado,* ed. J. S. Dean, pp. 27–56. Amerind Foundation, Dragoon, AZ, and University of New Mexico Press, Albuquerque.

Van West, C. R., and J. S. Dean
2000 "Environmental Characteristics of the A.D. 900–1300 Period in the Central Mesa Verde Region." *Kiva,* Vol. 66, no. 1, pp. 19–44.

Vargas, V. D.
1994 "Copper Bell Trade Patterns in the Prehistoric Greater American Southwest." Unpublished master's thesis, Department of Anthropology, University of Oklahoma, Norman.
1995 *Copper Bell Trade Patterns in the Prehispanic U.S. Southwest and Northwest Mexico.* Arizona State Museum, University of Arizona, Tucson.

Varien, M. D.
2000 Review of *The Chaco Meridian. American Anthropologist,* Vol. 104, no. 2, pp. 913–914.

Varien, M. D., W. D. Lipe, M. A. Adler,
I. M. Thompson, and B. A. Bradley
1996 "Southwestern Colorado and Southeastern Utah Settlement Patterns: A.D. 1100–1300." In *The Prehistoric Pueblo World, A.D. 1150–1350*, ed. M. A. Adler, pp. 86–113. University of Arizona Press, Tucson.

Villalpando, M. E.
1997 "La Tradición Trincheras y Los Grupos Costeros del Desierto Sonorense." In *Prehistory of the Borderlands: Recent Research in the Archaeology of Northern Mexico and the Southern Southwest*, ed. J. Carpenter and G. Sanchez, pp. 95–111. Arizona State Museum, University of Arizona, Tucson.

Vivian, R. G.
1990 *The Chacoan Prehistory of the San Juan Basin.* Academic Press, San Diego.
1991 "Chacoan Subsistence." In *Chaco and Hohokam*, ed. P. L. Crown and W. J. Judge, pp. 57–75. School of American Research Press, Santa Fe, NM.
2000 "Economy and Ecology, Chaco Synthesis Project." *Archaeology Southwest*, Vol. 14, no. 1, pp. 5–7.

Vivian, R. G., D. N. Dodgen, and
G. H. Hartmann
1978 *Wooden Ritual Artifacts from Chaco Canyon, New Mexico: The Chetro Ketl Collection.* University of Arizona Press, Tucson.

Von Habsburg, O.
1969 *Charles V.* Trans. M. Ross. George Weidenfeld and Nicolson, London.

Walker, W. H., and J. M. Skibo
2002 "Joyce Well and the Casas Grandes Religious Interaction Sphere." In *The Joyce Well Site: On the Frontier of the Casas Grandes World*, ed. J. M. Skibo, E. B. McCluney, and W. H. Walker, pp. 167–175. University of Utah Press, Salt Lake City.

Walker, W. H., J. M. Skibo, and E. B. McCluney
2002 "Joyce Well and the Casas Grandes World." In *The Joyce Well Site: On the Frontier of the Casas Grandes World*, ed. J. M. Skibo, E. B. McCluney, and W. H. Walker, pp. 1–10. University of Utah Press, Salt Lake City.

Walters, H., and H. C. Rogers
2001 "Anasazi and 'Anaasází': Two Words, Two Cultures." *Kiva*, Vol. 66, no. 3, pp. 317–326.

Ware, J. A., and E. Blinman
2000 "Cultural Collapse and Reorganization: Origin and Spread of Pueblo Ritual Sodalities." In *The Archaeology of Regional Interaction: Religion, Warfare, and Exchange Across the American Southwest and Beyond*, ed. M. Hegmon, pp. 381–409. University Press of Colorado, Boulder.

Washburn, D. K.
1979 "The Mexican Connection: Cylinder Jars from the Valley of Oaxaca." *Transactions of the Illinois State Academy of Science*, Vol. 72, no. 4, pp. 70–85.

Weigand, P. C.
1976 "Rio Grande Glaze Sherds in Western Mexico." *Pottery Southwest*, Vol. 4, no. 1, pp. 3–5.
1991 "The Western Mesoamerican Tlachco: A Two-Thousand-Year Perspective." In *The Mesoamerican Ballgame*, ed. V. L. Scarborough and D. R. Wilcox, pp. 73–86. University of Arizona Press, Tucson.

Weigand, P. C., and A. García de Weigand
2001 "A Macroeconomic Study of the Relationships Between the Ancient Cultures of the American Southwest and Mesoamerica." In *The Road to Aztlan: Art from a Mythic Homeland*, ed. V. M. Fields and V. Zamudio-Taylor, pp. 184–195. Los Angeles County Museum of Art, Los Angeles, CA.

Weigand, P. C., and G. Harbottle
1993 "The Role of Turquoises in the Ancient Mesoamerican Trade Structure." In *The Southwest and Mesoamerica: Systems of Prehistoric Exchange*, ed. J. E. Ericson and T. G. Baugh, pp. 159–177. Plenum Press, New York.

Weigand, P. C., G. Harbottle, and E. V. Sayre
1977 "Turquoise Sources and Source Analysis: Mesoamerica and the Southwestern U.S.A." In *Exchange Systems in Prehistory*, ed. T. K. Earle and J. E. Ericson, pp. 15–34. Academic Press, New York.

Wendorf, F., ed.
1953 *Salvage Archaeology in the Chama Valley, New Mexico.* Monographs of the

School of American Research No. 17. Santa Fe, NM.

Wendorf, F., and E. K. Reed

1955 "An Alternative Reconstruction of Northern Rio Grande Prehistory." *El Palacio,* Vol. 62, nos. 5–6, pp. 131–173.

Whalen, M. E., and P. E. Minnis

1996 "Ball Courts and Political Centralization in the Casas Grandes Region." *American Antiquity,* Vol. 61, no. 4, pp. 732–746.

1996 "Studying Complexity in Northern Mexico: The Paquimé Regional System." In *Debating Complexity: Proceedings of the 26th Annual Chacmool Conference,* ed. D. A. Meyer, P. C. Dawson, and D. T. Hanna, pp. 282–289. Archaeological Association of the University of Calgary, Calgary, Alberta.

1999 "Investigating the Paquimé Regional System." In *The Casas Grandes World,* ed. C. F. Schaafsma and C. L. Riley, pp. 54–62. University of Utah Press, Salt Lake City.

2001 *Casas Grandes and Its Hinterland.* University of Arizona Press, Tucson.

2003 "The Local and the Distant in the Origin of Casas Grandes, Chihuahua, Mexico." *American Antiquity,* Vol. 68, no. 2, pp. 314–332.

Wheat, J. B.

1955 *Mogollon Culture Prior to A.D. 1000.* American Anthropological Association, Menasha, WI.

Wilcox, D. R.

1986 "A Historical Analysis of the Problem of Southwestern-Mesoamerican Connections." In *Ripples in the Chichimec Sea,* ed. F. J. Mathien and R. H. McGuire, pp. 9–44. Southern Illinois University Press, Carbondale.

1991 "The Mesoamerican Ballgame in the American Southwest." In *The Mesoamerican Ballgame,* ed. V. L. Scarborough and D. R. Wilcox, pp. 101–125. University of Arizona Press, Tucson.

1994 "A Processual Model of Charles C. Di Peso's Babocomari Site and Related Systems." In *The Gran Chichimeca: Essays on the Archaeology and Ethnohistory of Northern Mesoamerica,* ed. J. E. Reyman, pp. 281–319. Avebury, Ashgate Publishing, Aldershot, Hampshire, UK.

1996 "The Diversity of Regional and Macroregional Systems in the American Southwest." In *Debating Complexity: Proceedings of the 26th Annual Chacmool Conference,* ed. D. A. Meyer, P. C. Dawson, and D. T. Hanna, pp. 375–389. Archaeological Association of the University of Calgary, Calgary, Alberta.

1999 "A Preliminary Graph-Theoretic Analysis of Access Relationships at Casa Grandes." In *The Casas Grandes World,* ed. C. F. Schaafsma and C. L. Riley, pp. 93–104. University of Utah Press, Salt Lake City.

Wilcox, D. R., and C. Sternberg

1983 *Hohokam Ballcourts and Their Interpretation.* Cultural Resource Management Division, Arizona State Museum, University of Arizona, Tucson.

Willett, E. R.

1996 "The Dual Festival System of the Southern Tepehuan of Mexico." *Journal of the Southwest,* Vol. 38, no. 2, pp. 197–213.

Willey, G. R.

1966 *An Introduction to American Archaeology,* Vol. 1, *North and Middle America.* Prentice-Hall, Englewood City, NJ.

1971 *An Introduction to American Archaeology,* Vol. 2, *South America.* Prentice-Hall, Englewood Cliffs, NJ.

Williams, M.

1996 "A Comparison of Classic Mimbres and Black Mountain Phase Ceramic Manufacture and Exchange Patterns." Paper presented at the 9th Mogollon Conference, Silver City, NM.

Williamson, R. A.

1987 "Light and Shadow: Ritual and Astronomy in Anasazi Structures." *Astronomy and Ceremony in the Prehistoric Southwest,* ed. J. B. Carlson and W. J. Judge, pp. 99–119. Maxwell Museum of Anthropology, Anthropological Papers No. 2. University of New Mexico, Albuquerque.

Wills, W. H.

2000 "Political Leadership and the Construction of Chacoan Great Houses, A.D. 1020–1140." In *Alternate Leadership Strategies in the Prehispanic Southwest,* ed. B. J. Mills, pp. 19–43. University of Arizona Press, Tucson.

Wills, W. H., and R. D. Leonard, eds.
1994  *The Ancient Southwestern Community: Models and Methods for the Study of Prehistoric Social Organization.* University of New Mexico Press, Albuquerque.

Wilson, J. P.
1995  "Prehistory of the Gallinas Mountains, Socorro County." In *Of Pots and Rocks: Papers in Honor of A. Helene Warren,* ed. M. S. Duran and D. T. Kirkpatrick, pp. 189–210. Archaeological Society of New Mexico, Albuquerque.

Windes, T. C.
1984  "A New Look at Population in Chaco Canyon." In *Recent Research on Chaco Prehistory,* ed. W. J. Judge and J. D. Schelberg, pp. 75–87. Reports of the Chaco Center No. 8. National Park Service, Albuquerque, NM.

1991  "The Prehistoric Road Network at Pueblo Alto, Chaco Canyon, New Mexico." In *Ancient Road Networks and Settlement Hierarchies in the New World,* ed. C. D. Trombold, pp. 111–131. Cambridge University Press, Cambridge, UK.

Windes, T. C., and D. Ford
1992  "The Nature of the Early Bonito Phase." In *Anasazi Regional Organization and the Chaco System,* ed. D. E. Doyel, pp. 75–86. Maxwell Museum of Anthropology, University of New Mexico, Albuquerque.

Winship, G. P.
1896  *The Coronado Expedition, 1540–1542.* Fourteenth Annual Report of the U.S. Bureau of American Ethnology, 1892–1893, Pt. 1, U.S. Government Printing Office, Washington, DC.

Winter, J., L. Casjens, P. Hogan, and B. Noisat
1977  "Site Descriptions." In *Hovenweep 1976,* ed. J. Winter, pp. 10–62. Archeological Report No. 3. Anthropology Dept., San Jose State University, San Jose, CA.

Wiseman, R. N.
1986  "An Initial Study of the Origins of Chupadero Black-on-White." Albuquerque Archaeological Society, *Technical Note* No. 2, pp. 1–6.

1995  "Reassessment of the Dating of the Pojoaque Grant Site (LA 835), a Key Site of the Rio Grande Developmental Period." In *Of Pots and Rocks: Papers in Honor of A. Helene Warren,* ed. M. S. Duran and D. T. Kirkpatrick, pp. 237–248. Archaeological Society of New Mexico, Albuquerque.

1996  "Socioreligious Architecture in the Sierra Blanca/Roswell Regions of Southeastern New Mexico." In *La Jornada: Papers in Honor of William F. Turney,* ed. M. S. Duran and D. T. Kirkpatrick, pp. 205–24. Archaeological Society of New Mexico, Albuquerque.

2001  "The Hinterlands in the Middle Rio Grande: A Look at Prehistoric and Historic Land-Use South of the Lower Jemez River." In *Following Through: Papers in Honor of Phyllis S. Davis,* ed. R. N. Wiseman, T. C. O'Laughlin, and C. T. Snow, pp. 161–181. Archaeological Society of New Mexico, Albuquerque.

2003  *The Roswell South Project: Excavations in the Sacramento Plain and the Northern Chihuahuan Desert of Southeastern New Mexico,* with contributions by N. J. Atkins, B. T. Hamilton, P. J. McBride, and S. M. Moga. Museum of New Mexico, Office of Archaeological Studies, Archaeology Notes 237, Santa Fe, NM.

Wiseman, R. N., and J. A. Darling
1986  "The Bronze Trail Group: More Evidence for a Cerrillos-Chaco Turquoise Connection." In *By Hands Unknown: Papers on Rock Art and Archaeology in Honor of James G. Bain,* ed. A. V. Poore, pp. 115–143. Archaeological Society of New Mexico, Ancient City Press, Santa Fe.

Wiseman, R. N., and B. Olinger
1991  "Initial Production of Painted Pottery in the Rio Grande: The Perspective from LA 835, the Pojoaque Grant Site." In *Puebloan Past and Present: Papers in Honor of Stewart Peckham,* ed. M. S. Duran and D. T. Kirkpatrick, pp. 209–217. Archaeological Society of New Mexico, Albuquerque.

Woodbury, R. B.
1959  "A Reconsideration of Pueblo Warfare in the Southwestern United States." In *Actas del XXXIII Congreso Internacional de Americanistas,* 2:124–133. San José, Costa Rica.

Wooldridge, H. G.

1981 (?)   *Implications of Trade in the Jornada Region of South-Central New Mexico,* R81–64, Espey, Huston, and Associates, P.O. Box 519, Austin, TX.

Woosley, A. I., and B. Olinger

1993   "The Casas Grandes Ceramic Tradition: Production and Interregional Exchange of Ramos Polychrome." In *Culture and Contact: Charles C. Di Peso's Gran Chichimeca,* ed. A. I. Woosley and J. C. Ravesloot, pp. 105–131. University of New Mexico Press, Albuquerque.

Woosley, A. I., and J. C. Ravesloot, eds.

1993   *Culture and Contact: Charles C. Di Peso's Gran Chichimeca.* University of New Mexico Press, Albuquerque.

Wright, B.

1994   "The Changing Kachina." In *Kachinas in the Pueblo World,* ed. P. Schaafsma, pp. 139–145. University of New Mexico Press, Albuquerque.

Young, M. J.

1994   "The Interaction Between Western Puebloan and Mesoamerican Ideology/Cosmology." In *Kachinas in the Pueblo World,* ed. P. Schaafsma, pp. 107–120. University of New Mexico Press, Albuquerque.

Young, R. W.

1983   "Apachean Languages." In *Southwest,* ed. A. Ortiz, pp. 393–400. Handbook of North American Indians, Vol. 10, William C. Sturtevant, general editor, Smithsonian Institution, Washington, DC.

Zubrow, E. B. W.

1974   *Population, Contact, and Climate in the New Mexican Pueblos.* University of Arizona Press, Tucson.

Zurita [Zorita], A. de

1992   *Relación de los Señores de la Nueva España,* ed. G. Vazquez. Historia 16, Madrid.

# Index